TABLE OF CON

Preface*

For many years I have wanted to write and tell my children and grand children about my experiences and recollections as a boy growing up in German occupied Holland. The desire to do this has become stronger the older I became. But not until I finally retired at the age of 71 in 2002 has it become possible to do so. Over the years my thoughts of how I should write these experiences have crystallized in to making the experience of WWII more encompassing, more informative, more educational and more interesting to read for not only the older generation but primarily for those who are at the age or younger at which I experienced that period in my life. Thousands of books have been written about WWII and continue to be written. Increasingly, however, these books are written by people who were too young to experience it themselves. Although my involvement and experience was naturally restricted by my age and limited knowledge of the why, what and where, I was sufficiently aware and sometimes even involved on the periphery of events as they unfolded during those years that shook the world. There are no revelations about the major events and battles of the war but merely how these events played a role in my young life and how they affected and sometimes even directly impacted my environment. I have been asked many times what it was like living under German occupation for all those years and my answer always included the desire to be free once again. Not have to be afraid or hungry. This desire to be free became an obsession for all of us in Holland. Out of the 1,815 days of occupation not a day would pass that we did not talk about it. But not all was gloom and doom. There were funny moments and we never lost our sense of humor. We had some good times and laughed but those moments were always experienced under the oppressive Nazi cloak. As freedom was our main goal and greatest wish I am titling this book: *"Countdown to Freedom"* It's the story of a young Dutch boy from the big port city of Rotterdam in The Netherlands whose symbols of freedom were the contrails of thousands of Allied bombers flying over Holland on their way to Germany or the lone Spitfire that one time swooped down low, rocked its wings several times, waved at us and then sped away. But it is not just Freedom for its own sake but rather what in the end the cost of that freedom was. That is the story and the message I would like to get across. "A Tear, a Smile and a Message!"

*Both my mother and brother contributed to this book with their recollections of the war, which I had asked them to put on paper. My mother *Coba* finally agreed to do so when she was already 88 years old. She made several attempts and each time she remembered more detail. She wrote it in Dutch and I translated it. The same was true for my brother *Henry* but he wrote it in English. *Henry* was 80 years old at the time. Throughout the book I am using their recollections of events as they unfolded. You may note that in some instances their recollections differ from mine.

MONDAY JANUARY 31, 1938

"This line is not moving at all. By the time we get inside there won't be anything left for us; there are just too many people here". I was talking to my mom as we were standing in a queue of people stretching around several blocks in the area of *"De Blaak"*, downtown Rotterdam in Holland. We had arrived there with a yellow streetcar of Line 4. To further support my concern I suggested that everybody in Rotterdam must have read the newspaper, Het Rotterdamsch Nieuwsblad, and the paper's promise of *"Beschuit met Muisjes"* (Dutch Rusk with Orange Sprinkles) when a prince or princess would be born. Princes Juliana had been expecting a baby and this morning she had given birth to Princess Beatrix.

1. Princess Beatrix born on January 31, 1938

The city was a sea of red, white and blue flags and there was a lot of orange bunting as well.

2. Dutch flags with the orange 'wimpel'
Many happy people were on the street and some were
dancing to the music coming from an old-fashioned
'draaiorgel' (barrel-organ)

3. A barrel organ (draaiorgel) in the early 1900s

Mom assured me that there would be enough *'Beschuit'* for all the people.
I was hungry for a snack and her assurance made me feel better.

I was 7 years old and a few months earlier I had undergone surgery for a double hernia. Maybe that is why she was holding my hand so tightly. Everybody had been so worried for me. The surgery had been done at the Children's Hospital on the Gordelweg. Although outwardly healthy I had been very skinny, listless and didn't want to eat much. My parents figured something had to be wrong with me. Sure enough, our doctor, who my mom had taken me to, had diagnosed a double hernia. I was told that that occurs when a small sac containing tissue protrudes through an opening in the muscles of the abdominal wall. Didn't make much sense to me but what really caught my attention was when the doctor told me I would have to have surgery. Now that was scary and I had worried about it. All of a sudden everybody that knew about my upcoming surgery had been nice to me. That part I enjoyed, particularly since these people promised to mail me picture post cards while in the hospital. My mom had told them that I collected those and already had several boxes full. The fact that people were so nice to me should have alerted me to the fact that what I was to undergo might well be dangerous and life threatening. However, at the ripe old age of seven, that never dawned on me. So, to the hospital I went. This had been the first time that I had been away from my family but I didn't cry or carry on: just another adventure of which I would have many in my life. What struck me most was the smell in the hospital; something very therapeutic, not unlike the smell of Lysol. I would experience that smell more often in the future as well. From the surgery I don't remember much other then a mask on my face and the nurse telling me to inhale deeply. Just like that I was gone and if I had died on the operating table I would never have known. The operation was a success however and from then on both hospital staff and visiting friends and relatives pampered me. During the two weeks in the hospital I received picture postcards every day. My collection quadrupled. One event in the ward caused everyone to laugh uproarishly. If you have ever been in a hospital and you are not allowed to get out of bed and walk, the nurse will give you something that looks very much like a big glass boot. That's what the nurse gave me and, for the life of me, I didn't know what it was for. But not to appear completely ignorant, I remarked the obvious reason to the nurse by suggesting that the neck of this *'boot'* was too narrow for my foot to go through. After the nurses and doctors got off the floor I was told that I would have to use it in case I needed to go to the bathroom. I would never make that mistake again. Following the surgery my appetite improved and I was finally putting on some weight.

Slowly shuffling our way forward, we finally made our way into the newspaper building and we got our "Beschuit met Muisjes).

4. Beschuit met Muisjes (Rusk with Mice)

Two and a half years later all of downtown Rotterdam where we had been on that January 31, 1938 and where we had waited so patiently with all those happy people would be no more.

5. The building in 1938

Gone, erased: totally and irrevocably destroyed in an unprovoked attack by Nazi Germany. Worse still would be the loss of our precious freedom. It would be five long years, 1,815 days of growing misery and despair before we would taste freedom again. The clock is ticking. This then will be my story.

INTRODUCTION

PART I
THE NETHERLANDS
AND THE DUTCH

If you ask the average person where the Netherlands is, he or she will tell you that it is somewhere in Europe and most likely in Scandinavia. Let me set the record straight. The Netherlands is NOT part of Scandinavia. Scandinavia is made up of Norway, Sweden and Denmark. The other Nordic countries Finland, Iceland and the Faroe Islands are sometimes included, because of their close historic and cultural relations to Norway, Sweden and Denmark. Those countries are located to the north of The Netherlands; often referred to as 'Holland'. I guess you may say that the names: Holland and the Netherlands, are interchangeable but that would be unfair to the people who live in the other ten provinces: provinces that do not carry the name *'Holland'*. You see there are twelve provinces in the Netherlands. Two of these provinces are called: North and South Holland. The other ten are called: Friesland, Groningen, Drente, Overijssel, Flevoland, Gelderland, Utrecht, Noord Brabant, Zeeland and Limburg.

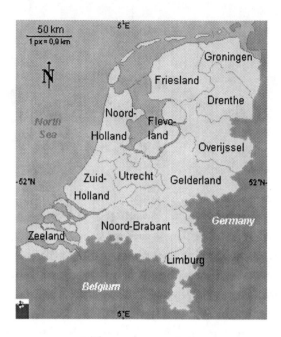

6. The twelve provinces

These twelve provinces make up the Kingdom of the Netherlands. The three largest cities are located in the two provinces called "*North and South Holland*": Amsterdam, Rotterdam and The Hague. Together these cities have a population of roughly 1.9 million or about 11 percent of the total population of the country of 16+ million. In the year 1830 the population was a measly 2.6 million. Of course, at that time the country was a lot smaller. There is a saying that goes something like this: "*God created the World but the Dutch created Holland.*"

They did that by building dikes out in the sea and then pumping out the water. That explains the many windmills. These were necessary to keep the water at the right level at all times. All that land is, of course, below sea level. When you are in Holland and driving your car from Amsterdam to The Hague and Rotterdam you will be amazed to see an occasional ocean liner sail across the freeway.

The Netherlands is a gem among the European countries – small, beautiful and many-faceted. From a soggy landscape, the industrious

Dutch have built one of Europe's most progressive countries. More than any other people, they have literally built the country with their bare hands, grain-by-grain of sand. The process of claiming the land from the water has never stopped. This industry has created much of the 15,770 square miles that is now the Netherlands. The country measures less than 320 km (200 miles) from tip to toe. And only about 160 km (100 mile) between the beaches of the North Sea to the west and the wooded Dutch/German border to the east. By comparison it is barely bigger than the thumb on the mitten-shaped State of Michigan or five thousand square miles smaller than the County of San Bernardino in California.

In February 1953* Holland experienced the worst flood in 300 years when the two worst components got together; an unusual high tide and a hurricane-force northwesterly wind. It flooded most of the islands in the province of Zeeland (New Zeeland got its name from that province) and about half of the province of South Holland. It killed 1,835 people and 47,000 heads of cattle drowned. It destroyed 3,000 homes and 300 farms. Since then the Dutch implemented a plan, known as the *'Delta Project'*. This Delta Project was one of the greatest post-war feats of hydraulic engineering in the Netherlands. When in Holland you must not forget to go see this wonder of the world. A huge storm barrier was built, with huge gates that can be opened and closed. The components for the moveable gates, each the size of a twelve-story block of flats, were built in special docks and floated into place before being sunk.

*I was called back to duty in the Netherlands Army to assist with the evacuation of people and animals from the stricken area.

7. Delta Works - Gates

They may have gotten the idea from the *'Mulberries'*, the two artificial harbors that were designed and constructed by the British to facilitate the unloading of supply ships off the coast of Normandy following the invasion of Europe on June 6, 1944. But that is another story.

8. Mulberries for the invasion on June 6, 1944

9. A Mulberry being towed into place

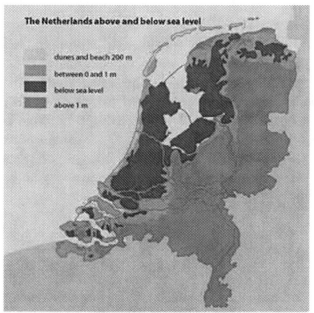

Map depicting the areas of Netherlands below and above sea
level. Source:
http://www.deltawerken.com/Before-the-flood-of-1953/90.html;
accessed January 11, 2006.

10.

The Netherlands borders on the North Sea, Belgium and Germany.
Belgium used to be part of the Netherlands but it seceded and formed
a separate kingdom in 1830. Some Belgians have very long memories
and still hold a grudge against the Dutch because, at the time, they
considered them selves *'occupied'* by the Dutch; an understandable
feeling. When driving there with my son Steve in the area of Waterloo
near Brussels in 1985 I cut off a Belgian car by mistake. The man

stopped, got out of his car; I rolled down my window to apologize but the man was ahead of me. He chastised me for doing what I had done and reminded me that they had been independent from the Netherlands since 1830 and the Dutch were no longer in charge. You see, although we had US Passports, the license plate on our rental said NL (**Netherlands**). There are many jokes back and forth between the two countries but it is usually good-natured banter and there is a great deal of kinship between these two freedom-loving nations. Germany, however, was another case altogether. I say, *'was'* because things have changed so very much since the end of World War II. The Dutch were always a little frightful of that *'juggernaut'* neighbor to the east. In May 1940 that *'fear'* was well founded. During WWI Kaiser Wilhelm was honorable enough to acknowledge our neutrality and although things were tough for the population they were spared the terrible devastation and hardships of our good neighbor Belgium. This neutrality in the First World War led to a flood of refugees and it is no secret that the Netherlands has been a refuge for many centuries. Kaiser Wilhelm himself took refuge in Holland after he was forced to abdicate from the throne following the Armistice in 1918.

11. Kaiser Wilhelm 1859-1941

Prior to WWII many Jews took refuge in the Netherlands in the hope that Hitler would honor its solemn oath not to invade the Netherlands. We all know that he did not keep his word.

The Netherlands is a constitutional monarchy with a parliamentary system. Queen *Beatrix* is head of state; but the prime minister, the cabinet, and the parliament wield the power. The seat of government is in The Hague, but Amsterdam is the capital city. One of the festive highlights in the capital city is the April 30 celebration of Queen Beatrix' official birthday. Originally that was the birthday of the late Queen Juliana, the mother of Beatrix. Queen Juliana's mother was Queen Wilhelmina. She was the reigning queen during the Second World War. On royal birthdays and other important days for the House of Orange, life is just a little brighter. A *wimpel* (fringed orange banner) flies above the Dutch flag.

12. Dutch national colors with orange "wimpel"

In some villages, children wear an orange *sjerp* (sash) draped over the left shoulder and tied at the right waistline. A splash of orange is the order of the day. Orange sprinkles decorate rusks and breads. Some cooks bake a special *'Oranje koek'* (orange cake). During the German occupation in WWII when all this was forbidden, carrying a *'carrot'* would do the trick.

Holland is proud of its history and particularly its glorious naval past and prides itself on the fact that it succeeded where Germany in the Second World War did not. It successfully invaded England. In June 1667 Admiral de Ruyter launched the Dutch *'Raid on the Medway'* at the mouth of the River Thames.

13. Raid on the Medway

After capturing the fort at Sheemess, they went on to break through the massive chain protecting the entrance to Medway and, on the 13th, attacked the English fleet that had been laid up at Chatham. This daring raid remains England's greatest military disaster since the Norman Conquest. Many of the Navy's remaining ships were destroyed, either by the Dutch or being scuttled by the English to block the river. Three ships of the line were burned: the Royal Oak, the new Royal London and the Royal James. The English flagship, HMS Royal Charles, was abandoned by its skeleton crew, captured without a shot being fired, and towed back to the Netherlands. Its coat-of-arms is now on display in the Rijksmuseum in Amsterdam. Fortunately for the English the raiders spared the Chatham Dockyard: England's largest industrial complex. It is easy to understand that a peace-treaty followed. The Dutch were keen to sign it as well because they had to deal with a French invasion of the Spanish Netherlands at the same time.

14. Michiel Adriaenszoon de Ruyter (1607-1676)

15. HMS Royal Charles

The country is equally proud of its explorers. For instance, did you know that the Dutch Sea Captain Willem Janszoon discovered Australia in 1606? He called it New Holland. That Abel Tasman discovered a large island south of Australia and called it Tasmania?

16. Abel Janszoon Tasman (1603-1659)

Then there was Henry Hudson, an Englishman in the employ of the Dutch who in 1609 explored as far north as the present site of Albany, New York.

17. Henry Hudson (1565-1611)

The Hudson River is named after him. In 1625 Peter Minuit bought the island of Manhattan from the Indians for $25 worth of European goods. The Dutch West India Company would offer large land grants to those who'd settle fifty or more people in the new colony within four years. In 1630 the Village of Beverwijck was founded at the present site of Albany. It later merged with Fort Orange.

18. Peter Minuit (1580-1638)

The first colony at the Cape of Good Hope (Africa) was founded by the Dutch East India Company in 1652. They wanted a port where ships could take on fuel, water, and provisions en route to the Far East. About thirty-five years later, the Huguenots joined the Dutch.

Later, when Napoleon overran the Netherlands, Britain sent troops to keep the Cape out of French hands and was awarded the colony. But, of course, the Dutch immigrant farmers (Boers) were still there and struggled to keep their independence but were defeated by the English general Sir Harry Smith at the battle of Boomplaats in 1848. Gold and diamonds had not yet been discovered and the British Government, finding the newly annexed territory of little value soon determined to retrocede the country to the Boers. The Boers thereupon set up a Republic, which under the name of the *'Orange Free State'*, enjoyed a period of peace and prosperity that lasted up to the Anglo-Boer War of 1899-1902. During that war, the Boers had the distinction of capturing Sir Winston Churchill, but he escaped. By that time gold and diamonds had been discovered and the "annexed territory" was all of a sudden of greater value to the British Empire.

The Dutch are recognized in the world for several reasons. Aside from wooden shoes, windmills and tulips they are considered successful and, in general, honest traders and outstanding seafarers. They are also tops in hydraulic engineering. They can be stubborn as a mule and display frugality better than anyone. They are also recognized for always being on the side of the *'underdog'*. They are fiercely independent and love their freedom. They are very tolerant of other's beliefs and one only needs to visit Amsterdam to see what I mean. Then there are the many world-renowned painters, writers, poets, inventors and scientists; too many to mention. All together an interesting amalgam of both good and annoying habits as well as skills. In general the Dutch are well liked and foreigners usually find themselves at home in that small country. In Stephen Ambrose's book 'The Victors, Eisenhower and his boys: The men of World War II', the GI's mainly made up of men from the U.S. 82d and 101st Airborne Divisions regarded the Dutch as: *"simply wonderful in every way"*.

When it comes to the typical traits of the European people I like to recite what many years ago a well-known publication (Elseviers) in the Netherlands described as the typical Common Market person. This was at a time when there were fewer countries member of that alliance.

This *'tongue-in-cheek'* description goes something like this:

The average Common Market person has: the *"generosity"* of a Dutchman, the *"sense of humor"* of a German the *"cleanliness"* of an Italian the *"flexibility"* of the French the *"efficiency"* of the British and the *"world-wide vision"* of a Luxembourger... In other words, a *"Belgian."*

In anticipation, I apologize to any citizen of these countries who takes offense.

Here follow some more statements concerning the Dutch:

About Frugality

"The trouble with the Dutch is that they offer too little and demand too much".

– Lord Chesterfield

"The Dutch invented copper wire. How? Two Dutchmen fighting over a penny". –

Author Unknown

Other things you need to know about The Netherlands:

Golf and Baseball

Back in the fourteenth century, many Dutch people played '*kolf*' with rubber or spun wool balls and a stick with curved end. Golf, a sport taking up a much larger playing area, is supposed to have come from '*kolf*' and is played according to the same principle. Another version was played on ice in the winter with a club resembling a hockey stick and a leather-covered ball the size of a grapefruit.

A 1628 copper engraving shows Dutch children in a school playground playing a game resembling present-day baseball called '*honkbal*'. Some historians maintain that Dutch emigrants took the original form of baseball with them to America in the seventeenth century.

Yankee

Did you know that this highly recognized and accepted word for an American from the northeast came from two Dutch names? <u>Jan</u> and <u>Kees</u>. The English would pronounce these two words as '*Yankees*'. What they were describing were Dutch colonials. I don't know if this is true but it certainly makes sense to me.

A Debt of Gratitude

It is said that the American bride-to-be who is showered with gifts before her marriage owes a debt of gratitude to a stubborn Dutch girl. According to legend, the girl's father refused her a dowry because she insisted on marrying a miller, her true love, rather than the farmer he had chosen for her. They married and she lost the dowry, but their friends, seeing their plight, sought to make up for it with what became the first bridal shower, *'raining'* china, linen, pots and pans and other household goods on the young couple.

From: *The Dutch Book: Celebrating 100 Years on Whidbey Island* by Dorothy Neil, Oak Harbor, Washington

Royal Reflections
Queen Juliana

Queen Juliana came to visit a campus – which shall go unnamed:

The professors in caps and gowns lined the sidewalks while the College President escorted the Queen and Prince Bernhard into the chapel for convocation. An elderly professor, too deaf to know how loud he talked, broke the solemn stillness by announcing to nobody in particular:

"Wat heeft zij toch dikke benen!" (What fat legs she's got!)

Everybody heard him including Queen Juliana.

She stopped in front of him, smiled, and said with a degree of playfulness:

"Mijnheer, daar moet het hele Oranjehuis op rusten." (Sir, these legs need to support the whole House of Orange.)

Everyone in earshot cheered.

19. Queen Juliana (1909-2004)

Queen Wilhelmina, the mother of Juliana

Queen Wilhelmina was entertaining the Frisian Cattle Breeder's Association at dinner. The Frisian farmers didn't know what to make of their finger bowls. They drank them down. The stylish courtiers from The Hague nudged each other and pointed and laughed at such lack of class.

Until the queen herself without a smile raised her finger bowl and drained it obliging all the courtiers to follow suit without a smile.

From Style and Class *by Sietze Buning.*
Middleburg Press. Orange City, Iowa. 1982

20. Queen Wilhelmina (1880-1962)

LAW OF THE DIKES

"Dike or Leave," the Frisians used to say. They meant that a Friesland farmer was expected to maintain his section of the dike perfectly, or he would be asked to leave. If a farmer decided to give up his land, he threw his spade into his section of the dike. Whoever pulled the spade from the ground and cared for the dike became the new owner of the land. Whenever a dike was in danger, immediate *'dike peace'* was in effect and all quarrels were forgotten.

The Famous Finger in the Dike

Plug a hole in a dike with your finger – hydraulically impossible. But in fiction and legend, anything is possible. Nineteenth-century American writer *Mary Mapes Dodge* penned *Hans Brinker, The Silver Skates,* and the tale of a Dutch boy who plugged the leak in a dike with his finger. The legendary boy hero and the story became world famous. The Dutch town of *Spaarndam* built a monument to the character *Hans Brinker,* to honor the courage of Dutch youth through the centuries and to please the many visiting tourists.

Windmill Lore

21. Windmills at Kinderdijk

A sense that justice will prevail is contained in the proverb, *"God's mills grind slowly, but surely."* The windmill is an important part of Dutch history, and as such has become an integral part of Dutch culture in the form of proverbs and folk sayings. As a warning that one may have to face the consequences of his actions, the Dutch say,

"Be careful or you'll have to face the wind." Cautious people are said to wait with a decision until they know out of which corner the wind will blow. Seizing an opportunity is known as pumping while the wind blows. When someone seems a little daffy, he is said to have been struck by one of the sails, or when someone's business is not doing well, the Dutch say, *"He cannot keep his mill going."*

KLOMPEN

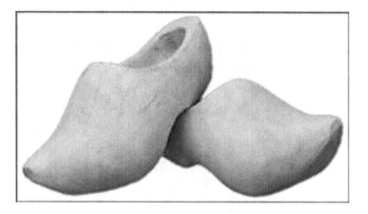

22. Klompen (Wooden shoes)

Wooden shoes, or '*klompen*' as the Dutch call them, began as inexpensive and practical footwear for farmers and fishermen. Carved by their wearers, they kept feet dry and were good insulation. The soil in Holland is usually wet and soggy and wooden shoes don't rot like leather boots would. They are also easy to maintain; a matter of fact they don't need maintenance other then scraping off any unwanted soil or dirt. The other advantage is that you easily slip in and out of them and leave them in front of the door. With a little bit of straw they are actually quite comfortable and warm in winter. I can vouch for that because during the war I wore them a lot. If one has a good quality toe corn, you can make a place for it by chiseling out some wood where it will have room to grow without getting pinched.

Proper, Orderly, Clean and 'Gezellig'.
Dutch Words to Know.

Deftig (proper) is a term respected by the Dutch. In the Netherlands, it is *deftig* to shake hands with all present, including children, when entering or leaving a home. Only when speaking to a social equal does a *deftig* person use first names. Going Dutch at restaurants is *deftig*. It is expected, unless different arrangements have been clearly stated in advance. Orderliness is a part of life, with a time and place for everything. Life is punctuated with regular coffee breaks. Housework is organized by days and hours. In Dutch the word *'schoon'* has two meanings: *'clean'* and *'beautiful'*. Saturday is *'schoonmaakdag'* (cleaning day). The Dutch are unmatched in their spotless housekeeping. The windows sparkle, and the sidewalks are scrubbed clean with soap and water. Each morning the bedding is hung from the windows to air. Visitors are expected to carefully wipe their feet upon entering a home. The annual *'grote schoonmaak'* (major spring cleaning) is the sole topic among traditional Dutch homemakers for two or three weeks each spring. You may notice that when you are visiting Holland most of the apartments and homes that you are passing will all have their curtains open as opposed to America and elsewhere where curtains are drawn. The Dutch just love light and openness, maybe because the weather can be so gloomy and they don't want to feel closed in. Another word that is very important to the Dutch is *'gezellig'*. It is impossible to translate into one single English word that would describe its meaning.

The Dutch/English dictionary provides: *companionable, convivial, sociable, clubbable, chummy, matey, pleasant, cozy, snug and chatty.* For example, getting together with good friends and enjoying a good meal, talk and drink is *"oer gezellig." (utterly fantastic)*.

Tulips and Bulbs

History relates that for one rare tulip bulb, an eager Dutch merchant once traded two loads of wheat, four loads of rye, four oxen, four pigs, twelve sheep, two barrels of wine, four barrels of beer, two casks of butter, 1,000 pounds of cheese, a bed, a suit, and a silver mug. That supposed bargaining occurred in the early 1630s; about fifty years after tulips were introduced into Holland from Turkey. They were an immediate craze. No well-to-do burgher with any taste could be without tulips. Prices skyrocketed, especially for exotic varieties. People thought the tulip mania would last forever. The bubble burst in 1634. Dutchmen who had mortgaged homes, estates, and industries to buy tulips were selling them at 5 to 15 percent of cost. Fortunes were lost, and it was years before this aspect of the economy recovered. The Dutch never lost their love for the tulip, however. It has remained a Dutch symbol, and people in the Netherlands and other growers have developed more than 2,000 varieties.

23. Bulb fields in Lisse

Holland and the 80-Year War with Spain

In those days Holland was part of a large sovereign state. Philip II, the king of that empire lived in Spain

24. Philip II of Spain (1527-1598)

It was very difficult to rule such a vast empire and he never knew what was happening in far-off Holland. Therefore the king appointed noblemen who would rule in his name. In the 16th century the king decided to rule again himself but the noblemen didn't take kindly to that. They did not want to lose their 'cushy' job and they rebelled. But that was to no avail. In those times there was only room for one religion, Roman Catholicism. All other religions were forbidden. But just in those days there were people who disagreed with Catholicism. One of these people was the Rotterdammer Erasmus.

25. Desiderius Erasmus Roterodamus (1466-1536) His statue in Rotterdam.

Others outside Holland were *Maarten Luther* and *Calvijn*.

26. Maarten Luther (1483-1546)

27. Johannes Calvijn (1509-1564)

The people that were non-catholic, for example the Calvinists, no longer wanted to be punished by the Spanish government. Not unlike the noblemen they considered Philip II an unjust king and they rebelled. When Philip found out about that he sent an army to suppress the rebellion. The noblemen and non-Catholics fled the country.

28. The Beggars (Geuzen)

They were called *Geuzen**. One of these "Geuzen" was the nobleman Willem van Oranje. Later on he was called Willem the Silent. Now abroad, the *'Geuzen'* formed an army and a fleet (the watergeuzen) to fight the king. On April 1, 1572 these watergeuzen entered the town of Den Briel south of Rotterdam.

29. Willem van Oranje (1533-1584)

The Spaniards fled and moved to Rotterdam where the city fathers kept the gates closed. They didn't want any Spaniards in their city. This so angered the Spanish soldiers that a few days later when the gates had been opened once again, they killed numerous Rotterdam citizens. Many Dutch cities kept their gates closed to the Spanish soldiers but while it kept the Spaniards out it also kept the citizens in. As a result they could not get food from the fields and farms surrounding the city. Sometimes the Spaniards lay siege for such a long time that there was mass starvation. They hoped that this would force those stubborn Dutchmen to surrender but that never really happened. Such a siege happened at the city of Leiden.

*The Dutch *'Geuzen'* comes from the French word for *'Beggars'* (Les Gueux), a name assumed by the confederacy of nobles and other malcontents, who in 1566 opposed Spanish tyranny in the Netherlands. The most successful group of them operated at sea, they were called *Gueux de Mer* or *Sea Beggars* (Dutch: Watergeuzen). On April 5, 1566 permission was obtained for the confederates to present a petition of grievances to the regent, Margaret, duchess of Parma. About 250 noblemen marched to the palace accompanied by Louis of Nassau. The regent was first alarmed at the appearance of so large a body, but one of her councilors was heard to exclaim, *"Madam, why is your highness afraid of these beggars (ces gueux)?"* The name caught on and from then on the patriots identified them selves as *Les Gueux or Geuzen.*

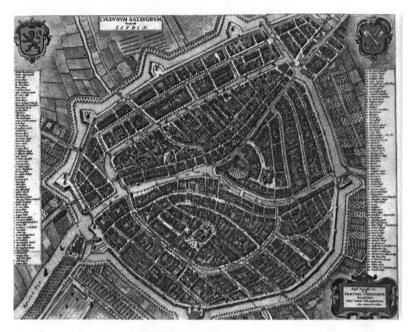

30. The Old City of Leiden

The siege lasted for months and there was much misery and starvation. At last, the leader of the Geuzen, Willem van Oranje found a good solution. At Rotterdam he broke through the dikes with the result that the polders between Rotterdam and Leiden flooded. With their ships the watergeuzen were able to sail up the polders and free the city of Leiden. That occurred on October 3, 1575. For the starving population they brought freshly caught herring and white bread.

31. Geus, a "Beggar"

HOLLAND IN THE 17ᵀᴴ AND 18ᵀᴴ CENTURY

In the year 1600 the port of Rotterdam had already grown considerably because more and more commerce was being conducted in the Netherlands. The Europeans were very interested in all products and spices from the East Indies (Indonesia), such as pepper, nutmeg and cloves. Dutch sailors tried to find an efficient route to haul all those products with their sailing ships. In seeking a better route they would invariably discover other countries. One of these discoverers was Olivier van Noort from Rotterdam. He sailed around the world from 1598 till 1601. A man from Rotterdam was the first one to do that. From 1602 the United East India Company conducted all trade in the East Indies. (Verenigde Oostindische Compagnie – VOC) One of the offices of the VOC was in Rotterdam and as a result many ships visited the Rotterdam harbors. The VOC also had a shipyard in Rotterdam. Things were going very well for the city during the *'Golden Age'* (1600 to 1700). Not only did Holland have excellent merchants, they also produced outstanding painters such as Rembrandt and Frans Hals and writers such as Vondel.

32. Rembrandt Harmenszoon van Rijn (1606-1669)

33. Frans Hals (1581-1666)

34. Joost van den Vondel (1587-1679)

Particularly writers liked Holland because they were allowed to express new ideas without the government getting upset. That was often much more difficult in other countries. It resulted in numerous writers coming to the Netherlands with new thoughts. For instance, Pieter Rabus and Pierre Bayle fled France for the Netherlands.

Pieter Rabus didn't think it was equitable or honest that only a few people (such as regents and princes) had anything to say in the country. Many people who read his books agreed with his ideas. Those people were called *'Patriots'*. The poor people hoped that the Prins van Oranje would help them improve their lot. Those folks were called the *'Orangists'*. The Patriots gained more and more power and very often had terrible rows with the Orangists. On April 3, 1784 there was even gunfire. On that occasion *Kate Mossel*, a real tough fishwife, led the Orangists.

35. Kaat Mossel, a real tough fishwife (1723-1798)

To this day the people of Rotterdam remember her name. By the year 1787 the Patriots had gained such power that the Prins and his family from Prussia (part of today's Germany) had to ask for help. The King of Prussia sent an army and on 20 September 1787 the Prussians also appeared in Rotterdam. Many Patriots then fled to France where a revolution had taken place and where they now had a more *'honest'* (more democratic) government. The French King had nothing to say any longer. France wanted a more democratic government in other countries as well and in 1795 they sent an army to *'liberate'* the Netherlands. Initially the Patriots were happy with the French soldiers and even assisted them.

36. Welcoming the French troops 1795

The Prins of Orange, however, fled to England.

The early pleasure of the French *'liberation'* quickly wore off. The French soldiers didn't pay with money but with pieces of paper that had to be exchanged first and were worth much less than the purported value.

37. The French paid with worthless money

On top of that the Emperor of France, Napoleon Bonaparte, was waging war with England and since the Netherlands was now also part of the French Empire it was not allowed to trade with England. Because of this the country (and also Rotterdam) was getting poorer than it already was. Additionally, more and more Dutch boys were conscripted in the French Army and had to fight for Napoleon. Many of these young men died in the many battles that were fought. The end for Napoleon finally came in 1813. By this time the Dutch people were so displeased that they were looking forward to the return of the Prins van Oranje. When in 1813 the country was liberated the government asked the Prins if he would be willing to return and once again govern the country. He agreed and in 1814 the Prins van Oranje became the first Dutch King of the Netherlands. King Willem I.

38. King Willem I (1772-1843)

PART II
THE HISTORY OF ROTTERDAM

In the year 1028 folklore refers to a place called *'Rotta'*. There were then only a few farmers and fishermen living in Rotta. There were no dikes because the water level was lower than it is today. However, in 1164 there was a flood and the old *'Rotta'* disappeared under the waves. Only after dikes were build did the population return. The population of about 1,250 lived on the dam constructed at the small river Rotte. That is how the town got its name *'Rotterdam'*. In 1340 Rotterdam had earned *'city'* status and Willem IV, Count of Holland granted Rotterdam its *'city charter'*.

In the old days only Roman Catholicism was allowed. All other religions were prohibited and sometimes there was even a death penalty. For instance, in 1539 *Anneken Jans* was bound hand and foot and thrown in the Maas River to drown because she had a different belief.

ROTTERDAM IN THE 19ᵀᴴ AND 20ᵀᴴ CENTURY

When in 1814 the French had disappeared from the country and the Netherlands had its first king, Willem I, the country became known as the Kingdom of the Netherlands. King Willem I ruled till 1840. During his reign he tried very hard to improve the living conditions. He sought many improvements and innovations, such as railways and steamships. The people, however, were poor and the people that did have money didn't think all those new things were necessary. They believed in a *'status quo'* and that was also the case in Rotterdam. What the poor people thought or wanted was not important. Nobody was interested in these people's fate. In the city this meant overcrowding, malnutrition, and illnesses. Without a functioning water and drainage system it eventually resulted in an epidemic that killed thousands of citizens. Now we know that they died of Cholera, the drinking of dirty water. However it was not until 1865 that they realized that.

Finally in 1840 some of the more progressive and wealthy citizens thought it was time to take action. Not to improve poverty; they could care less, but to stimulate commerce. They wanted Rotterdam to become an important port city. They were now interested in some of the very things that King Willem I had wanted all along. It resulted in numerous big projects. Railways were started, harbors were dug, a bridge was build across the Maas River and they started with digging a direct connection between Rotterdam and the sea. In the year 1863 this resulted in the 'New Waterway'.

39. Nieuwe Waterweg – New Waterway

Here and there factories were constructed and slowly but surely the Netherlands became an industrial nation. More and more trade was conducted and the Rotterdam harbors grew both in size and number.

From then on the situation in Rotterdam improved markedly. City architect *Rose* had originated plans for the construction of both a sewer and a clean water system. From the moment that this plan was initiated in 1874 cholera never returned to Rotterdam.

In 1874 Rotterdam had a population of more than 100,000 people. In view of the ever-increasing growth of the industry more people were required. Many of these came from the countryside. In 1890 the population of Rotterdam had increased to 200,000. Rotterdam was now bursting at the seams and new suburban areas were constructed around the old city. Within a short time Rotterdam had annexed Delfshaven, Kralingen and Charlois. Most of the construction was performed fast and slipshod but it was a real improvement over living in the old and dilapidated inner city. There the conditions were less than favorable to say the least. That situation remained until May 1940 when tragedy struck both Rotterdam and the country of the Netherlands. By that time the population of Rotterdam was close to 600,000 citizens.

I was one of those 600,000 people. Born on October 17, 1930 on the Hooidrift # 159A, next to the old city of *Delfshaven*.

40. Old Delfshaven

41. Old Delfshaven

42. Old Delfshaven

43. Old Delfshaven

My father Henk had also been born in Rotterdam, in 1899, and he instilled in me the pride of being a *'Rotterdammer'*. He would tell me never to forget that I was a citizen of *'The largest port in the world'*. He would emphasize that a Rotterdammer by his very nature is more macho, more manly and strong, never a *'crybaby'*. Always ready to do more work and preferably *'heavy'* work in the harbors, loading and unloading ships of all sizes, always active, always moving. Just like the water of the Maas River that flows through the heart of the city toward the North Sea. "Wim", he would say: *"Rotterdam is the biggest port in the world and we have something that Amsterdam does not have. We have the Maastunnel"*!

44. Maastunnel building and Euromast

45. Maastunnel Escalators

True enough, *"they"* did not have a tunnel. What made it all slightly difficult was the fact that my mother Coba had been born in Amsterdam, the capitol of the Netherlands and Rotterdam's rival city. All you soccer fans just think of Ajax and Fijenoord. But since I also loved my mother I always liked Amsterdam and its people and I always will. They were somewhat different from the Rotterdammers. They seemed more jovial, not so stoic, less inhibited or maybe not inhibited at all. They seemed to have more fun and laughed more. They were more exuberant. The Jewish influence played of course also a role. Before the war Amsterdam had a large Jewish population in the *'Jordaan'* district. They brought much art and commerce and not to forget comedians to the city. Amsterdammers were by nature more colorful, more *'smeuig'* (smooth). Their dialect sounded softer than the harsh *'Rotterdam'* dialect. People would always say that the Rotterdam people were better at speaking *'American'* rather than the King's *'English'*. I must admit, the Rotterdam dialect does not sound very pleasing. It is said that people from Rotterdam swear more and most likely more effectively. You must remember that many of Rotterdam's forefathers grew up on the high seas. All these differences only increased my sense of pride of being a kid from the big and tough port city of Rotterdam. Much the same as a U.S. Marine who needs to do more with less and through adversity and discipline becomes a *'proud'* marine and will <u>always</u> be a marine. So it is with me. Regardless of my status in life I will always be a *'Rotterdammer'*. Having said all this I must also tell you that Amsterdam had something that we in Rotterdam had lost. Amsterdam had a city center. Rotterdam's was blasted away on May 14, 1940.

PART III
HOME & FAMILY

Throughout the war we lived in Rotterdam–West, in the Dunantstraat 21a. The street was named after a Swiss citizen, Jean Henri Dunant who lived from 1828 to 1910. Henri was the founder of the Red Cross. I always felt good about the name of our street. It seemed of such a redeeming quality and sounded rather prestigious. Certainly better than most street names that I knew. Besides, everybody had heard of the Red Cross. It was a very short street; maybe 150 meters at the most. On the east side it opened up on the Pieter de Hooghstraat with on the corner a printing company by the name of *Wijt*. This company with its large curved windows and doors occupied about one fourth of the street on the south side. The remainder of the street was made up of 3-story apartments with some workshops on the ground floor. The north side of the street, where we lived, was build against a *'sleeper'* dike, which resulted in what the French call a *'souterrain'* (basement) The entrance to the first floor was at street level with a floor below that rested against the dike on one side and had a back yard at the other. A 6-foot wooden fence with a gate in the back fenced in each backyard. The gate opened up to some open land and a paved road that bordered the Coolhaven, an inland harbor that had been dug in the late 20th Century to make a connection with the Schie; an old waterway that went farther inland. At that connection there was also a bridge called the *'Lage Erf Brug' (Low Farmyard Bridge)* and the beginning of the Schiedamscheweg, which means: *'Road to Schiedam'*. Schiedam is a small town to the west, just a few miles from Rotterdam. Going west from Schiedam you quickly go through another town, Vlaardingen, then Maassluis and when you keep going west a few more miles you end up at Hook of Holland on the North Sea coast. Hook of Holland is now a large departure port for England and other places on the continent of Europe.

The Coolhaven connects with the Maas River; less than a mile to the south of where we lived. Since the water level in the Maas moves with the North Sea tides, locks were constructed between the Maas River and inland harbors. These locks were walking distance from our house and it was always fascinating to watch the ships going in the locks and seeing them either rising or moving down depending on where they were heading. These locks became of some significance toward the end of the war. Near those locks the government had constructed a large building, which was completed during the war and housed the offices of the Dutch Internal Revenue System. We called this building the *'lemon press'*. This building and all the other buildings near our house would play a role during the war.

From the Pieter de Hooghstraat you could get across the Coolhaven by means of the *Pieter de Hooghbrug* (bridge). Once over this bridge and by crossing the *Rochussenstraat* you would be on the *Heemraadsingel* (boulevard or promenade). This boulevard would take you north toward the inner city and the busy shopping area.

Our apartment was on the first floor and consisted of three rooms, a kitchen and a toilet on the street level. The *'souterrain'* below was made up of two large rooms, considerable storage space and another bathroom. One of the rooms in the souterrain had *French* doors that opened up to the backyard. From our balcony we had a great view of everything to the north, west and east of us, with the bridge only a few hundred feet away to the right. There was always a lot of activity in the harbor with sometimes three or four rows of long barges called *'Rijnaken'* (Rhine barges). Those barges would become of importance to the Germans during the first year of the war. Our *'bridge'* was operated from a small *'kiosk'* type house on the south side. On either side of the bridge were circular outcroppings from where you could observe the ships passing through when the bridge was raised. During the German occupation these outcroppings were put to immediate use as anti-aircraft gun positions.

On the Pieter de Hooghstraat were several large and imposing buildings that housed the offices of some big companies, the School of Seafarers, the University of Economics, an Embassy, a church and some apartments; quite a distinguished wide boulevard. By the way, *Pieter de Hoogh* was a famous Dutch painter. Behind the University of Economics was a small cemetery at the foot of the West Zeedijk. It was surrounded by a moat that always looked green from algae. On the cemetery with its imposing gravestones were huge trees. These trees made the place look forbidding and eerie. It was exactly the kind of place where we would play as kids and be scared. During the winter of 44/45 the huge trees on this cemetery would keep us warm. Another street that ended at the Pieter de Hooghstraat was the Willem Buytenwegstraat. This relatively wide street was at least a mile long and curved around the Dunantstraat toward the oldest area of Rotterdam, historic Delfshaven. The pilgrims left for the "new" country from here in the *"Mayflower"* and a famous admiral was born here as well. His name was Piet Hein (1577-1629) Ask any Dutch boy and he will tell you that Piet Hein captured the Spanish *'Silver Fleet'* in 1628 which at that time was valued at 15 million guilders; an enormous sum of money that financed the eighty year war with Spain. Understandably, Piet Hein is one of Rotterdam's favorite citizens

46. Piet Hein – Rotterdam Hero (1577-1629)

The Pieter de Hooghstraat ends at the West Zeedijk. This *'dike'* borders the Maas River with its many harbors with huge cranes and some of the largest and best-known shipping and ship building companies. Across the Maas at about that point is the famous

Waalhaven. The largest man-made harbor shaped like a *'bucket'* with *Waalhaven Airport* at the south end.

The Maas River, 560 miles long, originates in the *Langres Plateau* in NE France and at the town of Hertogenbosch it is joined by the Rhine River coming from Germany. Since the Rhine is the bigger river, most of the water in the Maas River is Rhine water that for many years was so polluted that one could easily develop film in it.

The Maas River points east, like an arrow pointing at the heart of Germany and the industrial Ruhr area. During the war the RAF and US 8th Air Force made good use of that direction beacon. As a result we saw more planes fly east during the five war years than anyone else.

What I have written so far is difficult to imagine without the help of an illustration. Unwittingly a Mosquito pilot did that for us. This pilot was on a photo recon mission on November 29, 1944 and took 10 photos of the Maas River at Rotterdam from a height of 30,000 feet. One of those pictures was taken straight over our house. *

47. *in the top-left-hand part of the photo is a bridge (light grey) spanning the Coolhaven. On the south side of the bridge and slightly to the left is a small white strip with a small bend – that is the Dunantstraat. From the back of our house we had a clear view of the harbor, both left and right. A large park can de seen bordering the river

on the right side.

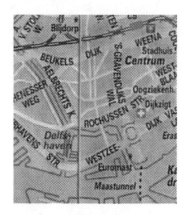

48. *Here you can also identify the Coolhaven (right below where it says 'Roc' of Rochussen') and the city center is indicated as 'Centrum'.

You will be able to identify the places and streets that I have mentioned without much trouble. It will give you a fair idea of our home's location in the west of Rotterdam.

As for the family that lived at number 21a of the Dunantstraat, we were with the seven of us. Aside myself there were: my father Henk, my mother Coba, my brother Henry, my sister Annie, my father's youngest brother Willem (Uncle Wim to us children), and a lady seamstress who occupied the room in the souterrain. She was called *'Juffrouw'(Miss) de Jong*, a *'spinster'* who worked at my father's place of business. She was tall and slender and had a wart on her nose that made her look a little bit like a witch. I am not very proud when I tell you that we played quite a few tricks on her. She got quickly irritated and that only stimulated us to do some naughty things. Interestingly enough, that stopped abruptly when the war started. When my father's parents died he had taken care of his two younger brothers Dirk and Willem. When Dirk got married my dad continued to take care of Willem until his death in 1982.

My dad worked at N.V. Kattenburg, a clothing manufacturer and retailer located on the exactly one kilometer (1000 meter) long Hoogstraat in the heart of the old city. The owners of N.V. Kattenburg were Jewish as were many business owners. The Hoogstraat was *'the'* place to shop and eat; it was old but it had character and a lot of atmosphere. *"Een echte gezellige straat"* (a real cozy street). My dad worked in administration and he knew all there was to know about clothing material and the many different styles. The company was the sole supplier of all police uniforms and other law enforcement agencies in the Netherlands. During the war they manufactured uniforms for the Germans.

It stands to reason that my dad was always very well dressed and expected us, his children, to follow *'suit'*. In this book you will see some pictures that illustrate what I have written. *'Henk'*, as my mother called him, was thin and slender. His poor eyesight forced him to wear glasses with thick lenses. I don't believe he was very strong because I don't remember him ever rolling over the floor or performing other wild stunts with us. He had his daily routine when he came home. He would sit in his easy chair and take a nap until my mom would be ready with dinner. He would sit at the head of the table and my mom would serve him first. After dinner he would sit in his easy chair again and smoke up a storm. My uncle Wim was also a smoker and I remember when, as a small child sitting on the floor, a virtual cloud of smoke would be hanging over me. I got my name from Oom Wim. When, upon my birth on October 17, 1930, my parents had suggested that they would name me after him he said: *"Please do the kid a favor and don't call him Willem Cornelius. They will only make fun of his initials WC."* In Dutch WC stands for Water Closet; the same as 'toilet'. So, they named me 'Willem' only and that's why I don't have middle initial. I have been grateful to Oom Wim ever since. When in the U.S. Army every soldier **must** have a middle initial and so they gave me one. From that point on my name was Willem 'NMNOI' Ridder. NMNOI stood for **No Middle Name Or Initial**.

I never really knew my father very well. Not until much later in life would I get to know him better. He was a very *'proud'* person who loved the city of Rotterdam where he was born in 1899. He never missed an opportunity to instill that love for Rotterdam in me as well. During my *'growing up'* years I remember him as a rather remote person. Mother Coba was, in my mind, the main person of the household. She ran the house. My dad was very good with tools and enjoyed *'knutselen'*, meaning he was a good handy man. For instance during the mid-thirties, together with my mother's cousin whom I called *'Oom Anton'*, he build a radio receiver. Stamp and coin collecting were his great hobbies as well and he had numerous albums with both. As a result I became interested as well and to this day have accumulated a good size stamp and coin collection. These hobbies taught me a great deal about history and geography. Dad was also the founder of a children's choir called *'Onder Ons'* (Among Us). Jacob Hamel, a famous Dutch conductor presided over the choir and his son played the piano for *Onder Ons*. Naturally, the three of us children had to attend the choir but we never liked it. Both Henry and Annie were exempted when they grew up but I had no way out. One time I had to sing solo. I was only 5 years old at that time.

49. A picture of the *'Onder Ons'* children choir. My father is the second and I am the sixth one from the left in the white shirt and tie.

In 1941 my dad contracted tuberculoses, which made him bed-ridden for most of the war. He came through the war OK and retired from his job in 1964. He then became interested in genealogy. He traced our ancestors back to the 1600's and Switzerland.

My mother was born in Amsterdam in 1900 and was the youngest of sixteen children. Her older sisters could easily have been her mother or, for that matter, my grandmother. I never knew a grandmother or a grandfather from either side of the family. They had all passed away by the time I was born in 1930. From my mother's family only seven children, all girls, survived birth. Four of these migrated to the USA where three married and had children. Three of their sons fought in World War II. Richard was a pilot of a B-26 Mitchell bomber in Italy. His plane crashed but he survived and was hidden from the Germans by the Italian resistance. His other claim to fame was that he attended Todd School in Woodstock, Illinois where he graduated in 1931 together with Orson Welles.

Henry and Frank Kriete both served in the U.S. Air Force in the Pacific Theater. Henry was a major in U.S. Air Force on the Island of Tinian in the Pacific. (See "The Atom Bomb" under Epilogue)

Sometime in 1939 our family was given the opportunity to migrate to the United States but my parents never followed through. Their decision would have been different had they known what was in store for us.

My mother Coba was a very caring and nurturing person. She had always wanted to be a teacher but was never given the opportunity to continue her studies beyond high school. She was a very good storyteller and always ready to help me with my studies when in elementary school. She had great energy that enabled her to clean the house, go shopping, cook meals and take care of us kids without ever complaining. She loved my dad and took extra good care of him. Although she was strong she had her problems. She had a bad wound on one of her legs that never healed and had to be cleaned and bandaged every day as long as I remember. When she was a very young girl she had walked into a pit of quick lime and it had burned her leg through to the bone near her ankle. Another problem was goiter. I remember vividly a time in 1935 or 1936 that her throat was so swollen that she could no longer breathe and would have died if not for a stranger in a black suit and coat had come to the rescue. He was a stranger to me, hopefully not to my dad. He instructed my brother Henry and me to go immediately in the back yard and get as many earth worms as we could. The soil was quite soggy and when we each put a spade in the ground and then shook it a little bit literally hundreds of fat juicy worms would come to the surface. We collected our worms and took them to this stranger who put them in a cloth and then proceeded to tie the bundle with the worms inside around my mother's neck. Then a miracle happened. In less than 15 minutes my mom started to breathe again and her goiter had greatly diminished in size. I was there when the stranger removed the cloth. All the worms were dead and where they had been pink before they were now totally black, like charcoal. I have always found this quite miraculous but it really happened. There must be an explanation for it and all I can think of is that the worms provided much needed oxygen and died in the process.

In doing the genealogy for my mother's side of the family, my dad obtained information that took us back to the year 1200 with roots originating in Denmark and Germany. Mother outlived my father by fourteen years. She died in Rotterdam at the age of 97.

PICTURES FROM BEFORE, DURING AND AFTER THE WAR.

50. Father and mother in 1939 under the Coolhaven Bridge with its round concrete pillars. We hid under this bridge during the early years of the war.

51. Author on the Beach in Scheveningen in 1934

52. That's me when I was 4 years old with the
neighborhood girls. The building behind us was a consular
building that the Germans confiscated. (See Pics 57 & 60)

53. The author and his horse in Kindergarten in 1935

54. On the Coolhaven Bridge with the neighborhood
girls. Annie is on the left.

55. At 6 years of age in 1936 with the neighborhood girls.
Annie, my sister, is on my left. We are sitting on a railing
of the Coolhaven Bridge parapet; a kind of outcropping
from where you could watch the passing ships. During
the war the Germans would have anti-aircraft guns (flak)
here.

56. In 1936 with my sister Annie and my *'big'* brother
Henry in front of our house in the Dunanstraat 21a.
We are standing in front of the window of the basement
bedroom(s). When the war broke out on the early
morning of May 10, 1940 we watched from this window.

57. The author beating his drum in the Dunantstraat in the spring of 1937 (The building in the back can also be seen on #52 & 63)

58. Tosca and I in the field behind our house. In the background the bridge where we would hide during bombing raids. The "skyscraper" in the background had AA guns on the roof throughout the war.

59. In 1941 with Tosca behind the fence of the backyard.
We lost Tosca during the *'hunger winter'* in '44/45

60. During 1943 in High School. I am the second one
from the right, second desk behind the girls, big tie and a
serious face.

61. Dad, Henry, mother, Annie and Oom Wim in 1943.
They all look underfed and very grim.

62. Dad, Henry, Annie and I in August 1945. Henry
moved from the Resistance into the new Dutch Army
and would serve in the Dutch East Indies (Indonesia). We
look a lot happier on this picture. Note the enamel plate
on the brick wall to my left. It shows my dad's designation
of *Assistant Air Raid Warden*. I removed it after the war.
The same plate is shown below.

63. The Dunantstraat in 2005, building in the back still there, see #51 and #54. The Printing Company of Wijt is on the right.

64. Assistant Air Raid Warden

65. Armband for Assistant Air Warden. "Blok Hoofd" literally translated: "Block Head" (not very flattering)

CHAPTER ONE

WAITING FOR THE INEVITABLE

Henry remembers:

"On September 3, 1939 I was listening to the BBC and heard Chamberlain declare war on Germany. I remember calling my parents and Uncle Wim (my father's brother who lived with us) to switch to the Dutch station; England had declared war on Germany"

England considered itself at war with Germany at 11:00am on Sunday, September 3, 1939. That was the time when the ultimatum expired that Prime Minister *Chamberlain* had presented the German nation as a result of the German attack on Poland. Six hours later, at 5pm, the French Government followed suit and also declared war on Germany.

66. Neville Chamberlain, Prime Minister of Great Britain
(1869-1940)

The western allies had tried to avoid the catastrophe till the last moment. England had demanded cessation of hostilities and withdrawal of the German military immediately following their invasion of Poland on September 1st. At that point they had not yet used the word "ultimatum". It still appeared conceivable that *Neville Chamberlain* and his French allies would concede once again. With the uncontested German invasion of democratic Czechoslovakia they had shown their willingness to do just about anything to keep the peace. Those first two days of September were a guessing game. They had turned down a proposal by Benito Mussolini because they had not wanted to negotiate while the Germans were still in Poland.

67. Benito Amilcare Andrea Mussolini (1883-1945)
PM and fascist dictator of Italy from 1922 until his
overthrow in 1943.

However, it was unclear whether England and France had the stomach for war. The time expired without there being any word from Berlin. Only on Sunday morning did the English ambassador in Berlin advise the Hitler-government that his government would take action after the expiration at 11 o'clock. From that moment forward Germany would be facing its first enemies in the Second World War. Around and between these belligerent countries were at that time still very neutral nations. Small democracies in the west: Norway, Sweden, Denmark, the Netherlands, Belgium, Luxemburg and much farther away, on the other side of the Atlantic Ocean, the United States of America under the leadership of Franklin Delano Roosevelt. These countries all declared themselves impartial in the conflict but it was clear that their sympathies went with the democratic nations as opposed to the fascists. At the last moment these countries had attempted to get the negotiations going again. King Leopold of Belgium was the spokesperson for the Western European countries. On August 24 he had suggested that differences be discussed in a large international conference; five days later both Queen Wilhelmina of the Netherlands and King Leopold offered their services for a peaceful solution. President Roosevelt was actively seeking diplomatic solutions in Berlin and Rome. All this was in vain. Fascist Italy had no influence what so ever in what was going on. In a boisterous speech to the Reichstag on September 1 Hitler had thanked his dictator friend Mussolini for his good intentions but that he was now taking control and would not ask for any *'outside'* assistance.

68. Adolf Hitler 'Der Fuehrer' of the German Third Reich
(1889-1945)

The greatest gift that he could have received from the outside was thrown in his lap by the sympathetic stand of Soviet Russia. In those last two weeks of August it became clear that as a result of the 1938 betrayal of Czechoslovakia by the west they had lost far more than a well-equipped and organized ally in Middle-Europe. The Soviet-Union concluded from this development that the western countries were not able and willing to honor their obligations. Even their ally Poland had acted criminally and shortsighted by wanting to participate in the partitioning of Czechoslovakia. An unshakable Molotov replaced the Russian Secretary of State Litwinov, a proponent of collective security. From that time forward there was only one policy applied toward international politics in the Soviet Union: security at any cost. The internationalism of the communist ideology was now replaced by pure Russian nationalism. The sovereignty of the Russian borders had to be guaranteed. All during the French and English negotiations which were kept going for months, the Russians met secretly with the German Nazis. The naïve English and French diplomats never suspected anything and on August 21 they were unpleasantly surprised by the German Russian non-aggression pact.

69. Molotov signed Pact with Germany. Ribbentrop is
standing to the right of Stalin.

The German Secretary of State, Joachim von Ribbentrop went to Moscow to sign the accord. The public opinion in the whole world was total bewilderment. The impossible had happened: reconciliation of fascism and communism. The agreement had been entered into for a period of 10 years and precluded the possibility of armed conflict between the two countries. At the same time, the two nations agreed to take a neutral position when either one would get into an armed conflict with a third party. A few weeks later it became clear that several secret clauses had been added to the agreement. On September 17th Russian troops entered Poland from the east and occupied a number of provinces that the Germans had allotted them. From the start of Hitler's rise to power on January 30, 1933, the foreign policy of England had based itself on the totally erroneous belief that Russians and Germans would never join hands. Communism had been an obsession of both French and English conservative politicians ever since the ending of the First World War. The downfall of the precarious Weimar Republic with its strong anti-communist opposition and in many eyes dangerous social-democratic leanings could have been the beginning of a stable conservative political period. France was afraid that such would also lead to a greater sense of German nationalism and a growing demand for a further dismantling of the Treaty of Versailles. But the English conservative politicians who had been dictating international politics for years appeared to be kindly disposed toward the new government of Adolf Hitler. At last, they argued, there would be a strong and self-conscious German state that would be a force opposing the communist hordes from the east. They further argued that the anti-Semitic rhetoric and numerous other demagogic points of the National Socialist program wouldn't be that bad and in time would lose emphasis and importance. In England they considered the French fear of German militarism exaggerated. Hadn't Germany's opportunities for waging war been significantly curtailed with the Treaty of Versailles? Even France had lately become more amenable to 'reasonable' German demands. They argued that the new countries in Middle-Europe that were so closely aligned with Germany would be strong enough to oppose the German *"Drang Nach Osten"* (Desire to go East). On top of that, they argued, Mussolini who in his own country had a minority of Germans would oppose any plans for revenge. What they had not bargained for was that with the National-Socialist government they were not

5

dealing with men who would play by the rules of the political game. The new German government was made up of criminals and lunatics and the German population followed them blindly. Anti-Semitism turned out to be the most important point on the Nazi agenda and they never gave a thought to dropping that point. On the contrary, it was exercised with unbridled harshness at every opportunity. In their foreign policies the Nazis replaced negotiations with blackmail and extortion. The Treaty of Versailles was unilaterally liquidated. The draft was implemented; the Treaty of Locarno was voided and the Rhineland remilitarized. Mussolini, who initially had been opposed to German annexation and even prevented an earlier annexation of Austria, was becoming more and more enamored with Adolf Hitler. He had considered him a novice and poor imitator but now became impressed with the corporal's successes and by his own words wanted also to "live dangerously". Mussolini had his own designs for expansion. He dreamed of a large Italian nation in Africa. Ethiopia, the English and French possessions in East-Africa, territory around the Mediterranean, the Mare Nostre .... Our sea. He therefore was looking for supporters and found those in Germany. The Nazis were happy enough to let Mussolini chase his crazy dreams in exchange for his non-involvement in their Central-European program. Mussolini, the imbecile, accepted. However, his adventure into Ethiopia brought him the animosity of the whole Western world. He eventually was able to conquer Ethiopia albeit at great expense of both material and loss of life. The gain of Ethiopia certainly did not weigh up against political influence on the European political stage. England and France were quick to observe that decisions within the Rome-Berlin axis were made in Berlin. Rome just played along.

Italy had its empire abroad and Germany decided European politics. Therefore, when in 1936 the Spanish Civil war started Germany and Italy would be standing shoulder to shoulder in support of Franco, who was rebelling against the legally appointed government of the Spanish Republic.

70. Francisco Franco (1892-1975)

Both German and Italian volunteers joined hands in this conflict. Particularly the German Luftwaffe was eager to participate and obtain some practical experience by bombing and strafing cities and villages.

71. Guernica, Spain, leveled by the 'Luftwaffe'

72. Picasso's Guernica: Testimony of War

The Western countries were deadly afraid to risk a national conflict and followed an uncertain course of non-involvement. The Republican forces, which also in the non-fascist countries were unfortunately and wrongly painted as communist terrorists, had to give up their battle due to exhaustion. In the meantime, without meeting any opposition or interference, Hitler crossed into Austria with the help of the Nazi: *Seyss Inquart.*

73. Seyss-Inquart (1892-1946)

From this moment on Hitler would be unstoppable. Within the Czechoslovakian border lived many Germans. Konrad Henlein would be Hitler's henchman. Czechoslovakia had solid connections with France; furthermore the country was a highly developed industrial state and a parliamentary democracy. There was no other country in the center of Europe with the strong orientation toward the west as

Czechoslovakia. In spite of that it was abandoned; the west did not want to use force. They didn't even want to threaten it. England had send Lord Runciman to the Sudeten who upon return concluded that Heinlein's demands were well founded. In September 1938 Hitler forced the English and the French to agree to Czechoslovakia ceding Bohemia & Moravia to Germany. Triumphant German troops entered their new possession. Jews and socialist workers who Lord Runciman had neglected to ask for advice now fled to Prague to get away from the Nazis. The Nazis followed them there when in 1939 they swallowed the rest of Czechoslovakia. At last England decided on a stronger position. In April it guaranteed the Polish borders. The Russian-French-English discussions had to lead to an agreement that would prohibit Hitler from further expansion. Too late. Germany was now firmly in control of Central-Europe. Russia understood that in order to protect its western border it would have to rely on the Nazis. In this way Western international politics went down the drain and the only thing left now would be brute force.

Credits: "Tomorrow At Dawn" by J. G. de Beus

CHAPTER TWO

"THE DIE HAS BEEN CAST"

Now that the two major Western powers had committed themselves to oppose Herr Hitler, it became quickly evident that all events were now leading inexorably toward war.

In one of his most aggressive speeches at the end of April 1939 Hitler cancelled both the naval armament agreement with England and the Treaty of Friendship with Poland. The die had been cast: Hitler had decided to force the issue. In fact, on April 3 he had already instructed the Oberkommando der Wehrmacht, the Supreme Command of the Armed Forces, to draw up plans for Operation *'Fall Weiss'*, (Case White) the war against Poland. He explained to his commanders that what he wanted was *'lebensraum'*, living space for Germans in the East. In June he ordered all preparations to be completed by August 20. In spite of the fact that all these decisions were conducted in the greatest secrecy the aim was becoming clearer and clearer taking on a most threatening shape. Holland's Military Attaché in Berlin was Major Gijsbert Sas. His old friendship with a German colleague would become of inestimable value. This German officer was a true German patriot who acted from moral indignation against Hitler's regime and methods. He was convinced that an offensive in the West would bring disaster to not only the neutral countries attacked and to Europe as a whole, but above all to Germany itself. In the end he paid with his life for trying to prevent it. Soon after April 3rd he had informed Sas of orders that had been given for full preparedness by early August for war with Poland. Forebodings of doom were expressed on June 22, 1939 in the following note to the Netherlands Foreign Office.

Memorandum
From: Her Netherlands Majesty's Minister in Berlin
To: Netherlands Foreign Minister, The Hague

"It appears that two weeks ago the decision was taken to force the Polish crisis to explode not after, but before the great Nazi party convention of September. Hence all military furloughs have been cancelled as of July 20 and the first signs of German activity can probably be expected from August 15 on. For this future military activity preparations are already under way in the shape of troop concentrations towards East Prussia and also towards Silesia and Slovakia. This has given rise to stories in the English and French press about an intended occupation of Slovakia, which stories, however, are premature. Plans now in the process of preparation at General Staff headquarters are to push forward simultaneously to the northeast and southeast, i.e. towards Memel and towards Slovakia as far as Ruthenia. Thus Poland would be completely surrounded, leaving only the theoretical possibility of rescue by the Russians. In that respect one is more and more inclined to doubt here whether Russia would be prepared to conclude an alliance with England.........If, however, such an alliance should come into being, it is assumed that Russia will first await what England would do, and it is believed that England would, in view of the situation in China, think twice before coming to the aid of Poland, which is geographically almost impossible".

Indications for the above suppositions are:

1. *The press campaign against Poland, which is on the rise again after having abated for a few weeks.*
2. *The vicious campaign against England, which is openly being accused of desiring the destruction of Germany by Russia and Poland.*
3. *A remark by the British Ambassador who, some ten days ago, said to me that he did not agree with those who expected a lull until September. Two other members of the British Embassy, who said they expected August to be the critical month, confirmed this view.*
4. *The reply of some officials of the Ministry of Propaganda to my question as to when I should take my holidays: "We all take our leave before August 1, and you would be well advised to do the same."*

Two very reliable sources informed me that the Fuehrer has made it abundantly clear to the General Staff that he wants the Polish question settled this year. In this connection I may point out that 'the Polish Question' is by no means limited to Danzig, but involves the Corridor and Posen, in other words the whole question of the previous German-Polish border".
The Minister:

> *Haersma de With*

When the Germans invaded Holland, all official documents were burned, both at the Legation in Berlin and at the Foreign Office in The Hague. This dispatch escaped because it had been sent for comment to the Dutch Minister in London, Count van Limburg Stirum. This was a man with a personality who, when he was Minister in Berlin, never hid his strong anti-Nazi feelings. In one of his reports from Berlin he wrote, *"Behind the shining shield of their love for peace they are whetting their sword"*

This sentiment was shared by almost all of the foreign diplomats in Berlin. During the summer of 1939 they had reviewed the crises through which they had lived since January 30, 1933, when internal weaknesses finally brought down the parliamentary system of the Weimar Republic and Hitler seized power. That evening when he stood at the floodlit window of the Reichskanzlei, the seat of German government, hysterically cheered by thousands of supporters, he could with some justification tell his followers that a new era had begun: *"the greatest revolution of world history, the revolution of the Germanic race against non-Aryans, Mongols, Bolsheviks, and liberals."*

He had taken firm possession of power in Germany. Equally firm was his determination to possess Europe. Europe had held its breath. It still refused to believe that Hitler would carry out the sweeping and aggressive program described in his book *'Mein Kampf'*.

74. Hitler's Mein Kampf

Even in Holland where public opinion had always resented the rising National Socialism next door, many believed that once Hitler was established in power he would not practice all he had preached. But he did. Western diplomats in Berlin were far more pessimistic about Hitler than their governments or public opinion at home. Everyday, the diplomats saw with their own eyes the symptoms of preparation for war – troops marching by, the economy being geared for self-sufficiency, the dwindling supplies of imported consumer goods, luxury items, food, and gasoline. Even more telling than the determined striving for economic self-sufficiency was the ruthlessness of the Nazi system, its cruelty to the Jews – crowds of whom filled the Dutch Legation waiting-room every day, trying to obtain a Dutch visa - and its disdain for all people who did not belong to the master race of Aryan and Germanic blood. The powerful resentment toward the Nazis was shared by almost all members of the Dutch legation, from relative newcomers to old hands, including the faithful German doorman. However, two unreliable elements had managed to push their way in. One was the new young German assistant doorman, taken on because of the flood of Jewish visitors applying for visas. He was diligent and eager to please – maybe somewhat too eager. He gave the impression that he was trying somewhat too often to listen at doors and to tidy up papers during one's absence. The other was a pretty girl, sent as a secretary from The Hague to cope with the flood of visa applications. She was easy on the eye, but when her background was checked they were shocked to find that she belonged to the small Dutch Nazi party, the NSB (Nationale Socialistische Beweging).

75. The "hated" Dutch Nazi Party Emblem.

Her recall had been requested immediately, but her appointment was indicative of the naiveté and lack of the Legation's security.

The Polish situation was hopeless, as it always had been when Poland's two powerful neighbors got together, as they were about to do again. Major Sas, when driving back to Berlin from Danzig witnessed a sign of things to come. On the badly paved road through the Polish Corridor there approached a heavy cloud of swirling dust from which emerged a squadron of Polish lancers. It was an impressive and stylish yet almost medieval sight. The long lances, carried straight up, made a solid block, as one sees in old paintings. Magnificent horses, magnificent riders – but as Sas described it: *"I shivered to think what would happen when these men with this equipment had to battle German tanks. On Hitler's birthday in April, I had seen them passing in review in Berlin, six abreast, like a wall of steel."*

Credits: "Tomorrow At Dawn" by J. G. de Beus

CHAPTER THREE

FALL WEISS – CASE WHITE

In the meantime, in Danzig the Greek tragedy continued toward a treacherous last act involving a Trojan horse. On August 25 a German training ship, the cruiser *Schleswig-Holstein*, arrived in Danzig for a friendship visit and moored opposite Westerplatte, the Polish military base.

76. The cruiser Schleswig-Holstein

The commander and his officers paid the usual courtesy calls on the High Commissioner of the League of Nations and on the representative of the Polish government, Minister Chodacki. The return calls proceeded with the perfect correctness one might expect on a German man-of-war. The official visitors to the *Schleswig-Holstein* did not know that before entering the harbor the cruiser had in open sea taken on 225 heavily armed shock troops from six German minesweepers. While the Polish Minister inspected the immaculate honor guard of cadets on the main deck, these 225 men sat packed in the hold, almost choking in their confined quarters. None on board knew the real purpose of this "friendship visit" except the Commander, Captain Wilhelm Kleikamp, for only he knew of the secret instruction "GK dos. 250/39." Its contents weighed so heavily on his conscience that during the reception given by High Commissioner Burckhardt, he could keep silent no longer and said to his Swiss host in a subdued voice, "I have terrible orders, which my conscience cannot justify." But he executed it precisely when following one delay he finally received the code word "Fall Weiss" (Case White) on August 31, at 18:35. The moment of attack had been fixed one hour earlier. While the black night sky slowly faded over East Prussia, Commander Kleikamp stood on the bridge of the *Schleswig-Holstein* tensely awaiting the moment: tomorrow at dawn, at 04:45. His eyes sharply fixed on the slow hand of his watch; he saw it reach the forty-fifth minute. At his command, "Fire!" all hell broke loose.

77. The Schleswig-Holstein firing at Westerplatte.

The thunder of the ship's guns rolled over sleeping Danzig, and a sea of fire and steel poured on the Westerplatte. The Second World War had begun.

The attack on the Westerplatte had to be abandoned around ten in the morning because the SS troops had been decimated by heavy Polish artillery fire for which they were not prepared. By then 127 of the 225 SS men had been killed.

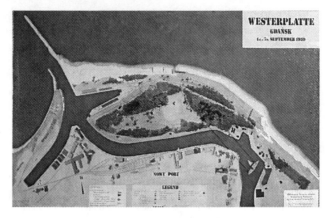

78. Westerplatte

The occupation of Danzig during the very first hours of the war was only a sideshow from the military point of view. The real attack took place farther south across the Polish border. For six days a group of SS men had been waiting on the Polish border to fake a Polish attack on the German radio station at *Gleiwitz* on the eve of the main offensive.

79. The German Gleiwitz radio tower

Dressed in Polish uniforms, the SS men captured the radio station by surprise, broadcast a brief anti-German speech, and left a few drugged concentration camp inmates, significantly code-named *"canned goods"*, dying on the spot as casualties to prove there had been a Polish attack. At daybreak, just as the guns of the *Schleswig-Holstein* were thundering destruction over the Westerplatte in Danzig, Hitler's armored columns roared across the Polish border and German airplanes swooped down on the Polish airfields, destroying most of Poland's 405 planes on the ground. The Polish campaign was quickly decided when some 1,000 German tanks, divided into a Northern and a Southern Army Group, rumbled across the Polish plains, seizing the bulk of the Polish army in an iron pincer movement. The Polish campaign made a horrifying display of the power and efficiency of the armed force Hitler had created from nothing. This was totally contrary to the belief that Polish and German forces were well matched and that this could lead to a stalemate that might open the door to a compromise peace. Some serious observers in Berlin even continued to repeat the fairy tale that many of the German tanks that had so gloriously occupied Vienna and Prague were made of cardboard. Pretty tough cardboard, as the Polish lancers found when they fell under deadly fire charging the German armor with their lances*.

Conquered Poland would be organized into a *General-Gouvernement Polen*, a high sounding title for a colony to be exploited to the bitter end. The mission of the Gouvernor-General *Hans Frank*: to exterminate the Polish intelligentsia and to turn the rest of the Polish nation into slaves for the master race of the Third Reich

80. Invasion of Poland, September 1939

*Although this is what you may find in many writings about the Polish Campaign, it is very doubtful that this actually occurred.

81. Hans Frank (1900-1946)

Holland's turn would be next.

Credits: "Tomorrow At Dawn" by J. G. de Beus

CHAPTER FOUR

EARLY WARNING

The first warning reached the Dutch Legation in Berlin on October 9, 1939. Seven months later on May 9, 1940 after more than eighteen or even as many as twenty-nine postponements by Hitler, mostly due to bad weather, the prophecy became reality. Major Sas was getting his information from a ghost informer, who was "very highly placed in the German military hierarchy." As a result of the many postponements, the Dutch Government in The Hague had lost faith in Sas and his informer. On Monday, November 13, the Netherlands Prime Minister, a stubborn old gentleman who had proved his distrust of Sas' warnings, delivered a radio speech intended to reassure the nation. He just wanted to say, "The disturbing rumor of the last few days about an imminent danger of war for Holland lacked all foundation;" the government had been misinformed. He ended his speech by quoting a little Dutch poem, which has since become famous in Holland:

Man often suffers most from fear
Of sufferance that may seem near
But that in fact does not appear

There may be some truth in the little poem quoted by the Prime Minister, but the reverse is equally true:

Most difficult we often find
To maintain awareness of the mind
Of a danger to which the eye is blind.

The truth was, as confirmed after the war, that Hitler did indeed postpone the attack maybe as many as twenty-nine times. And each time it was the weather.
Credits: "Tomorrow At Dawn" by J. G. de Beus

CHAPTER FIVE

THE MAN WHO TRIED TO SAVE THE WORLD

On November 8, 1939 Hitler delivered a rousing speech in the Buergerbraukeller in Munich to commemorate his attempted coup of 1923.

82. Buergerbraukeller - Beer hall

Contrary to his habit, he left the crowded beer cellar as soon as he had finished speaking. Twelve minutes later a bomb exploded in the very place where Hitler had just been haranguing his followers.

83. Hitler would not have survived this explosion.

Seven people died and sixty-three were wounded – but Hitler was still alive. To think that a difference of twelve minutes could have prevented the attack on Holland saved all of Western Europe from war and millions of deaths from battle and wanton killings, rid the world of this driving maniac, and perhaps open the prospect of a negotiated peace. Twelve minutes that could have saved the world!

Credits: "Tomorrow At Dawn" by J. G. de Beus

84. Johann Georg Elser, the man who tried to save the world. (1903-1945)

Chapter Six

The Venlo Incident

In *Tomorrow At Dawn!* By J. G. de Beus, the author gives a vivid report of what happened at the border crossing in Venlo on that fateful day of November 9.

Two British Secret Service agents were suddenly overpowered and kidnapped by Gestapo men who had lured them there by posing as representatives of a German opposition group. A Dutch lieutenant, Klop, a former assistant of Major Sas, who was accompanying the British and tried to resist was shot. The British intelligence officers were dragged over the border and abducted in a German car. As it turned out, Lieutenant Klop had been killed on the spot; Major Stevens and Captain Best survived miraculously for five and a half years in German concentration camps. The German Press revealed that both Intelligence officers had tried to precipitate a revolution in Germany. The involvement of a Dutch officer provided Hitler with proof that the Dutch did not adhere to their neutrality. That would come in handy as an excuse to invade Holland on May 10, 1940.

Credits: "Tomorrow At Dawn" by J. G. de Beus

Chapter Seven

How It All Began

Mother remembers:

"Thursday evening, May 9, your father had a meeting with the choir and Oom Wim was reading the newspaper and pointed to an article and said: "Coba that can mean War!" We didn't realize that it would be that soon. Later that night, toward early morning, we were awakened by the sirens and an enormous noise from low flying airplanes".

Henry remembers:
"The evening of May 9th is still vivid in my memory. Oom Wim was reading the paper and told my parents that the situation looked very bad and that he was sure that we would be drawn into the war as well."

Rotterdam, May 10, 1940,
Early morning

It sounds like a deep throaty bark from far away and the wailing of a million banshees. One moment it sounds very close and the next moment it fades only to come back with more insistence. It is at the same time all-encompassing and urgently penetrating. I know it is out to get me and I am terribly frightened but I can't see anything. Even so, I must get away from it. But my legs are stuck in what feels like quicksand. By trying to lift one leg up the other pushes deeper in the muck. Now it feels like I am going to drown in this muck and all the time that barking and wailing from above continues unabated. I am trying to scream for help but I just know that I can't get any sound out of my mouth. My breathing is now getting more and more difficult. With a final effort to catch some air I wake up and open my eyes. Thank God, it's only a dream and immediately I feel relief and happiness that I am still alive. But then I hear the wailing and that deep throaty barking again and I know that part was not a dream. It's for real. I look around the room and I can tell that it must be early in the morning because some light is coming through the high cellar window in my sister Annie's bedroom. Her bedroom is on the side of the street. My brother Henry with whom I share my bedroom is already at the window together with Annie and I can tell that they are peering at the sky above. Quickly I join them but because of my short stature, I am only nine years old, I can't see much of anything. I think I can see some small puffs of smoke in the early morning sky but they could be clouds. But no, they can't be because all of a sudden I see several more appear up high and then hear the accompanying explosions. That awful wailing is coming from the air raid sirens in our neighborhood. Henry and Annie can see more of what's going on and tell me that they saw planes flying over. We all knew that was not unusual. In the past couple of months we had heard and sometimes seen planes flying over Rotterdam. We were told that those planes were English because England was at war with Germany and they sometimes entered Dutch airspace by mistake. The sirens would start wailing and then we would hear the anti-aircraft guns in the harbor area near our house. We were told that the guns never fired directly at the planes and they would quickly fly west again. It must have been those guns doing the shooting this morning but this time it just kept on unabated and somehow it felt more real this time. After the initial shock the three of us ran upstairs to the living room where our mom and dad, who have an upstairs bedroom, were already in the living room listening to our new radio. A Philips bought in 1938. What a beauty. It had a polished bakelite exterior with lit dials and what looked like a green eye that could expand and contract depending on how strong and sharp the reception was. It had real loudspeakers that carried a superb clear sound. My dad and Uncle Anton had built our previous set. They had wound the coil themselves at Uncle Anton's factory on the Westzeedijk, about a mile from where we lived in the Dunantstraat. That set was big and must have weighed a ton. But it worked. The new Philips had now replaced this set and we were listening to the Hilversum Station this early morning of the 10th of May 1940. As long as I live I will never forget anything that happened from then on for the next five years. Everything made an indelible impression on me. At the age of 9 your existence is totally dependent on adults taking care of you, feeding and nurturing you. It is obvious to a child that those adults have total control over just about everything that goes on. You never worry because your parents seem so confident and knowledgeable in everything they do. They have an answer to every situation. That was about to change. The announcer was just now telling us something that sounded rather bizarre. He told us:*" Be sure to listen to the sound of my voice as the only true one and don't be fooled by imitators". He then proceeded to tell us: "At 3:55am Nazi Germany has violated our neutrality and without provocation has entered the Netherlands at numerous places along the Dutch/German border. German paratroopers are being dropped between The Hague and Rotterdam and also at the airport Waalhaven on the south side of the Maas River. The Dutch army, navy and air force are resisting the invaders and making them pay dearly for their treachery. As of this morning our country finds itself at war with Nazi Germany. Queen Wilhelmina will address the nation at 8:00am".*

With those words the world around us collapsed and our peaceful existence came to a sudden stop.

On May 10th Chamberlain resigned and was replaced as Prime Minister of England by Winston Churchill who immediately formed a war cabinet drawn from all political parties.

85. Sir Winston Churchill (1874-1965)

On this same day German paratroopers in gliders landed on the grounds of the Belgian fort of Eben Emael and in a brief struggle captured it together with its 1,200-man garrison.

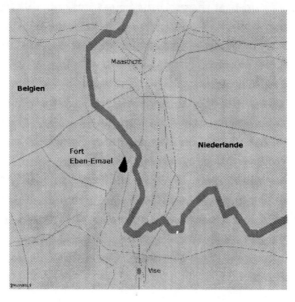

86. Location of Fort Eben Emael

87. Eben Emael Bunker

It is already clear, just hours into the German advance that the Belgian and Dutch armies will be unable to delay, let alone offer any significant defense against, the panzer Blitzkrieg.

Henry remembers:

"We went on the balcony to see what was going on. There were a lot of aircraft and one of them came straight at us. I remember telling my dad "He is dropping something". He sure did, it was a bomb that sailed over our house and hit the harbor area near the Rotterdam Lloyd docks. By then we saw the German crosses and the swastika on the aircraft and we knew."

Chapter Eight

The Waalhaven Attack

At 3:55 in the morning of May 10, 1940 German airplanes had appeared above airfield Waalhaven in Rotterdam. In order to surprise us they had flown to their targets from the west. For an hour the airfield was bombed and strafed; followed by the dropping of "fallschirmjaeger" (paratroopers) around the airfield.

However, things were not going all that well for the invaders. Two Heinkel 111 – C3 medium bombers would perform the first action of the morning.

In 1940 these were the heaviest bombers the Germans had in their arsenal. Two 1,350 hp Junkers Jumo 211F-2 engines powered these planes. It had 6 machine guns of different caliber, a maximum bomb load of 7,165 lb (3,250 kg) and a crew of 4.

88. A formation of Heinkel-111 bombers

Earlier that morning they had approached Rotterdam from the west, the North Sea side, and were now just about above their target area. The radioman had left his position to man one of the 13mm MG's in the dorsal blister and the gunner in the ventral gondola under the belly of the plane had been lying behind his downward pointing double barrel 7.9mm MG 81's during the whole flight, ready for action. The bombardier was counting down. The morning mist didn't allow for much vision yet and the pilot had to go down to about 750 meters before he could see in the distance that 'bucket' shaped stretch of water.

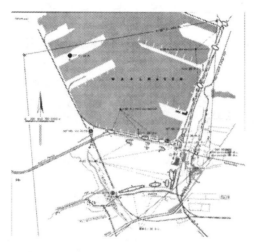

89. The 'Bucket' shape of Waalhaven with the airfield at its bottom.

"Now", the pilot yelled to his bombardier who immediately pushed the button of the automatic bomb release system and returned to his seat. The second Heinkel performed the same function at that same moment. The bomb bays opened up and before the bombers had reached the southern edge of the field the bombs tumbled down. First horizontal for a short while and then falling forward to aim straight at the earth. By the time the two Heinkels had reached the northern boundary of the field the bombs had all been released and were reaping havoc on hangers and planes. While zooming low over the water of the Waalhaven the pilots began their turn to once again take them over the airfield. In the meantime the gunners placed new bandoliers in their MG's and prepared for another strafing. In the first Heinkel the pilot looked at his bombardier and said: "Well, How'd we do?" "I think about eighty percent" was the answer. The pilot tried to figure out how many bombs had hit the target but gave up when he reached the target and saw flames and great clouds of smoke rising from the ground. When the field disappeared from his view the bombers headed east toward the fatherland and a new load of bombs. Unbeknownst to them the 3rd Royal Dutch Fighter Group made up of 11 Fokker G-1 planes, the most modern plane in the Dutch arsenal had been alerted and when the 2 Heinkels appeared at about 3:55am, their engines were already turning.

90. Fokker G-1's

91. Fokker G-1's in flight

92. Waalhaven Attack: Fokker G-1 chasing Heinkel-111

Bomb fragments hit three of the planes but eight of them were able to get in the air where they climbed and waited for the unsuspecting Heinkels below them. It was in that split moment that the two Heinkel crews knew they were doomed. From above, a fire spitting Fokker G-1 piloted by J. P. Kuipers and his gunner J. R. Venema scored hits left and right on both Heinkels and they saw both planes heading for what the Germans like to call 'Valhalla'. That is the place in the hereafter where the heroes would be drinking wine out of the skulls of their slain enemies. The G-1's then severely damaged a third Heinkel 111 which left the scene trailing smoke. Pilot Kuipers had to land his plane because of a damaged engine that he could not get started once he had landed back at Waalhaven. The second wave of bombers was met by a G-1 piloted by P. Noomen and his gunner H. de Vries. They scored direct hits on two of the Heinkels and saw them both go down in a nice wide spiral until they impacted with the ground where their occupants joined their brethren in the hereafter. Fokker G-1 #311 piloted by Pilot G. Sonderman and gunner H. Holwerda were at that same time involved in a dogfight with several German fighters, Me-109's.

93. German Luftwaffe Me-109
They shot down two of them.

94 & 95. Two Me-109's that did not make it.

96. Crash landing of a Ju-52 transport

Then they proceeded to destroy one of the German transport planes, a JU-52.

Pilot H. F. Souffree and his gunner J. C. de Man in Fokker G-1 #328 accounted for an additional two German planes shot down in flames. They had also been hit and had to make an emergency landing on the beach at Oostvoorne where they joined K. W. Woudenberg and J. A. Pauw, respectively Pilot and Gunner of G-1, # 329. They had made an emergency landing on the beach after shooting down a Ju-87 and a Ju-52.

Fokker G-1, #330 piloted by Wubalda and gunner Wagenaar were, at 4:00am, the last plane to get off the ground at Waalhaven but in spite of being severely damaged by enemy fire was able to shoot down two German planes. They had to make an emergency landing at Zevenbergen. These six Dutch planes had on the early morning of May 10 together accounted for thirteen enemy planes shot down and one severely damaged. A feat that I believe has never been fully appreciated.

CHAPTER NINE

AIRBASE DE KOOIJ

At about the same time up north, at the air base 'de Kooij' near Den Helder

97. Dutch Airbase 'de Kooij"

Bob Vanderstok, pilot in the Royal Dutch Air Force, and his squadron were in the air above their base. It was about six in the morning, the sun just barely sending its first hesitant light from the east.

98 *Bob van der Stok is on the left

The squadron of D-21's was divided in three sections of three and only the section commander's plane was equipped with a radio. They could talk to the ground station and the other section leaders, but not to the other pilots in their formation. Without warning they saw the Messerschmitts coming, one single Geschwader – a group of nine fighters with the highly recognizable black crosses on the wings and fuselage. Bob tried to say something on his radio: "We are being attacked by German Me.109's!" But there was a lot of talk on the radio, all on the same frequency, and it would have made no difference if they had no radios at all. The German fighters approached as if they expected little or no resistance. Two of them began strafing the buildings and some other planes on the ground, but then realized that they were being attacked. A dogfight of at least eighteen fighters developed, right above Den Helder airfield. Some of the Germans had used a lot of their ammunition on ground targets, and they had to fly a long way back to their own base in Germany. They had not counted on spending much time, or fuel, at their target. This unexpected situation probably caused a momentary hesitation, which put them at a disadvantage. Bob Vanderstok saw four Messerschmitts in their steepest turns with a D-21 on their tails. There was a lot of shooting as he saw the German tracer bullets streaking through the air. Wherever he looked he saw planes dog fighting; they were easily recognizable by their silhouettes. The Me.109's had sleek, liquid-cooled engines and retractable landing gear while the Dutch D-21's had stubby, radial-engine noses and a fixed landing gear.

99. D-21 formation

The D-21's ability to make shorter turns taught the Germans an unexpected lesson in the very first minutes of their well-planned attack on Holland. VanderStok closed in on a Me.109 and noticed immediately that he gained on him in a left turn. At close range, he opened fire with two machine guns and a stream of white smoke erupted from the enemy plane. VanderStok thought that he had done enough harm and knew that the Me.109 would never make it back over the Zuiderzee. Next to VanderStok was Dop, also on the tail of a Kraut and shooting. Then he heard Lt. Van Overvest (Spanky), who had a radio, say: "I got him. He is making a forced landing on our field."

Then he saw another Messerschmitt go down in a spin with black smoke trailing from the engine. Another Me.109 was attacking VanderStok's plane and he immediately threw the D-21 in a left turn, making it impossible for the German to adjust his aim at a moving target. The German tried to close in, but in three turns VanderStok was on his tail. Half a turn further and he had acquired the right angle to aim in front of him. He pumped him full with lead and the plane went down in the sea making a big white splash. The rest of the Geschwader disappeared in an easterly direction and the D-21's went in for landing. Over his radio Vanderstok heard, "German troops have invaded our Dutch territory, and the government considers itself in a state of war with Germany." They had known that before the government did.

Once on the ground, there was a great deal of excitement and a lot to talk about. VanderStok's plane was completely intact, but several of the others had bullet holes. One of the pilots had a wound in the calf of his leg. He had managed to land his severely shot up fighter, but then collapsed and had to be taken to a hospital. None of the others were injured, but the damage to the D-21's was more than initially had been thought. There was also some minor damage elsewhere. Ground crews immediately refilled the fuel tanks and reloaded the guns. Captain Hein Schmidt Cranz, the squadron leader called them together for a briefing. Four Germans had been shot down, one of them the commander of the German Geschwader. He had made that forced landing on the field. In the briefing room the radio was on and they heard the confusing news of the one-hour old war. Further attacks were obviously expected, and captain Hein quickly reorganized his remaining fighting units. Even planes with bullet holes and other minor damage were readied for flying. "All our D-21's up in the air, you are probably safer up there than here," Hein said. "We expect Stuka bombing of the airfield, so as soon as your plane is ready you go and attack any German aircraft you see." They took off for the second time, and made a few primitive rules for the use of the radios. Seven D-21's were once again above the air base of Den Helder. The radio was quiet this time. By this time the sun was up. It was 8:00 am. Suddenly they heard the ground station say that dive-bombers and fighters were attacking them. Simultaneously, VanderStok saw smoke coming from the hangars on the field and a number of German airplanes attacking. The air raid warning system was so slow that they never saw them coming. The attack was short but apparently very effective and in spite of the presence of the D-21's; quite a surprise.

100. A formation of Stukas

The Stukas disappeared quickly, but the Messerschmitts were still over the field and once again they were engaged in a fight. This time it was short. Van der Stok shot at one of them and registered several hits. The German turned tail and with his higher speed quickly outran the D-21. Then they were ordered to land and were warned about the condition of the field that had several bomb craters in and around the landing area. After having landed, VanderStok taxied to what had been one of the large hangars. When he reached the concrete in front of the destroyed building, a Me.109 came down in a dive and strafed the platform. VanderStok jumped out of his plane that had just now come to a stop. He started to run for shelter when he heard bullets hitting the concrete like a hailstorm. Something hit him on the left shoulder but he didn't feel any pain. He had a camera on a strap around his neck tucked away in his leather jacket. In those days planes did not have cameras installed in the wings. Pilots carried these on their person and hoped to be able to take a picture of a German plane going down in flames as confirmation of a 'kill'. When he looked back he saw his plane with billowing black smoke shooting straight up in the sky. He took a picture just before the remaining ammunition went off and rendered the plane in a twisted heap of aluminum. The Stukas had done immense damage to the buildings and the equipment. He took more pictures of the shambles. Then he saw the Messerschmitt that had made a belly landing on the field and he took a picture of it.

101. Me-109 of Hauptman Robitsch

The first photographic proof of a downed enemy plane. This was the plane of the leader of the Geschwader, Hauptman Robitsch, who had made the initial attack on the airfield. The Germans had thought that the D-21's would still be on the ground and they would be able to destroy the planes before they could take off. That was a very expensive mistake, but with their second wave the Luftwaffe achieved their objective anyway. As an air base, Den Helder was destroyed, except for seven D-21 fighters that could still fly. The German commander was, officially, the first German prisoner of war. Der Alte, as his comrades called him, tried to bluff:

"Friends," he said, "why put up resistance? You have no chance against the German Luftwaffe." No one was in the mood for that kind of talk and one of the pilots drew his pistol. Captain Hein quickly stopped

this confrontation and Der Alte was taken away to spend the rest of the war in POW camps in England and Canada.

*VanderStok escaped to England where he joined the RAF and flew a Spitfire. He participated in the D-Day landings in Normandy in 1944. He was shot down in France and was imprisoned at Stalag 17. He was one of three escapees that made it back to England. Fifty escapees were caught by the Gestapo and put to death. Bob's knowledge of the German language was of immeasurable value in his successful escape. Two of his brothers that were in the Resistance died in German concentration camps. His father lost his eyesight and became crippled as a direct result of Gestapo interrogation methods. Van der Stok is the author of 'War Pilot of Orange'. See the movie 'The Great Escape'.

CHAPTER TEN

GERMAN BLITZKRIEG

The Germans had made rapid advances on all fronts at the Dutch-German border. "Fallschirmjager" as the German paratroopers were called, took the airfields Ypenburg at The Hague, and Waalhaven near Rotterdam. The bridges at Moerdijk were in German hands.

102. German 'Fallschirmjaeger' landing at the Moerdijk
Bridge May 10, 1940

German tanks were moving along the rivers toward the south of Holland and Belgium. German JU.52 transport planes landed on the beaches on the North Sea coast, creating havoc and establishing some strongholds. German paratroopers in civilian clothing, one even disguised as a priest, landed between The Hague and Rotterdam. Dutch radio announcers spread news, which later turned out to be false information, supplied by Dutch-speaking Germans. There were rumors that all drinking water had been poisoned. Dutch soldiers were not to accept drinks or candy from any patriotic citizens; it could be poisoned. The pro-German political party, the N.S.B. (National Socialistische Beweging), would take over the government.

All of these rumors were just that, rumors and there was no truth to it. They were products of the German propaganda machine. But it caused chaos throughout the country. Talk of capitulation was now heard, and German troops were expected at any moment. There would be no more resistance.

In five days the German Luftwaffe had lost more than 500 planes or half of its planes used in the invasion of Holland. On a percentage basis it was the Luftwaffe's biggest loss of the war.

Many planes were lost in air-combat but most were lost on the ground, and while trying to land on beaches from where they could not take off and then subsequently were destroyed by strafing Dutch planes. Many Ju.52's crashed or force-landed on the main highway between The Hague and Rotterdam. It is believed that Dutch anti-aircraft guns shot down some fifty of them. Little has been said or written about this particular feat of arms. To my knowledge, little has been done by the Dutch Government to officially honor those relative few brave men in either the air force, army, navy or marine corps who, against all odds, held off the German Luftwaffe, their crack paratroopers and Wehrmacht personnel for 5 days. It was only when Rotterdam was bombed to smithereens with a promise to do the same to other cities in Holland that these men had to give up the good fight.

CHAPTER ELEVEN

"SO NAHMEN WIR WAALHAVEN!"

"How we captured Waalhaven"

So begins the report of a Hauptman Schulz, who will be awarded the "Ritterkreuz" for this daring feat.

103. German Ritterkreuz, Knight's Cross

He would be flying west, *"against Holland"*. *"My battalion had orders to take Waalhaven Airport and to render it safe for the follow-up paratroopers"*.

The 600 parachutists of Hauptmann Schultz' battalion will be transported to Waalhaven in 50 Ju-52's, flying in formations of nine each. Five of the planes will leave the squadron before reaching Rotterdam and will take a more northerly route. Their destination will be "The Kuip" (the Bathtub). That is the name the Dutch have given their Feijenoord Stadium The fifty men who will jump at the stadium are part of the 11th Company. Their commander is Oberleutnant Horst Kerfin.

104. Oberleutnant Horst Kerfin

His orders upon landing are to push for the bridges across the Maas River and to make contact with the 11th Company of Battalion Choltitz whose seaplanes would be landing on the Maas at 5am.

Hauptmann Schultz's orders also include taking and securing the two bridges across the Maas River in Rotterdam, and hold them until the arrival of ground forces. *"On the eve of the order my men were literally elated when they heard that very soon we would be going into combat. Many couldn't sleep that night. I asked them why they couldn't sleep. Herr Hauptmann, we can't, we are too excited!"*

The next day they take off in their Junker 52's. In her belly, the 'gute, alte Tante Ju' (good old aunty Ju) carried 12 paratroopers who were sitting close together on either side of the aisle. With their silk parachute packs slung low on their backs they are not very comfortable. In the Junker 52 that the 'Fallschirmjaeger' had given such an endearing name were, aside the crew of four and the 12 parachutists, two more men. These were the 'Absetzer' and the 'Uberwacher' respectively, jump master and the overseer.

105. Getting ready to jump

The jump master is sitting next to the pilot and will be responsible for the order to jump. The overseer will then stand at the jump door to ensure that the distance between the jumps is just right; as minimal as possible but not so fast that it would be dangerous. The overseer is not allowed to hasten the process by a forced push. The only thing that the overseer can do in case a parachutist hesitates is to immediately unhook the man from the jump line and quickly get the next man to jump.

Above Holland they receive anti-aircraft fire from the defenders but they don't care. "Mein Jungs, (my boys) think it's laughable", Schulz says.
When he spots many German planes all around him, he is reminded of a funny remark made by one of his men: "When Hermann (Goering) flies all his planes, the birds go on foot!"

106. Formation of Ju-52's

Schultz continues:

"The Dutch are looking up at us with their mouths wide open. Do they have any idea what our flying into their country means? In the distance we see black smoke columns rising from the ground and we are happy that our fighter/bombers have already done their work. Just before reaching Waalhaven the ack-ack gets more accurate. We can hear the explosions above the roar of our engines and feel the plane being hit. My boys look at each other and are no longer smiling. It's now getting serious. We are really concerned now and look forward to the signal to jump. It's definitely no fun to have your plane changed into a sieve. At last the signal to jump is given and in seconds we are all out of the plane".

107. Ju-52 dropping its Fallschirmjager while a Fokker
G-1 is preparing to attack

54

"We can clearly see that the defenses are all around the perimeter of the field. The Dutch seemed to have established several strong defensive positions. Upon landing we immediately get our weapons ready and start running for the airfield. From a slight incline at the edge of the field I can see that my men are already involved in heavy fighting with the enemy. The strong enemy resistance can't hold them back however and before long my men have taken most of the concrete pill boxes."

108. Attacking Waalhaven defenders.

So far Hauptmann Schultz' report.

Major General Droste, Assistant Chief of the Air Defense Command declares: *"At Waalhaven were a few primitive concrete bunkers constructed during the early days of the mobilization. They were more like toys but proved their worth during the bombing. The anti-aircraft guns that could still function have done a formidable job of bringing down enemy planes. That turned out quite a success story but it didn't take long before the gun emplacements and other defensive positions were taken by German paratroopers attacking into our rear."*

Hauptmann Schultz can be proud; he has captured Waalhaven airport! But he is not completely satisfied. In the broader area of the airport there are still some enemy strongholds.

109. Captured Waalhaven

Schultz continues:
"I send the captured Dutch Commander to them with the order to surrender. The Dutchman promises to do so and then return. He didn't come back. But this brave soldier deserves great honor! He was killed by friendly fire when approaching their position. He must have been mistaken for a German."

General Droste tells us:
"...Major Simon Thomas, the commander was put on the front bumper of a car and apparently forced to tell the defenders, who were still active, to surrender with all their weapons. In the end Major Thomas was killed by the Germans when he approached one of the anti-aircraft batteries, maybe intentionally, maybe not, who will know for sure?"

The capture of Waalhaven was part of a bold plan that entailed taking all the large river crossings in the west of Holland in one big swoop. This includes the new Moerdijk Bridge, the main bridge in the City of Dordrecht further north and finally the bridges spanning the Maas River in Rotterdam. By capturing these bridges intact the road to The Hague would be wide open for the invading ground forces. The objective is to take control of the Dutch Government and to capture Queen Wilhelmina, who has her residence in The Hague.
These operations are under the direction of General Kurt Student, commander of the 1st German Airborne Corps made up of two divisions.

110. General Kurt Student (1890-1978)

CHAPTER TWELVE

A BRIDGE TOO FAR?

<u>This will be the first time in human history that such a strategic attack would be conducted totally from the air.</u>
<u>A similar operation comes to mind conducted about 4 years and 4 months later by the combined airborne forces of Great Britain and the United States. That operation would be called "Market Garden". Even the results were similar and it may well be said that even for the Germans at Rotterdam it was also: "A Bridge Too Far"</u>

To the south of Rotterdam the German plan was executed successfully with the surprise attack on the large Moerdijk Bridge spanning 'Het Holland's Diep' and the main bridge in the city of Dordrecht, further north, spanning 'De Oude Maas'. Both bridges were taken intact.

Die große Autobahnbrücke vor Dordrecht ist genommen! Mit Maschinenpistole und Handgranate hält der Oberjäger der Fallschirmtruppe die Wacht   *Aufn. Oberjäger Jenuchowsky*

111. The Dordrecht Bridge has been taken. Note the stick hand grenade in the paratrooper's left hand.

112. Moerdijk Bridge from the air.

The southern approaches to the foot and railroad bridges, crossing the Maas in the city of Rotterdam, were very early in the morning of May 10th in German hands. The northern approaches to these two bridges, however, remained in the hands of the Royal Dutch Army and Marines.

To the north of Rotterdam where the German paratroopers under the command of General Sponeck had landed in fields between The Hague and Rotterdam it was a different story. General Sponeck's objective had been to penetrate The Hague and capture the northern approaches of the bridges across the river Maas in the heart of Rotterdam. He had failed miserably on both counts. Many of the Ju-52's were shot down or crash landed on the freeway between the two cities.

113. Ju-52 between The Hague and Rotterdam

114. Another Ju-52 crash-landed

115. Ju-52 crash-landed in the bushes

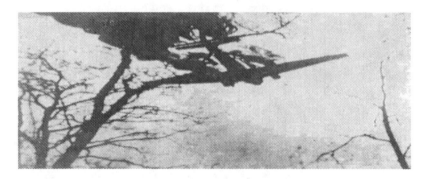

116. Ju-52 coming down in flames

Most of the paratroopers were scattered and unable to form a solid combat force. Many were taken prisoner. The Dutch Government and the Queen were able to escape to England. The 1,100 Germans that had been taken prisoner in that endeavor went to England as well but as POW's. Reich Marshall Hermann Goring was beyond himself when he learned of this disaster. Those 1,100 men were the cream of the crop of the German Airborne forces, all well-trained pilots and specialists.

It is abundantly clear that the city of Rotterdam held a key position in the German plans. The city would have to pay dearly for the failure of these German paratroopers.

The capture of Waalhaven Airport was a great German success. Transport aircrafts (Ju-52's), in great numbers, began landing at Waalhaven with troops and equipment. General Kurt Student also arrived with one of these aircraft.

In the meantime there were now also troops on the "Noorder" island and the bridges.

From what remained of Den Helder airport, seven D-21 fighters were transferred to a small, so-called secret airfield near Amsterdam. From there they made several ground attacks on German units. Volunteers now carried out the missions. On one of these raids, on Waalhaven airfield, which was already in German hands, they saw some thirty Junkers and Stukas neatly parked in two rows. Obviously, the Germans did not expect the crippled Dutch air force to be able to do any harm. As Bob Vanderstok tells it: "We attacked and pumped all we had into the enemy planes, until all thirty were kaput."

The other Dutch squadrons had similar encounters, and also suffered heavy losses – both in planes and in personnel. Even the old Fokker C-5 and C-10 reconnaissance planes were used. But they were no match for the Germans. The Dutch Air Force's only bombers, the T-5's flew a number of missions.

117. T-5 bomber of the Dutch Air Force

But these pregnant ducks did little harm to the advancing German troops. All of the planes were shot down or crashed when returning from these futile efforts to stop the German Blitzkrieg. Wim Rozenboom, a classmate of Bob VanderStok, was flying a Fokker C-10 when three Messerschmitts attacked him.

118. Dutch C-10's in flight

With no other options, he challenged the fight. Witnesses on the ground saw Wim and his gunner shoot down two of the attacking enemy planes. After that Wim himself went down in a spin, killing both Wim and his observer.

The war in Holland went on for five days, and there was not a single Dutch plane left that could fly any sort of mission. The last few D-21 fighters were now placed together at Schiphol and set afire by air force personnel. This was the end of the Dutch Air Force in the short war of May 1940.

Chapter Thirteen

The Early Morning of May 10, 1940

Most of the population of Rotterdam was still in a deep slumber when they were rudely awakened, as we were in the Dunantstraat, by the enormous din of low flying planes, gunfire and explosions. One of these people on the "Noorder Eiland" was Peter Jansen. He opened his window and stuck his head out to see what was going on. He reported seeing numerous planes flying low over the city. *"I thought that they must be German planes flying to England and I went back to bed. When the noise continued, I got up, dressed and went to the roof of the building."*

On the roof he joined some other people and they immediately identified the planes as German. Some of these planes appeared to be seaplanes that began landing on the river below them.

119. German Seaplane landing on the Maas.

Numerous other seaplanes had already landed between the Railway Station – North and the Maas Bruggen.

Peter continues: *"We went downstairs as fast as we could and right away noticed several Germans ashore with their weapons in the ready position. We saw others deplaning and getting into small rubber boats, then paddling to shore. More planes were coming down and one even landed under the bridge where it hit a plane already there. Their wings were intertwined and they appeared stuck together."*

Another observer on the Noorder Island was Dr. H. He tells it as follows:

"My sister Mary and I occupied an apartment on the second floor of Maaskade 161a. From our front window we had an unobstructed view of the Boompjes on the north side of the river. If we stretched our necks somewhat we could also see what was going on at the bridges and below in the water".

120. A view of the Maaskade on the Noorder Island

121. A view of The Boompjes

122. A view of the bridges spanning the Maas River. The
Noorder Island is on top.

"Soon after the Germans had occupied the approaches to the bridges the river became quite still. The barges still on the river were seen to be looking for a safe haven. But before they did we saw some take the rubber boats that were still floating on the river. The homeowners of the 'Noorder Island' were instructed to remain inside and it became very quiet on the Maaskade. Across the river on the Boompjes, on the other hand, we could see many people, mostly young men, who were clearly trying to see what was going on. They hugged the buildings and bunched together at the corners. It must have been around 5:30am when the first Germans in uniform appeared at the Boompjes. It was a group of 5 or 6 men and they came from the direction of the bridge. They were clearly being very careful as they moved furtively. They set up a machine gun but their position did not last long. About 30 minutes later they were very efficiently mowed down by a group of young Dutch soldiers under the command of an officer who had come to the scene with a heavy machine gun on wheels. I have to admit that the scene made me somewhat sick to my stomach but also very much appreciated the decisive action of the officer and his men. The public at the Boompjes who had been watching the action were clearly very pleased because we could hear their shouts of Hurrah! echoing from across the water. Several of the young civilians approached the bodies with the clear intent of stealing their belongings.
The young Dutch soldiers slowly withdrew from the scene on the Boompjes

and at 6:30am all was quiet again. At about 8 am we saw the first Germans on the Maaskade near our apartment. They carried light weapons and took up positions along the low wall bordering the river. Soon thereafter we saw, across at the Boompjes, a patrol of Dutch marines who were trying to get to the foot bridge from the direction of the Leuvehaven".

"They got only as far as the Vrij Entrepot (Tax Free Warehouse) because they were receiving fire from the Germans in front of our apartment on the Maaskade. Slowly the marines pulled back after leaving behind one of their man who had been killed in this action. What happened next is likely the most surprising event that occurred that miserable May 10th: From one of the side streets on the Boompjes, across from us, an old man and a boy pushing a hand cart unhesitatingly approached the fallen marine and carefully lifted him into the cart. The old man was speaking loud enough for us to hear him say something like: can't ....let him lie there...." When they completed their task they disappeared into the side street from whence they had come, without having been bothered by the Germans."

The military in Rotterdam were totally unprepared for the surprise attack by the Germans. Although there were some 6,000 army personnel from various branches in and near the city, there were only some 600 combat ready troops available. These were under the command of Colonel Scharroo.

123. Colonel Scharroo, Military Commander of
Rotterdam

Even with this small contingent he was able to consolidate his position. The Germans were unable to get any farther than the National Life Insurance Bank building, located straight across from the Willemsbrug (the name of the traffic bridge across the Maas River). On the other hand, the repeated attempts by the Dutch troops to recapture the bridge or blow it up went nowhere. As a result of these actions 200 Dutch Army personnel and 28 Marines were killed. Five marines were able to get under the bridge but in a location where they could not blow the bridge. They remained hidden under that bridge for about 5 days until Rotterdam capitulated.

In the meantime the Germans had now about 4,000 men in and around Rotterdam. They held the south of Rotterdam; they were on the Noorder Island and they were on the southern approaches of the 'Willemsbrug'. Some were under continuous fire from the Dutch troops on the other side of the bridge. That was the position on May 10 and it remained that way until Holland surrendered on May 15. The surprise had succeeded but they were not getting across the Maas River. These elite German Airborne forces were held back by tenaciously fighting Dutch soldiers among which were 900 raw recruits who had been in the army for a mere 2 weeks. Their commander Colonel Scharroo says of them: "They fought like lions, five long days."

Chapter Fourteen

"The Day My Father Cried"

Dick Hendrikse, the author of "The Day My Father Cried" was 15 years old when the war started on May 10, 1940. In his book's Prologue he describes his experience and what he felt that day. He also tells us what lessons he learned and his appreciation for those who fought for our freedom. It deserves repeating in this book because he expresses his feelings and observations so very well.

"On the morning of May 10, 1940 I was awakened by machinegun fire. Fokker fighters were zooming over our house near Schiphol Airport. I got to the window just in time to see a Dutch fighter destroy a German bomber with short sharp bursts of gunfire. The war had started. I was 15 years old. What followed were five very exciting, adventuresome days. Dutch soldiers were passing by our house and there were dogfights in the sky above. Known German sympathizers and possible traitors were being arrested and there was exciting news on the radio. I followed that war much like a soccer competition. Misery, death and destruction hardly made an impression. Then came the last day of that short war. The Germans had beaten our army, Rotterdam's heart was on fire and we were sitting at the radio listening to the announcer telling us that the Netherlands had capitulated. I experienced this news much like a 15 year old that reacts to his favorite soccer team being thoroughly beaten. Not more but also not less. I didn't know what 'war' meant. I didn't realize the consequences. Then when the announcer had concluded his somber and emotional talk I heard a strange sound. My father, that big, strong, hard working man was sitting there with his hands in front of his face sobbing like a child. Nobody spoke and I felt deeply ashamed. Because I was 15 years old and when a grown man cries with such passion you consider that childish. I believe that at that moment I actually despised my father. Yes, an ignorant boy of 15 year can be that cruel. I didn't understand why my dad cried that day. He cried because he understood that with that radio message the war for us had not ended. Because he knew that

71

our freedom was no more. What made him cry was the realization of that lost freedom. He had experienced ups-and-downs in his life, worries and happiness, sorrow and bliss. But one thing had always been constant: he had been a "free" man in a "free" country. At that moment he must have sensed, without being able to put it into words, what it meant to have lost that "freedom". I didn't know it because I was only 15 years old. Five years later I had learned it very well. I had learned about fear, I had learned to hate and with me millions of Europeans. At the end of those five years we knew that "freedom" was the only condition that made life worth living. We knew that many people had laid down their lives for that freedom because they could not tolerate living in slavery. That's why they rebelled against the German occupiers. People were resisting the German occupiers for different reasons. They resisted for political or religious reasons and some may have resisted for the sheer adventure of it. But whatever the motivation, they all had in common one single objective and that had been to regain their independence, their freedom. It was a fight against slavery. The resistance of these little, defenseless and common people against Hitler's mighty and all powerful war machine were, for that reason alone, not without merit." Some cynic had said: "What good did it do? Do you really believe that the war would have lasted one day longer without those Dutch resistance fighters?"

He was a little older than 15 years, but born too long after 1940 to understand. The question whether or not the war was shortened by the resistance will never be able to be answered. Even though the occupiers were forced to keep more troops in the Netherlands than they preferred because of those "pinpricks" by poorly armed resistance fighters. But that is hardly important. A father who does not work for his children is not worth those children. A person who does not defend his freedom was born to be a slave. Resistance, regardless how small and insignificant had earned us, five years after my father cried, our precious freedom. It was not something to be accepted with downcast eyes but to be savored thanks to the offers of those brave men and women, many of who laid down their lives. Without having been asked they had fought on our behalf. Often misunderstood and sometimes even taunted and distrusted. Does it make sense to be reminded of the suppression so many years after the liberation? Years ago, in a conversation that I had with Prince Bernhard concerning the post-war youth, he said something that may well be the best answer to that question. "I have noticed that to-days young people do not appreciate what it means to live in a free society. They accept freedom as self evident, a given. I would wish that they could learn to appreciate how fortunate they are in comparison with the youth of dictatorial countries." Freedom is a valuable asset. It has now been 60 years since common people like you and I, rich and poor, old and young, women and men, gave their lives for that freedom. I will be talking about these people and always in the background of their stories will be that lost freedom. When the young reader, who, thank God, has been spared the lessons learned by the youth of 1940, learns to appreciate the riches that his freedom holds then I have achieved my first goal. When additionally the reader in general, regardless of age, will develop admiration and respect for the dead and the living described in this book, then I will have achieved my second goal. They were not hare-brained adventurers; they acted in total consciousness with an open eye toward the consequences. They were of course not common people, even though you may not recognize them living among all others. They should never be forgotten. They were people who may have fought with a gun in their hands or the grandmother who hid a person going underground. Resistance that expressed itself in the printing of illegal news bulletins or smuggling Jews to the Swiss border. Who were these resistance people who in their own way resisted the hated 'Hun'? Statues are symbols of their fight and streets are named after them. But what do we really know about them? I hope therefore that my first picture of a resistance fighter will provide an answer to that question".

Dick Hendrikse
Credits: Uitgeversmij J.H.Kok n.v. Kampen 1962

CHAPTER FIFTEEN

THE DUNANTSTRAAT
MAY 10, 1940

Back in the Dunantstraat on that Friday, May 10th we continued listening to the radio. The announcer was given the listeners instructions on how to protect their homes. Sandbags in front of low windows and strips of tape over the windows to prevent broken glass from flying all over. This caused a lot of activity. In the meantime there was continuous shooting and explosions not very far from our house. They were hitting the harbor installations. I started to notice the difference between bomb explosions, artillery and anti-aircraft fire. It is interesting how quickly you learn these things. My mother suggested I run to the bookstore and buy tape for the windows. She gave me some money and as soon as the sirens gave a continuing high pitch sound to indicate that all was clear I was off and running. Out of the Dunantstraat, up the hill of the IJzerstraat and then across on the Willem Buytenwegstraat where the bookstore was. There were a lot of people with the same intent of purchasing tape and I had to wait in line. When it was my turn I could only get one roll. Further up the W. Buytenwegstraat I noticed some commotion near the butcher shop. I had to see what was going on and was just in time to see Dutch soldiers take the fat butcher into custody and shove him into a prison van. I was not surprised and actually delighted because we all knew that he was a Nazi sympathizer and a member of the NSB (National Socialist Party).

On my way back home, going the same way I had come, the sirens started up once again. At that point I was just at the bottom of the IJzerstraat where there was an open area where city maintenance had stored what I remember to be large, round tree trunks. I thought that those tree trunks would make a good hiding place from possible shrapnel and I therefore crawled in between and waited for the all-clear siren. While I was lying there I dug in the sand and low and behold I found what turned out to be a fountain pen. What a treasure. In those times there were of course no ballpoint pens and you wrote with a metal pen that you dipped in the ink or a pencil. That was also what we used in school. A fountain pen with its own reservoir of ink was something awesome. So you can imagine my glee of finding one in such a strange place. Who would have lost it there? When I made it home with the roll of tape and showed the pen to my mom and dad, my dad saw immediately that the pen was made of 18 karat gold. Hey, this war was turning out not too bad.

We then proceeded with putting the tape crisscross on the windows. It made the house seem like more of a fortress. I don't know how we got the sacks but I remember using my little go-cart to haul sand from the lot in the back of our house and filling these sacks. We were all out there on the street with the neighbors and all the other kids from the street. If things would not have been so serious it would have felt like a neighborhood party. Some people showed fear and then there were others who acted quite fearless. It felt good to be around those people because somehow you felt safer. I have often wondered about that and later on in life I met people who I felt the same way about. Was it charisma, a greater sense of confidence than most? I don't know but it was certainly a real feeling. I remember one of these men; his name was Tom de Mooy. He managed a small warehouse of dry goods in the Dunantstraat. He liked us children and was always very friendly and occasionally would fix our broken bicycles. Our house had a cellar on the street side and it together with other apartments at street level was chosen as temporary shelters during air raids. Occasionally he, together with other neighbors who lived on the floors above us, would come to our cellar for protection during these air raids. Our 'cellar' was not a real cellar as such. It had only protection from the side where our house was build against the sleeper dike. However, it did provide some protection. We learned very quickly that the safest place in the cellar was an area where there were multiple and intersecting walls. A matter of fact and this may sound funny but the safest place seemed to be the toilet. After a bombing it was not uncommon to see all the floors of a 5-story apartment collapsed but the toilets would all still be sticking out from the walls and attached to their plumbing. I figured that whenever there was an air raid I'd sit on the toilet and see what would happen. Fortunately that never was necessary. We would sit on the floor under the concrete stairway. Much later I would be thinking why we were sitting on that hard cold floor and not on a cushy chair. When I served in the Dutch Army in 1950-1953 I think I found the answer. I served in a 105mm howitzer Regiment. Whenever we were on maneuvers and were firing the guns 'at will' with several batteries of these guns lined up next to one another I would actually be hugging the ground. Everyone who was not directly involved in the firing did the same thing. We all hugged the ground. Other than the gun crews nobody would be standing straight up. I concluded that whenever there is a bombing and a lot of noise or explosions you want to get as close as you can near the ground and, better yet crawl into it if you can. Now to come back to Tom Mooy, when he would be sitting with us in our cellar and the sirens would be doing their banshee screaming and bomb explosions would rock our house I would feel completely safe. He exuded complete control and confidence. Nothing could hurt me. I don't know if other people felt the same. Of course I knew that he had no magic formula that would prevent bombs from hitting us but the feeling was there nonetheless.

Henry remembers:
May 10th, 1940
"We also heard the reports that paratroopers were landing all over the area. It was to the south and east of us so we could not really see it, but we could certainly hear it. We did see a couple of aircraft being shot down, which was quite a shock even if they were German. During the day there was a lot of shooting and many air raids. First we were staying in an air raid shelter at the large printing shop (Wijt) opposite our house. I only went in there once. When other raids came I stayed at home. I was mostly on the balcony, where I had a better view. Of course it was not smart, but what do you want, I was sixteen!
I was late for school, but nobody bothered. After a short speech by the teacher, expressing the hope, that he would see us back after it was all

over, we went home again. Walking back we saw a lot of fires and smoke, but more towards the center of the city. There were air raid warnings, which we generally ignored. Later we found out that one of the targets was the main hospital on the Coolsingel (where the Bijenkorf department store is now). It must have been easy to find with the big Red Cross on the roof. Most of the fighting was at Waalhaven airport and the main bridges across the river. We later found out that there were only a handful of soldiers defending the area. About 200 marines and 600 new soldiers, who had been drafted in the army 6 weeks before, had to defend the rest of the city, mainly the two bridges across the river. They were armed with World War I rifles that could hold 5 rounds and some machine guns from the same era. It is amazing that the marines and the few trained soldiers could hold off a German paratroop division for almost 5 days. Of course we were not aware of this at the time. The fighting was also near the Holland–America Line terminal, where the large passenger ship, the Statendam, was moored. It was undergoing engine maintenance and could not get away in time. Since the Germans were trying to capture the ship the marines set it on fire. It was destroyed and sank at the moorings in shallow water and was a total loss. The flagship of the line, the 'New Amsterdam', had left for New York just a few days before and later became a troopship. It did survive the war.

That first day, May 10th, a destroyer (Jan van Galen) sailed up the Nieuwe Waterweg and made it to the entrance of the Waalhaven. It opened fire on the airport where the Germans were landing and it kept doing that even after it sank with the guns still above water. It only stopped after the ship was completely destroyed. We could hear the artillery fire and the bombing which was not more than 2 miles from our house.

The bridge near our house (Pieter de Hoogh Brug) was protected by three or four marines. At some time that morning they started firing at a seaplane trying to land on the water of the Coolhaven in front of our house. That attempt was aborted and it barely skipped over the bridge. I don't know whether it crashed. A few weeks later they pulled a dead German out of the harbor. Of course we thought that was the best kind.

The second day (May 11) we saw some people stumbling along the harbor, a man, and a woman with a baby and I believe another little child. Mother called them and we took them in. The woman could not feed the baby she seemed to be in shock. They did not want to come upstairs, but stayed in the basement. They were literally scared stiff. Anyway they were fed and after a while the baby could be fed. We found out then that the Germans were in the Southern part of Rotterdam, but the marines were holding out at the bridges. The refugees got across the river thanks to a skipper who sneaked them over at night.

The military logistics were all fouled up, so the marines did not get any food. Mother made soup that day and I was going to bring it to them. I went out of the back of the house and walked along the harbor. I came under fire from probably some Nazi sympathizer taking potshots from a roof, most likely the Willem Buytenweg Street. (Notorious Nazi territory as we found out later) The marines waved me down and returned fire. I just ran with the container of soup and they got their food. I did feel and saw some branches fall out of the trees where I ran.

Pa and Oom Wim tried to get to their job in downtown Rotterdam. They managed to get close, but they were stopped by the police (ours) and advised to go home and wait till things calmed down. Close to home they were walking along the Coolhaven when there was shooting again from the Willem Buytenwegstraat. They both dived into the gangway of one of the barges. At least there they had a 3/8" steel plate as protection. When the shooting stopped they started running again until they were home."

CHAPTER SIXTEEN

THE BOOMPJES AND NOORDER ISLAND

The night of May 10th was uneventful for us living in the western part of the city but not so for the people on the Noorder Island and those living in the vicinity of the Maasbruggen. We could hear explosions, gunfire and an occasional plane flying over.

Dr H. continues:

"Late in the evening of May 10th the fighting intensified. Initially the initiative was with the Germans; they were shooting star shells at the houses on the Boompjes and bombing the National Life Insurance Bank with shells that were glowing white hot and were drawing beautiful, fiery, patterns above the bridges. When they hit their intended target they would explode in a great ball of fire. In spite of this heavy bombardment the National Life Insurance Bank building never caught fire and it seemed bomb proof.

124. The National Levensverzekering Bank building
across from the Maas Bridge

However, next and behind the building fires started and were swallowing one building after the other all the time moving in a south-westerly direction. Noteworthy is that the street lanterns on the Boompjes were brightly lit all through the night. This rendered the whole scene rather unreal."

SATURDAY, MAY 11, 1940

During the night of May 10 to 11 the fire at the Boompjes had already destroyed tens of buildings and the fire went on abated.

125. De Boompjes on fire

At about 10 am the initiative of doing battle switched to the defenders

Dr. H. continues:

"An important target was the big building 'Rhea' on the Maaskade that stretched all the way from the Prins Hendrikstraat to the Meeuwenstreet.

126. The Rhea building is in the center.

From our living room we could see a piece of artillery behind a barricade in the Pottebakkerssteeg on the north side of the Maas literally spitting fire. Although this was all very exciting we became quickly aware that our apartment was in great peril of being hit by this fire. We decided to move to the lower floor. The door opening up to the Maaskade had been blasted from its hinges and was lying among glass and other debris. The door to the ground floor apartment of a neighbor was locked but a door panel was missing and we were able to crawl through and move to the basement. At about 4 pm we became aware that our apartment building had been hit and was burning fiercely. That caused us to leave for the Prins Hendrik Lane where we arrived via the back door of the Catholic Church. We joined many other refugees in the school building on the Prins Hendrik Lane 10. Noteworthy is that nobody seemed to have saved anything from their homes. I was an exception, carrying my antique "viola d'amore" in its chest. Another exception was Wilem Keevin who carried his 40 year Anniversary plate of having been a fireman."

Fires on the Maaskade were going on unchecked and it was destroying building after building. People wanted to leave the island but the Germans did not allow anyone to leave to the south where conditions were relatively safe. Artillery fire from the north side of the Maas River went on unabated and the Germans were forced to find places to hide as well. Dr. H. who with many other refugees was still in the school building now decided that it was no longer safe and went outside where he asked a German NCO for help.

Dr. H continues:

"The Feldwebel (Sergeant) was quite courteous and helpful. He took us to a house where the front door was open. The house consisted of three large rooms that were dimly lit by a few candles. In one of the rooms we saw Germans sitting at a table sipping 'advocaat' (egg liqueur); they did this very neatly with the glasses placed on coasters. Other Germans were sleeping on the floor and an officer was lying on a double bed in another room. All of them were fully dressed and ready to jump into action at the first alarm.

At around mid-night a Feldwebel entered and in a mooted voice said: "Auf Manner, auf, er ist Unrat!" ("Get up men, get up, there is trouble!")

"Ist denn etwas los?", ("Is something wrong?"), a young soldier asked in a whiny voice but others made it clear to him that he should get up and do his duty. Discipline appeared excellent and there seemed a lot of camaraderie. The officer came up to the women and pointed to the bed that they were now free to use. They weren't interested.

More and more refugees joined us in the course of the night and in the morning the officer returned with some apples and pears. He offered them to the people but they all declined whereupon he put them on the table. It was clear that all of us refugees despised the Germans and when we learned that the school building was still standing everyone wanted to move back.

On the way to the school I noticed that the Germans were preparing for street fighting. They were carrying guns and stick hand grenades stuck in their belts as well as belts of bullets around their necks. Upon arriving in the Prins Hendrik Lane we saw the burned out buildings on the Maaskade among which was our house. On the Boompjes we saw the completely gutted remains of the buildings on that boulevard. We entered the school and joined 300 other downcast refugees who would try to make the best of it."

MAY 11, 12 AND 13, 1940

The night of the 12th to the 13th of May was relatively quiet as concerned the fighting outside the school building but inside some people went completely crazy and it was difficult to hold them down and keep them from hurting themselves and others. In the early morning hours a few brave men went out in the Sleephellingstraat and the Maaskade; their goal was to find any kind of food. They located a truck from Reederij Stanfries parked on the Maaskade loaded with tins of condensed milk. They confiscated several hundred tins that they brought to the school. They also found the body of a young woman who on May 11th, while trying to escape, had been killed in the Sleephellingstraat by fire from the Boompjes. A grave was dug in the strip of grass running through the middle of the Prins Hendrik Lane and she was buried in accordance with her Roman Catholic faith.

At this time the fighting had again intensified with grenades exploding close by. However, the priest went about his duty without showing any sign of fear.

At 0:30 in the morning of May 13 Colonel Scharroo received orders from his superior in The Hague, General Winkelman, to wipe out the small bridge head of the Germans on the north shore of the Maas River.

Generaal Winkelman

127. General Winkelman, Commander of all Dutch
Armed Forces (1876-1952)

He also ordered Scharroo to prepare the two bridges, spanning the
Maas in the heart of Rotterdam, for eventual destruction.

The small German bridgehead on this fourth day of the war was made
up of four separate strongholds. The strongest was the one under the
command of Oberleutnant (First Lieutenant) Kerfin in the building
of the National Life Insurance Bank. Then there was the group of
10 men under Oberfeldwebel Grauting (Platoon Leader) who were
located in a house on the Boompjes between the foot and railroad
bridges, the machinegun position of Oberfeldwebel Steinhoff on the
railroad bridge and a group of eight men under Unteroffizier (NCO
- Non-Commissioned Officer) Arntjen under the footbridge.
Arntjen and his men had already been under the bridge for three
days, like virtual prisoners. He didn't believe they would come out
alive. Continuous fire from the Dutch soldiers at the end of the
bridge prevented them from escaping their position. They had been
promised at the briefing four days earlier that the 'panzers' would be
there in three days.

CHAPTER SEVENTEEN

"IT'S ABOUT TIME YOU SHOWED UP!"

General Student who had his HQ in Hotel Rijsoord in the south of Rotterdam said this in an emotional tone of voice. But then good-naturedly he slapped the shoulder of Hauptmann (Captain) Gernott Matthaei. When he saw a column of light tanks in front of the hotel a heavy load had left his shoulders. Matthaei's 6th Company had won the race. That morning at 7am he had crossed the Moerdijkbrug and entered the Island of Dordrecht. They had found the bridge in Dordrecht firmly in the hands of the German paratroopers and had crossed it in great haste. They reached the HQ of General Student at 2pm. Full of pride he had reported to the commander of the 7th Airborne Division and pictures were taken. In the course of the day Student received other parts of Hubicki's 9th Panzer Division and at 6pm he had in his area of occupation: one battalion of infantry on "Zundapp" motorcycles, a company of tanks and a heavy artillery detachment with 15cm howitzers.

128. A column of infantry on Zundapp motorcycles.

129. A German half tracks entering the south of Rotterdam

130. A 15cm Howitzer

With the arrival later on in the evening of most of Apell's 9th Panzer Division the traffic got more and more congested. General Hubicki and his staff also arrived at the Hotel Rijsoord and were now waiting for the arrival of Rudolf Schmidt, commander of the 39th Army Corps. This corps was made up of the 7th Airborne Division, the 9th Panzer Division, infantry and the SS-Regiment Adolf Hitler. Until Schmidt's arrival expected at 9pm, Student would still be in charge.

All actions in the campaign against The Netherlands were under the command of the 18th Army Commander, General von Kuchler in the city of Uden.

131. General Georg von Kuchler (1881-1968)

The general and his staff were starting to get nervous. They were wondering whether it would be possible to force the surrender of The Netherlands before the British and French forces would come to their aid.

Rumors were coming in that reported French forces on the Island of Walcheren in the province of Zeeland and English troops in Den Helder, IJmuiden and Hook of Holland. They turned out to be just that – rumors but they didn't know that at the time. That afternoon von Kuchler received news that units of his 10th Army Corps had succeeded in breaking through the defenses of the Grebbe Line but had been stopped dead in their tracks at Scherpenzeel. On his right flank a division was held back at the head of the 'Afsluitdijk', the 20-mile long dike connecting the provinces of Friesland and North Holland.

132. The 'Afsluitdijk'

On May 13 at 14:50 hours von Kuchler issued the order for the attack on Fortress Holland. This attack would have to be decisive. On May 14 the 18th Army would attack 'Festung Holland' from the north, east and south.

Von Kuchler had come to the obvious conclusion that the city of Rotterdam was the key to the success of his plan. He decided that with its stubborn resistance the city of Rotterdam could no longer be considered an 'open city' and therefore felt justified to use brute force.

The 39th Army Corps was informed by radio at 17:05 hours: "Resistance in Rotterdam must be broken at all cost. If necessary it must be threatened with the destruction of the city and this threat must be executed"

This was the beginning of the end of the great port city of Rotterdam, as we knew it!

In Rijsoord the staff of General Schmidt, who had finally arrived and had now taken over the command from General Student, was feverishly working all through the night on the plan of attack for May 14.

In the city of Dongen, where part of the 9th Panzer Division had its HQ, Oberleutnant (First Lieutenant) Friedrich Plutzar was sitting at a table in a house that earlier in the campaign had been the HQ of General Hubicki. Before the war Plutzar had married a girl from Rotterdam and as a result he spoke and read Dutch better than he could write it. For that reason he rewrote the German text that he had been asked to translate into Dutch.

The German text had read:

An die Kommandantur der Stadt Rotterdam.
An den Oberburgermeister und die staatslichen behorden der Stadt Rotterdam.
Der Widerstand, der in der offenen Stadt Rotterdam gegen das Vordringen der deutschen Wehrmacht geleistet wird, zwingt mich dazu Ihnen mitzuteilen, dass, falls der Widerstand nicht unverzuglig aufgegeben wird, ich zu den notwendigen Mitteln greifen wired. Dies kann die vollige Vernichtung der Stadt nach sich ziehen.
Ich ersuche Sie, als Mann von Verantwortungsgefuhl darauf hinzuwirken, dass diese schwere Schadigung der Stadt unterbleiben kann.
Als Zeichen des Einverstandnisses ersuche ich Sie sofort um Hersendung eines Parlementars, der mit den notwendigen Vollmachten ausgestatte ist.
Ist binnen zwei Stunden nach Ubergabe dieser Mitteilung keine Antwort in meinem Besitz, so bin ich gezwungen, die scharfsten Vernichtungsmittel anzuwenden.

Der Befehlshaber der deutschen Truppen

Plutzar had translated the text into Dutch as best he could. It contained a few misspellings but in essence conveyed the meaning and intent very clearly.

To the Commander of Rotterdam.
To the Mayor and City Counsel members of the city of Rotterdam.
The resistance shown in the open city of Rotterdam against the German Army forces me to take the most decisive action unless resistance ceases immediately.
The effect of that action could mean the complete destruction of the city.
I am asking you as a man who possesses a great sense of responsibility to heed this warning and prevent immeasurable destruction and bloodshed.
As a sign of agreement I ask you to immediately send a parliamentary who has the necessary authority.
Unless I receive an answer within two hours following delivery of this communication I will be forced to take the necessary steps for the destruction of the city.

The Commander of the German Troops

Hauptmann (Captain) Raymund Hoerst, 33 years old, the Intelligence Officer of the 9th Panzer Division, had been designated to make a last ditch effort of convincing the defenders of Rotterdam to cease their resistance. Hauptmann Hoerst knew that complete destruction of the city could only mean one thing – a bombardment from the air.

At night, after the plan of attack had been completed under the direction of General Schmidt, a specialist from Fliegerkorps Putzier reported to the General. He was a communications officer of Kampfgeschwader 54, the bomber squadron that had been assigned to the 39th Army Corps to assist with the last decisive action against the defenders of Rotterdam.

CHAPTER EIGHTEEN

LULL BEFORE THE STORM

It was still Monday, May 13th. Walking in the city was practically impossible and most citizens remained safely inside.

Citizens had wanted to assist their soldiers by offering them food and drink but that had been refused for the fear of poisoning. This rumor had been around since May 10 and had later turned out to be unfounded.

From our balcony in the Dunantstraat we had a good view of the bridge near our house and the few Dutch soldiers that occupied the small guardhouse used for opening and closing the bridge. The bridge was in its 'raised' position and as a result no traffic could go across the harbor. These soldiers had been on the job for several days already and it was apparent that they had not received any food nor, to our knowledge, were they relieved of their guard duty at any time. Occasionally they were being shot at from the direction of our street and the street behind us. There were known 'Nazi' sympathizers living in that area and it must have been those traitors taking shots at these men. What struck me was that I could easily identify these soldiers when they were moving around the guard house and then it dawned on me that what made them so obviously visible was the Dutch Lion emblem on their helmets. While the helmet was green, the brass lion had to be polished and shiny. Every time the sun hit the emblem, it would reflect like a mirror.

After my brother Henry had taken some soup to them he told us that the soldiers were well aware of the problem and had asked if we had any paint. We had some black paint and I took it to them together with a brush. I ran up and nobody shot at me. They were very grateful and immediately went to work covering up those shiny brass lions. But the occasional firing continued. Fortunately no one was hit which made me wonder but I didn't give it any further thought until much later.

133. The shiny brass 'Dutch Lion' emblem on the helmet

There was also the fear that the Germans were using 'gas' as they had during World War I. This also turned out untrue. What many people took for gas was intense black smoke from the BPM (Bataafse Petroleum Maatschappij) Oil refineries that penetrated the whole area of Rotterdam.

134. Oil Refineries of BPM

These refineries in Pernis, to the southwest of Rotterdam, had been set afire by a detachment of English engineers for fear of it falling in

German hands. These English engineers had been the only assistance that Rotterdam received from the allied side.

The refineries were burning. The "Statendam" of the HAL, (Holland America Line) was burning.

135. ss. Statendam of the Holland-America Line
completely destroyed

The buildings on the Boompjes and the Blaak were burning, as were the buildings and houses on the Maaskade on the island in the middle of the Maas River. That night the sky was colored a crimson red.

CHAPTER NINETEEN

AN ATROCIOUS ACT

The night had passed and the 13,000 people on the Noorder Island were still alive. The weather was slightly overcast but it was already getting warm. At least warmer than Monday when the temperature had never reached 50 degrees Fahrenheit. A slight wind was blowing from the west on what would become a day never to be forgotten and always to be remembered.

The Commander of the Luftwaffe, Hermann Goering, had been beyond himself over the loss of so many aircraft in their attack on Holland. (Eventually the number of planes lost in the attack on Holland would surpass 500) as well as the failure of his 22d Airborne Division at Overschie, Valkenburg and Wassenaar, near the city of The Hague. For the most part these troops had been wiped out or taken prisoner. The remainder was holed up in an area to the north of Rotterdam. His sour mood must have influenced his desire for revenge and in his discussions with Kesselring, Commander of the 2d Air Force he urged the latter to be ruthless in the proposed bombing attack on Rotterdam.

136. Hermann Goering (1893-1946)

137. Albert Kesselring (1881-1960)

Three groups would execute the plan of attack developed by General Rudolf Schmidt: A, B and C.

Group A under Oberst von Apell of the 9th Panzer Division would attack across the bridge over the Maas River.

Group B under Oberst Kreysing, commander of Infantry Regiment 16 would cross the Maas River at the Kralingscheveer with barges that were available at that location and push through to Kralingen. (East Rotterdam)

Group C made up of units from the SS-Leibstandarte (Bodyguard) Adolf Hitler and a detachment of tanks would be on the heels of Group A push through the city and make contact with the 400 men of the 22d Airborne Division that were surrounded there.

The attack was supposed to start at exactly 1pm (Dutch time). At that precise moment the artillery on the Noorder Island (Group A) and on IJsselmonde (Group B) would begin with the zeroing in on the Dutch positions. Five minutes later at precisely 13:05 the artillery would begin a 43 minutes uninterrupted barrage. The last artillery shell would be fired at 13:48.

After that, at 13:50, the way would be open for the tanks and the infantry.

It was taken for granted that following the artillery barrage resistance on the other side of the river would be minimal. Particularly since during the barrage Kampfgeschwader (Bomber Squadron) 54 would be over the city with 90 Heinkels-111, carrying bombs of 100 and 500 pounds. Their designated target was a triangular piece of the city of which the river formed the base.

Friedrich Plutzar who had translated the ultimatum, and Hauptmann (Captain) Raymund Hoerst, the Intelligence Officer of the 9th Panzer division (Armored Division) had been chosen for the important mission of delivering the ultimatum. Dr. Pessendorfer, an Austrian, also accompanied them. The three were now on the Noorder Island and from the Van Der Takstraat they could see the Willemsbrug. Black clouds were rising from the end and left and right side of the Willemsbrug. Tanks and artillery were lined up in long columns in preparation for the assault. They were given white flags after reporting to the diminutive Oberstleutnant (Lieutenant Colonel) Von Choltitz.

138. Lieutenant Colonel von Choltitz (1894-1966)
(Choltitz would save Paris from destruction in 1944)

Plutzar thought he looked tired.

It was now 9am. The three officers left Von Choltitz's command post. Walking behind one another. First Pessendorfer, then Plutzar and then the most important one of the three, Hoerst. They climbed the stairs to the Willemsbrug and with their flags waving started to walk slowly forward. When they were halfway across the bridge Plutzar looked to his left to see where the black smoke was coming from. He recognized the ship that was burning fiercely. It was the 'Statendam' of the Holland-America Line.

Right then he wished he was back in Vienna with its bars and music.

Both Colonel Scharroo and Rotterdam Mayor Oud knew it practically at the same time: the final act of the drama was about to unfold. The Germans had send negotiators. Colonel Scharroo was advised by phone that three Germans were coming across the bridge with a message for the Dutch commander. He had instructed his men to blindfold them and take them to his command post. He waited, somewhat nervously. It was 10 o'clock.

Mayor Oud at City Hall on the Coolsingel received a telephone call from a citizen who reported that something important was taking place. *"There are three Germans with white flags. They yelled in German that they had a message for you."* *"For me? Can you understand them?"* Oud asked.
"Yes, I can understand them very well." They yelled: *"Holland in Ehre! Wir haben parlementare Briefe fur den Burgermeister!"*
"Is that what they said?" Oud asked somewhat surprised.
"Yes," the man said.
"And then what happened?" the mayor asked.
"Those Krauts were taken prisoner. They are no longer here," was the response.

139. Pieter Jacobus Oud mayor of Rotterdam
(1886-1968)

Mayor Oud called Scharroo immediately and asked him what he was going to do.

"You have nothing to say here!" Scharroo snarled. Oud responded that he was well aware of the fact that he had no authority here but suggested that it would be a good idea for the Colonel to receive the negotiators and listen to what they had to say. Scharroo's tone of voice improved somewhat. *"I will certainly do that Mayor," he said. "Will you keep me posted? Oud asked. "Of course," Scharroo answered. "The best thing you can do is to come to my command post. Make sure that you are here in 30 minutes. I expect you at 10:30!" "Excellent, Colonel," Oud said and hung up.*

The six soldiers that had stopped the three Germans were listening somewhat surprised to the accented Dutch from one of them but they didn't pay attention to what he was saying. "You may take my weapon but please don't throw it in the water!" Plutzar said. They took his pistol anyway and unceremoniously threw it in the water of the Oude Haven as they had done with the weapons of Pessendorfer and Hoerst. Plutzar contributed it to their nervousness. They were now walking next to each other over the Gelderschekade. As they understood it they were on their way to the Beursplein, the square where the stock exchange was located and where the command post was.

140. Beursplein (Stock Exchange Square) before the war.

When they arrived at the Beurs station an officer approached and told them to stop. "Who are you and what are you doing here?" he asked. Plutzar took a step forward and in several well-prepared Dutch sentences he said: *"Good morning, we are here on behalf of the German commander. We have a very important message for the Dutch commander!"* *"Wait here!"* the officer said, then turned on his heels and walked back to the station. He returned shortly with three blindfolds that the soldiers put on them and the three were then led to a car. After they were seated the car left immediately. A lot of time had been spent before the three men had made it this far and by the time they arrived at the Command Post of Colonel Scharroo it was already 10:30.

Mayor Oud had already arrived at Scharroo's command post and was asked to wait in a separate room because as Scharroo pointed out: *"This is a military matter and one that I rather you not join."* *"Naturally,"* Oud responded.

Scharroo was told that there were three Germans, the highest in rank being Hauptman Hoerst. The other two were lieutenants. One of them spoke Dutch and was the interpreter. *"My German is fluent,"* Scharroo snarled. *"I don't need an interpreter; just bring in the Hauptman!"* Hauptman Hoerst entered the room, clicked his heels, saluted and said: "Herr General!"
"Ich bin kein General," Scharroo said. *"Forgive me, Herr…"*
"Colonel!
"…Herr Colonel!"
"And…"
"Hauptman Hoerst, Herr Colonel, ich bin Offizier im General-stab einer Division," the German said, being careful not to identify the name of his division. (I am a staff officer of a division)

He handed Scharroo two envelopes. One was addressed to the Mayor of Rotterdam. *"Do you have anything else to say?"* Scharroo asked. *"I am not allowed to, Herr Colonel,"* Hoerst replied. *"What I can tell you is that your reply must be in the hands of the German commander within two hours. If not, bad things will happen."*

The time was now 10:40am.

"Twelve thirty!" Hoerst said.

That meant one hour and fifty minutes.

Scharroo told the Hauptmann to wait and told his aide to bring the other two in the room as well. Scharroo then left the room and walked to the quarters where Mayor Oud was waiting. He handed Oud his envelope addressed to the Mayor and Counsel Members of the city of Rotterdam. Carefully he opened the envelope.

Plutzar and Pessendorfer were sitting across from Hoerst. Plutzar asked Hoerst what had happened. Hoerst told them that the commander was a colonel and appeared rather nervous. "Right now he is reading the message. Let's hope that he replies quickly. Then we can go back." They were silent. The room they were in was shuttered. On the way to the command post they had not been able to see anything of the city. They did have the feeling that they were in the center of the city because the ride had been a short one. Hoerst addressed Pessendorfer, "You, with your experience in journalism, paint us a picture of the situation with the limited data that you have been able to gather."

From the start, Pessendorfer had been the quiet one but the most observant of the three. He thought for a moment and then said: *"The resistance of the enemy is improvised. The HQ of the Dutch troops is located in a common house where the atmosphere is one of chaos and confusion. Officers and soldiers appear to lack experience. They have old and antique weapons. In short, they are a weak opponent."*

"But they have been holding us at bay for four days already," Hoerst said skeptically. *"You know, Herr Hauptmann, that in a war the impossible becomes possible and the possible impossible. That is an old truth!"* said Pessendorfer.

"Didn't you see those dead paratroopers at the end of the bridge, elite troops, killed by inexperienced Dutch recruits?" Hoerst said.

"Hauptmann (Captain) Schultz of the paratroopers told von Choltitz on May 10 that he had seen Dutch officers still wearing sabers!" He repeated it: *"sabers…!"*

"The impossible becomes possible," Pessendorfer repeated.

It was now almost 11am.

Scharroo and Oud had read the letters from General Schmidt and they looked at each other. *"Complete destruction of the city…"* Oud said.

"That is quite clear," Scharroo answered.

"Colonel, you know what happened to Warsaw," Oud continued *"Of course, I know that,"* snarled Scharroo.

"What are you going to do?" Oud asked.

Scharroo told him that he would contact General Winkelman, the supreme commander in The Hague.

141. General Henri Winkelman (1876-1952)

When he was connected, he read the ultimatum to Winkelman. Winkelman asked if the ultimatum was signed. *"No, General"* replied Scharroo. *"It only states: "Commander of the German Troops", that's all."*

Following his conversation with General Winkelman, Scharroo summoned Hauptmann Hoerst to him. Upon leaving, the other two Germans gave him the sign of the cross.

Scharroo told Hoerst that he must go back and tell his superior that a Dutch Parliamentary would be send as soon as the supreme commander had rendered a decision. *"Er uberlegt jetzt."* (He is deliberating it)

When Hoerst asked him when that would be he was told that it would be prior to the deadline. *"Before twelve thirty then?* Hoerst asked with some emphasis. Scharroo confirmed that it would be before twelve thirty.

At exactly 12 o'clock Hauptmann (Captain) Hoerst reported to General Schmidt in Rijsoord and told him that the Dutch commander would send a Parliamentary before the deadline expired at 12:30am. Schmidt appeared disappointed. *"What is your impression?* Schmidt asked. *"That they will offer us the city."* Hoerst replied.

Schmidt then instructed Hoerst to immediately report to Hubicki and tell him to postpone the planned artillery barrage scheduled for 1pm.

General Winkelman in The Hague had made a decision and instructed Scharroo to send a Parliamentary. Captain Backer was appointed and Scharroo gave him a letter addressed to the Commander of the German Troops. The letter read:

"Ich habe Ihren Brief empfangen. Dieser war nicht unterzeichnet und erwahnte nicht Ihren militarischen Rang. Bevor einen derartigen Vorschlag in Ueberwagung nehmen zu konnen, muss dieser mich erreichen mit Ihrem militarischen Rang, Ihren Namen und Ihren Unterzeichnung versehen."

Der Oberst – Kommandant der Truppen in Rotterdam."

The letter was signed: P. W. Scharroo

By the time that Captain Backer set foot on the Willemsbrug it was 12:10am.

At that moment the first 90 Heinkels-111 took off from Quackenbruck in Germany destination Rotterdam.

Schmidt had postponed the artillery barrage but so far had neglected to postpone the bombing. Via the command post of General Student's airborne corps he had sent a message to General Kesselring's Airforce Command #2.

The message read: "Attack suspended due to on-going negotiations. Prepare new start schedule." At 12 o'clock noon the commander of the 39th Army Corps had instructed this urgent message to be transmitted but it went only out at 12:35.

At that time the Heinkels had already been in the air for more than 15 minutes on their way to Rotterdam.

142. Formation of Heinkels 111

Captain Backer went forward on the Willemsbrug with the white flag held high. He arrived in the van der Takstraat at 12:20. He crossed the Noorder Island onto the bridge spanning the Koningshaven. A short heavyset German officer came forward and he concluded that this was the man to whom he should direct himself.

143. Captain Backer with the white flag

He stopped and laid down the flag. *"I am bringing you the reply from the Dutch commander to the message that he received from your commander."* Backer spoke in fluent German. With that he handed von Choltitz the envelope for the commander of the German troops. *"Are you the commander,"* Backer asked. *"No,"* the Oberstleutnant said. *"But what is the reply? "I will ensure that the commander receives it immediately."* *"Your ultimatum can not be accepted because it was not signed,"* Backer said.

"That is a pity, but I will call the General immediately to come over here and you can hand him the letter."

All around him Captain Backer saw swastika flags spread out on the pavement.

It was for the obvious reason of showing German bombers to spare that area. It was now 12:30. The sky was clear but the temperature had come down somewhat. The wind from the west had increased.

Oberstleutnant (Lieutenant Colonel) Otto Hohne had been the pilot of a fighter plane in the First World War. He was 45 years old and was popular with his men. He had the eyes of a hawk and could spot things before everyone else. He was also the best observer of Geschwader (Bomber Squadron) 54. Left and right from his Heinkel-111 flew the two escorts that accompanied the commander's plane. His formation of 36 bombers was on the way to the target at a speed of between 300 and 320 kilometers per hour; 4 groups of 9 Heinkels spread out so as not to collide with one another but close enough to not loose sight of them. His Heinkels were flying at a height of 5,000 meters or close to 16,000 feet.

At first General Schmidt had said a few choice words but then told von Choltitz that he would be there shortly. By now 20 minutes had passed. Von Choltitz was getting impatient. Everything took too damn long at this battle for a bridge of only 400 meters (1,200 feet) long. He had been here almost five days. The moment that he had received his orders back in Neuhaus seemed like ages ago. Where was Schmidt? It was now 12:40. Like Schmidt he was convinced that the Dutch commander was playing games in order to gain time.

The Heinkel-111's under Oberst (Colonel) Lackner were now about 50 minutes from their target. They would fly into Rotterdam air space from the east. Hohne's group would fly in from the south. They were told that if the attack were called off 'red' flares would be fired up in the sky.

Both Captain Backer and Lieutenant Colonel von Choltitz were about at the end of their patience when three generals and their staffs finally arrived. Schmidt stuck out his hand to take the envelope from Backer and said: "Is it your intention to get a stay of execution?" He didn't wait for a response and turned toward Student and Hubicki. He opened the envelope and read the message in mere seconds. He then handed the letter to Student. The generals then conferred together with the staff officers. Captain Backer waited. It was now 12:45. Von Choltitz came up to Backer and told him to follow. Walking behind the three generals they crossed the Stieltjesplein and entered an Ice Cream Parlor with a guard in front.

Schmidt entered first, sat on a crate in the middle of the floor and started to scribble on the back of Scharroo's letter; in pointy gothic style letters.

The Heinkels were now about 30 minutes from their target: Rotterdam. To the north they spotted the city of Utrecht.

It took a long time before the commander of the 39th Army Corps finished writing; he seemed to weigh every word. The general laid down his pen and looked at Backer. "I will read to you what my demands are," he said. "After that you may return to your commander."

The general started to read:

"Conditions for the surrender of the city of Rotterdam to the 39th Army Corps,"

He cleared his throat and continued: *"1. The city of Rotterdam will immediately be surrendered to me. All matters concerning the surrender must be completed forthwith in order for the occupation to take place during daytime.*

2. The Dutch troops that fought so bravely must upon orders from their commander lay down their arms in designated locations. Those locations

must then be handed over to my deputies.
3. In close columns the soldiers must be marched by their commanders to a point to be designated.
4. Officers and officials with an officer rank will retain their weapons!
5. In addition, all other conditions for the surrender will be in keeping with the Geneva Convention.
6. Military supplies may not be destroyed."
"Seven", he said and then continued slowly: *"I am forced to proceed quickly and I emphasize that I must have your decision in hand within three hours, which is before 18:00 hours. I ask you to return this letter with your response!"*

Before he handed Captain Backer the letter Schmidt said sarcastically: *"I have signed the letter with "Schmidt, Generalleutnant und Kommandierend General eines Armee Korps"."* (Lieutenant-General & Commanding General of an Army Corps)
Captain Backer took the letter and waited for approval to leave the location.

144. Captain Backer leaving the Ice Cream Salon

He had to have a response before 18:00 hours, he thought. That was German time: 100 minutes had to be deducted to get the proper Dutch time: 16:20 hours then. Again there was no time to loose!
On the bottom of the letter Schmidt had still a little room to scribble that the document had been signed in the south of Rotterdam, May 14, 1940 at 14:45 hours. When he started his return to the Dutch

front line it was past 13:05 hours. They had three hours and fifteen minutes to get back to the German commander.

The 90 Heinkels-111 were now flying at 200 meter elevation above the green polders. They were less than five minutes from the target and they had still not received any flak from the ground.

145. Heinkels 111 on their way to Rotterdam

On the ground below, in and around the houses and farms of the Krimpenerwaard the people heard the deep drone of the approaching bombers. They flew over and disappeared in southwesterly direction. The population had not seen such a large force of bombers during the previous four days of war. It was clear that this force was on its way to Rotterdam where, if the radio was to be believed, the front line ran straight through the center of the city. In five days the moffen (krauts) had not been able to make any headway.

At a distant of ten kilometers from the target Kampfgeschwader (Bomber Squadron) 54 had split up in two groups. The bomb aimers were now bending over their bombsights. In the first two planes of Groups A and B the commanders were looking at the big port city. They were watching for red colored flares! It was 13:20 hours and no red flares had been spotted.

Halfway down the Willemsbrug von Choltitz and an Oberleutnant (First Lieutenant) who were escorting Captain Backer came to a halt. The Oberleutnant handed Backer the white flag that he had been carrying.

"You have to go on alone," von Choltitz said to the parliamentary. Captain Backer took a step forward on his last few meters to the other side. Then he lifted his head to concentrate on the sound that was coming from afar but getting louder by the second. The sound turned from a loud drone to a booming sound that shook the surroundings. The two German officers were also listening and looked up to see the Heinkels-111. Then von Choltitz said to Backer: "It is better that you don't go on. It is getting dangerous out there. Come back with me!"

Oberst (Colonel) Wilhelm Lackner had not spotted any flares above the city and dropped his bomb load. One after the other the planes followed his example and dropped their 100 and 500 pound bombs. The first bombs came down in Kralingen; the most easterly part of the triangle that overlaid the heart of the city. Group A of Kampfgeschwader (Bomber Squadron) 54 had done its duty. With Group B it was different. Oberstleutnant (Lieutenant Colonel) Hohne had recognized Waalhaven airport below him and knew that it would now only be seconds. He would have to see the red flares now; otherwise it would be impossible to stop the bombing of his group. He peered at the ground. Big clouds of smoke are all he saw. No red flares. The bombs would have to be dropped. The moment of decision had arrived. The observer, seated behind him, told him it was time otherwise they would be out of the target area. With an up-down hand movement Hohne gave the signal: "Drop the bombs". The mechanism started to run; only a short moment and the bombs would start going down where Hohne observed explosions and great clouds of smoke and debris. Lackner had done his duty!

Not a second had passed since he had given the signal and he was now right above the target area, still looking out. He moved his head to the right and then he gasped. "Flares, red ones! But it was too late!"

Too late?

Hohne turned to the wireless operator, kicked him in the back – an agreed upon sign – and yelled: *"Turn away from the target, turn away!* *"We are not bombing; turn away! Pass it on: turn away!* It was already too late for his bomber and his two escorts. The automatic mechanism could not be stopped and it dropped the bombs within the triangle. Hohne observed the impact of his bombs and then veered his plane sharply to the southwest. His two escorts followed.

Turning away from the bombing run?

In the 33 Heinkels that were following their leader there was great confusion. They had seen the leader and escort dropping their bombs and couldn't comprehend the order to turn away. But the command continued to be transmitted. The 33 Heinkels obeyed and followed Hohne and his escorts in southwesterly direction to a group of islands called Zeeland. They had been instructed that this was their secondary target.

Rotterdam had been saved 100,000 pounds of explosives that the 33 Heinkels had on board. But the disaster was complete even without the impact of these explosives.

Chapter Twenty

Catastrophe...

General Schmidt had used this word when he had seen the Heinkels come in from east and south:

"Mein Gott, das gibt eine Katastrophe!' (My God, this is catastrophic!)

He was standing with Generals Student and Hubicki on the Stieltjesplein and saw how Oberstleutnant von Choltitz came running from the bridge across the Noorderhaven as fast as his rotund body allowed him to.

"Flares!' Schmidt yelled, "Fast, Flares!" Von Choltitz* barked some orders and almost immediately flare pistols were fired into the air. General Student had taken the 'Very' pistol (flare pistol) from one of the soldiers and was firing it himself, perhaps thinking that his firing was more credible.

146. Flare pistol (Very)

The generals had not noticed that part of the Squadron had departed without dropping its bombs.

From across the Maas River a column of smoke was rising that became denser by the minute and was obscuring the sun.

147. Rotterdam is burning!

"The battle is over! We have a lot of work to do!" Schmidt said to his officers.

At this point the reader knows what will happen next, the destruction of the city well before the expiration of the ultimatum at 16:20 hours.

The answer to the ultimatum must be clear to everyone; the surrender of the city and cessation of hostilities in The Netherlands followed by capitulation. The city would have been saved from destruction and the loss of so many lives would have been prevented. Yet, in spite of the new ultimatum, 90 Heinkels-111 appear above the undefended city and executed the sentence. How is that possible?

What happened must be seen in its full context. The 39th Army Corps under General Schmidt is part of the 18th Army under General Kuchler. That army is one of the Heeresgruppe B under Generaloberst (Colonel-General) von Bock.

148. Generalfeldmarschall Fedor von Bock
(1880-1945)

This Heeresgruppe (Army Group) is in turn one of the two under Generaloberst Halder, in charge of the Oberkommando des Heeres

149. Generaloberst Franz Halder (1884-1972)

This OKH together with the command of the Airforce (Luftwaffe) and Navy (Kriegsmarine) falls under the OKW, Oberkommando der Wehrmacht, commanded by none other than Adolf Hitler.

Unser Führer Adolf Hitler

trinkt keinen Alkohol und raucht auch nicht. Ohne andere im geringsten in dieser Richtung zu bevormunden, hält er sich eisern an das selbstauferlegte Lebensgesetz. Seine Arbeitsleistung ist ungeheuer.

(Reichsjugendführer Baldur v. Schirach im Buch: „Hitler, wie ihn keiner kennt.")

ABB. 6.10.   Vorbild Hitler. Quelle: *Auf der Wacht* 54 (1937), S. 18.

150. Der Fuehrer Adolf Hitler (1889-1945)

They have been following the course of the battle in Holland and observed that the "bereinigung" (cleansing) of Holland is not progressing as expected. It is not difficult for them to see where the stagnation is. They draw a circle around the city of Rotterdam. Therefore the leadership insists on speed at all cost. With bigger problems brewing in Belgium and France, Hitler and his officers turn away from the Dutch situation and rely on the chain of command structure to deal with the question of Rotterdam.

Not so, however, for Goering, the commander of the 'Deutsche Luftwaffe'. His attention has been focused on Holland ever since the debacle that unfolded north of Rotterdam on May 10th; the first day of the war. In that attack he lost more than 500 planes and about 1,100 of his finest officers and NCOs were taken prisoner and ended up in England. What made it even worse was the fact that most of these men were experienced aviators who were doing the training in his vaunted Luftwaffe. They would be difficult to replace. Additionally, his 22d Airborne Division commanded by his friend Graf Sponek had failed in their task of taking The Hague and the northern approaches of the bridges spanning the Maas River in Rotterdam. They had become surrounded in a small pocket near Overschie to the north of Rotterdam.

Is it possible that as a result of these failures Goering played a revengeful role in the destruction of Rotterdam? It would certainly not have been beyond Goering's personality to be this diabolical.

If they had remained in Rotterdam, thirteen anti-aircraft guns could have made the difference that afternoon of May 14 but they were gone. For some reason they had been assigned elsewhere. Furthermore, the last two detachments of the Volunteer Anti-Aircraft Corps had departed from Rotterdam early that morning. No one ever found out what was behind these moves. But it is the reason that the bombers that appeared above Rotterdam did not receive any fire from the ground. It is sheer speculation that the presence of the guns would have made much difference but, at least, Rotterdam would not have undergone its destruction in such a docile manner.

*Dietrich von Choltitz' had been appalled at the wanton destruction of Rotterdam but his leadership at the bridge would earn him the Knight's Cross. Von Choltitz fought at Sebastopol and was promoted to major general. He served in Italy before moving to Normandy in 1944. His failure to stop the advance of the Americans displeased Hitler and he was moved to Paris where he became the city's military governor in August. He will be best remembered for defying Hitler's direct orders to raze the city of Paris. He remembered Rotterdam in 1940.

Chapter Twenty-One

"Surrender or I will kill your mother".

It was about 1 o'clock in the afternoon of May 14 when my father decided he would go to the office in downtown Rotterdam. He worked for N.V. Kattenburg, a clothing manufacturer and retailer. They had their main store on the Hoogstraat. This was one of the oldest shopping streets in the city and exactly one kilometer long (1,000 meters or a little over 3,000 feet).

Rotterdam — Hoogstraat

151. Hoogstraat, before and after the bombing

The street was very narrow with on either side hundreds of stores and restaurants. One can imagine a busy day when hundreds of people would be shopping and crowding the narrow sidewalks.

A colleague of dad, Tom van der Meer, lived in our street, Dunantstraat #40. He was married to Ansje and a few months earlier had been blessed with a baby girl. My dad had suggested to Tom that they go to the office together. They had decided to leave a little before one o'clock. My mother, who was somewhat psychic and would have occasional premonitions, told dad that she was deadly afraid that something would happen to him if he left and she begged him not to go. But dad insisted that it was his duty to go to work; he had been home long enough already. Mother insisted and suggested that he wait just 30 minutes and she would have the midday meal ready. *"Please, please!"* she said. *"Stay at least for lunch!"*

"But I promised Tom that we would go together." "Then tell Tom to go ahead and you will come later." Dad relented and went to tell Tom who then left shortly thereafter. It would take Tom about 30 minutes to walk downtown. The streetcars were no longer operating. Tom arrived at N.V. Kattenburg a little before 1:30 and sat down at his desk to do some of the paperwork that had accumulated since May 10th. At that moment he was aware of a loud noise coming from outside. Before his mind had time to identify the sound of low flying airplanes, the world around Tom exploded. In the last few seconds of consciousness Tom experienced a red glow and extreme heat that surrounded him, lifted him up and tore his body to pieces. He was dead instantly. With him hundreds of citizens underwent the same fate in the 30 minutes that it took the 90 Heinkels-111 to level downtown Rotterdam.

Mother remembers:

"City Hall had been spared because the killers would need that building. How we cried and how angry and powerless we were to see this. Afterwards we heard that the enemy had given the mayor an ultimatum. Unless the city surrendered by a certain time, it would be leveled and other cities would follow the example.

"Surrender or I will kill your mother".

We heard that the schedule had been moved up by one hour. By radio we heard that Rotterdam had surrendered but that the fighting continued in the province of Zeeland."

"However, little could be achieved against such might and what was it all for? This was only the beginning of 5 years of terror. Never did we think that it would last that long".

Henry remembers:
Until May 14th there were almost continuous air raids, but generally more on the other side of the harbor. Of course the object was to terrorize the civilian population. The bridges over the Coolhaven were raised and we were almost on an island with all the harbor installations. Except for that one bomb on the first day no bombs fell in our area. The Germans obviously wanted to save it for their own purposes. During the morning of the 14th we had some more bombing and shooting. Then in the early afternoon we had the heaviest air raid of all. The house was literally swaying, as we well know now from our earthquakes in California. Of course ignoring my mother's very strong advice, I had to have a look and saw the aircraft bombing the center of the city. After the war the Germans said they only dropped the bombs from three aircraft. The rest were recalled. That is a lot of hogwash; I saw more bombs fall than you could ever get into three Heinkel bombers. There were at least sixty or more aircraft in the air. In no time the city center was on fire. That turned into a firestorm that spread from one end of the horizon to the other. Then suddenly everything became quiet and the radio reported that the city would surrender; I believe at 5 or 6 o'clock.
We could get across the bridge again, but the marines had disappeared. They probably went to Hook of Holland and from there would try to escape to England.
Uncle Wim left on his own to have a look around. A little later Pa and I went also. Annie and Wim had to stay with mother under strong protests from Wim, who probably sneaked out later anyway. We crossed the PdeHoogh brug and were to cross the Rochussenstraat when a couple of German soldiers on a motorbike stopped us and yelled something. I have no idea what they said but since I probably did not give them a very friendly face I had to put my hands up. They yelled some more and left. We walked down the Heemraadsingel and turned on the Nieuwe Binnenweg to the Westersingel, where we could see the Oude Binnenweg burning near the Coolsingel. We walked along the Westersingel and saw the Jonker

Frans Straat on fire. There were a lot of refugees walking more or less aimlessly. We walked around some more and ended up near the railroad tunnel to Blijdorp.

Then shooting started again and columns of German troops were marching and driving towards the railroad tunnel toward the northern part of Rotterdam. The shooting later appeared to have been "friendly fire" and they had accidentally (?) shot their own general (Student). He was shot in the head and taken to one of our hospitals where he was repaired by a Dutch neurosurgeon. General Student survived the war.

To the southwest of us was also an enormous fire. Our own people had set the large Royal Dutch (BPM) and the Caltex refineries with the storage tanks in Pernis on fire. Closer to home an army depot on the Westzeedijk was also burning.

After seeing all this we made our way back home, not realizing that the nightmare would last 5 long years and get worse.

The schools in our area reopened in about a week. During that time I roamed around and had a look at a couple of crashed German planes, one a Junkers transport. It was shot full of holes. The other one was a burned wreck, no idea what type it was.

My dad wanted to go to his place of work and I could go with him. He also was looking for one of his colleagues, who had disappeared. They lived close by and his wife was very worried and with good reason.

The streetcars were not operating and we walked and walked, sometimes it was more climbing over the rubble. We made it to his place of work on the Hoogstraat, but it was all burned-out rubble at least 20 feet high. The street was a trail about 5 ft wide; the rest was total desolation. We detoured a little bit and had a look at the burned out St Laurens Church, which dated back to before 1500. I still have the charcoal sketch I made of it. We ended up at Crooswijk, the big cemetery. In a large open area were rows of corpses, most of them badly burned. My dad could have a look and to try to find his colleague. I was not supposed to follow him and stayed at the entrance, but could see more than enough. It gave me nightmares for some time and a very deep hatred for the people who had done that. The smell of the burned city was horrendous and it hung around for months.

About two weeks later they found the poor guy or what was left of him under tons of rubble.

We walked back again and when we were out of the burned area we stopped at a coffee shop. Everybody was very depressed and when the radio came with the news that we had to change the time to 'German time', some women started to cry. As for the men, they used some pretty good expletives; it was one of the very few times that I heard my dad curse. We walked near city hall, which was still standing, lot of shrapnel holes though. The main post office had been hit, but had not burned. For the rest the destruction was total.
Back in school everybody tried to get back to 'normal', several students were not back and we found out that the father of one of the girls had been killed aboard a navy ship off the coast.

Chapter Twenty-Two

Horror Stories

152. The Hoogstraat after the bombing

Frits Wehrmeijer, a student who lived on the Boezemsingel was running with his father over the Goudscheweg.

153. Goudscheweg

They had been visiting family when the bombing started. When the explosions subsided they had left the building that they had been taking shelter in. The building was about to collapse. On the street it was hell all around. Houses were collapsing and the fire fed by a strong westerly wind was howling and sucking oxygen away from tens of people that were running everywhere, screaming and crying; some fell and didn't get up again.
Running behind his father Frits ran into the Warmoezierstraat where he saw glowing pieces of metal, the leftovers of the bombs that had caused this destruction. He saw some people covering these twisted and glowing pieces with sand. *"Keep running!* " his father yelled.

They reached the Alkemadeplein that Frits remembered as a fun blue-collar area.

154. Alkemadeplein with the gazebo.

But now the place was in flames and many people were running everywhere, seeking shelter. His father entered a workshop and Frits followed but before he took another step his father had already turned around. *"Go back, go back!"* his father yelled over the howling of the fire outside. On the Alkemadeplein the High School building looked undamaged but the three other sides of the square were infernos with only the facades still standing. The gazebo on the square, where in better times music performances were given every week, was still intact.

They knew that next to the gazebo there were two air raid shelters. In front of one they crouched down and looked at the huge fire surrounding them. The heat was almost unbearable. From the third floor of a burning house Frits saw a man or woman, he couldn't tell, throwing furniture out of a broken window. Piece after piece came down to disintegrate on the street below. *"That doesn't make sense"*, Frits thought, but completely fascinated, kept looking at the person in the window. Then, all of a sudden, he saw a red glow rising up behind the person. The man or woman raised arms and collapsed backwards in the raging fire.

"Frits!" his father cried, *"We've got to leave here. I'd rather get hit by a bomb than be burned alive here!"*

They continued running to the Goudschesingel. When, what seemed like forever, they had reached the relative safety of the Kralingerhout, Frits knew that they had forever said *"Goodbye"* to the neighborhood that he, like all other boys from Rotterdam, had enjoyed so much.

A shout was heard on the Coolsingel and then more people were shouting: *"The Coolsingel Hospital is on fire!"*

155. Coolsingel Hospital

Four bombs had hit the hospital with its broad façade on the Coolsingel: in the stairwell, in the operating room, the boiler-room and the warehouse. The fire started almost immediately in the new addition on the Van Oldenbarneveltstraat and spread to the top floor of the old building via the connection between the old and the new building. Even the bushes in the garden caught fire. As soon as the bombing had ceased people who happened to be in the area of the hospital were running to its aid. The hospital had 750 beds but fortunately most of the patients that had been able to walk had been sent home on the first day. This afternoon there were only 100 patients that had been brought in as a result of the fighting and occasional bombings since the first day: 59 soldiers (including 3

Germans) and 50 civilians. Twenty-five of these people had died and several had been discharged. When the bombing started the doctors and nurses had moved the patients to the basement.

156. Coolsingel Hospital after the bombing

Across from the Doelen: a large theater complex, Karel van Hagen was standing next to his motorbike. On May 10th he had volunteered his services to the police in the Oostervantstraat. They had provided him with an armband that he was wearing now. He had seen bombs dropping on the Doelen and adjacent buildings. The City Hall and Post Office buildings, however, were still intact. Behind Hotel Atlanta he saw how flames were shooting from the roof of the hospital and figured that it must have received direct hits.

157. Hotel Atlanta on the Coolsingel prewar

He hesitated what he should do. Should he go to the Doelen where without doubt there had to be many casualties, the hospital that required evacuation or to the place that his heart told him to go: The Lucia Institution on the Rottekade? His two daughters Tinie age 7 and Bep age 5 were living there since the divorce from his wife. He made his decision and rode as fast as he could through the rubble to the Rottekade. As far as he could see everything was in ruins with fires raging everywhere. Building facades were crashing down in front and behind him. He knew that his two children were in this hell. At the Boschjeskerk next to the Lucia Institution he jumped off his bike and ran onto the inner court.

158. Boschjes Church after bombing

For a moment he stood paralyzed. He saw that bombs had fallen on the institution and the church: flames were already erupting from the ruins. He figured he was already too late because nowhere did he see any sign of life. He looked at the school building adjacent to the building. He remembered that the school building had a cellar. He felt some sense of hope. When he came closer to the school building he heard a strange sound: like buzzing bees. The sound came from underneath the building. He saw a heavy wooden door that provided entrance to the basement but it was obstructed by a heap of debris. Frantically he started to remove the debris and tried to open the door but it didn't budge. When he held his ear closer to the door he could hear what the buzzing was all about: the shrill voices of tens of children praying to the Holy Mother. They kept repeating: Holy

Mother of Jesus, full of grace etc. etc, over and over again. His two children had to be there.

The Mother Superior had already given up hope that her 71 children and 12 nuns would be rescued in time. A priest was going around the cellar giving his salvation to those about to die. Then, all of a sudden, they heard loud banging on the door at the top of the stairs to the cellar. One of the nuns had nailed the door shut in order to *"keep out the evil from reaching the children"*. Somebody on the outside was calling. One of the sisters yelled: *"Help, help!"* She ran up the stairs and quickly tore away the lumber that had been used to barricade the door. With a bang the door opened and a blinding ray of light entered the dark cellar. Against the bright light they saw the shape of a ghost. The ghost descended into the cellar and came closer. The praying had stopped and there was now only sobbing. *"Help, thank God, Help!"* someone yelled again. Then the ghost talked and said:
"Get out, all of you must get out now, everything is on fire!" Two children ran forward into the arms of their father. Tinie and Bep van Hagen had recognized their dad.

Mother remembers:
"The sirens now gave the "all clear" over our burning city. We could go outside now and those who had some knowledge of First Aid were going in the city to see what could be done to help. I also left and had to leave Annie and you in the care of Henry who was old enough at 16. I was afraid and prayed to God that I would be strong enough to face the terrible things in the city. I prayed to God to please make me strong so that I could help others and be of support to them in their anguish. Your father left with other men from the area on a truck toward the center of the city. We didn't get any farther than the end of the Nieuwe Binnenweg and the corner of the Westersingel. The first part of the Oude Binnenweg was still standing. From that direction came a column of marching German soldiers. It was the most horrible experience to see the victorious smiles on those 'kraut' faces. We did the only smart thing we could do; all of us turned around and showed our behinds. If we would have done what was really on our minds they would have killed us."

Leo Ott, a reporter of Het Rotterdamsch Nieuwsblad was on the Beursplein and he saw them coming, the triumphant Germans. He shuddered.

159. German tank columns entering Rotterdam

At the head of the column walked an officer with a map in his hands. He stopped on the Beursplein and with his legs spread wide he looked at the fires around him. He then pointed at the Noordblaak and the column started to move again. Black clouds everywhere. Ott knew that they were the messengers of more fires to come. He heard the falsetto sound of the flames, roaring and wailing. It was like music that was coming to him as the finale of the symphony of the bombers. Then he notices the beginning of a wide smile on the round face of the officer. *"One can just read it from that hated "kraut" face,"* Ott wrote later when he was home again: *"They had done their job well."*

Following behind the column of paratroopers and airborne infantry drove the tanks of General von Hubicki. Shortly thereafter the motorized columns of the SS-Leibstandarte Adolf Hitler crossed the Willemsbrug over the Maas River.

160. German 'panzer' entering the city on the approaches of the Willemsbrug.

161. Tanks crossing the Willemsbrug. View of the city is
completely obscured by smoke from the burning city.

They appeared in a great hurry. Then followed detachments of the 254th Infantry Division. The SS-regiment was on its way to Overschie to free the men of Sponeck's 22d Airborne Division. The order to push through regardless of the negotiations concerning the surrender of the Dutch forces came direct from the Oberbefehlshaber der Luftwaffe, Field Marshall Hermann Goering.

Via General Kesselring, the Commander of the 2d Luftflotte (Air fleet) he had instructed that the following order be transmitted to Rotterdam: *"Field Marshall orders to immediately break through the enemy lines to free Sponeck without regard to the capitulation. The attack to take place between 19:00 and 20:00 hours with three groups. Use bombs if I am not immediately notified of breakthrough."*

That would be between 17:20 and 18:00 Dutch time.

General Schmidt who was notified of this order by the 18th Army radioed back immediately: "North of Rotterdam has been occupied. Do not bomb." That was at 17:15 hours. Schmidt's message was premature because aside from a handful of soldiers that had relieved the bridgehead across the Maas River there were no troops across the bridge in any great numbers. It was sent in time to prevent a second bombing of the city.

Oberleutnant Helmuth Stamm found himself once again in his Heinkel-111 above the Netherlands. At Quackenbruck airfield in Germany, where they had landed after the first bombing, they had been given a rest. Not for long because quickly three *'staffels'* received orders to get ready for another raid on Rotterdam.

The men asked: *"Why?"*

"The city has still not surrendered, that's why!"

Twenty-seven airplanes were once again on their way to Rotterdam to satisfy Goering's order.

At 17:43 they were approaching the target. They saw big, black clouds over the city at a height of 4,000 to 4,500 meters. (12,000 to 14,000 feet): their flying height. The acrid burning smell of the city below was entering their aircrafts. Fortunately they had not yet pulled in their trailing radio antennas and they were able to receive the radio message: *"Attack cancelled. Capitulation a reality."*

Helmutt Stamm was looking down at the triangle of destruction; that looked a lot different from what he had been told at the earlier briefing: *"military and harbor installations"*. Instead, what he saw encompassed virtually the whole heart of the city. After the Heinkels turned away to the east, Stamm felt that Hauptmann Schaede was making the plane rock from left to right, back and forth. Via the radio he spoke to his staffel: *"Thank God, the war with Holland has ended!"*

A little later all the planes were rocking their wings; in Kampfgeschwader 54 that was the way they expressed their satisfaction.

Mother continues:

From there we walked up the Oude Binnenweg, the streets on either side had been destroyed. That is where the blue-collar workers had lived. Most had fled and were now on the open land called Hoboken with only the clothes on their backs. The department store of Vroom & Dreesman was partly in tact. There were still clothes and mannequins displayed in the windows but the following day also this part of Rotterdam had been destroyed by fire. Not by the bombs but by fire whipped up by the strong wind. The Coolsingel Hospital had been completely destroyed. It is impossible to describe what took place there. I saw nurses walking around in circles, like in a trance. Even though it has been 48 years ago, one face I will never forget, she said: "My mother, what happened to her, she lived here": pointing to a street that was no longer there.

In the Mauritsstraat, part of a school was still standing. It was bursting with people that had fled the bombing and fire. We would try and find housing for these poor people in the western part of the city. The people clung to us in their despair and begged to be taken along. Neighbors from across our street had a large house and they met some friends in that school. Fortunately, the parents with their daughter could go with them. The neighbors of these people who had been with them all the time could not join them and therefore I took them under my wing. It was a woman whose husband was in the service and her brother-in-law who lived on IJsselmonde had come to Rotterdam to see how his sister-in-law was doing. He couldn't return home. Together we went back to the Dunantstraat.

I had not seen any dead or injured people, only people that were half out of their minds, looking for children or relatives. Your father returned home in shock. Tom had not returned home and your father had gone to the Crooswijk Cemetery. Hundreds and hundreds of bodies were taken there and he was asked to see if he could identify any. He was not allowed in the burning city but did get a pass later on that authorized him to go in the ruins to look for anything that was left from the business.

Your father was able to get these two people in the house of a neighbor who had gone to the Veluwe and who had given your father the keys to her house to use in case of emergency. The next day they came back to our house where they decided to walk to IJsselmonde. But the woman had no shoes. I went to our neighbor where I knew that Jo had small feet and might have shoes that fit. At first she didn't want to but when I told her that the woman had lost everything and that it could happen to all of us, she relented. She brought shoes that fit the woman perfectly. They then left for the house of her sister. Later on I received a "thank you" letter from that sister.

On the following day, May 15, bulletins were posted all over telling us what we could and could not do. We had lost our freedom. A German was now in the guardhouse on the bridge. We lived on # 21 and on # 25 lived an NSBer. The Dutch soldier must have been fired upon from there. From now on we had to be careful what we said and how we behaved. In the Coolhaven were a few Rhine barges that had been confiscated to serve as living quarters for the displaced people. They slept on these barges and camped out in front of our house where they did some cooking. I don't know how long they were there but soon the Germans came and burned everything that they had brought to the barges, blankets, sheets, clothes etc. Much to the dismay of the people but maybe just as well because the Germans were afraid of a possible epidemic."

Free but utterly confused a small monkey was making its way across the ruins and debris of houses surrounding the Oostplein. It was far away from the place where it had been born. This little monkey was just one of the many animals that had joined the many refugees from the bombing and fire that were trying to flee the city. On the Coolsingel people saw several deer jumping from one heap of rubble to the next, on the railway terrain of the Delftsche Poort station, buffalos were running around in mortal fear.

At the same time, zebra's were seen calmly grazing on the grass on either side of the Westersingel. Almost all the buildings of the zoo on the Kruiskade were in flames.

162. Entrance to the zoo on the Kruiskade before the war.

Following the bombing the cages and enclosures had been opened to save the animals from certain death by asphyxiation or burning. Not all the animals took flight.

Especially among the apes there were many that had stayed close to their old quarters. It was total chaos in the zoo. The stable where the elephants were housed had escaped the fire. Rumba, a female elephant had gone berserk and none of the keepers had dared to get close to her. Sonny, the male elephant had been no problem and he was now chained to a big tree in the park. Several firemen were keeping four polar bears wet with their hoses. A rhinoceros, that like several other animals could not be allowed to run loose, received an occasional shower as well. Members of the Volunteer Fire Brigade would be busy all night taking care of these animals. The city water system was no longer operating in that area and they pumped the water from the Diergaarde Singel. Among the animals that disappeared from the zoo were many parrots and other tropical birds. They didn't fly out on their own but were taken by citizens who were fleeing the city and on their way passed the zoo. Their intent was undoubtedly to save the creatures but it is a fact that none were ever returned to the zoo.

I remember when my mother and father left to help out in the burning city. I cried my heart out and begged them not to go. I was afraid I would never see them again. It was one of the worst feelings I ever experienced in my life. They were given improvised white armbands with a red cross painted on it. When they returned I took those armbands and kept one to this day.

163. Red Cross armband my mother wore on May 14, 1940

On the afternoon of May 14 thousand of people were fleeing from the inferno in the city. Most of these refugees would end up on a large piece of open land called: "Land van Hoboken".

164. Refugees are gathering at the *Land of Hoboken* near
the Boymans Museum

There they would stay for a long time: camping out in the open. This large area was adjacent to the Boymans Museum on the Mathenesserlaan and not far from our house on the Dunantstraat: bordering the Coolhaven.

Hundreds of refugees would also be streaming past our house on their way west, away from the terrible conditions in the city.
Two things have stayed with me ever since:
First is the penetrating smell of the disinfectant *'Lysol'*. In fear of a possible epidemic, several officials of the city health department were spraying refugees liberally with this liquid. All this happened in front of our house. The smell of this disinfectant and the acrid smell of the burning city will stay with me forever. I remember that many years later one could still smell the strange, pungent odor of the many different spices that had burned and were still smoldering for months after the bombing. The second thing was *'empty'* birdcages. Numerous refugees, mostly older people, were carrying cages without a bird in it. It would be the only possession they had saved before fleeing the fire. But why empty cages. All I can think is that when they fled their homes they took the cage with a bird still in it and on their way through all the smoke the bird died. They ended up with an empty

cage and since it was the only belonging they had, they held on to it because it was the only object that reminded them of their past life.

Throughout the night the evacuation of the burning city continued. Thousands of people fled to the *Kralingerhout* and *Land of Hoboken* where some stayed in improvised tents. Most of the people were camping out in the open. Nobody was able to sleep: they were silently watching the burning city. Volunteers brought in food. They had collected it in the undamaged parts of the city.

The Dutch soldiers that had been defending Rotterdam until the bombing had crushed their resistance spend the night in several collection centers. They had been disarmed on Tuesday afternoon and were marched by their commanders to churches and schools in Feyenoord – 1,500 men -, the Museumpark, the Ice Hocky Arena in Kralingen, schools in Hillegersberg, the court-yard of the Heinekens Brewery, the Marine Depot in the Mecklenburglaan and the building of the St Laurens Institution on the Binnenweg.
There were also soldiers that had left the city with the intent to fight another day.
However, when they heard the proclamation of General Winkelman over the radio, they had also laid down their arms. They were sad, had cried and some were swearing profusely. I remember several hundred of these men coming through the Dunantstraat on their way to Delfshaven. They looked beaten and had tears in their eyes. I felt very sad.

That same night the victors continued to advance through the city. The SS-troops of General Sepp Dietrich had finally made contact with Sponeck's forced that had been isolated near Overschie.

165. SS-Obergruppenfuehrer Sepp Dietrich (1892-1966)

They had then moved in the direction of The Hague. Parts of the 9th Panzer Division reached the city of Delft midway between Rotterdam and The Hague. They would reach The Hague the next day and on Thursday the 16th would move toward Amsterdam.

There was a clear blue sky on May 15th but it was almost totally obscured by the dirty black smoke columns rising from the ashes of the city. The wind had increased and was still blowing from the southeast. The temperature had risen to about 73 degrees Fahrenheit equal to 22.4 degrees Celsius.

That day many people made their way to the city to try and help or just wanted to see for them selves what damage had been done. Very few made it to the heart of the city: much of it had already been barricaded. A school principal in Rotterdam made such a pilgrimage. In a small note-book he recorded where he went and what he saw. He saw the first heaps of smoking and smoldering rubble along the Schiekade.

166. The Schiekade with the Schie having been filled with debris from the bombing.

From this point onwards he no longer recognized the city; it was a realization that made him feel sick. In a grassy area he saw a piano surrounded by some arm-chairs. A stack of dinner plates was leaning against one of the chairs. The beginning of the Schiekade was like a row of big ovens, separated by pieces of wall. Part of a kitchen was sticking through the roof of one house. Coughing and with his eyes burning he was trying to find the old stately St Laurenskerk through the thick mist hanging over everything. When he saw it rising up out of the glowing mist it appeared to him more touching and pathetic than a fairytale. It was a mere skeleton with the façade totally burned away.

167. St Laurens church after the bombing.

The beautiful pipe organ was reduced to rubble. His eyes went up to the top of the tower. It had been rendered a deep dirty yellow like old porcelain. Time had stopped the big clock at precisely 1:30pm.
He walked on. Near the Karnemelkshaven he passed a garage that had collapsed. In the process of collapsing it had crushed numerous cars. He looked up and realized why the ruins of the St Laurenskerk dominated the scene: it lacked a background. The 1,000 meter long Hoogstraat had ceased to exist.

168. Hoogstraat after the bombing

It had received direct hits and was one long heap of stone and rubble. At the end of this heap of rubble he saw the big undamaged grain mill on the Oostplein; it seemed unreal like it had been an oversight.

169. The Mill on the Oostplein

(The miller had given the wings free reign during the fire. The outward pressure from the wind had kept the fire and flames away from the mill. It had saved itself)

He passed Het Boschje; the well-known church had disappeared.

170. Het Boschje after the bombing

The school behind it was now totally visible and it showed its completely unacceptable name of: *"Immaculatae Conceptioni"* – Immaculate Conception. He walked on the Goudschesingel, the Pompenburg, passing big stacks of smoldering paper.

171. Goudschesingel

Then he was back again on the Hofplein and had to step across the electric wiring of the streetcar system lying all around him.

172. Hofplein

At the Coolsingel he could not get any farther. A long fence spanning the width of this main artery had hastily been erected. Looking through the fence he was trying to find familiar landmarks but all he saw were smoking skeletons all the way toward the

173. Coolsingel

Westzeedijk. On the Noordplein he got the impression that the apartment buildings appeared self-conscious because of their undamaged status. All of a sudden he saw that on the corner of the Noordsingel there were a growing number of people.

174. Noordsingel

When he joined the crowd he saw a group of Royal Dutch marines pass by in torn and dirty uniforms. He wrote: *"From their tired and dirty faces I could read the tragic sorrow of their unrivalled bravery and the forced surrender." "Surrender or I will kill your mother!"* On the corner of the square they turned with shorter steps and in this slowdown the eyes of the silent civilians met the eyes of this silent *"honor"* guard. He saw that not all the people that were crying and sobbing were women. One man spoke. He said only one word with great passion: *"Goddamn!"*

Ton Loontjens was one of those young marines. He was only 17 years old and had signed up for the Royal Dutch Marine Corps on February 5, 1940; just 94 days before the war started. He had only just finished his basic training. Ton fought the German paratroopers at the Maasbruggen for several days and prevented them from securing a foothold at the north end of the bridge. Then on May 14 he witnessed the bombing of the city... Ton's story does not end there. He was able to escape to England in a small sailboat. He wrote a book about his exploits and if you can read Dutch I suggest you buy it*:
"Eens marinier, Altijd marinier, een leven vol afwisseling en avontuur".

Qua Patet Orbis 1940 – 1972 (Once a marine, Always a marine, a life full of diversity and adventure)
To my knowledge the book has not been translated in English.

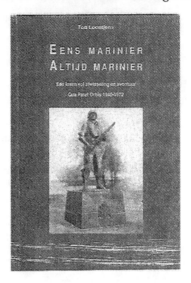

175. Eens marinier, Altijd marinier by Ton Loontjens

176. Ton Loontjens is on the left

In silence the principal made his way to his home in Blijdorp. He had seen it all.

He knew it now: *"The dirty victory of a mechanized superior lie. A lie remains inferior even if the lie is gigantic. Warsaw and Rotterdam"*, he noted in his little notebook, *"they were merely stages"*.

Dirk van Veelen was trained in first aid and on the afternoon of May 14th he and 30 other trained and licensed medics had rushed to places in the city that required their help. He and his partners lived in the south of Rotterdam. They had watched the bombing of the city from the relative safety of the Noorder Island.

They didn't know what to expect. At any rate it would be different from their routine of the last few days when they had treated mainly wounds.

On the Pompenburgsingel they came upon the first two bodies of the many they would recover in the course of the month of May. Near the Hofplein they had that night recovered thirty bodies of people that had found shelter in a lodgment.

177. Hofplein

The place had received a direct hit and the building crushed them when it collapsed on top of them. They had cleared the debris and in a mountain of broken glass they had found the bodies. Van Veelen had thought that you could also have said that in the thirty bodies, they had found glass. It really didn't make much difference. They had asked the undertaker located in the Zwaanhals for a hearse. The all-black hearse with a silver skull & bones insignia had arrived and they had taken the remains to Crooswijk Cemetery.

178. Crooswijk Cemetery Angel

They had performed this chore every day without let-up. How many of these trips had they made already and how many dead?

It was the most gruesome work that they had ever performed. They had started that Tuesday, May 14, with thirty-one and now with the month coming to the end he had only eleven men left. The work had been too terrible to perform for very long. He had understood it only too well. There had to be people to do this work he had reasoned and he had stayed on. At times when the work was just too gruesome they had encouraged each other. One of his men didn't wear rubber gloves. That was Joop Praag. He was in charge of the administration. He recorded the place where they had located the body or body parts, the sex, approximate age and any other objects that might identify the person. Further identification would be attempted at the cemetery. Most bodies were completely unrecognizable as human beings and the task would almost be impossible.

CATO, KOBA AND TRUUS

Today it was time to go home. Van Veelen's men made their way through a narrow lane that had been cleared between the rubble of the Hoogstraat. They were on their way to the Willemsbrug across the Maas. To the left and right they saw only heaps of rubble intersected occasionally by what must have been a side street. Near the St Laurenskerk (church) a man approached through one of those streets. The man called: *"Stop gentlemen, please stop!"*

Van Veelen waited. *"Am I correct in assuming that you people belong to the recovery team?"* the man asked. Van Veelen nodded. He knew what would follow. It had happened so many times. They would be asked to quickly dig here or there for people that were missing.

The man grabbed on to van Veelen's coat and begged him to help him. *"Please, please"*, he said. *"I am from the Old Catholic Church in the Torenstraat. Please help me. There are still three servants missing...!"*

179. Catholic Church on the Kaasmarkt

Van Veelen hesitated: it had been a long and difficult day. Three waitresses missing.... They would certainly not be alive any longer....

"Must that be done today?" he asked the man. *"Please, please, I have already been waiting so long for people to help me!"* he begged. Van Veelen turned to his crew, *"What do you say guys, do we still have time to go to the Torenstraat..."* Joop Praag was the one who made the decision. *"Let's go"*, he said.

With his team he followed the man to the ruins of the church. When they reached the huge heap of rubble he regretted his decision. This would be a much bigger job than he had anticipated. "Those three girls are supposed to be under this heap?" he asked the man from the church. *"They are most likely in the vault of the church,"* the man said somewhat timidly. *"That safe is still reachable. They went in there when the bombing started: Cato, Koba and Truus."*

"Cato, Koba and Truus..." Van Veelen repeated to him self while he climbed over the rubble and located the huge safe surrounded by big chunks of brick and steel. *"And you say they are in there, those three..."* He experienced intense dread of what to expect. "If they are in there, Cato, Koba and Truus, there will be very little left of them. That safe must have been red hot when the fires were raging here...." *"Joop!"* he yelled. *"Come here with a few strong guys!"*

Many years later Dirk van Veelen told a visitor what had happened that afternoon at the Old Catholic Church in the Torenstraat. The recovery team had gathered at the big safe and was waiting for instructions.

I said to a few of the men: *"Boys, let's first remove that debris from in front of the safe and maybe we can open it."*
The boys removed the stones and yanked at the heavy door. Then one of the men said to me: *"Dirk, there is a real foul smell coming from that safe! I can't stand it, it's horrible!"*
"Weren't you afraid of what you might find?" the visitor asked. *"No,"* Dirk replied, *"and I don't know why not."*

"I also smelled that foul odor. It was indeed horrible". I remember telling Joop Praag: *"Joop, we take a real deep breath, go to that door, pull it open and then run back!"* It was a distance of some hundred feet. The two of us walked up to the door and pulled it open. Immediately a bluish cloud appeared. It was unbelievable...
That safe had been in the inferno for hours. Everything inside had been boiling, red hot. When the cloud had dissipated, I said to Joop: *"I think I can see them sitting there."* I said to him: *"We get in there as fast we can and pull them out one after the other!"*

We grabbed a hold of one; she was sitting on a bench or a chair, I forgot. With Joop and me pulling she got longer and longer and continued to grow. Completely cooked!

Cato, Koba and Truus were there names; we recovered all three. I can't go on.

THE DEATH OF THOMAS VAN DER MEER

On May 23d my dad was asked to come to Crooswijk cemetery to assist with the identification process. Body parts had been recovered from the debris of N.V. Kattenburg & Co in the Hoogstraat. They had also found a wedding band. My dad had no doubt. They had found the remains of his colleague Thomas van der Meer, age 27. The ring and a torso were all. Dad had the unpleasant task of notifying Tom's wife. Ansje had already given up hope that Tom would be found alive and she received the news stoically but then collapsed in my dad's arms. He had given her the wedding band but didn't tell her what had been found.

Tom was buried at Crooswijk Cemetery on Monday, May 27th at 2 o'clock in the afternoon.

The death announcement read:

Due to circumstances we are only presently able to let you know that on the 14th of May 1940 because of a fatal accident was taken from us my beloved husband and father, our son, son-in-law, brother, brother-in-law and uncle

Thomas van der Meer
At the age of 27 years

From all of us:
A.J. Van der Meer – v. Dijk
Ansje

Rotterdam, 24 May 1940
Dunantstraat 40

Please No Flowers

If not for my mother's premonition my dad would have undergone the same *"fatal accident"*. Instead he lived. He died in 1982 at the age of 83.

CHAPTER TWENTY-THREE

STATISTICS OF THE BOMBING

Fires had been raging over an area of 633 acres, of which 390 acres had been built up. The remaining 243 acres were parks, city squares, avenues and streets. The following numbers give an impression of what was lost:

(Alphabetical order)

Banks:	13
Buildings:	11,000
Cafes & Lodgments:	527
Charitable Organizations:	10
Churches:	24
Cinemas:	12
City buildings:	21
Consulates:	19
Entertainment centers:	22
Factories:	31
Parking Garages:	Untold
Hospitals:	10
Hotels:	26
Insurance offices:	287
Large department stores:	31
Living Quarters:	24,978
National buildings:	4
Newspapers:	4
Opera Houses:	2
Other offices:	1,150
Railway stations:	4
Retail stores:	2,320
Schools:	62
Warehouses:	675
Workshops:	1,319

Zoos: 1

The number of dead has never exactly been determined but it is a fact that 900 bodies are buried at Crooswijk Cemetery in a mass grave. Many people died as a result of their wounds; many of these years later.

See the results of the bombing in the following three pictures:

180. The heart of Rotterdam has been removed. Photo taken by a German reconnaissance plane on May 19, 1940

181. The area around the White House, May 1940

182. The area around the Hofplein, May 1940

Chapter Twenty-Four

Generalfeldmarschall Albert Kesselring testifies in 1946

The following is an excerpt from Volume 9 of the Nuremberg Trial Proceedings of German Major War Criminals held in Nuremburg in 1946.

The witness is **Generalfeldmarschall Albert Kesselring,** (born August 8, 1881, died July 16, 1960) who commanded Army Group C during WWII. One the most respected and skillful German generals, he was nicknamed "Smiling Albert".

183. Generalfeldmarschall Albert Kesselring, (1881-1960)

Prosecutor: Sir David Maxwell-Fyfe

(Prosecutor turning to the witness) Now, I will come to the tactical position at Rotterdam: Will you just tell the Tribunal who were the officers involved? There was a Lieutenant General Schmidt and with him was major general Student, who was in charge of the troops that were attacking Rotterdam. Do you remember that?

Kesselring: Only General Student. General Schmidt is unknown to me.

Sir David Maxwell: Well, the evidence that is given in this case is that the negotiations, the terms of capitulation, were actually written out by Lieutenant General Schmidt in a creamery near Rotterdam. I suppose he would be General Student's superior officer, would he not?

Kesselring: General Student was the senior German officer in the Rotterdam sector and the responsible commander. General Schmidt I don't know.

Sir David Maxwell: So that General Schmidt would be junior to General Student, would he?

Kesselring: He may have been called in for the special purpose, but I do not know of him.

Sir David Maxwell: I want you to have the times in mind. Do you know what time in the day the bombing of Rotterdam started?

Kesselring: As far as I know, in the early afternoon, about 1400 hours, I believe.

Sir David Maxwell: Well, I was going to put to you 1330.

Kesselring: Yes, that is quite possible.

Sir David Maxwell: Do you know that negotiations for a capitulation had been in progress since 10:30 in the morning?

Kesselring: No, as I said yesterday, I have no knowledge of these facts.

Sir David Maxwell: And did you know that at 1215 a Dutch officer, Captain Backer, went to the German lines and saw General Schmidt and General Student, and that General Schmidt wrote out the suggested terms of capitulation at 1235?
Kesselring: No, that is unknown to me.

Sir David Maxwell: That had never been told to you?

Kesselring: It was not communicated to me. At least, I cannot remember it.

Sir David Maxwell: Well, you see, Witness, it is 35 minutes before the bombing began and....

Kesselring: The important factor would have been for Student to call off the attack as such, but that did not happen. The cancellation never reached me, and did not reach my unit either.

Sir David Maxwell: Well, I just want you to have the facts in mind, and then I will ask you some questions. The terms that were discussed at 1235 were to expire; the answer was called for at 1620. After Captain Backer left with the terms, at 1322 and 1325 two red flares were put up by the German ground troops under General Student. Did you hear of that?

Kesselring: I did not hear of that either. Moreover, two red flares would naturally not have sufficed for the purpose.

Sir David Maxwell: No, but in addition to that your ground troops were in excellent wireless communications with your planes, were they not? Will you answer the question?

Kesselring: I already said yesterday...

Sir David Maxwell: Will you please answer the question?

Kesselring: Yes and no. As far as I know, there was no immediate communication between the ground station and the aircraft, but, as I said yesterday, there was a connection from the tactical force, through the ground station, to the aircraft formation.

Sir David Maxwell: If it had been wanted to pass the communication to the aircraft and stop the bombing, it could quite easily have been done by wireless, apart from putting up these two red flares?

Kesselring: Yes

Sir David Maxwell: If that attack had any tactical significance about helping your troops, it could have been called off, could it not?

Kesselring: I did not understand the final sentence.

Sir David Maxwell: If the object of this attack was merely tactical, to help in the attack on Rotterdam, it could easily have been called off by a wireless message from General Student to the planes, could it not?

Kesselring: Yes, if the tactical situation had been communicated, or if the situation had been reported to the bombing units immediately, then there could have been no doubt.

Sir David Maxwell: But if in honest negotiations, Witness, terms of surrender have been given and are to expire 3 hours later, it is only demanded of a soldier that he will call off the attack, is it not?

Kesselring: If no other conditions have been made, yes.

Sir David Maxwell: But if he can stop the attack, it would have been the easiest thing in the world to do so. I want to make my suggestion quite clear – that this tactical matter had nothing to do with the attack on Rotterdam; that the purpose of the attack on Rotterdam was, in your own words, to show a firm attitude and to terrorize the Dutch into surrender.

Kesselring: May I repeat again, that I have said explicitly that this attack was only serving the tactical requirements, and that I disassociate myself completely from these political considerations.

Sir David Maxwell: Well, you know that General Student apologized afterwards for the attack; you know that? Apologized to the Dutch commander for the attack?

Kesselring: I do not know it and, as I explained yesterday, I saw General Student when he was seriously injured, and I could not even talk to him.

Sir David Maxwell: I am not going to take more time. I have made my point, I hope, quite clearly. I want to ask you on one other point on which you spoke yesterday in regard to bombing. You said that the attack on Warsaw on 1 September 1939 was made because you considered Warsaw a defended fortress with air defense. Is that fair?

Kesselring: Yes, certainly.

CHAPTER TWENTY-FIVE

THE FIVE FREEDOMS

Until May 15, 1940 the people of The Netherlands enjoyed basically the same freedoms as those guaranteed under The First Amendment of the Constitution of the United States of America:

Freedom of Religion
The First Amendment prevents the American government from establishing an official religion. Citizens have the freedom to attend the church, synagogue, temple or mosque of their choice – or not attend at all. The First Amendment allows us to practice our religion the way we want to.

Freedom of Speech
The First Amendment keeps the American government from making laws that might stop us from expressing rational opinions. People have the right to criticize the government and to share their opinions with others.

Freedom of the Press
A free press means we can get information from many different sources. The government cannot control what is printed in newspapers, magazines and books, broadcast on TV or radio or offered online. Citizens can request time on television to respond to views with which they disagree; they may write letters to newspaper editors and hope those letters will be printed for others to see. They can pass out leaflets that give their opinions. They can have their own Web pages and offer their opinions to others through the many means made available by the Internet.

Freedom of Assembly
Citizens can come together in public and private gatherings. They can join groups for political, religious, social or recreational purposes. By organizing to accomplish a common goal, citizens can spread their ideas

more effectively.

<u>Right to Petition</u>
"To petition the government for redress of grievances" means that citizens can ask for changes in the government. They can do this by collecting signatures and sending them to their elected representatives; they can write, call or e-mail their elected representatives; they can support groups that lobby the government.

"When Do You Know That You Have Lost Your Freedom?"

When:
- You are no longer allowed to worship your religion
- You are no longer allowed to state your opinion
- You are no longer allowed to criticize the government
- You are no longer allowed to obtain your information freely
- The government controls the press and all communication sources
- You are no longer allowed to form discussion groups for any reason
- You are no longer allowed to travel freely
- You are no longer allowed to listen to the radio of your choice
- You are no longer allowed to sing your country's patriotic songs
- You are no longer allowed to fly your country's flag
- You are forced to work for the government
- You are restricted to curfews
- Text books have been altered to eliminate or alter historic information
- You are not allowed to assist or fraternize with Jews
- You are not allowed to bear arms
- You no longer have elected representatives
- You no longer have free elections
- You can be arrested without due process
- As a Jew you are no longer allowed to live

Freedom Lost!
On Wednesday May 15, 1940 we lost our freedom in The Netherlands. But what is Freedom? You only know what freedom is after you have lost it. Just read the above list and draw your own conclusions. How do you think you and your family would be affected? Would you try to rebel or bow your head in acquiescence? Which of these losses matters most to you? It is a fact that one can go on living with all the above restrictions except for the last one. If you were a Jew you no longer had the right to live. Not all of these restrictions to our freedom were evident immediately. They were implemented over time and each time they were enforced more stringently. All of a sudden our country had a foreign power that spoke a different language, telling us what to do and more importantly what not to do. Human nature will automatically rebel when one is told that you are not allowed to do certain things. *"I had no plan to do it but now that you tell me that I am not allowed to I will start thinking about it!"* In that sense rebellion becomes a self-fulfilling prophecy. A government or occupying power that puts these restrictions on the people is fearful for its own existence. Such a government is made up of criminals and is corrupt to the core. Sooner or later it will rot from within and loose its grip and succumb. However, that may take a long time because as long as you hold a gun to a person's head he will usually obey. Another tool for such a power to wield is '*food*'. Deprive a person of food and his focus is no longer to fight for his '*freedom*' but for '*food*' instead. Food is the primary motivator for people to stay alive. Control the food supply and you control the urge to be free. Only when a person has a full stomach will he/she think of other needs. Just contemplate that for a moment.

From this day on forward until our liberation five years later the story must be considered in the context of the loss of all the above freedoms and restrictions. Every day of those 1,815 days we would think of our liberation and it would become an obsession. Almost from the beginning there were people, mostly young students that rebelled and didn't anticipate the violent reaction of the German occupiers. They committed minor acts of resistance that did little damage to the big German war machine. Those people were patriots albeit naive and paid for their *'crimes'* with their lives. They were our first *'freedom fighters'* but to the Germans they were *'terrorists'*.

GERMAN PROPAGANDA LIES

The following translation from the German language gives you a good idea of the Nazi regime controlling the press:

Friday, May 31, 1940: Epilogue in Leipzig
On this Friday in Leipzig, Germany, Number 22, Volume 77 came off the presses of Moritz Schaefer Verlag (Publisher). It was only a small weekly publication, both in size and circulation.
Its name was: "Die Muehle", (the windmill). It could be said that it was the Magazine of the German Association for the Preservation of Windmills. On a regular basis the publication would carry articles on The Netherlands; windmill country of pre-eminence.

Like that Friday, the 31st of May.

The front page of "Die Muehle" showed a large picture of the Rotterdam ruins, a picture of utter destruction. However, from this chaos rose the image of a completely undamaged windmill, a brilliant specimen of windmill construction, tall, with wide vanes and a broad platform surrounding the body. It was the windmill that for untold years had stood on the Oostplein in Rotterdam.

This was the news that "Die Muehle" had printed for its German readers on May 31, 1940:

Windmill on the Battlefield Rotterdam
"The Dutch Government is guilty of a serious crime when, in spite of being called upon several times to evacuate the big port city of Rotterdam, they decided to make it into a fortress. This criminal act that has its parallel in the shortsightedness of the defenders of Warsaw was therefore punished severely to the detriment of its innocent population.
Paratroopers had already landed on the first day of the campaign and

had taken a bridge. By trying to recapture the bridge they made the city into a battlefield. When the enemy was asked on May 13 to evacuate the north bank of the river in order to prevent the city from destruction, they refused. On May 14 they received an ultimatum to evacuate the city and surrender. The commander was prepared to negotiate but then all of a sudden changed his mind. When the time of the ultimatum expired several German seaplanes landed on the Maas and occupied several buildings. In this process they encountered barricades and defensive positions. Dutch bombs and incendiary grenades set the old city afire. In the midst of the ruins and heaps of rubble only an undamaged cinema and the tall slender 'Oost' windmill, reaching toward the sky, are left and shown on our picture".

184. The windmill on the Oostplein was the only structure
that remained.

<u>In Nazi Germany they now knew how it had all happened!</u>

<u>USA Armament</u>
On the same day that this article appeared in the 'Muehle', President Roosevelt introduced a massive armament program that would assure the United States of America's position as a dominant military power. It included the production of 50,000 military aircraft a year. Although the USA is not yet *'at war'* Roosevelt is preparing for the time when it will be. We don't know what Herr Hitler's reaction was and can only guess that he shrugged it off. Soon enough he would be in control of England and what could the USA do thousands of miles to the west without a base from which to conduct a war? No, *Hitler* wasn't worried.

CHAPTER TWENTY-SIX

ESCAPE FROM DUNKIRK

Also on this day, the evacuation at Dunkirk in northern France continues...

185. The escape from Dunkirk

On May 24th, to the utter disgust of Colonel General *Guderian* he is ordered to halt his advance into Dunkirk. Goering has assured the Fuehrer that his Luftwaffe will take out the remaining encircled forces and so avoid the need for *Hitler* to risk his tanks in the flat boggy fields in the area.

186. Colonel General Heinz Wilhelm Guderian (1888-1954)

In 1937 Colonel General *Heinz Guderian* had published a widely acclaimed textbook, *Achtung! Panzer!* (Attention! Armor!) in which he advocated his ideas about high-speed warfare (blitzkrieg). Most of the other officers in the German Army High Command were skeptical about his ideas; nonetheless he was selected to command XIX Panzer Corps, the vanguard of Kleist's Panzer Army. He gave a perfect demonstration of his theory, breaking through at Sedan, crossing the *Meuse,* and traveling so fast that the German High Command felt it had to put a brake on him.

187.Generalfeldmarschall Paul Ludwig Ewald von Kleist
(1881-1954)

Hitler's direct involvement in local strategy and tactics appalled many of his commanders on the ground, but it is destined to be repeated many times. The German pause allows the beleaguered Allied forces time to regroup. The evacuation has a chance of success. Later on it will be remembered as *'The Miracle of Dunkirk'*. It will become the greatest evacuation in history, made possible by British Ultra intercepts of German messages. It was called Operation Dynamo and 1,200 Allied naval and civilian craft succeeded in removing 338,226 military personnel, of which 112,000 were French, from the beaches between May 27 and June 4, 1940.

It was the most diverse armada ever assembled in ports along the English Channel coast; it included pleasure boats from the holiday resorts, fishing vessels, cabin cruisers from the Thames manned by their civilian owners, and tugs and ferries from the ports. It was called the *'Mosquito Fleet'*

188. The "Mosquito Fleet" heading for Dunkirk

By the time that *Hitler* rescinded his stop order, British ships had already begun to arrive to take French and British soldiers back to England. The action wasn't a complete surprise to *Hitler*, who had been told by *Goering* that an evacuation could be prevented. The Luftwaffe did stage constant bombing raids on *Dunkirk*, the site of embarkation, but failed to slow or prevent the operation. One reason was *Goering*'s decision to attack five different ports rather than *Dunkirk* alone. Another explanation was the effective covering operation of the Royal Air Force.

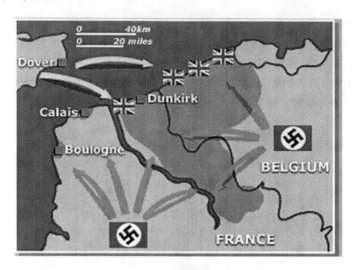

189. Map of the embarkation area of Dunkirk

Initially, the British had hoped to have two days to carry out the evacuation and save perhaps 45,000 men. The German time-out bought extra time. Still, what the British planned as a limited withdrawal became a mass evacuation after the Belgian army surrendered on May 28.

The two-day halt Hitler called made little difference in the short-run campaign to conquer the Low Countries and France. *Churchill* said at the time: *"wars are not won by evacuations"*. Still, the halt may have affected the outcome of the war because it ultimately allowed the Allies to save a significant portion of their forces through the evacuation at Dunkirk. These troops would return to the fight later. Had Hitler stayed on the offensive, these troops probably would have been destroyed or captured.

More than 1,200 vessels, from destroyers to fishing boats to private yachts from Britain (*) (**) carried out the ferry operation under almost constant attack. In nine days of bombing, the Luftwaffe damaged many vessels, but succeeded in sinking only eight destroyers. The RAF, meanwhile, shot down 176 German aircraft while losing 106.

(*) A retired naval commander, C.H.Lightoller, the senior surviving officer of the 'Titanic', owned one of the private yachts that evacuated soldiers from Dunkirk. His son was one of the first pilots killed in action in September 1939.

(**) Mrs. Miniver, a real classic movie of 1942 became the second biggest box-office hit of the decade. It portrays an English family where the husband takes his pleasure craft to Dunkirk and assists with the evacuation. The movie stars: Greer Garson and Walter Pidgeon.

On May 28 King *Leopold* of the Belgians agreed to capitulate while the evacuation from Dunkirk was still going on. Ever since, the British will be bitter about the Kings 'premature' action that caused the front to collapse behind the retreating Allied forces.

190. Leopold III, King of the Belgians (1901-1983)

On May 31 the air battles over the evacuation beaches became more balanced with the Spitfire now on active duty; more than 68,000 men are taken off that day. The German Stuka dive bombers that had been doing the bombing and strafing are quickly found wanting by the sleek and highly maneuverable British fighter. Many Stukas are shot down as a result.

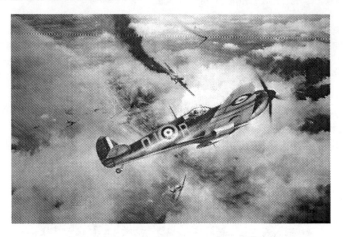

191. Spitfires over Dunkirk

As successful as the Dunkirk evacuation was, and as big a boost it gave British morale, it was not without its downside. More than 30,000 British soldiers did not escape and were taken prisoner. In addition, most of the BEF's (British Expeditionary Force) weapons had to be left behind, allowing the Nazis to capture a treasure trove of thousands of guns and vehicles, hundreds of tanks, and millions of tons of munitions.

192. British equipment abandoned at Dunkirk

After the evacuation from Dunkirk, the main concern of the British was whether Hitler intended to make them his next target. According to secret communications intercepted by British intelligence, the Germans planned to finish off France. The British people were still understandably fearful of *Hitler*'s next move. Churchill sought to reassure them, telling the nation:

193. Winston Churchill (1874-1965)

"We shall fight on the beaches, we shall fight on the landing grounds, we shall fight in the fields and in the streets, we shall fight in the hills; we shall never surrender, and even if, which I do not for a moment believe, this island or a large part of it were subjugated and starving, then our Empire beyond the seas, armed and guarded by the British Fleet, would carry on the struggle, until, in God's good time, the New World, with all its power and might, steps forth to the rescue and the liberation of the Old".

During the retreat of the British Expeditionary Forces toward Dunkirk, a British officer, Major *Cyril Barclay*, could not find his way to Dunkirk because the BEF could not get adequate tactical maps from the War Department. Major *Barclay*, therefore bought eighty *Michelin* maps in one of the small French villages and successfully led his unit to *Dunkirk*, but the War Office refused to reimburse him because *"regulations offer no provision for an officer to buy maps on active service."*

So much for bureaucracy!

CHAPTER TWENTY-SEVEN

THE NEW ORDER

May 29th saw the end of the military government under the control of the German Army in The Netherlands.

Seyss-Inquart, the man who in 1938 in his homeland of Austria had played his country into the hands of Adolf Hitler, would be the new German Government Minister for The Netherlands. This would be a day to remember and one that history would record as a day that followed a night of thunderstorms and rain, a very dark night indeed. It was a grey morning; intermittent rain would come down out of a leaden sky; sometimes in buckets. The sun would not make its appearance that day in The Hague.

Seyss-Inquart (*'six and a quart'* is what everybody named him, referring to his limp) made a speech in the *'Ridderzaal'* (Hall of Knights) consisting mainly of false and empty promises.

194. The Ridderzaal in The Hague

195. Seyss-Inquart gives the 'Hitler' salute

In essence he said the following:

"We will not introduce imperialism to this country nor will we force our political beliefs on you. We will only be guided by the necessities of the current situation."

He ended his speech with:

"We Germans do not hesitate, we are filled with the faith in our Fuehrer. We do not sing the silly songs of our enemy soldiers about the Siegfried Line, but we know that upon an order from our Fuehrer we can take any enemy stronghold. We know that what the Fuehrer desires is peace and moral order for all those that are of good will. The greatest happiness of every living German is to obey the will of the Fuehrer."

In mentioning 'the silly song of the Siegfried Line' he is referring to the British Song:

We're Gonna Hang out the Washing on the Siegfried Line

We're going to hang out the washing on the Siegfried Line
Have you any dirty washing, mother dear?
We're gonna hang out the washing on the Siegfried Line.
'Cause the washing day is here.
Whether the weather may be wet or fine.
We'll just rub along without care.
We're going to hang out the washing on the Siegfried Line.
If the Siegfried Line's still there.

The occupied territory of The Netherlands would from now on be governed by the following Nazis: Government Minister Seyss-Inquart, Government Commissioner; SS-Oberfuehrer Dr. Friedrich Wimmer, Commissioner General of Justice; Minister Fischboeck, Commissioner General of Finance and Economic Affairs; Reichsarmleiter Fritz Schmidt, recipient of the Golden Batch of the NSDAP, Government Commissioner of Special Cases and Brigade Fuehrer of the SS and Police; Hans Rauter, Commissioner General of Security.

Life under the 'New Order'

The Dutch Press was not completely fooled by any of this and a few saw fit to provide their own interpretation. It was abundantly clear to everyone that our democratic form of government had disappeared and had been replaced by a German-led dictatorship.

The press threatened to create confusion and therefore it became the first target of the new regime. Independent reporting and commentary were to be abandoned immediately. During the five war days the newspapers were still *'Dutch'*. The headlines reflected the indignation of the population; it had not been dictated by *'above'* and it was the heartfelt feeling of reporter and citizen alike. On May 15, *'while the field-grey worm is moving across the Berlage Bridge into Amsterdam'*, the editor of the 'Algemeen Handelsblad' writes his last headline without the intruder whispering in his ear what he must say.

He ended the article as follows:

"What our future will hold, nobody knows for sure. But one thing is very clear: the disruption of our normal social and economic life caused by the war will have repercussions on every level of our existence. The mutual cooperation of all the members of our Netherlands family will now be more important than ever. It will be a heavy burden for all of us but it will be less heavy if we bear it together. The deep sense of kinship of our people will grow as a result and will remain the source of its indomitable will to live."

May 16 was the beginning of the end of our *Freedoms of Speech and Press*. The aforementioned newspaper opened with the announcement:

The 'Algemeen Handelsblad' will from now on be issued under the control of the German Commander for the Netherlands.

With this announcement the game of *'Cat and Mouse'* began, as a result of which all pre-war newspapers would die by the wayside unless they were prepared to work hand-in-hand with the Germans.

Naturally, at 9 years of age, I was not directly aware of these events that would have such an impact on our future life. Whatever opinion I formed came directly from the attitude of my parents. I would hear them talk about *'die rot moffen'* (those rotten krauts) and my intense hatred for these Germans that had invaded our small country had no bounds. I needed little encouragement. On the first day I had witnessed a *'dogfight'* right above our house between several Messerschmitt Bf-109s and a lone Dutch Fokker G-1. In my mind the G-1 was the most beautiful plane I had ever seen. It was the *'Pride of the Dutch Air Force'*. With its double fuselage it was also very recognizable. That morning of May 10th it managed to shoot down one Bf-109. It went down in a wide spiral; trailing smoke as it went. We followed it going down until it must have crashed in the Maas River. How overjoyed we all were! We were dancing and jumping up and down. But then the G-1 went down in flames. That was a terrible thing to watch. I cried and it started my intense hatred for the Germans who were doing all this to us. A few days later, from our balcony on the Dunantstraat, I had seen the German Luftwaffe bomb our *'undefended'* city; they appeared to fly around at their leisure dropping bombs as they went. I remember the explosions, first a few and then too many to distinguish one from the other. I had then witnessed the city aflame from one side to the other; columns of black smoke rising up to great heights rendering the sun a small copper-colored disk. From this *'twilight'* I had witnessed the thousands of refugees streaming out of the heart of the city; carrying what little belongings they had been able to save from the inferno. I remember how frightened they looked. Grown people crying and sobbing for lost children and relatives.

I was only nine years old and my life up to that time had not prepared me for anything as horrible as that. How could it have? Your parents would shield you from anything that might be considered traumatic. You lived your childish fantasies and in those fantasies there was no room for death and destruction. You always looked up to grown-ups. They had all the answers and knew what was good for you. They always seemed in total control of any situation. You were totally dependent on those grown-ups for everything. All of a sudden my small world is shattered and my young life would never be the same again... Gone is the innocence; replaced by a complete feeling of despair. Here was something over which the *'grown-ups'*, my mom and dad, had no control. Worse yet, they were crying as well which added to my misery. It was like floating, all alone, in the middle of the ocean with sharks circling around. At the impressionable age of nine I was being exposed to events that would leave scars and stay with me forever. I believe that the *'hatred'* of a child can be greater than that of an adult. A grown person possesses the intellect to reason things out. A child can't do that. After Holland surrendered I saw the first Germans come across the bridge near our house. They came with their tanks, half-tracks and artillery, marching and singing soldiers in their field-grey uniforms. I will always remember the sound of their *'hobnailed'* boots on the pavement and the intense smell of leather and sweat.

196. German hobnail boots

From then on I would be able to recognize a *'kraut'* with my eyes closed. The sound and the smell would do it. Aside from *'hatred'* there was the element of *'fear'*. That fear would grow in time; particularly when the conquerors of the Maydays were replaced by '*occupation*' troops. It was then that I recognized that the Germans that had done the fighting were a lot different from the troops that replaced them. The regular Wehrmacht (Army) had done the fighting and in most instances were honorable. Except for their Nazi superiors, they, at least, had recognized the rules of the Geneva Convention. The troops that followed were a totally different breed. Schutzstaffel (SS), Siecherheits Dienst (SD), Geheime Stats Polizei (GESTAPO) and Hermann Goering Truppen. The '*cream of the crop*' of the Nazis. Without exception they were brutal individuals without a conscience.

197. SS and Gestapo Insignia

In those early days of the occupation when the regular Wehrmacht had not yet gone to fight elsewhere, life had returned to relative normalcy. My brother Henry, my sister Annie and I were again attending school. My father had located suitable premises for the business of N.V.Kattenburg that had been destroyed in the bombing and was back at work as was my uncle Wim. He was enlisted in clearing debris in the ruined city and would be doing that for a very long time. Brick-by-brick. My mother was back at her routine of taking care of the house and us. There was still enough food on the table. Maybe things wouldn't be so bad! But even so, I remember them talking about how long all this would last and would we ever be free again? After school I would be playing outside with my friends and we would talk among ourselves about the '*rot moffen*' (rotten krauts) and what we would like to do to them. One day, a large convoy of trucks and some half-tracks came from the direction of the city. A German on a Zundapp motorcycle was leading the convoy. He stopped where we were playing and now an opportunity presented itself to do our part for the war effort. He asked: *"Wo is der Weg nach Den Haag?"** (How do I get to The Hague?).

We knew that if the column continued on, they would eventually end up on the freeway to The Hague. Therefore he should not have asked us because I said in my best German:"Sie sind verkeerd', Sie mussen zuruck gehen. Die 'andere' richtung!" (You are going wrong; you have to go back in the opposite direction!) The German left on his motorcycle; driving alongside the columns; yelling: "Zuruck, Zuruck!" (Go back Go back!) It was great fun albeit a little scary to see the effect of my dishonesty. Fortunately for us kids there were no repercussions from this action. I remember another occasion of rebellion when the Germans were preparing for their invasion of England. Hundreds of Rhine barges were converted to landing crafts and parked five deep in the Coolhaven; the harbor in front of our house. Again we were stopped by a German on a motorcycle and asked for directions. We were able to understand him well enough but we acted as if we did not understand him and answered in Dutch: *"Dat weten wij niet!" (We don't know!")* The German, frustrated, said: "Was? Was sagen Sie? Was?"(What? What are you saying? What?) In Dutch the word 'was' is the English word for 'wax' and we then replied: "Dat moet je aan je achterwerk smeren dan kan je naar Engeland glijen!"

("Put that on your behind and you can slide to England!) The response of the German would again be the same: "Was, was sagen Sie denn?" Not understanding a word of what we had said. A good thing! He went on his way shaking his head and when he would be far enough away we would all burst out laughing. What a joke! That was our contribution to the war effort! The situation would become far more serious over time forcing us kids to refrain from such innocent childish pranks for the duration of the war.

In those early days of the occupation people with radios were still able to listen every day to the BBC (British Broadcasting Corporation). The transmitter from London called *Radio Oranje*. Thousands of people heard the voice of Queen Wilhelmina speaking to them and telling them to be steadfast and to have faith.

198. Queen Wilhelmina on Radio Oranje

It helped to enforce the hope of eventual liberation. People would wear silver dimes or quarter pins on their lapel or dress. Only the image of the Queen would be showing with the rest neatly sawed away. Some people expressed their love for the House of Orange by sticking a match with its orange head in their front pocket. People would greet each other with OZO (Oranje Zal Overwinnen), meaning *"Orange Will Win!"*

CHAPTER TWENTY-EIGHT

CELEBRATING A BIRTHDAY

June 29 is the Birthday of Prince Bernard, husband of Princes Juliana. In 1940 that day became the first large anti-German, anti-NSB and pro-Orange demonstration. It was totally spontaneous, not organized in any way or form. People appeared on the street wearing the color orange or a white carnation, Bernard's favorite flower. As usual, at the Palace Noordeinde in The Hague, registers were available for the signatures of well wishers.

199. Palace Noordeinde in the Hague scene of anti-Nazi demonstration.

200. General Winkelman receives applause and well-
wishers at Palace Noordeinde

General Winkelman went to the Palace and signed the register. His signature is followed by literally thousands from other citizens willing to stand in line for hours.

Many of these people would not have thought of making an effort to sign the register in the pre-war days. One person came with a bouquet of white carnations and laid it down at the entrance to the palace. In no time hundreds more would be bringing flowers. The city of The Hague was no exception. Elsewhere in the country people were reacting in the same spontaneous way.

The Germans were furious. They confiscated the registers; occupied the palace; beat up some people and arrested several who they suspected of being ring leaders. A few days later General Winkelman was taken into custody and transported to Germany. Two Dutch generals that had signed the register together with Winkelman are also arrested and shipped to jails in Zwolle and Groningen. The Mayor of The Hague was fired from his job. A member of the Dutch YMCA is also taken into custody and shipped to a concentration camp. His crime? Upon arrival at the Palace of General Winkelman and two other Generals he had led the singing of the Dutch national anthem: Het "Wilhelmus".

Holland took a deep breath. For a brief moment it had tasted *'freedom'*. At the same time it had experienced for the first time the methods used by the Germans to suppress that *'freedom'*.

Chapter Twenty-Nine

Rebellion & the Geuzen Movement

Henry remembers:

In June we had our finals and during our English finals the RAF showed up and started bombing the warehouses at the Wilhelmina docks.

As a rule we had to go under the desks when there was an air raid, but that was only theory. We were on the third floor and had a good view of the bombing only a few miles away from us. As usual lots of smoke and fire, but no homes were hit. I believe the bombers were Bristol Blenheim two-engine aircraft. Anyway I did very well on my English test!

After graduating from high school (they call it different in Holland), I could reconnoiter on my own. In September I would go back to school and start taking evening classes in school for business or economy as they called it then. I also took special classes in English, which was still possible at that time. I had preferred a technical school, but that would have been an invitation for the Germans to grab me and let me learn it the hard way in Germany. Learning how to become a bookkeeper was not a bad alternative, though I did not like it. The best part was that they thoroughly taught you English.

I could get to school on my bike and spent 4 days a week from 7 till 10 pm taking the classes. That lasted three years and I managed to graduate. However many things happened in the meantime.

I also had to get a job. In January 1941 I would turn 17 and could be picked up by the Germans if I were unemployed and taken to Germany to work there as 'slave labor'.

I got a job at Stokvis, a large commercial outfit that sold everything from bicycles to large machinery, chemicals, and electronics. My first work was to distribute the internal mail. Not very challenging, but it was a job and it also gave me time to study. My initial salary was 18 guilders a month! The place was rather crowded and I fell over some obstacle and hurt my

elbow, I had to go to the doctor to see that nothing was broken.
I think it was sprained and so he bandaged it. After leaving the doctor's
office I ran into a riot. Dutch Nazi's, the W.A. was marching and it did
not go over well with the rest of the population. Rocks were thrown,
nightsticks came out and it became a real street fight until the Gruene
Polizei (Gestapo police) showed up. There was some shooting and everybody
faded away. From a good distance I noticed that there were some bodies on
the ground that did not move.

THE '*GEUZEN*' MOVEMENT

Around the same time that kids like me were having their occasional
fun fooling the Germans there were other patriots that were prepared
to take more serious actions against the occupying forces. It started
soon after the surrender of Holland with Bernard IJzerdraat, 48 years
old, married with three children, two adult sons and a daughter of
almost eleven. Bernard was eager to do something about his country's
defeat. He started a hand-written newsletter. He was a school teacher
and he had majored in Dutch History.

In my earlier writing about Dutch history I mentioned the Eighty
Year War with all- powerful Spain. The freedom fighters of that
conflict had called themselves '*Geuzen*'. These "*Geuzen*" had united
under the leadership of *Willem van Oranje*
(William of Orange). He had liberated Holland from under the yoke
of the hated *Duke of Alva* and his feared inquisition. Bernard had
found a parallel in the Geuzen from that time and therefore called
his newsletter '*Geuzen Actie*'. His first hand-written newsletter:
Newsletter no.1 has been lost but a copy of no. 2 written on May 18,
1940 was saved and in short reads as follows:

The action of the Geuzen was started in Amsterdam on May 15, 1940.
Our first communication has already reached the city of Nijmegen. We
are not going to take our loss of freedom sitting down. We know what to
expect. All our supplies will be confiscated. Pretty soon everything will
be rationed and after a while we will not be able to buy anything with
the coupons. Our young men will be forced to work for the enemy. Soon

enough we will have another 'Alva' and the 'Inquisition' coming after us. But the Geuzen actions will slowly but surely unite us and we will regain our freedom like we did in the 80 year war. Be brave and have faith! Our country will never become part of Germany...

He had written five copies and distributed them to family members and to friends he could trust. He asked these people to make their own copies and pass them on to their friends and family. In this fashion he hoped the newsletter would receive wide circulation. He mentioned in his second newsletter that it had already reached the city of Nijmegen, a city about 60 miles from Rotterdam. Maybe that was wishful thinking on his part but people believed it as fact; it helped to lift the spirits and it awakened people to the thought of resistance. With nothing but propaganda from the German side, this innocent and rather naïve piece of patriotic writing acted as balm on the open wounds of our lost freedom. It provided hope in spite of the fact that the German war machine had by now captured practically all of Europe. Soon Bernard had build up a network of like-minded people that were eager to do their share. However, Bernard had not been completely honest with his fellow patriots. In order to appear more interesting and acceptable to new members of the Geuzen *'army'* he had continuously given the impression that there already existed a secret organization with a direct link to England. Only Bernard knew better but he felt that the end justified the means. The *'army'* now had the use of better stenciling equipment and in the beginning of August 1940 the first *'new'* *"Geus of 1940'* was published. The writing was now more professional. Several of the new members had demanded that the organization go beyond mere patriotic writing and commit acts of sabotage. For that to happen they would have to obtain guns, ammunition and explosives. Members went looking for these items. It was said that the retreating Dutch army following the capitulation had either destroyed or discarded their equipment in canals or buried them to be dug up later. Most of this was pure nonsense but a few handguns and a machine gun were actually discovered and rendered fire-ready by several *'member'* mechanics. Bernard and his co-conspirators decided to organize as an army and implement army ranks. This gave the organization an even greater feeling of secrecy and importance. Bernard made himself a *'colonel'* and he appointed *'lieutenants'* and *'NCOs'*. It was further agreed by the 'staff' that because of its many members and the real possibility of being discovered *'aliases'* should be used. What if you come upon a person and you don't know if he is a Geus? *'Watch words'* was the answer. They would have to be difficult words: just like those used by the Dutch army. They would have to include the letters 'SCH': the Germans can't pronounce Dutch words with SCH in it*. They also implemented a *'fool-proof'* ID system.

* Just ask a German to say words like: *'Scheveningen, Schoonhoven or Achtentachtig'*.
What you will hear is: *'Skeveningen, Skoonhoven and Aktentaktig'*. Then you kill him.

CHAPTER THIRTY

GOERING VISITS ROTTERDAM

On May 24, 1940 Reich's Marshall *Hermann Goering* visited the city of *Rotterdam* or rather what was left of it.

201. Hermann Goering in Rotterdam viewing his
Luftwaffe's handiwork.

There he stood at the *Leuvenhaven Bridge* with his lieutenants. There is a picture of this visit entitled: *"Hermann Goering viewing damage in Rotterdam"*.

He must have been very proud of his Luftwaffe having done such a thorough job. Not many people saw him that day when the ruins were still smoking. They had been kept at a distance in fear that somebody might assassinate him. There were a lot of Dutch citizens who would have gladly done so. He had arrived by Ju-52 at Waalhaven Airport and after the Rotterdam visit had driven to Amsterdam.

In early June we were told that *Adolf Hitler* himself had visited Rotterdam as well. However, that visit was kept a secret and there is no picture of that visit. Shortly after his alleged visit a very interesting story was told that connected both Nazi's visits. Even I, at my age, could appreciate it.

It is alleged that Hermann Goering during his visit on May 24 wanted to see the destruction up close and with his entourage took a stroll through the ruins. A narrow lane had been cleared between the heaps of rubble. With his Marshall baton in hand and his big stomach out front Hermann made his inspection. The area was completely deserted except for a little girl that he saw sitting on what was left of a flight of steps. Hermann noticed that she had a small basket on her lap with a towel covering the contents. It was a peculiar sight indeed to see that little Dutch girl sitting there among the rubble. Hermann walked up to her and greeted her in a most fatherly manner. The little girl smiled at Goering and acting very forthcoming, she said: "Do you know what I have here in my basket?" She said it in Dutch but Goering understood her and said: "No, what do you have in your basket?"

With that the little girl uncovered the basket and what Hermann saw were five little kittens. The little girl once again smiled at Hermann and said: "Do you want to know what their names are?" "Natuerlich!" said the Reich's Marshall. Pointing with her index finger at the little kittens she said: "Well, this one is Hitler, this one is Goering, this one is Goebbels, this one Himmler and the fifth one is Mussolini". Hermann was overjoyed. How could it be that in this devastated city there was a child who loved the Nazi leaders so much that she would call her kittens after them? With a full heart Goering left for Germany and in Berlin told Adolf Hitler about his amazing experience. Hitler was very much impressed and decided that he travel to Rotterdam and see the child for himself. It was the first week in June and Hitler flew in his private plane to Waalhaven Airport. From there he went by armored Mercedes to the inner city of Rotterdam. To his delight he found the little Dutch girl where Goering had told him she might be. Hitler walked up to her and greeted her in his most fatherly manner. The little girl looked sternly at Hitler but didn't respond to his greeting. Hitler therefore decided to take the lead and asked her what the names of the five kittens were that she had in her basket. She removed the towel covering the basket and again using her index finger named her kittens: "This one is Churchill, this one is Roosevelt, and this one is Wilhelmina, that one Juliana and this one Eisenhower!" Hitler was shocked with the names of his foes and said: "A few weeks ago when Hermann Goering was here you told him that their names were: Hitler, Goering, Goebbels, Himmler and Mussolini. What happened?" This time the little girl looked up at Hitler and with a smile on her face said: "Since then they have opened their eyes!"

We all enjoyed this story immensely.

CHAPTER THIRTY-ONE

THE GEUZEN MOVEMENT – (CONT'D)

They were now ready for *'sabotage'*. On August 14 they committed their first act by cutting five telephone cables connecting anti-aircraft batteries with searchlight units in the city of Vlaardingen. That night there were several English bombers over Holland and the German anti-aircraft batteries were unable to direct accurate fire because the searchlights were unable to assist in locating the bombers. It is very well possible that an English *'Halifax'* crew owes its life to Bernard and his men. Six additional cable cuttings took place. On September 11, the day following the seventh occurrence, the Mayors of Vlaardingen and Maasland were summoned to appear at the Ortskommandantur. Both were chewed out in typical Prussian fashion and threatened with the severest penalties. Somewhat shaken they returned to their offices. A few hours later bulletins appeared on walls and fences:

ONE THOUSAND GUILDERS
REWARD
For the SEVENTH time telephone cables have been cut in the city of VLAARDINGEN
The German authorities will apply the severest measures to the City of Vlaardingen and its citizens.
It is in EVERYONE's interest that the perpetrator(s) of the above crimes is/are arrested.
The individual who can point out the criminal(s), resulting in his capture, receives
A REWARD
OF ONE THOUSAND GUILDERS

In Vlaardingen and Maasland a city clerk on his bicycle makes the rounds of the city and delivers notices to hundreds of citizens. Under Article 12 of the Law governing 'Protection against Air Raids' they are ordered to guard the many telephone cables in the city. They will receive 2.50 guilders for 5.5 hours of duty. They only do this for one night because working at their jobs during the day and then guarding these cables at night from eight till half past one, or from half past one till seven o'clock is next to impossible. The City decides to enlist the *'unemployed'* instead.

This action puts a stop to further acts of sabotage. As a result, on October 16 there is an announcement in the *New Vlaardingen Courant* from the German Ortskommandant stating that the further protection of the telephone system is no longer required. This *'gesture of goodwill'* is, of course, on the condition that Vlaardingen and its citizens continue to be responsible for the protection of the cable system and immediately report any damage to the local police.

However, the perpetrators are very naïve. They have no idea of the tactical aspects of resistance. They have no idea of the risks they are taking. They never ask themselves whether they are suited for resistance, or: for what *'type'* of resistance they are suited? Different kinds of resistance don't exist for them. It's all or nothing. Any new member is welcomed because he is a *'good'* man, *'hates'* the Germans and is *'ready'* to commit any acts of sabotage: not because he has a specific skill that can be put to good use. The Geuzen *'army'* while made up of predominantly brave young men is little more than an expression of unbridled fury directed at the *'goose-stepping, hated Hun'*.

August 31 is Queen Wilhelmina's birthday but on this occasion there is little or no demonstration. People have learned their lesson of June 29, Prince Bernard's birthday. Only in cafes frequented by Germans and members of the NSB some men in a loud voice order *'oranjebitter'* (a potent Dutch drink like Gin). Yes, Orange bitter! On the afternoon of August 31 a man is walking on the street in a drunken stupor. He is singing loudly: "... *long live Queen Willemien*", looses his balance and falls down. He gets up again and a police inspector from Vlaardingen prevents him from entering another pub. He takes him in custody and locks him up. Two hours later: alarm. The drunk has set fire to the straw mattress. He is removed from the cell, handcuffed and only then is he searched. And what does the inspector find in his inside coat pocket? A stenciled copy of Geus Action Illegal newsletter No 3. In his report the Inspector of Police considered the contents of the newsletter insulting to the German Government and Wehrmacht. *"The Siecherheits Polizei must be notified"*. Three days later the man is picked up by the SD (Siecherheits Dienst). We don't know what happened to the man but the Nazis now know about the Geuzen and their newsletter.

CHAPTER THIRTY-TWO

JOKES AND PATRIOTISM

In the early days of the occupation when the population had not yet experienced the German methods of dealing with any kind of dissent many patriotic stories, songs and comedy were heard and then eagerly passed on.

Some of the comedy came from the well-known vaudevillian Johan Buziau:

Buziau enters a room carrying in one hand the portrait of Mussolini, in the other hand a portrait of Hitler. He looks at both pictures, a look around the room and then with some doubt in his voice says: 'What shall I do with these?' 'Shall I hang them or just put them against the wall?'

Buziau talks about the occupation. 'In the old days we had it good,' he says, 'but now we have it better, they say'. A short pause, then…. 'I really hope that once again we will have it good.'

Buziau enters the still empty stage. He is silent and then brings the stiff Nazi salute to the audience: his right arm shoots halfway up, his face a scrupulous mask. The audience holds its breath. Would he too? Then Buziau speaks loud and clearly: 'This is the size of the dog I have at home and he eats like hell…'

Everybody knows that the Germans will never admit that the British are bombing and destroying their cities. The British never seem to hit anything. Now then, on stage there is a basket overflowing with eggs. *Buziau drags a heavy boulder to the basket, lifts the boulder with all the power he can muster and drops it in the basket. He leans over the basket and looks. Then, to the audience: 'Only one cracked…'*

Here follow the bawdy lyrics of a melody sung by the British to the tune of the "Colonel Bogey March" (Bridge over the River Kwai)

<u>Hitler Has Only Got One Ball</u>

Hitler, he only has one ball.
Goering, he has two but very small,
Himmler has something simmler,
But poor old Goebbels has no balls at all.
Whistle Chorus:

Hitler has only got one ball,
The other is in the Albert Hall.
His mother, the dirty bugger,
Cut it off when he was small.

Everywhere in the country circulated satirical poems about the NSB (National Socialist Movement) and their leader Anton Mussert. The majority of the Dutch population hated him and his party; they were even more hated than the Germans. They had aided and abetted the enemy during the invasion of Holland and were considered traitors by one and all. One poem was especially well-known. It came from a person in Rotterdam and he picks on Mussert, the 'Fuehrer' of the NSB.

Here follows a rather loose translation:

Fuehrer, may I ask you something?
Do you still remember May the 10th?
When we were fighting the Germans?
And you didn't stick out your hands?
When our Dutch soldiers
Were cut down by German guns
And you were hiding cowardly
Among a group of nuns
Fuehrer, may I ask you?
What exactly do you do?

Hitler is Dead

During WWII in a small village in Holland were two parrots, one owned by a bar owner and the other by the protestant minister. Every time someone would enter the bar the parrot would say: *"Hitler is Dead!"* That was no problem until a couple of SS men entered. *"If in two weeks that parrot won't say something else, you and your parrot will be put to death!"*

The bar owner exchanges his parrot with the minister's. Two weeks later the SS-men come in and in order to prompt the parrot say: *"Hitler is dead."* The parrot answers: *"Thank God and Praise the Lord!"*

CHAPTER THIRTY-THREE

ORANGE PAJAMAS

Through the months of October and November the Geuzen 'army' continues to expand and now counts members in the major cities. But with this many members the resistance movement becomes more and more vulnerable to being found out.

Daan van Striep is employed at the Wilton ship yard in Rotterdam. The huge ship building yard was forced to work for the German war machine. In addition to ship repair jobs they were also involved in the construction of U-Boats. For several months Daan knows something is cooking. He hears people whispering about *'Geuzen'*. He concludes that those must be workers at the yard planning to do something about the *'krauts'*. He is merely guessing at this point because workers stop talking when he gets close. Nobody knows Daan very well; he comes from another area in Holland. His parents live in the city of Arnhem and he lives in a rooming house in Schiedam. Every week-end he goes home to Arnhem.

The week before, Jan Smit, his boss, had talked to him and had asked him a few questions. Jan had then given him a copy of the latest Geuzen Action newsletter, which he was told he should put in his pocket. *"If you are interested to join, come and see me!"* Jan had said. Join them? Well of course! He wanted nothing more!

Already the next day he had gone to see Jan. "Just tell me what you want me to do." *"For the time being just keep your trap shut; you will hear more in a few weeks."*, Smit had said. Daan was excited. He would be given a chance to do something against those bastards that are stealing his country dry and are ordering him around at work with their stupid swagger.

On Saturday afternoon, November 2, Daan is traveling to Arnhem in a train that is practically overflowing. He manages to get a seat and with a smirk on his face thinks about his role in things to come. He arrives at his parent's place on Saturday night. On Sunday afternoon he visits his older brother and they talk about, what other, the situation in the country. They agree that the *'situation'* is improving. Goering had lost his air battle over England and Hitler has given up on invading England. It's now only a question of <u>when</u> the British will come, not <u>if</u>. Daan is confident that it will be before Christmas. *"We are ready!"* Daan tells his brother. His brother is not that optimistic. *"What do you mean by ready?" "With what?"* his brother opines. Daan remembers his pledge for secrecy. But, this is his brother; that's different.

Excitedly he pulls the crumpled newsletter from his pocket. *"Here, go ahead, read this!"*

Brother reads it but doesn't appear to be very impressed. *"This is only a piece of paper; you can't fight the Germans with that".* Daan gets more excited. *"You want weapons; you want a new pistol with lots of ammo?" "I can get you one for fourteen guilders; we got plenty of them in Schiedam".* *"No, no, that isn't necessary, I believe you".* But nonetheless brother is somewhat impressed. Before Daan leaves he reminds his brother to keep his mouth shut.

'Keep your mouth shut!" naturally. The occupation had not even lasted six months. Just about no one had experienced how important it was to keep your mouth shut. Didn't you know whom you could trust? You knew who the Dutch Nazis were. So what? That Sunday night Daan returns to Schiedam. He doesn't realize that he has already violated his pledge of secrecy.

But, this is the beginning! The beginning of the end of the Geuzen movement. The beginning of the end for so many other resistance movements during the next five years. The excitement of the moment; unbridled enthusiasm; the exhilaration of a heart that is bursting with passion and pride. A heart that needs to share that passion with other like-minded souls. It is a human weakness but again so human and completely understandable. It is just not human to go through life distrusting everyone. All of us have a need to share our happiness and our sorrows. All that is very normal. But in November 1940, times are not normal. The time we live in now is very different. These are dangerous and perilous times for everyone. It will be years and will cost thousands of lives before the reality of that danger finally sinks in. But even then, in '43 and in '44, the heart, that brave heart of a resistance fighter will sometimes succumb to that tiny weakness, the unforgivable sin: *taking someone into your confidence*.

Daan's brother is actually rather impressed with his younger brother. Even somewhat proud. The following Sunday when one of his best friends stops by the house they talk about the *'situation'* and he can't refrain from telling his friend. *My brother told me...*
In Schiedam... Brand new revolvers with enough ammo... Fourteen guilders.
The friend, who is totally trustworthy, is impressed as well. *"But keep your mouth shut"*, the friend is reminded. Of course, that speaks for itself.

'Friend' is the secretary of a chess club. A few days later before they put the chess pieces on the board they discuss the *'situation'*. All good friends; most of them have been members for years. All are trustworthy because they keep NSB traitors out. There is good news from Africa. But North Africa is far away and everyone is hungry for some good local news. Friend can't resist and tells his trustworthy fellow members what he has heard the previous Sunday: *Schiedam... revolvers...fourteen guilders*.
Someone outside their small ring picks up on it. He is a pharmacist. The next day a customer comes in his store, a local NSB party official. While shaking his head the pharmacist tells the official what he had heard the previous night. *"Lousy communists!"* he adds. *"Something should be done about that!"* The official is in complete agreement.

We have almost completed the circle. The point of the calipers put on paper by Daan has by now traveled it largest distance. Via Brother, Friend and Someone to Comrade NSB. What happens next are mere formalities. Through proven SD interrogation methods one after the other of the Geuzen leadership and members are arrested during the next several weeks and transported to Scheveningen. There they are taken to the jail on the Van Alkemadelaan and put in cells of roughly

6 by 10 feet. There are a total of 500 cells and a political prisoner occupies every one. Half of these are *'Geuzen'*. They have no idea of the German interrogation tactics but they learn quickly. This is the first big job for the SD in Holland and they mean to do a good and thorough job*.

*The SD toward the end of the war destroyed most of the records in 1945. Only one 'Meldebuch' (Report) still exists. It covers the period of November 14 to January 28, 1941

One of the Geuzen who escaped his sentence wrote down his experiences.
Following his first *'rather mild'* interrogation in December two SD men interrogated him again in January 1941:

"All of a sudden this brute comes storming in and with all his might starts slapping me in the face with both hands. Ten, twenty, thirty times this bully hammers my face. After that he ordered me to sit down again and the smaller guy told me to fess up what I knew. I told him that I couldn't tell him anything. Then I had to stand up and face the wall. I heard them opening a drawer and they must have removed a revolver because I heard them cocking it and laughing softly. In those few seconds I still didn't think they would shoot me because a dead man can't speak. The idea was to get information out of me. Carefully I looked to the side to see what was happening. The big brute had obviously waited for that moment and started yelling at me to keep my head directed at the wall. He then hit the back of my head and I smacked into the wall. He then turned me around and started to hit me in the face with both hands…. I felt him groping for my shirt and make a twisting movement almost choking me…He then ordered me to remove my coat and told me to lean forward on the table. What followed was a terrible beating of my back and buttocks…"
The report continues for a while longer. But:
"I remained silent. In all my misery I kept telling myself to hold on, hold on…they had already been beating me for 5 hours. What a mentality. In these circumstances it would seem better to be the victim rather than the executioner…"

This is the story of one *'Geus'* who was not even officially a member of the movement. He had been rather calm because he really didn't know anything and couldn't tell anything. He was the lucky one and came out alive. In the absence of all interrogation reports and the fact that the SD destroyed them we can only guess what the SD interrogators did to the others. Brutality had no bounds with these criminals.

On February 24, 1941 the *'Geuzen'* case comes to court in The Hague. It would become a showcase for the Germans. It would show who is the boss in Holland and teach those reluctant and hardheaded Dutchmen a lesson they would never forget. The press has been invited and five reporters of the *'German controlled'* papers attended the proceedings. Even so, they needed sign-off from the authorities before publication. Forty-three Geuzen entered the court building and passed through the hallway. At one end of the main hall is a statue of the blind-folded Vrouwe Justitia (Lady Justice), with sword and scales.

202. Lady Justice under the hated Swastika

Above the statue and partly draped around it they see the Swastika flag. One of the forty-three recognizes its symbolism and whispers to the man next to him: *'Now all hope is lost!'*

One can imagine what the proceedings were like. It is a mere formality that will lead to death sentences for eighteen of the Geuzen. Twenty-one will receive sentences of 1 to 6 years and four will go free. *Bernard IJzerdraad*, our teacher, receives four consecutive death sentences.

At noon on March 13, 1941 eighteen freedom fighters are taken from their cells and they are read their sentences. They are told that the sentences will be carried out that same afternoon at 5pm. At the last moment the three youngest are saved from execution and receive jail sentences instead. IJzerdraat, the untamable, wears his pajama top over his clothes. The color is a vivid orange.

203. Bernard's orange pajamas

Outside, the trucks are waiting. They assist each other in climbing in the back. Then the trucks leave, through the Van Alkemadelaan, to the beautiful white sandy dunes bordering the North Sea. The trucks come to a halt at the Waalsdorpervlakte.

After a few minutes the volleys of fire and then all is quiet again.

204. Waalsdorpervlakte, scene of the executions

205. Bernard IJzerdraat's tombstone

206. The poem of the Eighteen Dead.

Jan Campert, a man of letters, wrote a now famous poem called:
"De Achttien Dooden" (the Eighteen Dead)
It is in memory of these first freedom fighters that gave their lives for
what they believed in.
Following is a translation of the first stanza:

The Eighteen Dead

A cell is a mere two meters long
And only two meters wide
Still smaller will be the piece of ground
That I know not yet
But where I will be resting
Together with my friends
We totaled eighteen
Not one will see the sunset

CHAPTER THIRTY-FOUR

THE NOOSE IS TIGHTENING

Henry remembers:

"In the spring 1941 the Germans tightened their hold. Every men or boy from 17 to 40 had to be registered at the Labor Department. If you did not do this you could not get your ration coupons.

So, I had to go too, but my Dad went with me. I was pretty skinny and had not grown to my adult height. I believe I was about 5 ft 3 in. To make me look even more like a kid, I also wore short pants. I probably did not look older than 13 or 14. I used that young, 'innocent' approach very well during the war years.

Also in early 1941 the Germans started their anti-Semitic campaign in Holland. As a matter of fact I did not even know who was a Jew or not. We were not brought up that way. Later I realized that two of my school buddies were Jewish, Lou Courant and Hank Ball, they disappeared and I never saw them back.

First the Jews were ordered to wear the (yellow) Star of David marked with Jood (Jew). That created riots and I saw several cases that (Dutch) people came over to them and ripped the star from their cloth and yelled at them not to wear it, "We don't do this in our country" and "the Germans are going to kill you". The poor people were scared out of their mind. That happened on the Schiedamseweg near the Princess Theater. Only relatively few were able to hide, or even wanted to hide. The German Gestapo police put a stop to the rioting quickly, in their typical way. They shot them or arrested them and then shot them anyway. Later in the year when they started deporting the Jewish people, there was an uprising and a general strike. The Germans took hostages (non-Jews) and publicly executed them. It still lasted about three days before it calmed down. The only thing was to try to hide those who wanted to, but it did not always work and too many were caught and murdered".

*As a note: In the Netherlands you could not own a firearm. The civilian population was unarmed. It took several years before we managed to get

weapons from England by air. We did not realize that they were so hard up themselves.

"After this resistance to their inhuman behavior and the rejection of their ideology by the great majority of the population, the Germans became really nasty and started taking more and more hostages who were deported to concentration camps or shot after a sham trial.

In spring 1941 I was ordered to report to the Labor Department. My Dad went with me; he was over the critical age.

When I was questioned he was talking to some other people and when I came out of the 'interrogation' room I had to go in a line with other people. My Dad told me: "you are in the wrong line, take the other one" and so I ended up with the 'rejects'. I remember we bought some flowers so mother could see them when we crossed the bridge to our house and know I was ok.

About a year and a half later they called me again. In the meantime I had an official document stating that I had tuberculosis. There was a German doctor to check you out. Since I was perfectly healthy that bothered me, until I saw the guy who handled the paperwork. I knew him; he was in the resistance. He told me:" Don't worry, the guy is totally deaf". And indeed I became a total reject again. We had obviously infiltrated into some of these organizations".

CHAPTER THIRTY-FIVE

THE BATTLE OF BRITAIN

On June 18, 1940 Churchill told the House of Commons, *"The Battle of France is over. I expect that the Battle of Britain is about to begin."* The night before, British bombers had attacked German factories in the Ruhr. As Churchill expected, it was now England's turn to learn about terror from the skies. Hitler wanted to invade Britain and had the forces to subdue it as he had Germany's other victims. That is, if he could get his troops across the Channel. Germany had no amphibious landing craft or any of the components the Allies would later use for their own crossing; nevertheless, Hitler believed Britain could be conquered if the RAF (Royal Air Force) was destroyed, or at least neutralized. He sent the Luftwaffe to accomplish that goal in early July. The attack intensified after the Germans established bases in France, and the Low Countries. For nearly five months, the Luftwaffe bombed ports, shipping, airfields, factories and cities.

Although Hitler's directive for Operation Sea Lion, the invasion of England, was not issued until July 16, the idea of an invasion first received his attention nearly two months earlier, on 21 May; this was the day on which German spearheads reached the French coast. Raeder, the Commander-in-Chief of the German Navy, was responsible for bringing it forward. It was coolly received. Raeder had an interview with Hitler on May 21.

207. Raeder and Hitler

It was Hitler's unpractical custom to rely upon the tête-à-tête rather than the inter-service conference when dealing with his commanders-in-chief, and there was only one occasion in the summer of 1940 – on September 14 – when he saw all three of them together. He trusted nobody. Things had not yet reached the stage when every visitor to his headquarters, no matter how distinguished, was searched for arms by SS guards before being admitted to his presence; but one puppet is always easier to manipulate than three, and doubtless – remote though the contingency was at this stage – Hitler thought it possible that his military triumvirs, if dealt with as a triumvirate, might one day sink their differences and combine to oppose his designs. He intensely disliked being disagreed with.

In the preamble to Directive No.16 it is possible to detect petulance and irresolution. The words in which Hitler defined his intentions *("I have decided to begin to prepare for, and if necessary to carry out, an invasion of England")* lack the crisp, compulsive, *'off-with-his-head'* ring which was a normal feature of his style in these situations. For instance, the first paragraph of Hitler's directive for the attack on Poland ends *"I have decided on a resolution by force"*. The corresponding words in the directive for Yugoslavia are *"Yugoslavia… must be crushed as speedily as possible"*. The warning order for Operation Barbarossa, the invasion of the Soviet Union on June 22, 1941, begins with: *"The German Armed Forces must be ready to crush Soviet Russia in a rapid campaign."*

It would however be wrong to suppose that Hitler's mealy-mouthed statement of his operational aims was due mainly to his misgivings about the possibility of the operation. He was still not only hoping for, but also actively working to bring about, that compromise which the beaten British had – "so far", as the Directive noted – shown them selves unwilling to accept. His strategy at this stage was schizophrenic. It reflected the strange mixture of esteem and spite, which underlay his attitude toward England. Hitler in some way respected England whereas he loathed the French. He felt a certain kinship with the British and would have hoped for an arrangement with the British where **they** would be in charge of the Oceans and their Empire and **He**, Hitler, would be the undisputed master of

Europe. Prime Minister Winston Churchill was definitely not the kind of person who would have considered such a proposal. He wanted nothing more than the total and utter destruction of the Nazi regime. As repeated so many times in history, tyrants underestimate their opponents' will to fight, not only for them but also for the suppressed. England was that kind of an opponent.

Paragraph 1 of Hitler's Directive 16 presumed *"a surprise crossing on a broad front extending approximately from Ramsgate to a point west of the Isle of Wight."*

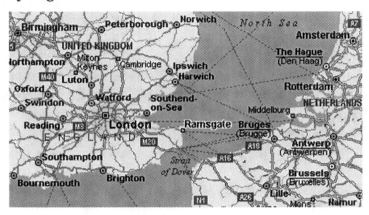

208. Invasion beaches from Ramsgate to the Isle of Wight

Paragraph 2 demanded the elimination of effective opposition by the Royal Air Force: the sweeping of mines from the sea-routes: the laying of impassable minefields on "both flanks of the Straits of Dover and the western approaches to the Channel: the domination and protection of *"the entire coastal front area"* by heavy coastal guns: and the *"pinning down"* of the Royal Navy in the North Sea and in the Mediterranean. That was a very ambitious plan and one that had more holes in it than Swiss cheese. For one, he had no landing crafts with which to make a landing of that magnitude and little or no planning had gone into this hare-brained scheme.

Hitler's strategic plan to attack Britain had met with what was turning out to be typical reluctance from his generals. The military men did not believe they had the naval forces necessary to mount a land campaign (and were correct)*.

Generals Raeder and Goering, representing the navy and the air force, were even more dismayed by Hitler's expressed intention (with the support of the army generals) to fight the Soviets and create the very two-front war that Hitler himself viewed as a cause of Germany's downfall in the last war. Even before the failure of the air war was obvious, however, Hitler postponed the invasion of Great Britain.

At its outset the Germans see the air battle as the precursor to invasion and the British as a *'last stand'* to prevent it. On Jul 13 Hitler decrees that the German air offensive will begin on August 5 even though the Luftwaffe will not be ready by then. He also talks of the likelihood of having to invade Russia. On July 16 Hitler's Directive 16, setting out the plans for Operation *'Sea lion'* – the invasion of England – gives no target date but stresses the importance of control of the sky over the Channel. It will also entail the use of submersible tanks; tests begin on primitive designs. Of Germany's 1.2 million tons of shipping capacity at this time, more than half may be needed to transport the invasion force across the Channel. On August 1 Hitler's directive 17 updates the plan for the invasion of England. The new target date is now 19 - 26 September, though this still assumes that the Luftwaffe will have gained air supremacy.
On August 2 Hitler orders the destruction of the RAF and the British aircraft industry and states that the necessary air offensive must start on 5 August. The significance of this is that it accords the Luftwaffe an independence of role and action that has not been permitted hitherto. Its *'offensive force'*, rapidly assembled in France, the Low

Countries and Norway; will consist of almost 1,700 aircraft including bombers, fighters, Stuka dive-bombers and fighter destroyers. Field Marshall Kesselring's Luftflotte 2 will play a major role because its bases are the closest to England; in support will be Field Marshall Sperrle's Luftflotte 3; General Stumpff's Luftflotte 5 will operate from Norwegian bases against sites in the English Midlands.

209. Albert Kesselring (1881-1960)
Luftflotte 2

210. Hugo Sperrle (1885-1953) Luftflotte 3

211. Stumpff (1889-1968), Luftflotte 5

At this point the Germans remain unaware that the fighters, which will be ranged against them, are controlled by ground radar, a crucial asset in the weeks to come. On August 8 the Head of British Secret Intelligence, Wing Commander F. W. Winterbotham, learns of Goering's orders for the air offensive against England. Air Chief Marshall Sir Hugh *'Stuffy'* Dowding, head of fighter command is alerted.

212. Sir Hugh Downing (1882-1970) – Head of RAF
Fighter Command in the Battle of Britain

On August 12 raids by Messerschmitt Bf 110's and Stukas on radar stations along the coast of Kent, Sussex and the Isle of Wight fail to break the system.

213. Radar towers

RAF HQ reports five German aircraft shot down and others damaged; the Germans report their air raid on Portland harbor with vessels damaged and ground installations destroyed. On August 13 bad weather causes a brief delay to the first major action of what will develop into the *"Battle of Britain"*. The day still sees nearly 500 bomber sorties and twice that number of fighter sorties. A German press report suggests that: *"…a lessening of the fighting spirit has been seen in the British fighter pilots confronting the waves of Luftwaffe aircraft."*

On August 15 more than 2,000 sorties over England mark this as the Luftwaffe *'truly at war'*; RAF Fighter Command deploys all three of its Groups for the first time. The propaganda war is at its height with Germany issuing no acknowledgements of RAF bombing raids against industrial sites or success in dog fighting over the Channel, preferring to assure Germans at home that Goering's forces are facing *"little opposition"* and recording *"great victories"*; British newspapers and official government releases overlook the impact of some German raids, the heavy fighter escorts accorded the most incoming bomber formations, and the poor return from some of the high-risk bombing missions to the German heartland. On August 16 some 1,700 sorties are flown by the Germans against military sites in the south and south-east of England. The RAF attacks the Ruhr* industrial area in

Germany and the FIAT manufacturing plant in Turin. From then on Hermann Goering's name would change to Hermann Meier*

* Early in the war Hermann Goering had made the statement: "If any enemy bomber reaches the Ruhr, my name is not Hermann Goering. You can call me Meier!"

On August 17 Hitler orders a total blockade of the UK; all vessels, including those of neutral countries, will be sunk without warning. On August 18 *Kenley* and *Tangmere* airfields are severely damaged and other Surrey and Kent RAF stations hit by Germans bombers, but the Luftwaffe loses 71 aircraft. On August 19 using reactive rather than offensive patterns, the RAF is succeeding in confusing the Luftwaffe hierarchy and gaining advantages for itself. The Germans, expecting fighter confrontations, find instead selective heavy concentrations of opposing fighters interdicting their routes to and from target areas. The use of radar is enabling the RAF to concentrate its fighters where they are needed; fuel is saved, pilots are given the best chance of success, and the impact of the huge German bombing missions is reduced. On August 20 Churchill, in a typical inspirational speech, will speak his memorable words:

__'Never in the field of human conflict was so much owed by so many to so few'.__

214. The Few

The *'Few'* are the RAF fighter crews that on a daily basis are fighting the best that the Luftwaffe has to offer. Churchill's words will become engraved into British history together with the words he spoke on June 18 when he addressed The House of Commons:

"Let us therefore brace ourselves to our duties, and so bear ourselves that, if the British Empire and its Commonwealth last for a thousand years, men will still say, "This was their finest hour."

On August 24 through an accidental navigational error, a German bomber offloads over the center of London with some loss of civilian life. On August 25 in a reprisal for the London bombing of the night before, the RAF attacks Berlin. On August 26 the German High Command admits to RAF bombing raids on Berlin but denies any damage has been caused there or elsewhere. The United Press Agency, based in the city, claims, however, that ten heavy explosions were felt in the first few minutes of the raid. Reuters in London tells of damage caused by fires started by German incendiary bombs dropped in clusters. Since mid-August the RAF and Luftwaffe have suffered combined losses of more than 800 aircraft, of which the German count is 467 fighters and bombers. The Germans have also lost more aircrew; their British opponents can bale out to safety and return to duty, the Luftwaffe personnel are usually taken prisoner. September 4, Hitler, stung by the bombing of Berlin on 25/26 September, orders an all-out air assault on London. This ill-advised, reactive move gives the embattled RAF bases and their crews a respite from the raids of the past weeks. The back-room planning centers can also regroup and continue to develop their radar systems and air warfare strategies. The change of Luftwaffe policy sees 60 tons of bombs dropped on London. On September 7 more than 900 German aircraft attack London. Goering observes the sorties from the French Channel coast at Cap Gris Nez.

215. Goering and entourage viewing the white cliffs of
Dover. They would never get there.

A new escort tactic sees fighter aircraft flying cover for the bomber
formations. The German High Command reports a huge cloud of
smoke from the center of London to the Thames estuary.

216. The London blitz has started

By this action the Germans effectively '*invade*' England from the
air, but within another ten days Hitler will have cancelled his plans
for Operation '*Sea lion*', the full- scale invasion of England. It can
be said that England was saved from invasion by the loss of life of
thousands of Londoners.

By September 12 the Channel ports of France, Holland and Belgium
hold more than 1,000 assorted German vessels gathered for the

cancelled invasion and are raided by the RAF. More than 80 barges in Ostend are sunk. On September 15, which will come to be known as *'Battle of Britain Day'*, the RAF scrambles all its fighters for the first time. The Germans lose nearly 25 percent of their force – 56 aircraft – for a British loss of 26; the Luftwaffe hierarchy is convinced that it cannot continue to bear such losses. It has failed to gain control of the skies, the invasion cannot proceed, and its first opportunity to function as a separate arm has been a failure. It will change its strategy to night bombing, but the British have survived and the German advance to the west has been stopped at the English Channel.

On September 17 Hitler announces the postponement of the invasion of England. On September 22 the RAF bombs Berlin once again. On September 30 in a final daylight raid on England, the Luftwaffe loses 47 aircraft to the British twenty. The month has seen the Luftwaffe deliver more than 6,000 tons of explosive bombs and 8,500 tons of incendiaries on London. The German High Command decided to drain British morale and resolve by night bombing. On October 12 Hitler postpones Operation *'Sea Lion'* until the spring of 1941. His priorities are now elsewhere and Goering has been unable to achieve the vital air superiority. Sea Lion will never receive the go-ahead. Great Britain has been saved!

British intelligence greatly overestimated the strength of the German air force until deciphering the Luftwaffe's messages. Still, the true size of the force was about 1,300 bombers, more than double the number of fighters available to the RAF, and 900 fighters. As the Americans would do when they entered the war, the British people were asked to contribute whatever scraps of aluminum they had to be turned into aircraft. Britain's economy then went into overdrive to produce all the materials needed for war.

The duration of the *Battle of Britain* is still being debated. For the purposes of this book, my choice has been arbitrary: August 12 – September 15, the five crucial weeks when the battle for air supremacy was most closely linked with the planned invasion of England, *"Operation Sea Lion"*.

Battle of Britain Statistics

As concerns the types of British planes that were involved, British legend obstinately gives pride of place to the Vickers-Supermarine Spitfire, Mark I and II – most of them armed with eight Browning .303 machine guns, capable of climbing 2,530 feet a minute, a maximum speed (at 19,000 feet) of 355 miles an hour. But, in fact, only nineteen Spitfire squadrons took part in the Battle: at its peak, on August 30, exactly 372 Spitfires were ready for operations. By contrast, Hawker–Hurricane squadrons totaled thirty-three with 709 planes available for front-line operations on August 30. Reliable up to 20,000 feet, with a sturdy gun platform, the Hurricane was essentially a slower performer, with a climbing rate of 2,380 feet a minute and a maximum speed of 342 miles per hour.

The German star performer was the Messerschmitt Bf-109, whose worth was proven in the Spanish Civil War; most of Fighter Command's spiraling losses could be laid at the door of the eight single-engine fighter groups, accounting for 805 of Goering's August 10 front-line strength that took part in the Battle. As fast as the Spitfire (maximum speed 354 miles an hour), faster than the Hurricane, it could out-dive and out-climb both; its sole drawback was that a Spitfire could out-turn it. Less certain were the 224 ME-110 Zerstoerers (destroyers) that took part, initially successful as a long-range fighter, its speed (340 miles an hour maximum), its weakened tail unit, made it no match for the agile Spitfires. Among German bombers: the short-lived JU-87 Stuka dive-bomber, withdrawn after ten days' fighting; the Heinkel-111, inadequately armed with its hand-operated gun; the slim-nosed Dornier 17, '*The Flying Pencil*' originally a high-speed Lufthansa commercial plane; the Junkers-88 medium dive-bomber, best suited to the pin-point bombing of industrial targets.

On August 13, '*Eagle Day*', the German Quartermaster General's reports show 4,632 aircraft in all countries – with an average of 3,306 serviceable at any one time. Total front-line strength, though, whittled down to 3,358 aircraft – with 2,550 planes immediately serviceable. The breakdown: 80 close and 71 long-range reconnaissance planes, 998 bombers (in Kampfgeschwaders, or bomb groups, of 74 planes, 261 Stukas, 31 ground attack planes, 1,029 single and twin-engine fighters (each Jagdgeschwader, or fighter squadron, totaled 120 planes), 80 coastal reconnaissance planes. By contrast, Fighter Command had only 708 fighters, 1,434 fighter pilots, immediately available on August 3 to bear the brunt of the battle – though the trained pilot strength of other commands were 1,147 (Bomber), 889 (Coastal), 206 (Army Co-operation), 702 (Overseas Commands)

CHAPTER THIRTY-SIX

OPERATION SEA-LION OR "DO YOU WANT TO DROWN ALSO?"

In Holland we were aware of the events unfolding on the French Coast at Dunkirk; only 115 miles from Rotterdam. We didn't have any details but it was sufficiently clear that the BEF had been able to escape to England to fight another day, albeit without their weapons; their equipment had been left behind on the beaches.

We were also very much aware that Germany had won the war on the continent of Europe. Belgium and France had surrendered. Only the island of Great Britain stood in Hitler's way and we were all sure that he would invade England shortly.

From the balcony of our apartment in the Dunantstraat we had an unobstructed view of the Coolhaven, the harbor that via locks flows to the river Maas. Starting in July we began to see a lot of activity in the harbor. Rhine barges were brought in and berthed five deep in front of our house and stretching all the way to the Lage Erf Brug; a mile to the north. At the same time, several metal sheds were erected and heavy lifting cranes set up near the barges.
It was clear to us that this activity had to do with the planned invasion of England.

"From the German merchant marine, about 1,300 ships, fishing vessels, motor cutters, tugboats, motor sailing boats, ocean- going barges, and ferries could be gathered, increased by about 600 ships that were already in the employ of the Kriegsmarine. With this ship capacity, about 200,000 men and 3,000 vehicles could be transported. On the Rhine,

Dutch and German passenger ships for 4,000 vehicles, and 1,500 barges for the transport of a further 120,000 men and 4,500 vehicles, were to be requisitioned. In total this came to a capacity for 300,000 men and 8,500 vehicles".
From Egbert Kieser's Operation Sea Lion, the German Plan to Invade Britain 1940, page 115

For the next month and a half we witnessed the frantic activity of converting these barges to landing crafts.

"The modifications required a substantial effort in time and material. Ships and hulls and barge bottoms had to be strengthened for loading tanks and artillery, unloading ramps installed and new towing gear affixed. Some of the barges had aircraft engines mounted for propulsion and huge portal ramps for the loading of tanks and guns; in addition the bows were cut off and hinged... It was not only a matter of transportation but also about protecting the men from rifle and machine-gun fire during the crossing and while disembarking. Therefore the sides were strengthened with concrete and iron bars; bridges, helmsmen's positions and unloading ramps were fortified...."
Credits: Egbert Kieser's Operation Sea Lion

While work on the barges was continuing the Germans installed multi-barrel anti-aircraft guns on the four corners of the Pieter de Hoogh Bridge near our house. This was obviously done to protect the barges from bombing and strafing by the Royal Air Force.
Sure enough, the English knew what was going on and on several occasions Spitfires came in flying low over the Coolhaven taking pictures. These fighters flew extremely low over the surface of the harbor, which prevented the guns from declining to that height. I still remember the Germans, manning the guns, frantically yelling:

"Achtung! Achtung! Spitfeuer!
(Attention, Attention, Spitfire!)
Although this was not without danger for us we were happy that something was being done about those landing crafts. The English knew where they were and they might come back and bomb them. Fortunately for us, they never did.

Much later we heard that there had been one landing exercise.

This exercise was carried out, just off the coast at Boulogne* in France.

Fifty vessels were used for the exercise, and to enable the observers to actually observe, the exercise was carried out in broad daylight. (The real thing was due to take place at night/dawn)

The vessels marshaled about a mile out to sea, and cruised parallel to the coast. The armada then turned toward the coast (one barge capsizing, and another losing its tow) and approached, then landed. The barges opened, and soldiers swarmed ashore.

However, it was noted that the masters of the boats let the intervals between the vessels become wider and wider, because they were afraid of collisions. Half the barges failed to get their troops ashore within an hour of the first troops, and over ten percent failed to reach the shore at all. The troops in the barges managed to impede the sailors in a remarkable manner – in one case, a barge overturned because the troops rushed to one side when another barge *"came too close"*.

Several barges grounded broadside on, preventing the ramp from being lowered.

In this exercise, carried out in good visibility, with no enemy, in good weather, after traveling only a short distance, with no navigation hazards or beach defenses, less than half the troops were put ashore where they could have done what they were supposed to do.

The exercise was officially judged to have been a "great success".

*The RAF devastated Boulogne-sur-Mer, the lower part of town hosting the port, during WWII to prevent it from being used in "Operation Sea Lion".

*Just outside the town towards Calais the Colonne de la Grande Armee dominates the vista. This is the site of the Boulogne Camp where Napoleon kept his troops from 1803 to 1805 in preparation for an invasion of England.

217. German invasion barges lined up in the harbor.

All during that time of heightened expectations and the real possibility that the Germans would indeed invade England, German troops in Rotterdam were heard singing the *'Engelland Lied'*:

Heute wollen wire ein Liedlein singen,
Trinken wollen wir den kuehlen Wein,
Und die Glaeser sollen dazu klingen,
Denn es muss geschieden sein.
Reich mir deine Hand,
Deine weisse hand!
Leb wohl, mein Schatz, leb wohl, lebe wohl!
Denn wir fahren, denn wir fahren,
Denn wir fahren gegen Engelland, Engelland!
Ahoi!

Kommt die Kunde, dass ich bin gefallen,
Das ich schlafe in der Meeresflut,
Weine nicht um mich, mein Schatz, und denke:
Fuer das Vaterland, da floss mein Blut!
Reich mir deine Hand,
Deine weisse Hand!
Leb wohl, mein Schatz, leb wohl, lebe wohl!

Denn wir fahren, denn wir fahren,
Denn wir fahren gegen Engelland, Engelland!
Ahoi!

The second stanza of this song, translated loosely, tells us:

When the time comes that I die
That I will be sleeping in the sea.
Do not cry for me, my darling but know
That for my country I gave my blood.
Give me your hand, my darling
Your beautiful hand.
Live well, my darling, live well!
Because we are sailing against England, Against England.
Ahoy!

Lots of jokes were making the rounds:

A little boy was marching behind a column of krauts singing their song. The little boy's mother seeing her son marching with the Krauts yells from the third story of her apartment: *"Jantje come in, right now, you want to drown also?"*

"Say, the Germans are already in three places in England!" "What are you saying?"
"Yes: in hospitals, insane asylums and cemeteries."

A shark is swimming with her young behind her through the English Channel: *"Just be quiet son, in a little bit you will get a nice piece of Kraut." "Yak, Kraut again?"*

"The statue of Admiral Michiel de Ruyter* is broken!" "How come?" "He burst from laughing when he saw the Kraut invasion fleet."

*Admiral of the Navy Michiel Adriaanszoon de Ruyter was Holland's most famous Admiral. He is best remembered for his 'Raid on the Medway' at the mouth of the river Thames, England in June 1667.

On October 12 Hitler postponed *"Operation Sea Lion"* until the spring of 1941. Goering had been unable to achieve the vital air superiority and the mandated destruction of the Royal Air Force had not succeeded. However, it had been a close call. Hitler's priorities were now elsewhere. *'Sea Lion'* would never receive the go-ahead.

Of course, we didn't know that at the time. From the German side all we were given was propaganda of hundreds of English planes shot down. My father kept daily track of the British losses that were reported in the *'controlled'* press and he came to the conclusion that the Royal Air Force, at the outset, had far more fighters than what the German Luftwaffe had reported initially. He concluded that either the Germans were lying or the British were able to quickly replenish their losses from new production. Either way, we figured that there was a very positive side to all this.

CHAPTER THIRTY-SEVEN

CENSORSHIP, SPYING, RULES & REGULATIONS AND THE DUTCH NAZI PARTY

CENSORSHIP

In the middle of July 1940, Seyss-Inquart's representative in the province of Groningen, Conring, happened to read a 'General History of the World' book used in the elementary school system. It contained a paragraph about Adolf Hitler that was not very flattering. Conring found this totally unacceptable and it resulted in the book being removed from all the schools that used it in their curriculum. This action was followed by a review of all study material and libraries. Nine thousand books were reviewed with four hundred being removed from circulation and at least two hundred books were altered. During the first half of September, libraries were no longer allowed to lend out a single book. Following a complete review of all material they were given the green light with the exception of any book written by German immigrants and several Dutch authors who were known to be anti-German. In time the works of two hundred authors were forbidden and taken out of circulation.

I remember that over time our school books were returned to us with whole paragraphs, passages and pictures blacked out. It goes without saying that all of us in our school in the Havenstraat were trying very hard to find out what had been printed under that black ink. Often enough we were able to figure it out and most of the time it had to do with the Royal family or history of World War I and beyond; Hitler's rise to power in particular.

Publishers were the next target of the Sicherheitspolizei and Sicherheitsdienst. About 140 new publications were forbidden and destroyed. Additionally, Dutch readers were enlisted to review thousand of books. They were paid ten guilders a day. Until the end of 1941 about 300,000 books were taken off the shelves and destroyed. The result of this 'cleansing' was the genesis of a flourishing underground *'banned'* book exchange.

SPYING

During this same period and actually throughout the war there were a considerable number of people who were eager to spy on German military movements and pass information on to the British. These people were working entirely on their own and were always looking for ways to communicate their information to the British. In the beginning of the war that was next to impossible. One of these people was 65 year old Sieds van Straten. He had been a reserve officer during the First World War.

Following the surrender on May 15, 1940 he began traveling throughout the country. He didn't have much money and many times slept in Railway stations. During these travels he made military observations that he wrote up in lengthy reports. He enclosed these reports in green bottles that he dropped in the Nieuwe Waterweg, the waterway from Rotterdam to the North Sea.

Of the twenty bottles that he dropped in the water, five were picked up on the English coast and directly taken to British Intelligence. Starting in the summer of 1942 van Straten was able to transmit his reports via the connection Delfzijl – Stockholm in Sweden. Van Straten died in July 1943. Just before his death he received news via the Swedish connection that for his contribution to the war effort he had been appointed to Officer of the Order of Oranje-Nassau.

RULES & REGULATIONS

During the occupation it was the responsibility of the Dutch police to ensure that the population was adhering to the numerous German rules and regulations. One of these regulations was the ban on listening to English radio stations. The police was not very enthusiastic about this order and did little to enforce it; they could always say that they had not *'heard'* anything. The order for the nightly *'blackout'* was another question however. This was an order that had to be enforced. During the second half of 1940 in Amsterdam alone it resulted in 10,000 violations that were brought to court. Small fines were usually the result of these misdemeanors and this action by the police was one that did not endanger the lives of its perpetrators.

The reporting of acts of terrorism to the Siecherheits Dienst (SD), however, was one that had grave consequences for the perpetrator. In too many instances did the police report these people to the German authorities and the results were usually fatal, concentration camps and summary executions.

One could argue that the police should not have reported its own citizens to the authorities but that might be asking too much. It is a fact that many Dutch policemen did not report acts of sabotage but if they were caught withholding information they, themselves, would be in the same jeopardy as the perpetrators. It was definitely not easy to be a policeman in those days and many quit their jobs, only to be replaced by people who were considered pro-German.

THE DUTCH NAZI PARTY

The Nationaal Socialistische Beweging (NSB) was the Nazi Party in The Netherlands during its occupation by the Germans. The members of this political party were considered traitors by the majority of the population and in the early months of the occupation there was a great deal of open revolt to these people whenever they appeared on the street. Their weekly publication was called: *'Volk en Vaderland'* (People and Fatherland). On August 17, 1940 in Naaldwijk it came to a serious clash between outraged citizens and these Dutch Nazis that were selling their newspaper *'Volk & Vaderland'*. Because of problems they had encountered the previous week they had now come in force. The Dutch regular police was also present to keep order but it was clear that they sympathized with the people. The eighty Dutch

Nazis were dressed in black; the hated uniform of the SS. Soon after their arrival in town they were met by hundreds of citizens that were yelling: *"Shoot them; Hang those Bastards!"*

Forbidden patriotic songs were sung as well. The Nazis singing their party song: *'The Black Soldiers'*, countered this. It quickly resulted in a huge fight with guns being fired. Nobody got killed however but the *'Black Soldiers'* were beaten up quite badly. When they noticed the lackluster attitude of the regular police and their obvious support of the population they attacked the main police building. There they found a few German SD men who notified their HQ in The Hague. Within a short time *'marechaussee'* (national police) appeared on the scene and order was restored quickly. From then on Naaldwijk's police force was strengthened to twice its size.

On another occasion when shots were fired, a Dutch Nazi member of the NSB was shot and he died in the hospital. Naturally, he became a martyr of the *'Party'* and with much fanfare he would be re-buried in a mausoleum in Lunteren, the headquarters of the NSB. In order to make the funeral the most imposing display of support for the Nazi cause, all party members throughout the Netherlands were ordered to attend the service. Anton Mussert, the party leader, ordained that employers give the day off with full pay to those attending the funeral. There were many employers that refused this order and what follows is the dialogue between a Dutch WA Nazi member and the Chief Executive Officer of the Nijmeegse Papierfabriek. (Nymegen Paper Factory):

CEO: *You are not getting the day off. I don't accept anything that the NSB says.*

WA-man: *The Commander of the WA has ordered me to attend.*

CEO: *I don't know any 'Commander'.*

WA-man: *That you will find out soon enough. On top of that it has been announced in the paper that you must give the day off with full pay.*

CEO: *You are my employee and I have nothing to do with the WA. What kind of people are those anyway?*

WA-man: *It is the Police arm of the NSB party.*

CEO: *You already don't earn much and now you want the day off.*

WA-man: *Yes, but you must pay me for that day.*

CEO: *I suggest you try to get that money from the NSB party. They have stolen enough.*

WA-man: *You insult the whole party and me.*

CEO: *Just shut up! You won't get the day off unless I am ordered by a higher source. I don't consider the NSB as such; I am not familiar with that trash.*

In spite of this, the worker took the day off and was then promptly fired. Naturally none of this sat well with the NSB party officials or with the German authorities. People were arrested or were made to pay substantial fines. In doing so they only succeeded in fanning the flames of further covert resistance.

CHAPTER THIRTY-EIGHT

A DOUBLE ESCAPE

Following the surrender on May 15, 1940 the Germans took over Schiphol airport as well as the Fokker Airplane Manufacturing plant nearby. At that time there were two Fokker G-1's in the final stages of assembly.

Upon completion these planes would be flown to Germany.........

"I can still see him walking through our village. How we despised that man". It was during the last few months of 1940 and Engineer Vos of the Fokker Airplane factory was known as a *'kraut' lover. "I just don't understand it,"* one of the citizens had remarked shaking his head, *"he was such a nice man and on top of that an engineer. You would think that such a person would have brains."* But apparently airplane designer Vos didn't have those because the Germans appeared to be his best friends. He was often seen in an army vehicle talking and carrying on with the German officers.

Stories were circulating of parties that he was enjoying with his new friends. They were all the same at the factory. Test Pilot Leegstra who was a fantastic pilot was just the same. How was that possible! Had they forgotten the May days when their planes flown by their friends had done battle with the German fighters? Whenever Vos walked through town he must have felt the loathing of his neighbors and acquaintances. But it didn't seem to face him. People that greeted him received a polite nod back.

Only much later did we realize how difficult it must have been for him, how he would have wanted to tell these people: *"Friends, I hate those krauts as much as you do. It makes me sick to my stomach to be friendly and subservient. But it must be done, it's all part of the resistance work I decided to do."*

Vos was chief engineer at the Fokker plant and Leegstra was a test pilot. Nobody at the factory could understand why these men had remained at work after the capitulation. The Fokker plant got new German management; increased security and the two men were now working for the German war machine. Nobody understood it except for the two conspirators. Vos and Leegstra wanted to get to the other side, to England. They wanted to continue the fight and they knew that the RAF (Royal Air Force) needed experienced flyers. For that reason they had focused on one of two *'purebreds'*, both Fokker G-1 fighter planes, captured by the Germans in the final stages of completion and now almost ready to fly. Both knew the plane like the back of their hand. If they were given just one minute opportunity to get in the plane and start the two engines, they would be able to get across the North Sea. *"Its not very difficult for you, Leegstra,"* Vos said, *"You are a test pilot and they will certainly let you test the plane before handing it over to the Luftwaffe. But how do I get into that crate? That would be very suspicious. There is only one thing for us to do: we have to get chummy with these krauts. We have to become such good friends that they will not dare to refuse us."* They discussed their plan in detail. A trusted employee became an accomplish and would see to it that the gas tanks of the Fokker G-1 were topped of. Every day he would steal a few jerry cans and hide them somewhere. In the meantime they were becoming good friends with the Germans. To the outside world however Vos and Leegstra would become bitter enemies, who would quarrel openly and threaten each other with words. They would, independent from each other, befriend the most important German officers. At first the Gestapo was suspicious but when they decided that they were indeed pro-German and the factory workers were showing their hatred more and more they were received with open arms. They sat in on confidential meetings, received secret orders and were invited to all the parties. They used the winter months to further foster their relations with the Germans. In the spring of 1941 they received notice that the two Fokker G-1's would be flown to Germany. They knew this was their opportunity; now or never.

Leegstra did the talking. On Monday May 5th 1941 he had a long discussion with the German management. He explained that although the G-1 was an excellent machine it did have its peculiarities. Pilots would have to be aware of these. If the pilot didn't, it might mean his last flight. Therefore it was definitely necessary that Leegstra make a final test flight. He would not want to endanger the life of a German pilot. Weren't we there to help each other? It was not because he was eager to fly once more, rather not. Therefore, if management dared to take responsibility it would be OK with him. But he had warned them... The Germans nodded their approval. That was very nice of Mr. Leegstra. They would appreciate it very much if he would conduct the test flight. Oh, Mr. Vos had to come along as well? A few of the officers in the conference room smiled. That would really be something. Those two together in the plane. What if they had a fight; they couldn't stand each other. Leegstra admitted it with a sour-sweet smile on his face; he didn't like Vos. But if it was in the interest of the German cause then personal feelings would have to be set aside. And Vos was the only engineer at Fokker who could identify any problem in less then five minutes. Didn't the officers know that? This time it was Vos' friends who nodded their approval. Vos was an experienced technician and he was highly trustworthy. They had a difficult time keeping a straight face when together they walked to the field. They were on their way. The tanks of the G-1 had been topped of.

Now they would start at last..."*Halt!*" A German soldier blocked their way. Where were they going? Ach so, they wanted to fly? But in that case they would have to get approval from the officer in charge of captured booty. He was not there; therefore the gentleman would have to wait. They did not give themselves away and somewhat annoyed they returned to their friends. "*What? Back so soon? Ah, they had forgotten about that officer*". He was summoned immediately. He looked at both Dutchmen. He didn't like the idea and refused permission. A mere officer did not easily put off the German management. "*Who did he think he was? Didn't he know that both men were completely trustworthy? That they were the only people believing in the German cause? Didn't Herr Oberleutnant know that Leegstra was a famous test pilot who would give demonstrations for the Luftwaffe and from whom they could learn so much?*" However, they understood his concern and therefore they would make sure. The German pilot Emil Meinecke flew the escort. The planes took off at 16:20 and both flew in the direction of the IJsselmeer. Over the IJsselmeer Leegstra started to do some aerobatics, *"to test the G-1"*. In reality he was trying to get rid of Meinecke. With the help of cloud cover he deceived Meinecke and was able to escape his attention. Meinecke returned to Schiphol with the thought that Leegstra had crashed in the IJsselmeer. By that time Leegstra was already flying over the North Sea (in a Dutch plane with German markings). They looked straight ahead. Would the Germans follow them? Would faster fighters take off to come after them? Nothing happened. Every minute that passed the English coast was getting nearer. They were both well aware that they would have new problems once they got there. In the eyes of the British air defense their G-1 was an enemy plane. They would use fighters and anti-aircraft guns. It was essential that they land as quickly as they could on English soil before fighters and anti-aircraft guns would have a change to shoot them down. When they approached the English coast three Hurricanes came to take a look. Leegstra was flying low over the coast at East Suffolk, about six miles to the south of Great Yarmouth, when they were fired upon from the ground. Leegstra decided to make a belly landing. In sight of the coast the G-1 lowered its wheels; that might be a sign for the English. An enemy plane would never fly to its target with its wheels down. But the two friends couldn't blame the English if they thought it might be a ruse. From somewhere a machinegun was firing and bullets were ripping through the wings and fuselage. Then he spotted a suitable field. Leegstra went even further down and pulled the wheels in. While they were receiving fire from several directions the pilot pushed the plane down to the ground over the tops of some trees. Vos held tightly on to his seat, he knew that a belly landing would give a pretty good shock. At the last moment Leegstra could not find it in himself to wreck this beautiful plane. He quickly lowered the wheels and the Fokker G-1 made a perfect landing. British soldiers, guns at the ready, immediately surrounded the plane. Vos and Leegstra were both laughing when they were taken prisoner. Just in time, because there above them were the three Hurricanes. Five minutes later and they would not have made it. Their escape had succeeded. Leegstra and Vos were in England to continue the fight against the Nazis.

218. This is the actual plane but now with RAF roundels

219. This G-1 is similar to the one flown by Vos &
Leegstra. The number of their G-1 was #362

The big news had gone around like wildfire; in the Fokker factories;
at Schiphol airport and in the neighborhood of Amstelveen. *"Aha, so
that's why! That was the reason why those two had acted so pro-Nazi!"*

CHAPTER THIRTY-NINE

THE JEWS IN HOLLAND

In May 1940 there were a total of 137,000 Dutch nationals with some Jewish blood in their veins living in The Netherlands. Additionally, there were another sixteen thousand Jews that had fled Germany and about eight thousand from other countries, including two thousand from Poland.

That made for a total of over one hundred-sixty thousand. Most of these Jews lived in the city of Amsterdam. According to the 1930 census, forty-five percent earned a living in commerce, thirteen in the textile industry (mainly as tailors and seamstresses), and eight in the diamond industry. Most were quite poor; earning a mere eighteen guilders a week. Quite a few Jews earned a living in independent occupations: about three hundred as engineer or architect, the same number as attorneys, about seven hundred as medical doctors and roughly thirteen hundred as artists and entertainers.

Although they were Jews, they didn't display a strong religious ideology. In the fall of 1939 when The Netherlands mobilized its army, more than 3,000 Jewish inductees were asked if they would prefer the appointment of a Rabbi. Fewer than twelve percent replied in the positive. Two-thousand six-hundred and fifty could have cared less. The Jews in Holland had assimilated quite well and this trend was continuing as a result of numerous inter-faith marriages. With very little exception there was no anti-Semitism in The Netherlands.

The German occupation of Holland in May put an end to these people's peaceful existence. Every uniformed German was a threat to them. A threat that already had run its course in Germany and had been the reason for so many Jews having fled to The Netherlands, a country where they felt free.

Anne Frank and her family were among these people. The story of Anne Frank and her family is well known as a result of Anne's diary. While initially successful in hiding from the Gestapo, her family was betrayed and deported to concentration camps. Anne and her older sister Margot died in Bergen-Belsen in 1945.

220. Anne Frank (1929-1945)

221. Anne and her sister Margot's Grave in Belsen

With the occupation, the Jews in Holland expected pogroms and massive arrests; a kind of repeat of the Reichskristalnacht when Jewish shops in Germany were vandalized. But, that didn't happen. For the time being all was quiet. The process would be gradual because Seyss-Inquart was well aware of the bond between the Jews and the Dutch population. He had direct orders from Adolf Hitler to bring the Dutch nation into the German fold in the most peaceful manner because he, Hitler, regarded the Dutch as pure Germans with a different language. Given some time he felt they could be won over to the Nazi philosophy.

How wrong he was.

In spite of all this rhetoric, Mussert, the leader of the NSB, had been informed by one of the top Nazis in Holland that soon enough the Jews would be deported. To where, he did not say.

It started in the first half of 1941 with the mandatory registration of all Jews, the identification of all Jewish businesses and the removal of all Jews from cultural endeavors. The idea was to separate and isolate the Jews from the rest of the population. Jewish businesses were required to show a sign in the window that said: *Jewish Store*'. This resulted in windows being broken by members of the Dutch Nazi party, the NSB. This was not what Seyss-Inquart had in mind and he punished the perpetrators. He wanted a *peaceful*' administrative solution that would not result in any big protests. As we will see later, the Nazis in their *Final Solution*' were quite successful in leading the Jews in Europe to their *slaughter*'. This was done without the least rebellion. In this process the Nazis were very often assisted by the Jews' own organizations that they had created when they separated the population in Jews and non-Jews. Very diabolical to say the least.

Following the registration and identification, the logical next step of the Nazis was the removal of all Jews from their professions in all of industry as well as the education system and government.

DUTCH UNIVERSITIES REBEL

The first people in Holland to rebel against these measures were students from the nine largest universities. The reason was the removal of Jewish professors from the faculties. Of the twenty-four hundred students at Leiden University, seventeen hundred signed a declaration of protest. Other universities did the same and half of all university professors in the country also signed a letter protesting the action and sent it to Seyss-Inquart. Protestant churches (not yet the Catholic Church) joined this protest.

The churches in the Netherlands, without exception, were totally opposed to any form of anti-Semitism and gave expression to that position in a historic meeting on June 25th of the seven protestant faiths. This was also the first time in Dutch history that these seven different faiths got together and would speak as one. They represented close to four million Christians.

CHAPTER FORTY

"... To Oust The Tyrants That Have Pierced Our Hearts".

To understand what it took to oppose Nazi actions against the Jewish academia, it is important to tell you the story of one professor, Rudolph Pabus Cleveringa.

222. Professor Rudolph P. Cleveringa (1894-1980), a
brave man.

223. Holland's oldest university in Leiden

At the country's oldest university in Leiden, ten Jewish teachers including two professors were removed from the faculty. One of the two professors was E. M. Meijers. He taught civil rights and international civil law.

Cleveringa had studied under Meijers. They had become close friends. On November 26 Cleveringa visited Meijers after the latter had received his notice of dismissal. Cleveringa copied the text. Meijers knew what Cleveringa was planning to do; his protest could harm him but he kept quiet. Cleveringa went home to Hiltje his wife and his three daughters. He had already told Hiltje what he was planning to do. She had understood the reason and supported her husband even though she realized the great danger that he exposed himself to. Cleveringa said goodbye and walked to the university campus. The faculty room was already crowded; professors from other faculties were present as well. The main auditorium was overflowing with professors, teachers and hundreds of students. A second, smaller auditorium filled up very quickly as well. Loud speakers would carry Cleveringa's words.

He started with the reading of the message that Meijers had received from the Nazi authorities. He then said that it would be below his dignity to further highlight the message and its German originators.

"Instead", he said, *"let us focus on the man whom it concerns: Meijers, the scholar, pushed aside after thirty years of teaching by a ruthless power that can only support itself"*. He continued with describing the man Meijers. Occasionally there was the beginning of applause from the audience but with an impatient show of his hands he stopped it.

He finished his speech:

"It is this Dutchman, this noble and true son of our people, this human being, this father of the students, this scholar who is being removed from his position by a hostile stranger who is now in control of our country! I told you that I would not talk about my own feelings; I will stick to that even though my head and heart are about to burst. But in this faculty, whose aim is the practice of righteousness and justice, it must be said that in keeping with our Constitution and the Dutch tradition that every citizen in this country has the right to occupy any position regardless of belief or religious faith. In keeping with Article 43 of the Rules of War the occupier must honor this country's laws unless there is a question of absolute hindrance to the occupier. We can't see it any other way than that there is not the least of hindrance to the occupiers and that Meijers should have been kept in his position. The implication of his removal and that of others in the way that I told you can only be considered as unjust. We had hoped that we would be spared this miscarriage of justice. Unfortunately it did not turn out that way and there is now nothing else we can do but to give in to the superior occupying force."

He had spoken.

For a brief moment it was quiet. Then there was an eruption of applause that would not stop until one person started to sing the *'banned'* Dutch national anthem, *'Het Wilhelmus'*. Everybody sang it with great passion; the first stanza, tears streaming down their faces. The sixth and last stanza of the anthem that includes the 'appeal', "to oust the tyrants that have pierced our hearts", followed this.

Immediately afterwards his colleague *van Bemmelen* asked Cleveringa for the written text: *"so that I may read it once more"*. He handed him the pages but asked for their return when he was through. *Van*

Bemmelen was of the opinion that the text should be multiplied. He enlisted the services of a typist who produced six readable copies. He kept one copy and the five remaining copies were once again multiplied, this time by ten female students. In the end, fifty copies were produced. These were mailed out with the sender's name: *Santa Claus*. The people that received Cleveringa's text made their own copies and before long there were thousands of copies in circulation. It helped a lot of people getting through the first winter of the occupation.

224. Faculty and students leaving after Cleveringa's speech

The Siecherheits Polizei arrested Cleveringa on November 28. He was taken to Scheveningen, to the same jail where the *'Geuzen'* were being held at that time. He was well treated and went free after eight months. In 1944 he was again arrested and held hostage for other *'crimes'* against the Germans. He survived the concentration camp and went back to Leiden University. The motto of the University: 'Praesidium libertatis' *(Bastion of Freedom)*

CHAPTER FORTY-ONE

RETALIATION

When in November 1940 all Jews were suddenly dismissed from the civil service, the students of two of the nine universities went on strike. A little later Dutch Nazis, who represented no more than 1.1/2 percent of the population, were told to foment street riots against the Jews in all big cities. When in the course of these riots, a Dutch Nazi was killed in Amsterdam, and a German police patrol was attacked by a small Jewish resistance group, the Germans decided to retaliate. On a Saturday afternoon and a Sunday morning in the Jewish center of Amsterdam (Jordaan) over four hundred Jewish men and boys were brutally and viciously rounded up in full view of Jews and non-Jews alike. Indignation was so intense that, on February 25, 1941, virtually the entire working population of Amsterdam and a few other cities in the vicinity went on strike. The strike continued for two days, until the Germans broke it by force.

225. "The Dockworker", monument to the '41 February
Strike in Amsterdam

Dr. Louis de Jong, author of *'The Netherlands and Nazi Germany'* provides the following observation: *"This strike, which, I believe was the first and **only anti-pogrom** strike in human history, had an important effect on German policy. It made Seyss-Inquart and the other representatives of the Third Reich realize that they had to proceed with extreme caution. In doing so they made effective use of several important weapons: the weapon of fear and the weapon of deception."* He goes on to say: *"The weapon of fear was directed against both Jews and non-Jews. The non-Jews were given to understand that every act of assistance to Jews was punishable".* Vagueness being an important element of the entire German strategy, what sort of punishment would be imposed was never made clear, but virtually every non-Jew who tried to help Jews expected, that if found out, he would be sent to a German concentration camp."

Action against the Jews was more specific. In the course of 1941 over nine-hundred Jewish men and boys that had been picked up in Amsterdam were sent to the concentration camp of Mauthausen, in Austria. Only one of these men survived. The Jews in Holland knew that to be sent to Mauthausen was tantamount to a death sentence. In July 1942 the Germans announced that Jews would be sent to *'labor'* camps in Eastern Europe. A statement from Himmler's personal representative in the Netherlands accompanied the announcement: *"every Jew who was detected in hiding, would be sent to Mauthausen".* In fact, not a single one of those who were discovered in hiding was sent there; all were deported either to the concentration and extermination complex of Auschwitz-Birkenau or to the extermination camp of Sobibor in eastern Poland.

CHAPTER FORTY-TWO

THE WARSAW GHETTO

During the month of December 1940 I remember my parents talking about a 'Ghetto'. I didn't know what that was and they explained it to me. *"A Ghetto is an area where people, of a specific racial or ethnic background or united in a given culture or religion, live together as a group, voluntarily or involuntarily".*

They told me that they had heard of such a ghetto having been created in the capitol of Poland, the city of Warsaw. Like Holland, the Nazis occupied Poland and not unlike Holland there were a lot of Jews living in that country. In Holland few, if any, had any idea of the horrible things that were happening in that ghetto. We would only learn about it after the war.

In *'The Holocaust Chronicles'* there is a brief history of that Warsaw Ghetto and it needs repeating:

Warsaw Ghetto

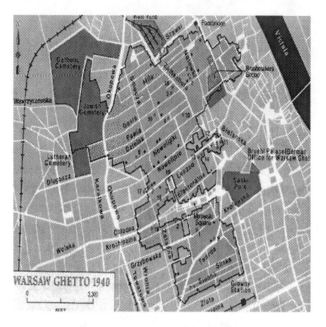

226. Map of the Warsaw Ghetto

The Warsaw Ghetto was the largest of the ghettos organized by the Nazis in Poland. A tiny section of the city, an area of 3.5 square miles, imprisoned a half million Jews. The ghetto covered merely two percent of the city's area but contained 30 percent of its population. Unimaginable overcrowding intensified the suffering. Ten percent died from starvation and epidemics during the first year of the ghetto's existence. With the fall of Poland, the Nazis subjected the Jews of Warsaw to a series of repressive measures, including identifying armbands, property confiscations, and forced-labor requisitions. The Nazis created the ghetto by concentrating Warsaw's Jews in the northern part of the city, the most heavily Jewish-populated district. The announced purpose was to isolate the Jews in order to keep them from spreading typhus. In fact, ghettoization actually spread the disease. In October 1940 the Nazi governor of Warsaw ordered the remaining 160,000 Jews of the city transferred to the ghetto. An endless stream of bewildered people moved slowly through jammed streets, pushing carts and wheel-barrows and carrying small bundles in a desperate search for shelter. Some found a tiny space in overcrowded rooms. Others took refuge in courtyards, under stairways, or in cellars of bombed-out houses. Each building housed an average of 400 people; rooms held an average of six to seven people.

227. Warsaw Ghetto overcrowded streets

The barbed wire and wooden fences hastily put up by the Germans gave way to an 11-foot-high brick wall topped with broken glass. It completely enclosed the area and covered 11 miles. About 20 gates allowed limited access to the outside world. These were heavily guarded and locked at night. In November 1940 the gates were permanently sealed, permitting no contact with the outside world. No longer allowed to leave the ghetto even to work, the Jews somehow had to find subsistence. Workers jostled for the few available jobs. Those without work sold jewels and clothing for food. The Nazis provided only minimal food supplies, rationing them in exchange for the output of forced-labor battalions and the products produced by ghetto craftsmen. Daily food allocations, distributed through the Judenrat (Jewish Committee), equaled roughly 200 calories* per person. The Nazis permitted no fresh fruits, vegetables, meat, fish, or milk inside the ghetto. Even safe drinking water was scarce. Dozens of soup kitchens helped the most needy. Many subsisted on boiled potato skins and water. Beggars with skeleton bodies roamed the streets.

228 & 229 Starving children in the Ghetto

During the winter, when sewage pipes froze, human excrement was dumped into streets. Without food, heat, or medical supplies, dozens of ghetto residents died daily. Old people and children, too weak to move, simply lay down in the streets and died. Corpses were covered beneath newspaper. Orphaned, naked toddlers sat amidst refuse in gutters, wailing pitifully. All told, about 500,000 residents of Warsaw lost their lives during the Nazi occupation.

* Each of the following has 200 calories:
1-16 fl oz bottle of Coca Cola
2-1 oz slices of bread
8-6 gram teaspoons of sugar
2-45 gram Turkey Frankfurters
7-3.5 oz Chicken Nuggets

CHAPTER FORTY-THREE

ARSENAL OF DEMOCRACY

In November 1940, for the first time in the history of the United States of America, a president was elected for the third consecutive time: Franklin D. Roosevelt.

A clear majority of the population had faith in Roosevelt and agreed with the support given by the USA to England while staying out of the war itself. However, Roosevelt knew that sooner or later the United States would be involved in the war and the question was how to win that war? In August 1940 he had sent a military delegation to London under the guise of discussing standardization of the weapons industry. What he really wanted to find out was what the English Chiefs of Staff were planning. All they were able to find out was the British intent *'to deliver the final death blow to Germany.'* Not more and not less.

Roosevelt, after having been briefed, found that overly optimistic. From the end of January till the end of March 1941, the military delegations of America and England met in Washington, in the greatest secrecy, to discuss the whole world situation. They reached agreement on almost all points. The exception was the desire of the English that the Americans would view the defense of the large British base of Singapore of utmost importance. President Roosevelt and his military advisors did not agree with that suggestion: defending a base that distant would only mean the weakening of available forces. The reader will understand that all this talk was merely theoretical. However, behind these *'paper'* plans stood the immense potential of the strongest industrial nation in the world.

In 1941 that did not amount to much but in time, with the changeover of factories to weapons production, the construction of new factories and shipyards, the United States of America would become *'the arsenal of democracy*'. These had been Roosevelt's words in December 1940.

CHAPTER FORTY-FOUR

SOME GOOD AND SOME BAD NEWS

In Holland we had no idea of any of these plans. We were forbidden to listen to the BBC but did that anyway. We listened to the news, which was mostly '*bad*', but there were several rays of hope. Roosevelt had been re-elected and Italy was losing one fight after the other on the African continent.

The fact that England had won the '*Battle of Britain*' and that the English under General Wavell were beating the Italians in Libya, strengthened the confidence we had in our English allies.

'FILOTIMO POLI!'

What further boosted our morale was the story that went around about a Greek pilot by the name of Marinos Mitralexis.

In the early stages of WWII he had defended his country from aerial attacks by the Italians, Germany's ally and one of the three axis members; Japan was the third. On November 2, 1940, twenty-seven Italian Cant Z. 1007 bombers with Fiat CR42 fighter escorts crossed into Greece intending to ravage Thessaloniki. The P-24s of the 32 Mira, Mitralexis' squadron, responded quickly and destroyed three of the bombers. The remaining bombers turned tail after jettisoning their deadly payload harmlessly in the sea below. Mitralexis, who had already shot down one bomber, gave chase. Out of ammunition, he used his plane's propeller as a weapon and severed the tail of a retreating bomber. The Cant Z.1007 went down and so did Mitralexis. After a dead-stick landing near the crashed Italian plane, the Greek pilot grabbed his sidearm, jumped from his plane, and captured the entire crew of the Italian bomber. 'Filotimo poli!' a Greek expression that to defend your country is the highest achievement for any Greek citizen. Actions of selflessness for the defense of one's country are the essence of 'Filotimo'.

COVENTRY, ENGLAND

The name of this city will always be remembered in conjunction with the city of Rotterdam. Both cities were practically destroyed by the German Luftwaffe: Rotterdam on May 14 and Coventry in the Midlands, exactly six months later, on November 14, 1940. A massive German Luftwaffe bombing destroyed most of the historic city center and Coventry's historic cathedral.

230 & 231 Coventry after the bombing

Huge firestorms devastated most of what remained of the city. The city was targeted due to its concentration of armament, munitions and engine plants, which contributed greatly to the British war effort. Almost 1,000 inhabitants were killed within a few hours. It is said that Winston Churchill, through Ultra* intercepts, had knowledge that the Germans would be bombing Coventry in retaliation for the British bombing of German cities. Churchill is said to have ignored warning the population so as not to alert the Germans that through Ultra the British had broken the German code.

*Ultra was the name used by the British for intelligence resulting from decryption of German communications in WWII. The name arose because the code-breaking success was considered more important than the highest security classification available at the time (Most Secret) and so was regarded as being *Ultra* secret.

232. Enigma Code Breaking Machine

CHAPTER FORTY-FIVE

WINTER 1940/1941

The first winter of the occupation was not too severe. We had enough fuel to keep us warm even though there was a growing shortage of coal. I remember getting time off from school because there was not enough fuel for the whole day. I did not mind that one bit; there was a lot of snow to be enjoyed with my friends in the Dunantstraat.

If the temperature was acceptable, the darkness in the afternoon, night and early morning was not. Curfew was from 12:00 midnight till 4:00am. Blackout was strictly enforced; walking outside at night could be hazardous. With all the harbors, canals and waterways in Rotterdam, Amsterdam and everywhere, a lot of people ended up in the water and too many drowned.

In Amsterdam ninety-three people drowned out of almost five hundred people that fell in the water. * Much higher 'numbers' were talked about when it came to Germans** drowning but then, they had received a little bit of help. I doubt whether this was true but it did a lot to bolster our morale.

*Following the winter of '40/41 the quay borders were painted white. From May 1941 till May 1942 one hundred and forty-five people fell in the canals of Amsterdam. Fifteen of these people drowned.

**Up till December 31, 1940 sixty-three Germans, of which five were drunk, ended up in the canals of Amsterdam. Twenty-one German soldiers and one German civilian drowned.

Among the population there existed such a desire to be free, to be liberated, that any good news improved the longer it went around.

The writer Henriette Mooy wrote in her diary in December 1940: *"The wildest rumors are going around that Germany will soon 'collapse'. It gives me a brief burst of pleasure even when I don't believe it.*

I think that these rumors originate from a desire to be free and the feeling: 'I can't stand it any longer, the revolting situation with the Nazis, the blackout, at home, on the street, everywhere. The loud wailing of the sirens in pitch darkness and the narrow fingers of light from the searchlights scanning the sky for prey, the food shortages, the coercion and the threats in all matters; the worry and fear of so many people. Oh, how I wish that somebody would get me out of this nightmare by telling me: "It's only a dream."

Chapter Forty-Six

Wierden – On the Farm

In the early spring of 1941 a decision was made by the Counsel of Churches to evacuate young children out of the city of Rotterdam and place these children with foster families in the countryside. The thought was that the children would be safer in less populated areas in the eastern part of the Netherlands. The harbor installations, the oil refineries and the German U-Boat pens in the general area of our house in Rotterdam were constant targets of the Royal Air Force. Unfortunately, bombs didn't always hit their intended targets and instead destroyed homes and killed innocent civilians.

My parents had put my name forward and shortly thereafter I was included in the first evacuation. All of us children wore tags showing our name, a number and destination

My destination was the town of *Wierden* near the city of *Almelo* in the province of *Overijsel*. I had never heard of *Wierden* before. It was a small farming and dairy community. Upon arrival in *Wierden* the family Beverdam received me. I would live with this family for the next 18 odd months.

The family consisted of Roelof Beverdam, the father of Miene, Bertha, Jan and Tine. Roelof's wife had died several years earlier.

In 1942 Miene married Jan Waalderink and I attended their wedding. Jan Waalderink worked for the Milk Cooperative. He would go around with his horse drawn wagon and collect the milk from the dairy farms on a daily basis. Miene and Jan W. had twin girls in 1956 and I visited them in 2005 when they told me some very sad news.

233. The farm on Zuidbroekseweg in Wierden

234. Family Beverdam and the Ridder family. I am sitting
next to Roelof Beverdam, the father of Tine, Bertha
and Jan, 2d, 4th and 5th from the left. Uncle Wim is in
the middle and my parents are on the outside. Note the
wooden shoes.

235. Mom, Dad, Annie and Uncle Wim visited me in Wierden during 1942. I am the one in the white shirt.

236. In my Sunday's best in Wierden in 1942

237. School met de Bijbel (Bible School) in Wierden. I
am the third one from the left on the back row.

Life on the farm was indeed a lot less exciting than wartime Rotterdam but it had its moments. Sometime in 1942 there were hundreds of Russian POW's in Wierden. They were kept behind heavily guarded barbed wire and it was obvious that they were poorly fed. In their free time when they weren't digging large trenches, they made wooden toys from old telephone poles. They exchanged these toys for bread. I bought a loaf of bread and exchanged it for a small airplane with a propeller that would spin in the wind. These guys were very clever with just a pocketknife and their hands. Later on when they had left I wondered how many would still be alive.

Although bombers weren't necessarily flying over Wierden on their way to Germany, they would often fly back home to England across the area. On August 9, 1942 a Wellington III was shot down by a German night fighter and crashed near the farm. The next morning I made it out to the crash site. The plane had attempted to make a crash landing and was destroyed in the process. Part of it had burned. Four of the crew had been killed and Flight Officer S. D. Read was taken prisoner.

238. Wellington wreck after crash landing.

I managed to take a small piece of thick Plexiglas. I had seen rings that were made from this material and in Wierden there was a jeweler who made a few for me. I don't know what happened to them. They would make a nice souvenir today.

In addition to bombs, the RAF would drop leaflets to the Germans. Wierden was close to the border and occasionally I would find these pamphlets in the fields. It was strictly forbidden to keep these leaflets and if you were caught with them you could be send off to a concentration camp. In spite of that, I kept them and I have included them here:

239. Pamphlet I. Note: Die Vier Freiheiten on the last
page (The Four Freedoms)

240. Pamphlet II. "Und Alle versprechen Euch den Eindsieg!" And All of them promise you the war's end!

241. Pamphlet III. Wer ist dieser Mann? (Who is this man) We don't know his name. If you, German man, and you, German woman, know him, put his name on your Black List. After Hitler's fall we will prosecute the guilty!

242. Pamphlet IV. Text to do with "After Hitler's Defeat".

Sometime in 1943 I returned to Rotterdam because I got homesick. I had learned a great deal about cows, horses, pigs and other animals as well as gathering rye, hay and straw. I even learned to milk a cow. They worked me pretty hard but they were very caring people.

CHAPTER FORTY-SEVEN

FREEDOM OF THE PRESS

In the United States of America and numerous other countries with a democratic form of government, 'Freedom of the Press' is guaranteed under its constitution. We take that for granted as we do all our other 'freedoms'. Occasionally, we read articles or commentary that involves 'criticism' of the press on the part of our elected government officials for articles that 'criticize' them. That is our right. That is our 'freedom of speech' as well as our 'right to petition'. Our forefathers knew only too well that any form of control of its people would lead to its own destruction. On November 19, 1863 Abraham Lincoln, in his Gettysburg address, reminded his audience of that fact with these final words: "...that this nation, under God, shall have a new birth of freedom – and that government of the people, by the people, for the people, shall not perish from the earth."

Now let us take a look at what happens when a totalitarian regime takes away those 'freedoms'. It will become more realistic if you can imagine for a moment that this is happening right here; in this country; in your state; in your town, in your street.

It started shortly after the occupation of Holland by the German Nazi regime on May 15, 1940. It became more pronounced when in May 1941 all journalists and reporters were forced to sign a declaration, the so-called: 'Journalistenbesluit' (Journalists Resolution). In essence it was an instrument that would exercise permanent control of the press. Only journalists that had signed this resolution were allowed to continue in their profession. Jews were not allowed to become a 'member'. The acting secretary-general of justice, Hooykaas, had refused to sign this declaration; only one signature appeared on this document: Goedewagen, a pro-German. Hooykaas was dismissed.

Frans Goedhart, the editor of the 'illegal' publication: Het Parool (Word of Honor) wrote in the edition of the end of May 1941:
'...this Journalist Resolution is a 'shameful' document.'
There was little or no open resistance and most journalists and reporters ended up signing the resolution in order to stay employed. This was not the case with many of the senior staff of the newspapers and many other publications. The only *'positive'* element of the *'organization'* was that it strengthened the social position of the fourteen hundred reporters that had signed the declaration. Frans Goedhart concluded in his article that:
'The untrustworthiness, incompleteness and mendacity of our press will now get far worse than it already was.'
Of course, he was right.

'Press Conferences' had already become an important element of putting pressure on the press. In the future these conferences would be held under the direct control of the Germans. All reporting would have to be in keeping with the overall German aims. Pressure was exercised to write and publish pro-German articles and commentary. In addition to the daily instructions there were general rules to be adhered to at all times. That was not very easy because who could remember in 1943 what had been banned in 1940 and 1941. Toward the end of 1943 there were about 2,200 of these *'prohibitions'*.

What follows is a sampling:
- It is not allowed to publish photos of senior German personalities sitting down for dinner
- It is not allowed to publish any photos, regardless of circumstances, of Negroes or half-negroes.
- It is not allowed to write about replacements when members of the government die while in office.
- It is not allowed to write about the Dutch East Indies regardless of topic.
- It is not allowed to copy from German papers the results of Allied bombings.
- It is not allowed to write defeatist articles, propaganda or advertisements, such as: 'Buy furniture NOW, tomorrow it

may be too late.

- It is not allowed to show pictures of extra wide or long attire. This includes large hats that require a great deal of material.
- It is not allowed to write about topics concerning taxation.

Additionally, it is of interest for the reader to know to what length the German authorities went to ban American, English and French influence from the press. In July 1941 it was no longer allowed to discuss American and English books. Someone asked whether this included books that had been translated from American or English authors. The reply was: *'Of course!'* 'What about the works of Shakespeare, Shaw, Carlyle and Longfellow?' *'We will have to look into that further'* was the response.

In January 1942 they went a step further; all English and American terms would have to be removed from everyday life. For instance, advertisements were no longer allowed to use American and English words or terms. This led to the following exchange at a Press Conference:

Question: *'There are still a lot of businesses that carry English names. Is it realistic to change all those names before this coming Monday?'*

Answer: *'Yes, why not. A business called: Forty Four will be called 'Vier-en-Veertig' (Dutch for 44)*

Question: *'What about the names of hotels?'*

Answer: *'It is important that no mention is made of those names in advertisements'.*

Question: *'What about sport clubs? Do those have to be changed as well? For instance, I have been a member of the soccer club 'Be Quick' in Groningen'.*

Answer: *'I do believe that there are quite a few things that need to be clarified'.*

Question: *'Our advertising department has a problem what to do about words like: 'racket', 'mecanodoos', etc. We don't know where that fits in'.*

Answer: *'It is difficult to draw a line by saying: 'This is right and that is wrong'*

We will leave that interpretation to you. It concerns exaggerated English or American expressions'.

In 1942 the Sicherheitsdienst (German Security Service) in their secret report to Berlin complained that most of the cigarette brands in Holland were English or American. *'This'*, they reported, *'led to a continuing pro-English or pro-American demonstration, because the smoker was continuously in contact with the English language'*.

Ridiculous? Of course! If it would not have been so serious, you might even think it comical.

There is much more that can be said about the loss of *'freedom of the press'* but I believe you get the picture.
I am sure that you will never for a moment believe that the loss of this *'freedom'* here in the US could lead to all the prohibitions that were enacted by the Germans in all the countries they occupied.
I can already hear you say: *"It can't happen here"*. Never be too sure! There are always elements in government that like nothing better than control the people. Those people know what is good for you because they don't think you are capable of making that determination yourself. All this under the guise of "law and order". Who doesn't agree with that? It can slowly creep up on you until you wake up one morning and find out you have lost your freedom of expression. Just don't be fooled by overly nationalistic rhetoric.

CHAPTER FORTY-EIGHT

RUDOLF HESS

An interesting piece of news came to us on May 10, 1941, exactly one year after the German invasion of Holland. The German press announced that Rudolf Hess, the number three-ranked German behind Hitler and Goering, had flown to Scotland alone in a Messerschmitt fighter plane and had parachuted on the estate of the Duke of Hamilton. It stunned the Allies and Axis alike. Hess apparently believed he could conclude a peace treaty with Britain. His mental condition was thought to have been a key factor in the famous flight, but Hess' notions of concluding the conflict reflected the belief of many Germans that the real struggle was not between them and the British but with the Soviet Union and a peace should be concluded. Considering the fact that on June 22, 1941 the Germans invaded the Soviet Union; of which Hess must have been aware, his intention of seeking peace with the British prior to the attack on Russia seems plausible. However, at no time did the British authorities take him seriously (although the Russians could never accept that fact and always assumed Hess was being kept available for an eventual separate peace).

(After the war, Hess was tried as a war criminal, but the flight probably spared him his life. He received a life sentence instead of being executed).

243. The remains of Hess' Messerschmitt

CHAPTER FORTY-NINE

"SINK THE BISMARCK!"

The German battleship *Bismarck* was one of the most famous warships of WWII. Its fame came from the Battle of the Denmark Strait in which the flagship and pride of the British Royal navy, the battle cruiser *HMS Hood*, was sunk by the *Bismarck* on May 24, 1941. It was a terrible loss for the British. Only three of *Hood*'s 1,416 crew were saved; the vessel's quick demise was put down to the penetrative gunfire of the German ships firing from a distance of some 28,000 yards, and its own weak, antiquated armor, but a shell from the German battleship may have hit an ammunition store. The ship sank in a matter of seconds.

Photo # NH 50741-KN   Sinking of HMS Hood, by J.C. Schmitz-Westerholt

244 & 245. HMS Hood before and after

In Britain a cry went up for immediate revenge and retaliation; *Churchill* ordered the British navy to: "Sink the *Bismarck!*"

A relentless hunt for the *Bismarck* was started and concluded three days later about 500 miles west of Brest on the French coast. On May 23d a 'miracle' torpedo from a British "*Swordfish*" bi-plane hit the ship's rudder, jamming it.

246. A Swordfish bi-plane with torpedo

This rendered her virtually unmanoeuverable, only able to steam in a large circle in the general direction of *HMS Rodney and King George V*, two front-line battleships that had been pursuing *Bismarck* from the west. The largest and most powerful warship yet commissioned had now been rendered a sitting-duck by a single aircraft. After extensive efforts to free the jammed rudders, the fleet command finally acknowledged their by-now impossible position in several messages to naval headquarters. Admiral *Guenther Luetjens*, the commander, promised that the ship would fight until its last shell was spent.

The next morning, May 27, 1941, *Rodney and King George V* drew closer to *Bismarck*, with their enemy well illuminated by the morning sun in the background. *Rodney* steered to the north so that her gunfire would work the length of *Bismarck*, while *King George V* took the side. They opened fire just before 09:00. *Bismarck* returned fire, but her inability to steer and her list to port severely affected her shooting capacity. She was soon hit several times. One salvo destroyed the forward control post, killing most of the senior officers. Within half an hour, *Bismarck*'s guns were all but silent and she was ever lower in the water. *Rodney* now closed to point blank range (approx. 2 miles) to strike the superstructure while *King George V* fired from further out.

Bismarck continued to fly its ensign. With no sign of surrender, despite the unequal struggle, the British were loath to leave the *Bismarck*. Their fuel and shell supplies were low; a demonstration of how difficult it was for a battleship to sink a similar unit in a balanced engagement. However, when it became obvious that their enemy could not reach port, *Rodney, King George V* and the destroyers were sent home. The heavy cruiser *Dorsetshire* launched four torpedoes, which may have hit the *Bismarck* at comparatively short range. Although the battleship's upper works were almost completely destroyed, her engines were still functioning and the hull appeared to be relatively sound; therefore rather than risk her being captured, the order to scuttle and then abandon ship was given. Many of the crew went in the water, but few sailors from the lower engine spaces got out alive. It's not clear who gave the order to scuttle the ship, as Captain Lindeman was presumed killed with all officers after the bridge was hit by a 16" shell. Some of the survivors, though, believe they saw him go down alive with his ship.

*Bismarck** went under the waves at 10:39 hours that morning. In all 2,100 German sailors had lost their lives. Only 115 sailors were rescued together with the *Bismarck*'s black cat, named *Oscar. Oscar* was then on board the destroyer *HMS Cossack* when it was sunk and was again rescued, and later on the carrier *HMS Ark Royal* when it was sunk. Apparently, this cat really did have nine lives.

247 & 248. The Battleship Bismarck before and after

*The sinking of the *Bismarck* was popularized in 1960 by the film *Sink the Bismarck!* Dr. Robert Ballard, the marine archaeologist also responsible for finding the Titanic, discovered the wreck of Bismarck on June 8 1989. *Bismarck* rests upright at a depth of approximately 15,500 feet, about 400 miles west of *Brest, France.*

CHAPTER FIFTY

RADIOS AND SABOTAGE

In 1941 there were about 1.1 million radio receivers in the Netherlands and about 300,000 households with a cable connection. Cable reception came from pro-German sources and programs contained basically the same news and commentary published in the *'controlled'* press. The radios were used primarily to listen to the BBC (British Broadcasting Corporation). The whole *'radio'* business was dominated by the German Rundfunkbetreuungsstelle (Radio Service Organization). Religious broadcasts were banned with the exception of individual pro-German religious figures. Both the Protestant and Catholic faiths were considered anti-German. Before the war there was no official registration of radio receivers. The only record that was kept of radios sold was by the stores that sold them. This information was private and the government had no control over these records. That situation changed radically with the implementation on January 1, 1941 of *'luistergeld'* (fee for listening to wireless broadcasts)

The PTT (Post, Telegraaf & Telefoon) kept a record of all the licenses issued and these records showed a total of about 1.1 million sets. Listening to the BBC and other foreign broadcasts was strictly forbidden but most listeners ignored that ban. That fact became evident when on September 8, 1943 there was great happiness everywhere in the streets when the BBC announced the capitulation of Italy.

The Jewish population had been ordered to turn in their receivers as early as June 1941. In several other towns where there had been demonstrations against the Germans the population was ordered to do the same. But until May 1943 most people were still enjoying the broadcasts from London, in spite of the fact that listening to the BBC was illegal.

Henry remembers:

In 1940 we were "forbidden" to listen to foreign broadcasts except German stations. Of course we could listen to the Dutch stations, but they were under German control. Not many people obeyed that order, but if you were caught, you ended up in jail or a concentration camp. In 1941 the Germans decided to confiscate all the radios. The Dutch government before the war required a yearly fee for the privilege of listening to the radio. They kept accurately count of the people with radios so that now the Germans had a perfect checklist. Holland was and is a very organized country. What nobody knew was that we had two radios. An old one, that my Dad and uncle built in 1928 or 29; before there was registration. It still worked, so that's the one that got confiscated. The good one, a pretty modern Philips (1938) went in hiding, but so that we could still use it. I built it in a file cabinet in the back of the drawers, which were filled with all kinds of junk. We had to use an unconventional antenna, so I used the gutter pipe. It worked fine and was not obvious. The Dutch broadcasts from London (thirty minutes a day: "Radio Orange"), were jammed. By using an indoor directional antenna you could still pick it up, but not very well.

Since I had no problems with English, I listened to the BBC and later (1943) to the US Armed Forces Network. On a few occasions I could pick up an American station. I still remember the call sign, WRUL, Boston Massachusetts. It depended on the atmospheric conditions. I also could on occasion receive Moscow in Dutch. This was just as bad as the Germans, if not worse. We became very adept at recognizing propaganda. The camouflaged radio was in the basement. Our apartment had two stories built against a "sleeper" dike. The basement opened up into the backyard, which had a 6ft. wooden fence with a gate. It opened up on open land and the inland harbor (Coolhaven). It made a good emergency exit as well.

In the back of the basement were two small rooms, one a bedroom and the other for storage.

Hidden in the back of the room behind boxes I made a fake wall, where I could sit, do my homework and more importantly, listen to the radio.

I had to disconnect the speaker and use a headphone. You could not just buy a headphone, so I stole one! In most telephone booths the telephone had a second ear piece to eliminate extra noise. I "liberated" two of them and they made a very nice headphone.

I was all set to start my once-a-day 'newsletter'. At the place where I worked were typewriters available and enough paper. I also had enough people there that wanted a daily bulletin.

Every morning I picked up the BBC transmission at dictation speed, translated it into Dutch and typed it out on onionskin paper at a maximum number of copies. This brought me in contact with a number of people, who were getting involved in the resistance. One of them was Piet Jesse.

For safety we never knew each other's last name, however since we both worked at Stokvis in the same department, it was unavoidable.

Soon after the Germans had invaded us, they started stealing the food supplies our government had stored for the population in case of war. These were not military supplies, but the Germans took it anyway, again in violation of international law, the Geneva Convention was a joke. Day in and day out large convoys of trucks transported everything to Germany including medical and industrial equipment essential for the civilian population.

At Stokvis they had a lot of heavy machinery equipment, such as large lathes, planing machines, polishing equipment, etc. Some German semi-military person was to oversee anything they wanted to 'buy' with worthless Reich marks.

Stokvis also carried the necessary lubrication oil and carborundum powder for polishing. Grinding wheels are made of the same stuff. We used it to commit our first act of real sabotage. We mixed the carborundum powder in the lubrication oil. It is so light that it does not settle down, but remains in suspension. I politely asked that German character whether the machine-reservoir, the oil cups, etc. should be filled with the (spiked) lubricating oil. "Ja, ja dass ist gut." Since this story should be rated G, except for violence, I better not write what I was thinking.

We estimated that the bearings in this precision equipment would get polished very well and would not be precision for very long thanks to excessive wear, especially if they kept using the 'spiked' oil, hopefully for their other equipment as well. Of course it would have had dire consequences, if they had caught us.

The situation in occupied Holland became worse by the day especially for the Jewish people. They started deporting them to two camps in Holland, Westerbork and Vught. From there they were taken by train to Germany and, as we later found out, to Poland.

There occurred more acts of sabotage, more hostages taken and shot.

After the Germans invaded Russia they started actively recruiting for the Labor Service and for the SS. They had some success in getting the Dutch Nazi's to go. We did not mind that at all. At least the Russians would kill them and save us the trouble.

In the latter part of 1941 I had a narrow escape, which I did not bother to tell at home. We had a barber close by on the W.Buytenweg straat, where my Dad, uncle Wim and I always went. In early 1941 he suddenly was gone. We found out he was in the Oranje Hotel, the prison for people who had violated some German law. They had caught him listening to the BBC. Punishment was still moderate in those earlier days and they gave him three months in prison. He lost his radio too.

After he was back all his old customers came back and he gained some new ones!

I went there one afternoon, probably Wednesday and while waiting I did my homework, which happened to be my German lesson. In my pocket I had my latest newsletter and my 'schooltas' (schoolbag) against the chair. The barber had just finished with his customer and it was my turn. When the guy left, two SS men walked in. Neither the barber nor I were happy campers, but all they really wanted was a haircut. As a polite little boy I let them go ahead of me. One of them sat next to me and asked what I was doing. I told him in my best school–German that I was doing my German homework. He appreciated that very much and they talked about it among themselves. I had to open my briefcase and show them my other German schoolbooks as well.

It took the barber about half an hour each to take care of them. For him and me that was the longest hour ever. The barber was still shaking after he had cut my hair. I am glad I did not need a shave at that age. Survived again!

Several times that winter the RAF visited us. They came very close to our house while bombing the docks. They also hit Stokvis and burned the top story off. All the Germans lost were a couple of hundred bicycles that were stored there. A couple of houses nearby were also hit. A couple of days later we could go back to Stokvis and clean up our department. They were still pumping out the basement when we were sent away again. When the water was gone they found a bomb halfway in a wall, obviously a dud. The Germans had to come to get rid of the thing. Our department had little damage and I could still do my newsletter again after about a week's interruption.

They also cleaned up the burned out top floor and put asphalt on it. We often went up there to look at the results of some air raids.

I had been able to get some film for the old Kodak box camera, which I used to take pictures of the damage. Naturally, this was not allowed.

During all that time I got my newsletter out with very few interruptions.

Early spring the RAF came over just when we were leaving Stokvis. Several aircraft (Bristol Blenheim) were hedgehopping and one flew right over the Heyman Dullaert Plein. The people were waving at them and the crews waved back. Too bad they lost two of them; one crashed near the Noordsingel jail and the crew was killed. The other one crash-landed in the old Zoo near the Kruiskade. According to some people some crewmembers disappeared in the crowd. One had a broken leg and was taken prisoner. The Germans were ticked off and we got an early curfew for a few weeks. The city was fined, but that was only worthless paper money.

We had another night raid by the RAF a few weeks later. We were just leaving school, when it started. I was going to get my bike, but in the absolute pitch dark I walked into the corner of a wall. I did not knock myself out, but was bleeding from a good cut above my eye. In school they put a couple of band-aids over it and I sat till the bleeding stopped. Then I got my bike again and rode home during the air raid, which was still going on. Suddenly bombs were falling close by and I got off my bike to walk along the houses. There must have been an explosion very near, I did not hear it, but found myself sitting against the door of a house.

I had to walk home because my bike did not work anymore. The chain had come off and some spokes were bend or broken. Well, better the bike than me. When I came closer to home I saw the red glow of fires from that direction.

However, everything was ok there, a whole rack of incendiaries had fallen in the middle of the Rochussenweg and had lit it up. By the time I was home, the air raid was over. You can imagine my reception, dirty with dried blood all over my face, but no further damage. The next day I could repair the bike.

CHAPTER FIFTY-ONE

OPERATION BARBAROSSA

Unable to force Britain's capitulation – though vacillating toward an invasion – lacking sufficient naval assets and a strategic bomber force, Hitler was impatient to get on with his long desired invasion of the *'east'*. He was convinced that Britain would sue for peace once the Soviet Union was knocked out of the war.

"We have only to kick in the door and the whole rotten structure will come crashing down" – Adolf Hitler

Hitler was overconfident due to his rapid success in Western Europe, as well as the Red Army's ineptitude in the Winter War against Finland 1939-40. He expected victory in a few months and did not prepare for a war lasting into the winter; his troops lacked adequate clothing.

This was Hitler's mindset when on December 18, 1940 he issued Directive No. 21; the invasion of the Soviet Union, given the code name: Operation Barbarossa.

The original goal was the rapid conquest of the European part of the Soviet Union and Ukraine. At the time of his directive a Non-Aggression Pact signed in 1939 was still in place between these two contrasting ideologies. It never made any sense to the western world but it had been signed simply for (mutual) short-term convenience.

Operation Barbarossa opened up the Eastern Front, which ultimately became the undisputed biggest theater of war in human history, with some of the largest and most brutal battles, deadliest atrocities, terrible loss of life, and miserable conditions for Soviets and Germans alike.

When we heard about the Nazi invasion of Soviet Russia in Holland, we were overjoyed. We were confident that Nazi Germany would eventually undergo the same fate as Napoleon's invasion of Russia in 1812. The Russian winter would do them in. It would only be a matter of time.

At 4:45 am on June 22, 1941, the Nazi Army attacked. It is difficult to precisely pinpoint the strength of the opposing sides in this initial phase. A reasonable estimate is however that roughly 2.6 million German soldiers went into action on June 22, and that they were facing a roughly similar number of Soviet troops. The surprise was complete: Stavka, (General Headquarters of the Soviet Union) had at 00:30 am ordered to warn the border troops that war was imminent, but not a single unit was alerted in time.

The shock of impact stemmed less from the timing of the attack however than from the sheer number of Axis troops that struck into Soviet territory all at once. Aside from the roughly 3.2 million German land forces engaged in or earmarked for the Eastern campaign, some hundreds of thousands of Romanian, Hungarian, Slovakian and Italian troops eventually accompanied the German forces, while Finland made a major contribution in the north. The Soviet forces directly facing them (not including forces in the interior and the Stavka reserve) were reinforced on such a scale that their strength had grown from roughly 2.6 million men on June 22 to more than 4 million by year's end, despite having had to make good more than 4.5 million casualties of all types.

The overall scope of the battle involved a total of almost 8 million men with about 80,000 guns and mortars, manning 18,500 tanks and flying 14,200 airplanes. These men fought at a front that extended from the Baltic Sea in the north to the Black Sea in the south.

Hitler's aim was to obtain *'lebensraum'* (room to live) for the German nation. Following the capture of *'lebensraum'* his intention was to enslave the population by relocating them to Siberia to *'work'* camps or kill them. Either way would guarantee the same outcome. He regarded the Russian Slavic population, as inferior beings, *'untermenschen'* (sub-human) whose only purpose was to be slaves of the German *'master race'*.

The immediate result of this conflict was that the Soviet Union became our ally in the struggle to be free from Nazi rule. Churchill made the statement that: "any enemy of Nazi Germany is our Ally". But Churchill knew also full well Stalin's reputation. During the late 1930s, Stalin had killed and imprisoned millions of people during the *'Great Purge'*, including large numbers of competent and experienced military officers and strategists, effectively leaving the Red Army weakened and leaderless. The Nazis often emphasized the brutality of the Soviet regime when targeting the Slavs with their propaganda.

While initially successful, the Germans ultimately ran out of time. The climax of Operation Barbarossa came when Army Group Centre, already short on supplies because of the October mud, was ordered to advance on Moscow; forward units came within sight of the spires of the Kremlin in early December 1941. This was as close as they would ever get. Stalin's troops, well supplied and reinforced by fresh divisions from Siberia, defended Moscow ferociously in the Battle of Moscow, and drove the Germans back as the winter advanced.

With no shelter, few supplies, inadequate winter clothing, chronic food shortages, and nowhere to go, German troops had no choice but to wait out the winter in the frozen wasteland.......................................

CHAPTER FIFTY-TWO

MEMORIES

Henry remembers:

"For Christmas 1941 the best news was; the Germans did not manage to take Moscow and were freezing their tails off.

With the Japanese attacking the United States, England and the Netherlands, it was really a World War.

The Japanese were really at it and the loss of Singapore and the Dutch East Indies was a bad blow, but there were so many problems close to home. It really was of the greatest concern to the people who had family there. Our main interest was to survive and foul up the Germans anyway we could without being caught. The Japanese would come later and pay their dues and that they did.

Since my mother's sisters were in the US we could sometimes send a 'letter' to one of her sisters via the Red Cross. The letter was maximum 25 words in English. The Red Cross office was in a building in the Park. Since I had to write the letter, I asked them how their little kids were, not indicating that their little kids were of military age. It took a year before you could get an answer, but we did find out that they were ok. After the war we found out that my cousin Richard had been shot down in his B25 over Italy, but was rescued by the Italian resistance and taken back across the lines to our side. For six weeks he was listed as missing in action"

Mother remembers:

"It was now 1941. Food was becoming more and more scarce. Then your father got sick. TBC (tuberculoses), that was very hard to take. He was no longer allowed to work and had to rest. He did get extra food coupons for butter, meat and milk. Fortunately he had a good boss who continued his salary. That year I remember visiting Jacob Hamel* in Amsterdam. He and his wife were in terrible shape. They lived in an apartment at street level and had drawn heavy drapes for fear of people seeing them. They would sit for a spell and then get up and walk around the room in total

desperation. They talked about Jack and his new wife whom they loved so much and now had been taken away. Every time somebody would pass or stop in front of their house they would physically shrink.

249. Children Choir of Jacob Hamel

I had to go back to Rotterdam and when I got ready to leave Mrs. Hamel clung to me for dear life and didn't want to let go. But I could not help them. Where would I hide them? A short time later all Jews in Amsterdam were picked up; Jacob Hamel and his wife among them. What had these people done wrong? Were the krauts afraid because they were Jews? I returned home a broken woman but I could still go home because I just happened not to be Jewish. In the train on the way back to Rotterdam the Germans checked our ID's. I thought how fortunate I was not to be a Jew. It was then that I realized what 'Freedom' meant. Jo Landzaat, a friend of Christien, worked in a nursery. Some Jewish mothers had been able to take their babies there before being picked up by the Germans. But in vain, at night the Germans came for the babies and small children. Jo and her nurses told the Germans that the children were fast asleep and please come back tomorrow. "Nein" was the response. With that they had taken these sleeping babies and children and thrown them in the waiting trucks. Where would they take them? We didn't know. Then the time came when all the Jews in Rotterdam were rounded up and marched off to the Central Railway Station. They were only allowed to carry a rucksack. Those who did not go voluntarily were later on picked up from their homes. They had to leave everything behind. Their houses were sealed off. One day your sister Annie came home crying. She had witnessed two sisters of her school being picked up on the Heemraadsingel. The parents were picked up the next day".

* Jacob Hamel (1883-1943) and his wife were sent to Sobibor concentration camp where Jacob died on July 9, 1943. The date of death of Mrs. Hamel is not known.

CHAPTER FIFTY-THREE

"A DATE THAT WILL LIVE IN INFAMY".

Henry remembers:

"In December the war changed. It was Sunday night, December 7th and I was at the radio in my 'hole in the wall' in the basement listening to music and doing my homework. The BBC interrupted their normal broadcasting (Victor Sylvester) and announced an unconfirmed report that Japan had attacked the Hawaiian Islands. Later in the broadcast it was confirmed. I tried my short wave connection and sure enough I got WRUL in Boston, weak but audible. They were really saying the same thing that the BBC had given us. In the meantime I ran upstairs and yelled that America was in the war. It took a while before they believed it. I really had a headline for the next morning. It did boost our morale, but the news for many months to come was very bad. We did not realize that it would take another 3 ½ years before we would be liberated".

250. A Day That Will Live In Infamy.

The news of the sneak attack by the Japanese fleet on Pearl Harbor on the island of Oahu, Hawaiian Islands* was another occasion when it became clear that not every Dutch household had turned in their radio(s). The news spread like wildfire that the United States of America was now '*in the war*'.

251. Roosevelt signs the Declaration of War on Japan.

On December 8, within 24 hours of the attack, President *Roosevelt* called a meeting of both the House of Representatives and the Senate. He didn't need to ask for approval to declare war on Japan. He only asked that Congress agreed that as a result of the '*unprovoked*' and '*cowardice*' attack on Sunday, December 7, 1941 a state of war existed between the United States and the Japanese empire. (It made that decision with one vote against)

It is of note that in his speech *Roosevelt* never mentioned Germany.

That was intentional. It was based on the erroneous assumption that the Axis' Three Powers Pact, (Germany, Italy and Japan) was a well-coordinated conspiracy.
It was believed that the attack on Pearl Harbor was just as treacherous as Hitler's specialty, the *Blitzkrieg* (lighting strike) and that it had all the earmarks of a well-prepared, coordinated plan. At the first meeting in the White House when news of the attack was being

analyzed there was total and undisputed agreement that Germany and Italy would now declare war on the United States. *Roosevelt* decided to leave the initiative to *Hitler* and *Mussolini*. He reasoned that such would have a positive affect on American public opinion.

Hitler addressed the Reichstag on December 10 and in his speech referred to Roosevelt as a lunatic whose actions were totally understandable: *"We know what power stands behind Roosevelt. It is the eternal Jew who thinks his time has come."* From *Hitler*'s almost endless tirade it was not clear whether he had declared war on America or was going to. His reticence can be seen as hesitation. If that assumption was correct, it may have been caused by the prevailing somber mood** in the Reichstag.

No wonder! Not only was Germany fighting a war on two fronts as in '14–18 with the United States giving the decisive blow, it would now be facing the United States with its practically limitless resources – and again, against Germany! The similarity was frightening.

One day later, on December 11, 1941 *Hitler* declared war on the United States. Italy followed the German example. *Roosevelt*'s expectation became reality. The direct result of America entering the war was a complete review by the German High Command of all their operational war plans. New instructions under Hitler's signature went out and included: the construction of an Atlantic Wall in Western Europe, the elimination of all British forces

252. Hitler and Mussolini

*For 61 years, from 1898 to statehood on August 21, 1959, the Hawaiian Islands were called the U.S. territory of Hawaii.

**The somber mood in the Reichstag is very much akin to the statement attributed to Admiral Yamamoto when after the attack on Pearl Harbor and when he learned of the late delivery in Washington of Japan's declaration of war he said: "All we have managed to do is wake a sleeping giant" ("Tora! Tora! Tora!)

From the Mediterranean; the fortification of French West and Northwest Africa; the possible occupation of Spain, Portugal and Sweden in order to form a 'Festung Europa' (Fortress Europe) German troops would have to be withdrawn from the Russian front in order to boost the strength of German forces in Western Europe.

In all these actions we can already start to see the beginning of the end for Nazi Germany. But it would take another three and a half years for this to play itself out and would result in millions of casualties and capital destruction running into the multi-billions of dollars.

In the Dunantstraat and everywhere in Holland there was great optimism now that America had entered the war. We could now really start to count down the days to our liberation. We didn't realize that America was not yet prepared for war on two fronts, Pacific and Atlantic. However, the *'sleeping giant'* had been awakened and would in short order become the *'arsenal of democracy'*. It would then only be a matter of time and the Allies would be storming onto the continent of Europe and defeat the hated Huns. We could hardly wait.

With the US in the war the situation at the end of 1941 looked a little better than the year before and we quietly celebrated the New Year.

- January 1, 1942 was day 596 of our occupation.

CHAPTER FIFTY-FOUR

THE ATLANTIC WALL

On March 23, 1942 Hitler ordered the construction of a barrier that was supposed to hold back the expected allied invasion forces. This order, which became soon obvious to us in Rotterdam because of construction activity, was in our minds a positive move. It confirmed our belief that sooner or later our liberators would invade the continent of Europe and set us free. This barrier would extent all the way from Norway in the north to Spain in the south. It started in the spring of 1942 and would involve the construction of mine fields, concrete walls, concrete bunkers, barbed wire fences, *asparagus* fields and fortified artillery emplacements. Since it stretched for 3,000 miles along the Atlantic Coast it became known as 'The Atlantic Wall'. Field Marshal Karl Gerd von Rundstedt, at age 69, was in over-all command of this endeavor. In 1943 when Hitler appointed Field Marshal Erwin Rommel to command Army Group B the project received a great deal of attention. Rommel had inspected the beach defenses and had found them altogether inadequate. It was clear to us in Rotterdam that while a Dutch coast landing would bring the Allies closer to the '*heart*' of Germany, particularly the industrial '*Ruhr Area*', the soggy soil of below sea level ground would preclude a landing in force in Holland. Even so, the Germans enlisted the male population of the immediate area bordering the North Sea to construct concrete bunkers and position poles in fields to prevent their possible use as landing areas. My brother Henry and Oom Wim were drafted to perform this work. When they returned after a month of work on the Dutch coast they told us how they had sabotaged the construction of the concrete bunkers by mixing twice as much sand with the cement. The mixture would dry and would appear solid but a direct hit would pulverize the concrete very quickly. The same was true for the placing of '*telephone*' poles in fields. Two men could easily carry one pole but they did it with five instead. It made me feel good and proud of my big brother and uncle. Construction also took place in the city. Throughout the city a concrete wall was built across the width of the main thoroughfares. These concrete walls had just enough space for a streetcar or automobile to pass through. The wall had a base of about 10 feet, was about 10 feet high and was tapered with the top neatly rounded off. I remember watching the construction of a concrete bunker at the base of the Dunantstraat near our house. Workmen had constructed a three-legged hoisting device. It was made up of three, very tall, wooden poles that were connected at the top. This contraption was used to hoist the large canon in the bunker before the roof could be poured. A man was hoisted to the top to connect something and it was then that the whole contraption toppled over. The worker was successful in jumping free before it hit the ground but then one of the poles landed smack on his body killing him instantly. I can still see it happening in my mind in slow motion. It took quite some time before this bunker was completed and a lot less when in May 1945 our liberators, Canadians from Saskatoon, blew it up in little pieces.

One more thing about the Atlantic Wall. Streetcars moved through these walls with little room to spare and it was essential to be inside the streetcar. That wasn't always easy particularly not when the streetcar was full and you happened to be German. There would then be very little *'give'* on the part of the natives when approaching the *'gauntlet'*. It was just fun to see the fear on those *'kraut'* faces when they couldn't get inside the car. Always at the last moment there would be room for them and no German was ever killed.

CHAPTER FIFTY-FIVE

TOKYO AND COLOGNE RAIDS

Toward the end of April 1942 we heard of an American bombing raid on Tokyo, Japan. Everybody now remembers it as the "Doolittle Raid". We were anxious for any good news and this certainly did the job.

On April 18, 1942 sixteen B-25 *'Mitchell'* medium bombers had taken off from the flight deck of the carrier USS Hornet and had bombed Tokyo. They had been under the command of Lieutenant Colonel Jimmy Doolittle. Jimmy would receive the Congressional Medal of Honor for this heroic feat. Little damage had been done to Tokyo but it boosted American morale as well as ours in occupied Holland. It had the opposite affect on the Japanese.

Henry remembers:
"Both 1941 and the first part of 1942 was a very bad time for almost everything including shipping. The Germans were bombarding us with news about all the ships that they had sunk, loud music and bragging about their U-boats. A lot of it was propaganda, but without rebuttals by the British it worried us that it was not all propaganda. Practically every Dutch ship not in a Dutch harbor in May 1940 had made it to England or the States. In the second half of 1942 the Japanese had slowed down or stopped. We knew there had been some large sea battles, but not that there had been a decisive defeat for the Japanese. The US did not give too much info about it; also the Germans kept quiet about it, but did report the American landings on Guadalcanal.
At night we heard the RAF fly over with hundreds of bombers blasting Germany. I remember the first 1000 bomber raid on Cologne; it kept going the whole night. We did not mind losing some sleep over it. "He, who sows the wind, will reap the storm" and they sure did. We remembered Rotterdam in 1940".

"Gentlemen, the target for tonight is Cologne!"*

"The time is 6pm, Saturday, May 30th, 1942. On scores of airfields along the east coast of England, the preparations have been pressed forward feverishly all week. For this is to be the biggest bomber raid yet launched by either side in World War II.

In this single raid, Bomber Command has committed its entire force… every plane that will fly, and every man, including service squadrons, flight instructors, student bomber crews, and volunteers who have finished their tours of duty. This night one thousand planes will take off to bomb Cologne. They will encounter overcast and icing conditions, radar controlled night fighters, searchlights, and intensive flak.

By morning the result will be known---either Cologne has been smashed or R.A.F Bomber Command *will have ceased to exist!*"

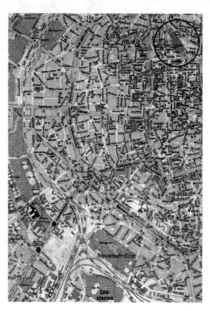

253. Bombing map of Cologne

"That Saturday in Cologne had been a mild and pleasant day, overcast but dry. For most people it had been a day of work and of week-end shopping, followed by a walk in the park and a quiet evening. Tomorrow was Sunday. That at least for most of Cologne's 800,000 citizens would be a day of rest…"

* From 'The Thousand Plane Raid' by Ralph Barker

That Saturday in Rotterdam, at about midnight, I was sound asleep in our basement. So were Henry and Annie. From a deep sleep our parents awakened us. I can still hear them now: "Get up, Get up! Can't you hear the sirens? They have been at it for a while already. Hurry! Put your clothes on over your pajamas; and also put your coats on. It's cold outside. We are going under the bridge (Pieter de Hooghbrug) Hurry up, quickly, before it's too late."

I will always remember this particular night. (1) It was always a shock to be awakened by a lot of noise out of a deep sleep. (2) I had never seen or heard so many bombers (3) I never returned to my bed that night and (4) never again would I find so many '*beautiful*' and '*jagged*' shrapnel pieces for my collection.

This was not the first time that we had been called out of a deep sleep. We knew the routine. The three of us quickly dressed. Annie was still half asleep and we helped her. All the time the sirens were wailing; an awful sound that goes straight through your body. It's a very fearful sound and it makes the adrenaline flowing. In short order we joined our parents and via the gate of our backyard we ran the 200 feet to the bridge. This bridge spanned the Coolhaven (harbor) as well as the road along the harbor. Where it crosses the road, the bridge was resting on a series of three-foot wide concrete pillars. When we arrived at the bridge there were already a lot of people huddling together. Mostly families from our street, including all my schoolmates. Naturally it was dark but my eyes grew quickly used to it and I spotted quite a few of my school buddies that had gotten there before us. Then the '*fun*' started. The sirens were no longer wailing and we could hear the drone of literally thousands of aircraft engines. A most exciting sound! Immediately there were searchlights scanning the sky and the anti-aircraft batteries on the bridge above us were testing their guns. Those guns, however, were of a caliber that could not possibly reach these bombers and their firing only served the morale of their crews. This was not the first time that we were under this bridge. We had experienced many bombing raids but this one seemed different somehow. The real scary moment is when you ask yourself: "Are they going to bomb us or fly on to Germany?" (We had experienced some of the first kind)

There was a '*full*' moon behind a low cloud cover and occasionally when there was a break in the clouds we would get a glimpse of the moon and the silhouettes of large bombers. Immediately the 88's* of the Germans were blasting away at those planes.

*The famous German 88 with a bore of about 3.5"

They could be Wellingtons, Halifaxes, Manchesters, Stirlings, and the new Lancasters. Also twin-engine planes: Hampdens and Whitleys. I knew them all. As it turned out, it was all of these, a total of 1,047 aircraft. This would be the first time that a bombing raid with the 'magic' number of 1000+ aircraft would be made on a German city.

602 Wellingtons, 29 were lost.

131 Halifaxes, 3 were lost

88 Stirlings, 2 were lost

79 Hampdens, 1 was lost

73 Lancasters, 1 was lost

46 Manchesters, 4 were lost

28 Whitleys, 1 was lost

254. The bombers that took part in the raid on Cologne

Thank God, the first planes were flying over and away from us. We would not be the recipients. We didn't know where they were heading and only found out the next day. For almost two hours these planes from the Royal Air Force were flying over the southern part of South-Holland and our city of Rotterdam. It was as if the rhythmic drone of thousands of engines were telling us: "Tonight we will avenge the German bombing of Rotterdam and Coventry!"

German *'night fighters'* from airfields in Holland had been alerted and were in the sky above us. With the cloud cover we couldn't see anything and besides, even without a cloud cover we would not have seen much because it was much too dangerous to stand out in the open. A great many searchlights were poking in the sky and most of the time only hitting cloud cover. The beams reflected off the clouds and lit up our whole area. In this intermittent *'strobe'* light affect I could occasionally see people's faces and bodies that seemed like dancing skeletons. It was unreal and eerie. Today I find it difficult to express how I felt that night under the bridge; I have thought about it often. I was only eleven years old. It was a mixture of total excitement and ultimate fear; as well as a feeling of *'privilege'* to be participating, with all the people under that bridge, in this *'Dance Macabre'**

*Dance Macabre or Dance of Death is a late-medieval allegory on the universality of death: no matter one's station in life, the dance of death unites all. La Dance Macabre consists of the personified death leading a row of dancing figures from all walks of life to the grave.

With the aid of searchlights several bombers were shot down by the Luftwaffe and crashed in the area; causing huge explosions (their bombs had not been jettisoned) The anti-aircraft batteries had then fallen silent. That could only mean one thing; the night fighters were out there and the German gunners, understandably, didn't want to hit their own planes. We all prayed for these brave young men in the bombers who were up there in the darkness risking their life and limb and, in too many instances, would give their lives for us.

The bombers were first following the river Maas that more toward the east becomes the river Rhine; leading them straight into Germany. At the German border the Rhine bends south. From that point it would only be a short distance to the cathedral city of Cologne*.

Over an extended period of several hours more than a thousand planes bombed the city. Wave after wave of heavy bombers dropped high explosives and incendiaries. The last planes to bomb were the *'newer'* Lancasters. By the time they were unloading their bombs, the defense in terms of searchlights and anti-aircraft batteries had just about collapsed. This accounted for only one Lancaster crashing near *Niederaussem*, killing its seven men crew.

*From Rotterdam to Cologne is about 125 statute miles

At about 2 am the flow of aircraft stopped to a trickle and there was momentary calm. We breezed a sigh of relieve but we knew it would not be the end. All these aircraft would be coming back; back to England. No longer was there a question of *'formations'*. They would fly back any way they could. In all, 41 planes were lost in this raid on *Cologne*: about four percent of the total force. One-hundred ninety six crew members lost their lives, sixty were taken prisoner, thirty-four were injured and six escaped to fight another day. Fourteen bombers had crashed in Holland. There was one Wellington, piloted by P/O R. L.W. *Ferrer* that had been hit by flak and with only one engine was trying to make it back to England. The plane's crew included three Canadians of the RCAF (Royal Canadian Air Force) *P/O A. Lucki, Sgt K. H. Buck and Sgt J. D. McKenzie. Flight Sergeant R. Grundy* was the only other Englishman. They had taken off from *Chipping Warden* at 23.20. By the time it was flying over the bridge and our house it was already down to 4,000 feet altitude. We watched *Ferrer's Wellington* as it was struggling its way toward the Dutch coast; 15 miles to the west

This is the story of what happened to this particular plane and crew.

"Even when the last bomber had left the Dutch coast on the homeward flight the danger was not over. Many crews were struggling across the grey spume of the North Sea with faltering engines and damaged controls. Another hazard was that of dangerous cumuli-nimbus cloud in the later stages of the crossing and over the east coast (*of England*). Those who got across safely faced deteriorating visibility and lowering cloud over the bases. With a large number of bombers returning in a short space of time, many of them crippled and facing crash-landings, runways and circuits were congested.

Pilot Officer *Bob Ferrer*, of *Stetchford, Birmingham* was one of the pilots who were struggling to get home in a crippled plane, the old drogue-towing *Wellington 1c* from No.12 O.T.U. (*Operational Training Units*) at *Chipping Warden*.

Home for *Bob Ferrer*, as for his wireless operator for the night, *Ronald Grundy*, meant furnished rooms in a row of cottages in a village outside *Banbury*. Both men were hoping to get back to their wives that night.

255. A Wellington 1c two-engine bomber

They had bombed the target about halfway through the raid, when the huge column of smoke belching up into the moonlight was flattened out at about 8,000 feet and spewing away to the south-east. Up to that time the danger to the *Wellington* had seemed general and impersonal. But soon after leaving the target they had been shadowed and then attacked by a Me-110. The fighter's first burst had been right on target. *Grundy*, sitting at the radio behind the pilot, had seen blue tracers darting from behind along the fuselage and ricocheting off the electrical panel on the starboard side. As he ducked, there had come a stifled groan from *Mackenzie*, the Canadian rear gunner, over the inter-com. To *Grundy*, unused to these '*extrovert*' Canadians, it had sounded like something out of an American film.

"They got me, *Bob*."

Ferrer put the Wellington into a steep dive, determined to shake off the fighter, and they had lost nearly 10,000 feet and were well clear of the target before he leveled off and set course for home. Then *Grundy* and the flaxen-haired *Lucki* went back to help *Mackenzie*. They made their way along the catwalk, negotiated the drogue winch, opened the turret doors and pulled *Mackenzie* clear. But as they lifted him forward they stumbled over the winch and fell in a heap around it. *Mackenzie* was in great pain and the fall was a disaster, but at last they got him on the rest-bed in mid-fuselage. *Ferrer* was calling for radio bearings, so *Buck* went back from the front turret to help *Lucki* while *Grundy* returned to his set. They gave *Mackenzie* morphine, and then returned to their crew positions.

One of the engines was running roughly but they made steady progress across Holland to the North Sea, losing only a little height. They were at 4,000 feet as they crossed the Dutch coast. *Grundy* began to use his loop aerial, tuning in to *Ely* radio beacon to take a bearing, but when he switched in the fixed aerial to try to sense the bearing the needles wouldn't respond. He looked out of the astrodome and saw that the fixed aerial had been shot away. As he reported this to *Ferrer*, the starboard engine failed.

At once they began to lose height more rapidly, though *Ferrer* still hoped to complete the sea crossing on the remaining engine. "Get me a fix," he called to *Grundy*. "Make it priority." *Grundy* reeled out the trailing aerial and called the D/F station at *Hull*. He passed the fix to *Lucki* who plotted it on his chart. It put them forty miles from the English coast, heading straight for the bulge of *East Anglia*. "There's a chance we may have to ditch," called *Ferrer*. The port engine was complaining now as *Ferrer* struggled to maintain height. Below him the sea was like glass, bathed in moonlight. The altimeter showed 1,500 feet. "Send an S.O.S." he told *Grundy*, "and get another position." *Grundy* sent the distress message and got an immediate acknowledgment. The fix put them less than thirty miles from the coast. Fifteen minutes flying. If only *Ferrer* could coax the plane along just a little longer they would be safe.

Back in the row of cottages at *Wardington*, the wives of *Bob Ferrer* and *Ronald Grundy* were asleep, unaware that their husbands were flying at less than a thousand feet over the North Sea, fighting for their lives.

"Ditching stations."

The port engine was faltering. *Buck* came out of the front turret and took up his ditching position next to the bed, under the astrodome. *Lucki* sat on the floor of the cabin, to the right of the radio, his legs splayed out into a V to make room for *Grundy*. As the port engine finally cut, *Grundy* clamped down the key, shut the ply-wood door leading to the cockpit and slotted his body into the opening made by *Lucki*, bracing his legs against the main cross-member of the wing a few feet in front of him. Alone in the cockpit, *Ferrer* was facing the almost impossible task of judging his height above the still mirror of the sea.

Within another thirty seconds the plane hit the water; before *Ferrer* was ready for it; slightly nose-down. The force of the impact sprang the trap-door under the nose and precipitated a tidal-wave of water through the fuselage, smashing the plywood door and flooding the cabin with a wall of green. As the waters rushed in, *Grundy* and *Lucki* were catapulted forward, doubling the impact. *Grundy* was hurled through this wall of water into the cockpit and then sucked out through the trap-door as the *Wellington* floated to the surface, suffering multiple injuries as he went. By this time he was unconscious. Somehow the *Wellington* passed over *Grundy*'s body and allowed it to float away freely. As he came to the surface his first awareness was of opening his eyes and feeling like a blinkered horse, unable to see anything except in a narrow aperture dead ahead. He was staring straight into the guns of the rear turret, which constituted his entire horizon. On either side of the turret was complete darkness.

He was so confused and concussed that he didn't have the presence of mind to pull the gas bottle on his *Mae West*. Somehow he started swimming, and then he saw the dinghy and struck out towards it. He wondered why it was that he couldn't swim properly, but even when he reached the dinghy and lifted his arm round the outer tube to hold on he was too bemused to take stock of his injuries. In fact he was suffering from compound fractures of both legs and one arm, several ribs were broken, his lip had been cut open and was flapping like a letter-box and he had lost his front teeth. Unaware of why he was doing so, and with no hope of being heard, he found himself shouting weakly for help.

The *Wellington* was rising and falling gently on the swell. All the others must still be inside. Then *Buck* appeared as if from nowhere, swimming powerfully across to the dinghy, pulling *Mackenzie* behind him. Somehow *Buck* had got *Mackenzie* off the bed and pushed him through the astrodome before climbing out himself. Even *Buck* didn't have the strength to get into the dinghy, still less to hoist up *Mackenzie*, and the three men huddled together at the rim, with *Buck* holding on to *Mackenzie* to keep his face clear off the water. There was still no sign of *Ferrer* and *Lucki* when, a minute later, the *Wellington* settled deeper into the water and sank slowly down.

It was still dark when they were picked up by a naval launch and taken to *Harwich*---- *Grundy's* S.O.S. had been quickly acted upon. They had been very near the coast when the aircraft came down; they had so nearly made it. There was even a report, which found its way later that morning to *Bob Ferrer's* wife that they had all got down safely. She even called on *Grundy's* wife to tell her the good news. *Mackenzie* died from his wounds later that morning; Buck's great effort to save him had been in vain. The bodies of *Ferrer* and *Lucki* were never recovered. Telegrams were sent later in the day to the two cottages in *Wardington*. One brought *Ronald Grundy's* wife to see him in the naval hospital at *Shotley* that evening. The other, to *Bob Ferrer's* widow, doubly cruel after the false report that he was safe, seemed to signal the end of all meaning to life.

Kenneth Buck, his crew gone, joined another one and was posted to a squadron a few weeks later. He was reported missing almost exactly a year afterwards and was subsequently presumed dead. *Ronald Grundy* made a partial recovery and was transferred to the technical signals branch with a commission, but he developed tuberculosis of the spine as a result of his injuries and spend two years in bed before being invalided out of the Service in 1947. His most ironic moment, however, came about a month after the raid, when he lay completely immobilized in the R.A.F hospital at *Ely*, one leg in plaster, the other leg in a splint, one arm in plaster, his face and ribs still only partly healed. It was fairly obvious that he would never fly again. It was at this moment that he had a visit from a clerk in the hospital orderly room.

"Flight," said the clerk, *"I've got some good news for you. Your pilot's course has come through."*
*Credits: 'The Thousand Plane Raid' by Ralph Barker

256 & 257. Cologne after the bombing raid.

It was already getting light when the *'all clear'* sounded. Annie had fallen asleep under the bridge and we had to wake her up to return home. She never knew what had happened that night. I never went back to bed, being too eager to go outside and see if I could find some pieces of shrapnel that had rained down from the sky minutes after the shooting had died down when we were still under the bridge. I had heard pieces hit the pavement all around us. What some people forgot to their detriment was that gravity would cause anything shot up in the sky to come back down again. That Sunday morning, May

31, 1942, I found some beautiful jagged pieces of anti-aircraft and on-board cannon shrapnel that I added to my collection.

CHAPTER FIFTY-SIX

THE JEWISH SITUATION

During 1942 we saw the gradual tightening of the noose around the necks of the Jewish population in the Netherlands. In spite of vehement protests from the churches, universities, city councils and numerous social organizations, the Nazi's enacted one law after another that affected the Jewish population. In the end it resulted in the deportation of over 100,000 Dutch Jews to the 'East' where most were either killed outright upon arrival or succumbed from mistreatment, illnesses, malnourishment and epidemics. What we were told was that the Jews were being *'resettled'* in the East. No one, for a moment, could have imagined what was in store for these unfortunate people. It is just humanly impossible to contemplate the actual act of driving innocent human beings to their death after their arrival in crowded box cars where, depending on the weather conditions, many may have already died. Then the SS process of *'selection'*. *"Men on the right, women with children on the left"*. Then the walk to the facilities for a welcome *'shower'*. First undressing with the admonishment: *"Be sure to remember the number of where you hung your clothes."* Then entering the large shower rooms where instead of refreshing warm water, Zyclon-B gas would be released through the showerheads.

258. Zyklon-B

Then the bluish haze coupled with a noticeable bitter almond odor and the realization of what was really happening. The resulting panic, the gasping for air when the gas vapors combined with red blood cells deprive the human body of vital oxygen. The momentary, incredible fear and then…death. Death through oxygen starvation. The bodies were then incinerated in ovens built for the purpose and the ashes discarded as best as possible to hide all signs of the atrocious act.

We only learned of the *'Death Camps'* at the end of the war when only a few Jews returned to tell us about it. Even then it would be difficult to comprehend that six million Jews had been destroyed by this means.

The following laws and actions taken by the Nazis in Holland during the year 1942 will give you an idea of the Jews' gradual descent into Hell:

<u>January</u>

Jews are no longer allowed to engage non-Jewish help in the household.

Jewish ID's must show 2 'J' stamps.

Jews are no longer allowed to drive a car.

<u>March</u>

Jews are no longer allowed to sell their furniture and household goods.

Jews are no longer allowed to marry non-Jews. Relations with non-Jews will be severely punished.

Enactment in Holland of the German anti-Jewish Neurenberger laws.

<u>April</u>

Jewish owned butcher shops must all close for business.

<u>May</u>

All Jews must wear the yellow six-pointed Star of David.

Jews are no longer allowed to have a bank account.

Jews are no longer allowed to rent safe-deposit boxes.

Jews are no longer allowed to go fishing

<u>June</u>

Jews are no longer allowed to travel.

Jews are no longer allowed to visit out-door markets.

Jews are no longer allowed to buy vegetables and groceries at non-Jewish stores.

All Jews are ordered to turn in their bicycles.

Jews are no longer allowed to participate in sport activities.

Jews are no long allowed to use public transportation.

Curfew for the Jews is 8pm till 6am

July

Jews are no longer allowed to make phone calls and visit non-Jews.

The first Jews are transported to Westerbork concentration camp.

Large scale round up of Jews in south and central Amsterdam.

First shipment of Jews from Westerbork to camps in Poland.

Jews are only allowed to do their shopping between 3pm and 5pm.

August

All Jewish street names to be changed.

Continuing large scale round-ups of Jews throughout the country during this month.

September

All Jews in a mixed marriage must report to the authorities.

Jewish students are no longer allowed to go to school.

October

Large scale round up of Jews in the country continues. In total 14,000 Jewish men, women and children are deported this month alone to Upper-Silesia

259. The Jewish Star of David

Chapter Fifty-Seven

"AF is short of water". The Midway Atoll

260. The Midway Island Atoll

For centuries, thousands of albatrosses have lived on the desolate islands that comprise the Midway Atoll. Beautiful in flight, but ungainly in their movement on land, the albatrosses were called *'gooney birds'* by the men stationed on the islands during World War II. The birds soiled the runways, clogged the engines of departing aircraft, and were always, always underfoot. Today, the shadows of their huge wings still dapple the glassy sea as they glide towards the islands to nest. They still perch on the airport runways and the old ammunition magazines and gun batteries, but they no longer need to do daily battle with America's armed forces for possession of the islands.

261. Old bunker and a baby "gooney"

Inhabited by humans for less than a century, Midway dominated world news for a brief time in the early summer of 1942. These tiny islands were the focus of a brutal struggle between the Japanese Imperial Navy and the United States Pacific Fleet. The U.S. victory here ended Japan's seemingly unstoppable advance across the Pacific and began a U.S. offensive that would end three years later at the doorstep of the Home Islands.

The Battle of Midway lasted from June 3 through June 6, 1942 and was a turning point of the war in favor of the Allies. A similar turning point would be the Battle of Stalingrad. That battle started a few months after Midway on August 21, 1942 and ended more than five months later on February 2, 1943 with the destruction of the German Sixth Army and other Axis forces around the city. A decisive Soviet Victory!

The story of the Battle of Midway is an interesting one not only because our side won but also because it involved the breaking of the Japanese Naval Code.

In late spring of 1942, the Allied war effort in the Pacific was in a precarious state. The combined elements of the Japanese Empire's armed forces had moved from victory to victory. The Pacific fleet, save for several aircraft carriers, had been left in ruins. It appeared that Japan's plans for reducing American and Western hegemony in the Pacific would become a reality. In order to prevail, Admiral Chester Nimitz, unlike his counterpart, had little room for error and he had to have a sense of Japan's intentions. The task of obtaining the critical information required to turn the tide in the Pacific fell to OP-20-G, the Navy radio intelligence organization tasked with providing communications intelligence on the Japanese Navy. Laurence F. Safford, the 'Father of Navy Cryptology' OP-20-G was key to Nimitz's planning. In addition to his earlier crypto logic efforts, Safford had played a major role in placing Commander Joseph Rochefort in command of Station Hypo, the Navy's code breaking organization at Pearl Harbor.

262. John Joseph Rochefort (1898-1976)

In 1942 Rochefort and his staff began to slowly make progress against JN-25, one of the many Japanese command codes that had proven so challenging to the Station Hypo team. JN-25 was the Japanese Navy's operational code. If it could be broken, Rochefort would be able to provide Nimitz the information he needed to make wise and prudent decisions concerning the dispersal of his precious naval assets.

The Japanese JN-25 code consisted of approximately 45,000 five-digit numbers, each number representing a word or phrase. Breaking the code meant using mathematical analysis to strip off the additive, then analyzing usage patterns over time, determining the meaning of the five-digit numbers. Prior to the attack on Pearl Harbor, only 10% to 15% of the code was being read. By June of 1942, however, Rochefort's staff was able to make educated guesses regarding the Japanese Navy's crucial next move.

In the spring of 1942, Japanese intercepts began to make references to a pending operation in which the objective was designated as *'AF'*. Rochefort and Captain Edwin Layton, Nimitz's Fleet Intelligence Officer, believed *'AF'* might be Midway since they had seen *'A'* designators assigned to locations in the Hawaiian Islands. Based on the information available, logic dictated that Midway would be the most probable place for the Japanese Navy to make its next move. Nimitz, however, could not rely on educated guesses.

In an effort to remove any doubt, in mid-May the commanding officer of the Midway installation was instructed by under-ocean cable to send a message in the clear: *"The installation's water distillation plant has suffered serious damage, fresh water is needed immediately"*. Shortly after the transmission, an intercepted Japanese intelligence report indicated, *"AF is short of water"*. Armed with this information, Nimitz began to draw up plans to move his carriers to a point northeast of Midway where they would lie in wait. Once positioned, they could stage a potentially decisive nautical ambush of Yamamoto's massive armada.

Due to the crypto logic achievements of Rochefort and his staff, Nimitz knew that the attack on Midway would commence on June 3rd. Armed with this crucial information, he was able to get his outgunned but determined force in position in time. On June 4 the battle was finally joined. The early stages of the conflict consisted of several courageous but ineffective attacks by assorted Navy, Marine, and Army Air Corps units. The tide turned however, at 10:20am when Lt. Commander Wayne McClusky's Dauntless dive-bombers from the USS Enterprise appeared over the main body of the Japanese invasion force.

Photo # 80-G-17054 SBDs over the burning Japanese cruiser Mikuma, 6 June 1942

263. Dauntless dive-bombers in the Battle of Midway

After a brief but effective attack, three of the four Japanese carriers, the Akagi, Soryu, and Kaga were on fire and about to sink. Later that day, Navy dive bombers located and attacked the Hiryu, the fourth and last major carrier in the invasion force, sending her, like the previous three, to the bottom.

264. The Akagi, Soryu, Kaga and Hiryu

The Japanese were able to sink the USS Yorktown with 2 torpedoes.

Photo # 80-G-17061   USS Yorktown being abandoned, 4 June 1942

265. USS Yorktown

As in any great endeavor, luck did indeed play a role, but Nimitz's *"Incredible Victory"* was no miracle. General George Marshall, the U.S. Army Chief of Staff, in his comments on the victory, perhaps said it best, *"as a result of Cryptanalysis we were able to concentrate our limited forces to meet their naval advance on Midway when we otherwise would have been 3,000 miles out of place."*

From that time forward, Japan would be on the defensive for the rest of the war. The Rising Sun of Dai Nippon, which had shone so brightly for so many months, was beginning to set.

CHAPTER FIFTY-EIGHT

1942/1943/1944

Henry remembers:

"In 1942 we started to see the British stopping Rommel near Egypt and later the German defeat at El Alamein and their retreat towards Tunis, the Allied landings in (French) North Africa and there were American troops involved. The Russians had stopped the Germans in Stalingrad, encircled them and after killing most of them took the rest prisoner, about 300,000 men. Only long after the war we heard that only about 5,000 came back, the rest died in the Gulags. We were hoping for a second front, but that would take a little longer. In the meantime our family managed to survive, Pa sick, and most of the time everybody was hungry. I remember the onion soup for breakfast; hot water with dried onions. Believe me; if there is nothing else you will eat it.

At one time we managed to get a couple of dozen boxes with custard pudding. We thought it was pretty good cooked in water without sugar. And that was just the beginning; the worst time came in the last half year of the war.

Sugar beets, tulip bulbs, and some kind of foam (whipped cream) that filled your stomach and within half an hour it passed into the open air. (I said it would be G-rated)

1943 was not a good year in occupied Holland. The deportations were going on, and by now we knew that they were killing the Jews, but we did not realize the scale of the murders. If they caught you helping them, you could join them and end up in one of the concentration camps or be shot out right."

"What was it like to be 13 years old and growing up during the Nazi occupation of Holland?"
I have been asked that question many times during the past sixty years and there was never an easy and quick answer. It always turned out that I would tell a story of the later years of the war when the

327

situation of our livelihood got worse and worse. It always centered on fear of one kind or another. Fear of getting killed, fear of getting picked up and tortured by the *'bad'* guys. Fear of losing your parents, siblings and friends. Fear of betrayal. Fear of losing your home. Fear of having nothing to eat. Fear of having nothing to keep you warm during the winter months. Fear for the allied flyers that on a daily basis flew over our country on their way to Germany as well as for the soldiers fighting on our behalf in far-off places around the world. Fear of losing the war and being forever stuck with the Germans. Whatever happened, there was always that fear factor. Next to this *'fear'* factor there was the occasional *'excitement'* of coming through unscathed. The 'highs and the lows' that we experienced were like a roller coaster ride. Just think how good you felt when you finally left the damn ride and told yourself: "Never again!" When exposed to these feelings day-in and day-out it becomes almost 'routine' and since everyone in the city was undergoing basically the same pressures and experiencing the same events it became bearable and we endured it stoically. As I said in the opening of this book: *"In spite of everything we never lost our sense of humor"*. It is true that we never completely lost that sense but it became harder and harder the longer the war dragged on.

Let me try and tell you what it was like for me during a typical day in 1943 Rotterdam:

At the age of 13, I attended a Junior High School. It was called ULO or MULO but it can best be compared with Junior High in the States. At the time in Holland it was not uncommon for one teacher to teach just about every course; languages, sciences, mathematics, geography; world, local and natural history and art. You always stayed in the same classroom. There were never any facilities for sports and I don't recall ever playing games during school hours. Classes would start at 8am in the morning and last till 3pm with an hour for lunch in between. Wednesday afternoons were free. I would leave the house at seven and with friends from the neighborhood would walk about 5 miles to school. Since the city had been leveled we took short-cuts across the heaps of rubble that covered most of downtown. We would always pass a spot with all kinds of signs pointing to German locations in the city.

266. German traffic signs in Rotterdam

Once in school we were seated at wooden desks; two to a desk. The only two girls in class were sitting together in front of me. Teachers were under strict orders from the German controlled Department of Education. Political discussions were not allowed and least of all criticism of the Nazi government. Teachers had to be very careful because they couldn't always trust their own students. Over time it became quite obvious who was on what side of the war. In my class we were all anti-German. The curriculum called for lessons in Dutch, English, French and German. Two years into the war we were no longer allowed to study English and had to double up on German. Our teacher ignored that and it resulted in the students doubling up on English instead and no German lessons at all. Suited me fine; all of us felt that we had to prepare for our liberation by the English speaking Allies. Toward the end of the war I was a lot better in English than German.

As I mentioned earlier, our history books had been removed during the first year of the war and came back to us with passages blacked out. Our teacher would tell us what had been eliminated and we drew our own conclusions. School cafeterias were unknown in Holland. You either went home to have lunch or you brought your own sandwich and apple.

Often enough the air-raid sirens would sound and in a short time allied bombers would be flying over.

267.A typical air raid siren

Unless it was obvious that they came to bomb we would not seek shelter. Planes on their way to Germany would usually fly at a very high altitude leaving hundreds of contrails in the sky.

268. B-17 formation leaving contrails

Rarely would the German anti-aircraft guns be shooting at these planes: undoubtedly because they were flying too high. With all the Germans around day-and-night those contrails were like constant reminders that sooner or later we would be liberated; we had not been forgotten. If it were a real bombing mission of targets in the harbor area we would go into the air raid shelter and wait until the all clear sounded.

269. A typical air raid shelter

All of this became routine but it didn't do much for continuity of our lessons. In the beginning of the war when there was still unlimited electricity we would be given home-work. That changed when our electricity became rationed and we would only have a few hours at night. During the last year of the war we didn't even have that and it became *"A world lit only by fire"*. (The title of a great little book by the famous author William Manchester)

At three o'clock we would leave school and walk home the same way we had come. I remember that we always tried to avoid the Germans but that wasn't always possible.

We always had to pass by the Headquarters of the SD (Sicherheitdienst); the German Security Police; a big building on the corner of a wide boulevard, the Mathenesserlaan and Heemraadsingel. We knew that there were political prisoners being held and tortured in that building. Occasionally we could hear screaming when we passed by and we would quicken our step. On November 29, 1944 Typhoons from the Royal Air Force, some flown by Dutch pilots who knew their way around Rotterdam, strafed and bombed this building. The RAF had been requested by the Dutch Resistance Movement to destroy the building because it held files on thousands of Dutch citizens that were implicated in anti-Nazi activities. When this attack happened we were still in the classroom. We could hear the planes and explosions but didn't know what the target was. After the 'all clear' we were allowed to leave and then found out what had occurred.

Typhoons are fighter planes carrying rockets. They had come in flying low over the wide boulevard and had actually fired rockets straight through the large front doors of the building. Unfortunately, the bombs these planes were carrying were released a fraction of a second too late and they hit a building behind the SD Headquarters where it killed innocent civilians. Nonetheless a lot of damage was done to the SD building and quite a few Nazis were killed as well as several prisoners. A few prisoners were able to escape.

Het SD-kantoor aan de Heemraadssingel 226 na
het bombardement

270. The SD building after the attack by Typhoons of the
RAF on November 29, 1944

271. The back of the SD building after strafing and
bombing

272. Some of the inside damage

273. The air pressure made one Nazi connect with the
wall.

One of the phosphorous bombs had hit the overhead cables of the
streetcar system nearby and then came apart against the side of
a building. It didn't explode but there was white phosphorous all
over the street and wall. Naturally I had to have some of it. I must
mention that it had been raining and the chunk of phosphor that I

took home was wet. When I came home I proudly showed it to my brother Henry. He got angry and called me names. How could I be so stupid as to pick up phosphor? *"Don't you know that when it dries up it will ignite automatically?"* No, I didn't know that. Henry put it in a metal bucket and sure enough, when the piece dried up it started to burn with a nice rosy flame.

274. White phosphor

He must have doused it with more water and I don't remember what happened to it. That was a good lesson.

Henry remembers:

"We had an interesting air raid that year. The alert sounded and I went on the roof at Stokvis and saw several fighter-bombers diving at an area fairly close and fire a bunch of rockets. They had attacked the Sicherheitsdienst Headquarters on the Heemraadsingel corner Mathenesserlaan.

We saw later some big holes in the walls and the front of the building had been damaged. We were glad that they did not hit the building next door where the archives of the City were stored. In between somewhere were also some Jewish people hidden. They did not have a scratch.

I believe that this is the air raid where Bill picked up some phosphorus from a rocket that hit the overhead tramline. It had been raining and there were puddles of water, some phosphorus fell in the water. Bill was under the mistaken assumption that I could make a bomb out of it. He took it home in his (wet) handkerchief and showed it to me. I made a few excited remarks, took him downstairs to the bathroom and stuck his hand in the tub with emergency water and washed his hands. The phosphorus was buried in the backyard. We had already some holes there where some incendiaries had fallen during another raid. They went too deep to dig them out. May be they are still there.

I emphatically explained to Bill that when the phosphorus dries out it starts burning and will not readily stop. He was lucky in keeping it in a wet rag".

On another occasion I found an unexploded incendiary bomb on *'Het Land van Hoboken'*. (You may remember that this was the area where the refugees from the German bombing of Rotterdam had taken refuge and camped out for months). It was lying there among the debris. It had the shape of large six-sided pencil about 20 inches long and three inches wide. Suffice to say I left it where it was but it would have made a nice addition to my collection of shrapnel.

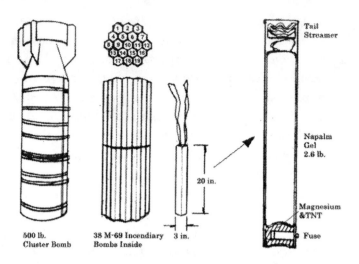

500 lb.
Cluster Bomb

38 M-69 Incendiary   3 in.
Bombs Inside

20 in.

Tail
Streamer

Napalm
Gel
2.6 lb.

Magnesium
&TNT

Fuse

275. Incendiary bomb cluster

I remember being always hungry. Food was rationed but in 1943 there was still enough to eat. No great variety but enough potatoes and veggies to fill you up. Whatever meat we could buy with our coupons went to my dad who was bedridden with tuberculoses. Mother took extra good care of him. Occasionally we would get some fruit; an apple or a pear; never a banana or an orange. I had forgotten what they looked like. To compensate for the lack of much needed Vitamin C we were given little white tablets at school. They were sour tasting but quite good. Bread, milk, sugar, cookies and candy were rationed as well as everything else. During the last year of the war we had coupons for food and clothing but no where to buy it.

In the Dunantstraat I had several friends and we would play the usual children games. I also enjoyed being home and tinker around in our cellar. My dad had started my interest in stamp collecting and occasionally I would go to the 'Stamp Market' on the Noordplein in the city to trade or buy used stamps for pennies. The Dutch Nazi Regime had replaced the pre-war Dutch stamps showing the likeness of the Queen with designs of famous Dutch seafarers. In 1942 the Post Office issued a set of stamps devoted to the Dutch SS volunteers, called 'Legioen Zegels'. (Legion Stamps)

276. The set of Legion Stamps issued in 1942

277. 1943-1944 stamps of Dutch Naval Heroes

Our pre-war silver and nickel coins were replaced by coins made from zinc.

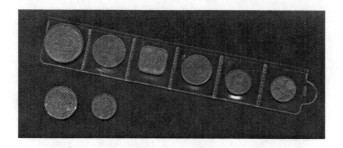

278. Zinc wartime coins, front and back

At night our movement was restricted by a curfew and, depending on the time of the year, we were no longer allowed to be outside after a certain hour. That resulted in a lot of in-door time and we would play cards or table games, like *"Mens Erger Je Niet"*: a well-known Dutch board game. My father and his younger brother Willem (Oom Wim) would be smoking cigarettes. (My dad would smoke in spite of his illness. He only stopped smoking a few years before he died from emphysema at age 82). I remember the cigarette brand: 'Rhodesia'. They smelled terrible but for staunch and addicted smokers it was all they could get. People said that 'Rhodesia' stood for: **R**egering **H**olland **O**ntdekte **D**eze **E**llendige **S**igaretten **I**n **A**frica. Translated in English: *Government Holland Discovered These Horrible Cigarettes In Africa*

At night my brother Henry could be found in the cellar listening to the BBC. A cave had been hollowed out at the end of the cellar where it extended under the street. It had a phony wall with shelves that hid the space from view. Henry had tapped into electrical cables under the street and according to Henry: "Whenever the Krauts in the bunker at the end of our street have electricity, so do we!" In that small cave was our Philips radio with the loudspeakers disconnected in favor of head phones. Otherwise the speaker sound might give us away. On the wall was a map of Europe extending all the way to the Ural Mountains in Russia. It also showed the coast of Africa all the way from Morocco to Egypt. Little pins were used to show the war's progress.

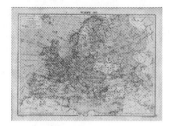

279. Map of Europe and North Africa 1942

Henry was then 19 years old. He was employed at Stokvis N.V. on the Westzeedijk He would take the news down in shorthand and after work he would find time to translate it and type it up in Dutch; five copies at a time. More copies with the black stencil paper in between would make it unreadable. Henry was by that time involved in the resistance but we didn't know it.

280. Stokvis N.V., Henry's employer.

Henry remembers:

"As far as the Resistance movement went we could not do much, except resist passively any orders from the Germans or their Dutch Nazi friends. Sometimes we could take a more active role.

The German losses in Russia were horrendous and they needed manpower for their war industry. The Germans themselves were drafted into the army from 17 years up to retirement age, which took a lot of people out of the war industry.

They started to take inventory of foreign labor. Every company had to fill out a form with all the vital information of everybody working there and what they did. Those forms were called "Q-cards". Everybody was dragging their heels, but eventually the cards at Stokvis were ready.

Piet Jesse and I found out where the cards were stored. There were always friendly people that would tell you.

We did get a hold of the two boxes with Q cards including the copies, but to get them out of the plant was something else. We decided not to take them out, but simply store them in the old archives. You could never find anything there anyway. We put them behind stacks of dirty boxes and paper. They never found them. We were questioned by the personnel director (his nickname was 'the tapeworm'). Of course we did not know anything, we could prove we left with other people and were not carrying any packages.

A couple of weeks after the liberation we stopped by at Stokvis to tell them "WE QUIT".

We went to the personnel director who turned very white when he saw us. We were well armed! When we told him we were quitting he was obviously relieved until we asked him: "Do you remember the Q cards?" I thought he would pee in his pants. He started heehawing, telling us he could not help it, etc.

We listened to his apologies and then told him:

"If you still want them, you can find them in the old archives".

Henry, Annie and I slept in the souterrain cellar. Annie had her own room with a small window high up in the wall at street level. In wintertime that cellar was colder than a witch's "you-know-what". If we only would have had light and fluffy eider-down blankets but all we had were heavy woolen blankets. It was like sleeping under a cover of lead. It would always take us a long time to get warm. In the morning we would wash ourselves with cold water. We didn't have a regular water heater. I don't believe anyone in our street had one either. I don't think they existed. Only in the bathroom in the basement did we have a contraption for the bath water. That was a dangerous appliance. It had to be lit every time you wanted to heat the water. First you lit a match and then turned on the gas. By the time the match was manipulated under the cover so much gas had accumulated that it would result in an explosion that shook everything. It was outright dangerous and I hated the thing. We would take a bath maybe every other week. Deodorant was unknown in those days but there was soap. Clothes were washed by hand. Washing machines, clothes dryers and refrigerators only came much later after the war. With so much rain in Holland, mother would hang the clothes after washing in the basement to dry. Not only would the cellar be cold but it would then be clammy as well. Our house upstairs at street-level was heated by one regular coal-burning stove. That stove would have to heat three rooms and the kitchen and then only when we had coal. In winter time with little fuel we would wear our overcoats all the time. Not having a refrigerator necessitated the purchase of food every day except in winter time when we could keep it outside on our balcony in the freezing cold. Venders would come through the street: the greengrocer, the baker and the milkman. A horse pulled the greengrocer's wagon. The milkman and the baker came on their peddle-driven tricycle. This three-wheeler had a large rectangular box, containing their wares, resting on the axle of the two front wheels.

We had a very small kitchen with one small natural gas burner for the cooking, a small sink for the dishes and storage cabinets around the wall. There was just enough room for two people to stand next to each other. To this day I find it remarkable how my mother was able to cook a meal of meat and potatoes, vegetables, gravy and whatever else and then serving it all nice and hot at the same time. She would even make some dessert in that *'closet'*. Breakfast and lunch would be bread with margarine spread and cheese, jam or chocolate sprinkles. I liked it with plain sugar. Cheese was also a favorite and in Holland we produce a lot of different cheeses, Edam, Gouda, old or new and *'cumin'* cheese (my favorite). Sometimes when there was enough money we would get a soft-boiled egg. After Field Marshall Montgomery's fiasco at Arnhem (part of Operation Market-Garden in September 1944), we would no longer get any of this food. A matter of fact, toward the end of 1944 we wouldn't have any food at all. But that is another story.

During the night when there was an air raid alert our parents would awaken us. That happened often enough. Sirens would be wailing like a bunch of banshees. For a long time we would hide under our bridge at the Coolhaven and as a result lost a lot of sleep. After a while we stopped doing that and decided that if it is our *'time'* so be it. We just stayed in bed and ignored it.

In the Dunantstraat we had to our knowledge only one *'verified'* Nazi collaborator, a woman of about 35. She kept to herself but on many occasions was visited by high-ranking officers of the Abwehr, not the Gestapo; their automobiles parked on our street. The Abwehr was the secret police of the German Army. The Gestapo was the Secret State Police of the Nazis. We concluded that she was a German spy reporting on possible anti-Nazi activities in our neighborhood. With this German collaborator in our midst we had to be extremely careful and circumspect. We always tried to avoid her as much as possible and never made eye contact. It dawned on us that she might have been the person shooting at our Dutch soldiers on the bridge during the first days of the war. We figured that we would deal with her after our liberation. On November 11, 1944 there was an occasion when we wondered about that action._

CHAPTER FIFTY-NINE

THE DIEPPE DISASTER
VICTORY AT EL ALAMEIN

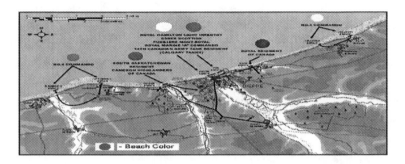

281. Map of the Dieppe coastal area.

The Dieppe raid was an allied attack on the German-occupied port of Dieppe on the Northern Coast of France on August 19, 1942. Over six thousand infantrymen, predominantly Canadian, were supported by large British naval and air forces. It was intended to seize and hold a major port for a short period, both to prove it was possible and to gather intelligence from prisoners and captured material while assessing the German responses; the raid was also intended to use air power to draw the Luftwaffe into a large planned encounter.

The raid was generally considered to be an unmitigated disaster, with no major objectives accomplished. 4,384 of the 6,086 men who made it ashore were killed, wounded, or captured. The RAF and RCAF failed to lure the Luftwaffe into open battle, and lost 119 planes, whilst the Royal Navy suffered 555 casualties. The only redeeming value of this catastrophe at Dieppe may have been the lessons learned. It influenced Allied preparations for Operation Torch and Overlord, the landing in Normandy on June 6, 1944.

Naturally, the German controlled Dutch press made hay from this event. First we didn't know what to believe but then the BBC confirmed the fact that it had failed to achieve its objectives and that the landing force had been withdrawn back to England. To say it shocked us was an understatement. But then we reasoned that it had been more of an exercise than the real thing. Nonetheless, we realized that we would have to wait a lot longer for our liberation.

El Alamein

Two months after the disastrous Dieppe Raid the BBC provided some good news. Field Marshall Montgomery had won the battle at El Alamein in North Africa. Rommel, the Desert Fox had been defeated. This battle marked a significant turning point in the Western Desert Campaign of World war II. The battle lasted from October 23 to November 3, 1942. The Allied victory at El Alamein ended the German hopes of occupying Egypt, controlling access to the Suez Canal, and gaining access to the Middle Eastern oil fields. The German defeat at El Alamein marked the end of German expansion.

282. Map of the Battle of El Alamein

CHAPTER SIXTY

IKE AND PAUL

On November 5, 1942, preparatory to the invasion of North Africa, a B-17 Flying Fortress named *Red Gremlin* flew General Dwight D. Eisenhower to Gibraltar. What is interesting about this flight is that the B-17 was piloted by the man who would less than 3 years later pilot the B-29 Enola Gay and drop the first atomic bomb on Hiroshima, Japan. His name: Paul Tibbits Jr.

He also piloted the first B-17 to cross the English Channel and bomb German-occupied Europe in the Rouen-Sotteville raid, which was the first mission of the Eighth Army Air Force of World War II.

Eisenhower had planned to go to Gibraltar on November 2, to take command of the Rock, the best communications center in the area, and direct the invasion from there. Bad weather prevented the flight on November 2 and again on the third; on the fourth Eisenhower ordered his reluctant pilot, by reputation the best flier in the Army Air Force, to ignore the weather and take off. Six B-17 Flying Fortresses, carrying Eisenhower and most of his staff got through safely, but only after engine trouble, weather problems, and an attack by a German fighter airplane had been overcome.

Credits: The Victors by Stephen E. Ambrose

CHAPTER SIXTY-ONE

BATTLE OF STALINGRAD "THE BIGGEST BATTLE EVER FOUGHT"

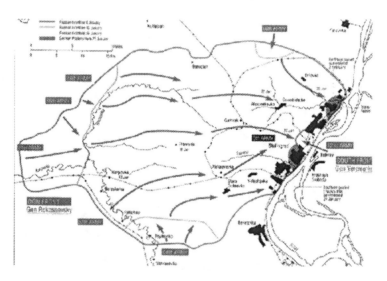

283. Map of the Stalingrad battlefield

The Battle of Stalingrad was a turning point in World War II and is considered the bloodiest battle in human history, with more combined casualties suffered than any battle before or since. The battle was marked by brutality and disregard for military and civilian casualties on both sides. Total casualties for both sides are estimated to be over two million. The axis powers suffered roughly 850,000 casualties, ¼ of their strength on the Eastern front, as well as huge sums of supplies and equipment. The Axis forces were never able to recover from this loss and were eventually forced into a long protracted retreat out of Eastern Europe. For the Soviets, who also suffered great losses during the battle, the victory at Stalingrad marked the start

347

of the liberation of the Soviet Union and leading to eventual victory over Nazi Germany in 1945.

In December 1941 the Soviet forces counter-attacked in the Battle of Moscow. The German forces, ill equipped for winter warfare and with overstretched supply lines, were stopped in their drive towards the capital. The Germans stabilized their front by spring 1942 but Hitler discarded the taking of Moscow as too predictable. Following the Japanese attack on Pearl Harbor in Hawaii, the United States had entered the war and the German high command knew that time was running out for them. Hitler was eager to end the fighting on the Eastern front or at least minimize it before the US had a chance to get too deeply involved in the war in Europe. For all these reasons, new offensives in the north and south were considered. A drive into the southern USSR would secure control of the oil-rich Caucasus, as well as the Volga River, a backbone of Soviet transportation from Central Asia. A German victory in the southern Soviet Union would severely damage Stalin's war machine and the Soviet economy.

Army Group South was selected for a sprint forward through the southern Russian steppes into the Caucasus to capture the vital Soviet oil fields. These oil fields were a key goal for Hitler and instead of focusing his attention on the key capital of Moscow like his generals advised, he continued to send his forces and supplies to the southern Russian front. Hitler then intervened and split the Army Group in A and B. Army Group South (A) under the command of Paul Ludwig Ewald von Kleist, was to continue advancing south towards the Caucasus. Army Group (B) including Friedrich Paulus' 6th Army and Hermann Hoth's 4th Panzer Army was to move east toward the river Volga and the city of Stalingrad.

The capture of Stalingrad was important to Hitler for several reasons. It was a major industrial city on the banks of the river Volga. Its capture would secure the left flank of the German armies as they advanced into the Caucasus. Finally, the fact that the city bore the name of Hitler's nemesis, Joseph Stalin, would make the city's capture an ideological and propaganda coup. Joseph Stalin had his own ideological and propaganda reasons for defending the city that bore his name.

Army Group South began its attack on June 28, 1942. It started well. Soviet forces offered little resistance in the vast empty steppes, and started streaming eastward in disarray. The initial advance of the German 6th Army was so successful that Hitler intervened once again, and ordered the 4th Panzer Army to join Army Group South (A) to the south. A massive traffic jam resulted when the 4th Army and the 6th Army both required the few roads in the area. Both armies were stopped dead while they attempted to clear the resulting mess of thousands of vehicles. The delay was long, and it is thought that it cost the advance at least one week. With the advance now slowed, Hitler changed his mind and re-assigned the 4th Panzer back to the attack on Stalingrad.

By the end of July the Germans had pushed the Soviets across the Don River. The 6th Army was only a few dozen kilometers from Stalingrad, and the 4th Panzer, now to their south, turned north to help take the city. To the south, Group A was pushing far into the Caucasus, but their advance slowed. Group A's forces were deployed far to the south and provided no support to Group B in the north.

Now German intentions became clear to the Soviet commanders: in July Soviet plans were developed for the defense in Stalingrad. Soviet troops still moving eastward before the German offensive were ordered into Stalingrad. The eastern border of Stalingrad was the broad Volga River, and over the river additional Soviet units were deployed. This combination of units became the newly formed 62nd Army under the command of Vasily Chuikov.

284. Vasily Chuikov, Hero of Stalingrad

Its mission was to defend Stalingrad at all cost. The battle began with the heavy bombing of the city by the Luftwaffe. The sprawling metropolis became a graveyard. Many died once the battle began and the city became a shell of what it once was. Still, many buildings survived and Soviet patriotism shone through. Many factory workers joined in the fighting.

Stalin prevented civilians from leaving the city on the premise that their presence would encourage greater resistance from the city's defenders. Civilians, including women and children, were put to work building trench works and protective fortifications. A massive German air bombardment on 23 August caused a firestorm, killing thousands and turning Stalingrad into a vast landscape of rubble and burnt ruins; 80% of the living space in the city was destroyed.

The burden of the initial defense of the city proper fell on the 1077th Anti-aircraft regiment, a unit made up mainly of young women volunteers who had no training on engaging ground targets. Despite this and with no support available from other Soviet units, these women stayed at their posts and took on the advancing panzers. The 16th Panzer Division reportedly had to fight the 1077th gunners *"shot for shot"* until all 37 AA batteries were destroyed or overrun.

The Soviet need for equipment was so great that tanks were driven to the front line, often without paint or even gun sights. Fighting in the city was fierce and desperate. The life expectancy of a newly arrived Soviet private in the city dropped to less than twenty-four hours. Stalin decreed that all those who retreated or otherwise left their positions without orders could be summarily shot. *"Not a step back!"* was the slogan.

German military doctrine was based on the principle of combined-arms teams and close co-operation by tanks, infantry, engineers, and artillery and ground-attack aircraft. To counter this, Soviet commanders adopted the simple expedient of always keeping the front lines as close together as physically possible. Chuikov called this tactic *"hugging"* the Germans. This forced the German infantrymen to either fight on their own or risk taking casualties from their own supporting fire; it neutralized German close air support and weakened their artillery support. Bitter fighting raged for every street, every factory, every house, basement and staircase. The Germans, calling this unseen urban warfare *Rattenkrieg,* 'rat-war' and bitterly joked about capturing the kitchen but still fighting for the living room.

Fighting on Mamayev Kurgan, a prominent, blood-soaked hill above the city, was particularly merciless. The height changed hands many times. During one Soviet counter-attack, they lost an entire division of 10,000 men in one day. At the Grain Elevator, a huge grain processing complex dominated by a single enormous silo, combat was so close that Soviet and German soldiers could hear each other breathe. Combat raged there for weeks until the German Army reduced the opposition. In another part of the city, a Soviet platoon under the command of Yakov Pavlov turned an apartment building into an impenetrable fortress.

285. Yakov Pavlov and the Pavlov House

The building, later called "Pavlov's House" oversaw a square in the city centre.

286. Monument of Children at Play in Stalingrad

The soldiers surrounded it with minefields, set up machine-gun positions at the windows, and breached the walls in the basement for better communications.

With no end in sight, the Germans started transferring heavy artillery to the city, including a gigantic 800 mm mortar. The Germans made no effort to send a force across the Volga, allowing the Soviets to build up a large number of artillery batteries there. Soviet artillery on the eastern bank continued to bombard the German positions. The Soviet defenders used the resulting ruins as defensive positions. German tanks became useless amid heaps of rubble up to eight meters high. When they were able to move forward, they came under Soviet anti-tank fire from wrecked buildings. Soviet snipers also successfully used the ruins to inflict heavy casualties on the Germans. The most successful sniper was Ivan Mihailovich Sidorenko of the 1122nd rifle regiment who had made approximately 500 kills by the end of the war. Vasily Grigoyevich Zaitsev was credited with more than 400 kills during the battle.

Vassili Zaitsev a Stalingrado, Ottobre 1942

287. Vassili Zaitsev (Jude Law in the movie)

For both Stalin and Hitler, the battle of Stalingrad became a prestige issue, on top of the actual strategic significance of the battle. The Soviet command moved the Red Army's strategic reserves from the Moscow area to the lower Volga, and transferred aircraft from the entire country to the Stalingrad region. The strain on both military commanders was immense: Paulus developed an uncontrollable tic in his eye, while Chuikov experienced an outbreak of eczema that required him to bandage his hands completely. The troops on both sides faced the constant strain of close-range combat.

Chuikov's plan was to keep pinning the Germans down in the city, and then to punch through the overstretched and weakly defended German flanks and to surround the Germans inside Stalingrad.

288. Chuikov and his commanders

The attacking Soviet units consisted of three complete armies.

The Romanians, who continued to push for reinforcements, only to be refused again, could hear the preparations for the attack. Thinly spread, outnumbered and poorly equipped, the 3ʳᵈ Romanian Army, which held the northern flank of the German 6ᵗʰ Army, was shattered after an almost miraculous one-day defense. On November 20, a second Soviet offensive was launched to the south of Stalingrad. The Romanian forces collapsed almost immediately. Soviet forces raced west in a pincer movement, and met two days later near the town of Kalach, sealing the ring around Stalingrad. Because of this brilliant pincer attack, about 250,000 German and Romanian soldiers found themselves trapped inside the resulting pocket.

A planned air supply mission failed almost immediately. Heavy Soviet anti-aircraft fire and fighter interceptions (many flown by Soviet women pilots) led to the loss of many German transport aircraft.

289. Soviet Women Pilots

290. Natalya Meklin, Fighter Pilot, Order of "Hero of the
Soviet Union"

In general only ten percent of the needed supplies could be delivered.
The 6th Army slowly starved. One general at the German high
command, moved by the troops plight at Stalingrad, began to limit
himself to their slim rations at meal times. After a few weeks of

such diet he'd grown so emaciated that Hitler, annoyed, personally ordered him to start eating regular meals again.

291. "Stalingrad" Movie Poster
Credits: Internet Movie Database

292. "Enemy at the Gates" poster
Credits: Internet Movie Database.

In spite of a lack of food and ammunition the Germans continued to resist stubbornly, partly because they believed the Soviets would execute those who surrendered.

Hitler promoted Paulus to Generalfeld Marshall on January 30, 1943. Since no German field marshal had ever been taken prisoner, Hitler assumed that Paulus would fight on or take his own life.

293. Friedrich von Paulus (1890-1957)

Nevertheless, when Soviet forces closed in on Paulus' headquarters in the ruined GUM department store, Paulus surrendered.

294. Friedrich von Paulus and his generals following their surrender.

The remnants of the German forces in Stalingrad surrendered on February 2, 1943; 91,000 tired, ill and starving Germans were taken captive.

295. The Battle has been won

To the delight of the Soviet forces and the dismay of the Reich, the prisoners included 22 generals. Hitler was angry at the Field Marshall's surrender and confided: *"Paulus stood at the doorsteps of eternal glory but made an about-face".*

The battle of Stalingrad was the largest single battle in human history. It raged for 199 days. Numbers of casualties on the axis side are estimated at 850,000 of all types among all branches of the German armed forces. The Red Army suffered 478,741 men killed and 650,878 wounded (for a total of 1,129,619)

For the heroism of the Soviet defenders of Stalingrad, the city was awarded the title *Hero City* in 1945. After the war, in the 1960s, a colossal monument of *'Mother Russia'* was erected on *Mamayev Kurgan*, the hill overlooking the city.

296. *"Mother Russia"*

The statue forms part of a memorial complex that includes ruined walls deliberately left the way they were after the battle. The Grain Elevator, as well as Pavlov's House, the apartment building whose defenders eventually held out for two months until they were relieved, can still be visited. One may, even today, find bones and rusty metal splinters on *Mamayev Kurgan*, symbols of both the human suffering during the battle and the successful yet costly resistance against the German invasion.

Where before the German controlled press in Holland had been trumpeting the German victories in the Soviet Union at every opportunity, toward the end of December 1942 and beginning January 1943 the press had become noticeably less optimistic and it was only at the end of January 1943 when the papers were giving hints that things were not going according to plan with statements such as: *"Heavy fighting of man to man is continuing in the city of Stalingrad. Enemy casualties are running into the thousands. The victorious German 6th Army is continuing its push toward the river Volga"*. Everyday we would be reading between the lines what we already knew from listening to the BBC in London. (The Germans were indeed approaching the Volga River because unrelenting Soviet forces were driving them there). That we were overjoyed was an understatement. Our hatred for the Germans at that time was such that we relished the fact that thousands upon thousands were being killed every day. To us in Holland, the only good German was a dead German. Today it is difficult to imagine how we felt in those war years and how bloodthirsty we had become. The true extent of the battle could only be imagined. The battle lasted for 199 days and history now shows that there were about two million casualties on both sides. Only 6,000 of the 91,000 German prisoners of war survived their captivity and returned home.

CHAPTER SIXTY-TWO

"I WANT MY BICYCLE BACK!"

When in Holland you can't help noticing that the Dutch like bikes. In fact, the 750,000 people who live in Amsterdam own approximately 600,000 bicycles.

297. Bicycles in Amsterdam

At the present time there are alternatives to the bike but during the war, aside from streetcars, the only transportation to and from work was the bicycle. The bicycle therefore is an integral part of Dutch life.

During the spring of 1942 the Germans started to prepare for the expected Allied invasion and they began constructing the Atlantic Wall. In spite of the fact that the land behind the Dutch coast would not be suited for heavy tanks from an invasion force the Germans nonetheless were anxious to prepare for the eventuality. On July 9, 1942 the Commander of the Wehrmacht Christiansen wrote a letter to Seyss-Inquart telling him that he needed a minimum of 100,000 bicycles within 8 to 14 days. *"These bicycles"*, according to Christiansen, *"are of the utmost importance for a more rapid movement of the reserves to the invasion beaches. A delay of half an hour can make the difference between success and failure." The question was how to get 100,000 bicycles in short order?* They had already taken 10,000 from the Jews in Amsterdam and surroundings. However, these bicycles were in a reportedly poor shape and only about 1,000 were usable. Bicycle factories were no longer producing bikes because there were no longer any tires.

Seyss-Inquart decided on July 14 that the quickest way to obtain the bikes was to confiscate them from the public at large. And that's how the *"grand theft bicycles"* started in the 144 municipalities with more than 10,000 inhabitants. Quotas were established for the big metropolitan areas: Amsterdam 8,000 bikes, The Hague 4,000, Rotterdam 3,300 (somewhat less than the other cities because it was felt that the people had suffered already enough as a result of the May 14, 1940 bombing by the Luftwaffe). Mayors of the 144 municipalities were notified by phone immediately with orders to confiscate the bicycles from the population. Exceptions were made for people in the Police and Fire Department, as well as farmers and those people involved in the Air Defense. The results were not encouraging. Word had gotten out and people were hiding their bicycles or taking them apart and burying the parts. After some time however, when people thought that the danger had passed, they were back on their bikes. That's when the Germans decided that the quickest way of obtaining the bikes would be right on the street. Another advantage of that action would be that these bikes usually still had rubber tires. That's how the Germans finally got their bikes. To say that the Dutch population was upset is a gross understatement. The loss of a bike was akin to people in the *'Wild West'* having their horse stolen. Or, in general terms of today, losing their automobile. That is also how our family lost their bikes with the exception of my father who was bedridden with Tuberculoses. His bike was hidden in our basement. Over time we were able to scratch together enough parts to manufacture two bikes but we never had the tires for them and we rode these bikes on the rims. Our bikes were never returned to us and having long memories the Dutch never have forgotten the fact. On one occasion in 1966 we were once again reminded of the loss of these bicycles in 1942/1943.

Princess Beatrix, the current Queen of the Netherlands, married Prince Claus von Amsberg, a German who as a youngster had served in the Hitler Jugend and the German Army. The Dutch population was not pleased with the choice of a German so soon after the war. In time, Claus* was accepted by the public and became the most popular member of the royal family. In 1966 however, that was not the case and there were protests.

The wedding of Beatrix and Claus took place in the Westerkerk in Amsterdam on March 10, 1966. It was televised and Diny my wife and I were watching it in our home in Huizen, t'Gooi, Holland.

298. Wedding Picture of Beatrix and Claus

The procession, watched by thousands of people along the route, moved slowly through the heart of the city when all of a sudden the television camera panned up toward the Keizersgracht patrician houses. What we saw was hilarious and gave the Dutch people who watched something to smile about. From two third-story windows about 20 feet apart several people were holding what looked like a large white bed sheet that, in Dutch, read:

Ik wil mijn fiets terug!
(I want my bicycle back!)

*The reasons for the change in Dutch opinion were Claus' strong motivation to contribute to public causes, especially third world development, his sincere modesty, his candidness (within, but sometimes on the edge of, royal protocol), and his approachability to all layers of society.

The public also sympathized with Claus for his efforts to give meaning to his life beyond the restrictions that Dutch law posed on freedom of speech and action of the royal family (lest they get involved in political controversy). Many also believed that these restrictions were at least partly the cause of his severe depression, which lasted many years. As a result, restrictions were loosened; Claus was even appointed as senior staff member at the Department of Developing Aid.

A fine example of his mildly rebellious attitude toward protocol was the "Declaration of the Tie". In 1998, after presenting the annual Claus Award to three African fashion designers, Claus told *"workers of all nations to unite and cast away the new shackles they have voluntarily cast upon themselves"*, meaning the necktie, that *"snake around my neck"*, and encouraged the audience to *"venture into open-collar paradise"*. Then Claus removed his tie and threw it to the ground.

Claus suffered various health problems during his life, such as depression, cancer and Parkinson's disease. He died on October 6, 2002 after a long illness. His embalmed body was placed in the royal family's tomb in Delft on October 15. It was the first full state funeral since Wilhelmina's in 1962.

CHAPTER SIXTY-THREE

THE FIVE HOSTAGES OF ROTTERDAM

In the course of 1942 a resistance group was formed made up of mainly members of the illegal Dutch Communist Party (CPN) The group called itself the *"Dutch People Militia"*; its leader was Samuel Zacharias Dormits. In 1937 he had fought in Spain on the side of the Republicans and as a result had military experience. In the summer of 1942 he proposed a *'spectacular'* attack. His plan involved blowing up a train loaded with German soldiers on leave. He had done considerable research and knew when the train would depart the Beurs station on its way to the Delfse Poort station. A large load of explosives would be detonated at the moment that the train would pass over this part of the rails. The explosives had come from the National Coal Mines in the province of Limburg. On August 7 at 6:45 they succeeded in attaching the explosives. A trip wire was attached and extended under the viaduct to the two perpetrators that would be waiting for the train. The train was delayed for several minutes and just during that time a railway employee on his bicycle was passing along the rails. One of his pedals caught one of the wires and part of the explosive charge detonated. The railway employee was seriously hurt and the Germans were alerted. They located the explosive charge and removed it. Not a German had been harmed but Commander Christiansen of the German Army wanted revenge. He demanded of Seyss-Inquart that twenty hostages were to be executed. An example had to be set. At that moment more than 1,000 hostages were held in a jail in Noord Brabant province for that exact purpose. These were all prominent Dutch citizens well known to the population.
Seyss-Inquart had to make the decision and in the end decided on five hostages.

An effort was made to find the perpetrators and a reward of 100,000 guilders would be awarded the person reporting the guilty.

On August 8 Hans Rauter placed an announcement in the local media.

299. SS Gruppenfuehrer Hans Albin Rauter, Head of
Police in the Netherlands. (1895-1949)

The deadline for bringing the perpetrator(s) forward was August 14. Nobody came forward however, least of all the actual perpetrators. They concluded that their confession would jeopardize the whole organization and cause the death of far more that the five hostages. Relatives of the more than one-thousand hostages, that were being held, were beyond them selves. Their concern and dread increased by the minute the closer it moved toward the deadline. When the deadline passed, five prominent and innocent Rotterdam citizens were chosen and without further ado were executed. The next day the following announcement appeared in all Dutch Newspapers.

300. Announcement of the five executions

Epilogue

Understandably, Rauter became the most despised and hated senior SS Police Officer in the Netherlands. On the night of March 6, 1945 six members of the Dutch resistance were instructed by their commander to capture a German truck loaded with 3,000-kilo meat. The resistance movement needed both the truck and the meat. An employee of the meat plant in Epe had advised them of this shipment. At 10pm that night, dressed in German uniforms, they were hiding in the bushes next to the Woeste Hoeve Inn. At around mid-night a BMW cabriolet approached. Unbeknownst to the resistance fighters the most hated man in the Netherlands, Polizeifuehrer Hans Rauter, was in that car seated next to his driver. In the back of the car was Oberleutnant Exner.

Since they thought they also heard the sound of a truck, the resistance men ordered the BMW to stop. Rauter however, realizing that something was amiss, ordered his driver to keep going. Thereupon, the resistance men opened fire with their *Sten* guns.

301. British Sten gun.

In a few seconds all was over. They approached the car to ensure that everyone was dead.

302. Rauter's BMW Cabriolet

Rauter, however, was severely wounded and at six in the morning a German patrol finally found him and transported him to a hospital in Apeldoorn.

303. Rauter before and after

In an act of reprisal, several hundred prisoners were executed on March 8, 1945 at the scene of the attack. *One German Oberwachtmeister of the Ordnungspolizei who refused to participate in this killing was executed as well.*

304. Announcement of the execution of several hundred
prisoners.

Rauter was apprehended after the war and on April 1, 1948 the case
against him went to trial in a Special Tribunal in The Hague. On
May 4, 1948 he was sentenced to death and on March 25, 1949 was
executed for his crimes. His replacement, Schoengarth, who was
held responsible for the reprisals was sentenced to death by a British
tribunal and hanged.

CHAPTER SIXTY-FOUR

"JUST ONE CREW OUT OF THOUSANDS"

A Lancaster, Type III, with the markings ED423 VN-N from 50 Squadron took off from Skellingthorpe, England at 1905 on March 1, 1943. The plane was one of 302 aircraft – 156 Lancasters, 86 Halifaxes and 60 Stirlings. Their mission: Berlin

ED423's crew were:
Sergeant-Pilot David Thomas, 25 years old
Sergeant-Flight Engineer Clifford Howard Lewis, 19 years old
Sergeant-Navigator/Bomber Edward James Gray, age unknown
Sergeant-Gunner Leonard Arthur Ketley, age 20
Sergeant-Gunner Rupert Sutton Whittcombe, age 23
Sergeant-Gunner John Hughes, age 20
Sergeant-Gunner Robert Emmerson Stockburn, age 32
(Average age of the crew 23 years)

With the exception of Sgt Whittcombe who came from the Royal New Zealand Air Force the other six were from the RAF.

The RAF Bomber Command War Diaries provide the following report on this mission:

The Pathfinders experienced difficulty in producing concentrated marking because individual parts of the extensive built-up city area of Berlin could not be distinguished on the *H2S* screens. Bombing photographs showed that the attack was spread over more than 100 square miles with the main emphasis in the southwest of the city. However, because larger numbers of aircraft were now being used and because those aircraft were now carrying a greater average bomb load, the proportion of the force, which did hit Berlin, caused more damage than any previous raid to this target. This type of result – with significant damage still being caused by only partially successful attacks – was becoming a regular feature of Bomber Command Raids.

Much damage was caused in the south and west of Berlin. Twenty-Two acres of workshops were burnt out at the railway repair works at Tempelhof and 20 factories were badly damaged and 875 buildings - mostly houses – were destroyed. 191 people were killed. Some bombs hit the *Telefunken* works at which the *H2S* set taken from the Stirling shot down near Rotterdam was being reassembled. The set was completely destroyed in the bombing but a Halifax of 35 Squadron with intact set crashed in Holland on this same night and the Germans were able to resume their research into *H2S* immediately.

On January 30, 1943, *RAF bombers used H2S radar* for the first time and so became the first ground mapping radar to be used in combat.

The Germans were eager to get their hands on one of these sets and within a relatively short time they had developed an antidote.
Later in WWII the Luftwaffe night fighters used Naxos radar detectors to home in on the transmissions of *H2S*.

The above are all *'cold'* facts but what about the crews that flew this mission and so many others, every day, day-in, day out, for weeks and months and years.

Of this particular mission, out of a total of 302 aircraft, 20 aircraft were lost – 9 Lancasters, 6 Halifaxes and 5 Stirlings.
Thus far, these numbers are mere statistics.
With 20 aircraft lost out of 302, the overall loss is 6.6 percent. Not good, but *'acceptable'*. Still: *'cold'* facts.

But what about the 143 human beings involved in these 20 crashes?

Killed: 123
Injured: 4
POW's: 15
Evaded Capture: 1

Overnight 143 families in England and New Zealand were, in time, informed of the fate of their loved ones. The sorrow would be shared by a multiple of at least a few hundred friends and relatives for each of these men, totaling roughly 30,000 people. And this was just one raid on March1/2, 1943.

We tend to forget that these young men paid the ultimate prize so that in time we would be free and could go on with our lives, but not these young men. They died a horrible death at a young age.

On its return flight a Luftwaffe night fighter attacked ED423 VN-N over Holland. The plane was severely crippled and Sergeant Pilot Thomas was struggling to keep the plane in the air. Then in the area of Rotterdam it was attacked for the second time and the plane went into a dive from which it could not recover.
The plane crashed on March 2nd at 0044 at Ridderkerk (South Holland), 10 km SE from the center of Rotterdam.

All seven men of the crew were killed instantly and the bodies or what was left of them were taken to the Cemetery Crooswijk in Rotterdam. The graves were located in the immediate area of the entrance to the cemetery and thousands of Dutch citizens visited the graves and paid their respects as a sign of solidarity with our Allies. The Germans were bothered by this overt expression of sympathy for these fallen fighters. They ordered the bodies exhumed and reburied in a dark corner at the very end of the Cemetery. As a result more Dutch patriots then before visited the graves.

Edward James Gray is buried in Plot LL. Row 1, in a joint grave with his 19-year-old friend Clifford Lewis.

Immediately after the war my sister Annie, who had lost her boyfriend in a bombing in Germany, adopted the grave of one of these men: Sergeant–Navigator Edward James Gray and took care of it for a very long time until the Commonwealth War Graves Commission took over the maintenance.

305. Annie's Grave Adoption Certificate

When in Holland in 2005 at the 60th anniversary of the end of WWII on May 8, 1945, I visited Crooswijk Cemetery and found the graves of all seven men from Lancaster ED423. It is a beautiful and peaceful spot where these young men will be forever young while we grow old and remember them.

In Memory of
Sergeant Edward James Gray
1391377, 50 Sqn., RAF Volunteer Reserve who died on 02 March 1943
Remembered with honour
Rotterdam (Crooswijk) General Cemetery

Commemorated in perpetuity by the Commonwealth War Graves
Commission

306.

CHAPTER SIXTY-FIVE

"A VERY ACCURATE BOMBSIGHT!"

"IT CAN DROP A BOMB IN A BUCKET"
(AS LONG AS THE BUCKET IS LARGE ENOUGH)

During the spring of 1943 the German air *defense* got the upper hand over the Allied air *offense*: the German defense, executed primarily by their Luftwaffe fighters, had become so strong that the American Eighth Air Force and Bomber Command of the RAF were taking losses in bombers and resulting casualties that were considered totally unacceptable.

This resulted in the Americans ceasing bombing operations in the fall of '43 with the intent to start again as soon as they were able to have long-distance fighters accompany the vulnerable bombers: the *Mustang P-51*. It was only during the early months of '44 that a sufficient number of *Mustangs* were becoming available. During the 12 months from January '43 till January '44 Bomber Command lost approximately 5% of all planes during each nightly raid. But when by March '44 that number had risen to about 10%, Bomber Command decided to make important changes to its tactics. Bomber Command had few long-distance fighters; the one they had were usually unable to locate the German fighters in the dark of night. For the Luftwaffe, on the other hand, it was quite simple to locate the bombers on their radar screens; the bombers were always flying in concentrated formations and usually heading for one specific target. Their concentration rendered them extremely vulnerable. Instead Bomber Command decided to bomb multiple targets at the same time. Losses diminished and the numbers lessened even more when, preparatory to the invasion, targets in France, Belgium and Holland were chosen: railway emplacements and large German installations for the launching of *Vergeltungswaffen*, 'V' for *vengeance* weapons. Additionally, the Mustangs accompanying the bombers were shooting down so many German fighters that starting in March '44 the Allies had clearly achieved air superiority over Western Europe; at least during daylight. Bomber Command took advantage of that fact and began flying during the day. However, the British bombers were more vulnerable than the American planes; they flew lower and slower and had fewer and less effective machine guns on board. German anti-aircraft fire remained dangerous but most of the planes that were hit were able to make it back to their base in England.

Although the population of Holland appreciated the pounding that Germany was receiving from the RAF and U.S. 8th Air Force (almost on a daily basis) it had to accept that targets in Holland and particularly those around Rotterdam were also on the agenda of the allied bombers. These bombing raids had already claimed a considerable number of innocent lives. The December 1942 bombing raid on the Philips factories in Eindhoven claimed almost one hundred and fifty civilians. However, the bombing resulted in heavy damage to the factories with 1/6th completely destroyed. A second bombing of the Philips plant on March 30, 1943 claimed twenty civilians; a completely failed mid-day bombing of harbor installations in the Rotterdam area claimed more than three-hundred innocent civilians; another failed late afternoon bombing on April 16 of railway installations near the city of Haarlem in the vicinity of Amsterdam – eighty-five deaths.

The bombing of Rotterdam on March 31, 1943, claiming more than three-hundred lives, led to a great deal of criticism. It was the first bombing by the U.S. 8th Air Force of a target in Holland. Almost one hundred American bombers had lifted off from airfields in England for this *'precision'* bombing mission to be executed at a height of five miles. The target was the large ship building installation of Wilton-Fijenoord on the west side of Rotterdam. Because of heavy clouds over the approach and target area about two-third of the planes couldn't find the target and the remaining one-third, thinking they had located the target, misjudged the Rotterdam geography and dropped their bombs on a heavily populated area in the west of the city. This disaster caused the deaths of three hundred and twenty six civilians; about four hundred were badly injured and more than twenty-thousand people lost their homes. Some people compared this bombing with the German bombing of Rotterdam on May 14, 1940 and what was worse; our American friends had done it.

Among the dead were friends of our family that had been their neighbors on the Hooidrift where I was born. The van Wingerden family, Mrs. van Wingerden and her two children, Kees and Annie, lived on the Schiedamscheweg, the area devastated by the bombing. The irony however was that their house had survived the bombing. Mrs. van Wingerden and Annie had found themselves on the street at the time and when the sirens had sounded, had entered an air raid shelter together with many other people. The air raid shelter had received a direct hit and both Mrs. van Wingerden and Annie had been killed instantly. Son Kees was home at the time and survived.

After the United States entered the war in 1941, Great Britain and America made an arrangement that resulted in the American 8th Air Force bombers, B-17's and B-24's to fly during the day and the Royal Air Force's plethora of planes to fly at night; this changed prior to the invasion on June 6, 1944 when the Allies had achieved air superiority. Many of these planes would fly across Holland on their way to targets in Germany.

When it came to bombing targets in our area we would fear the Americans more than the British and let me tell you why. This was our interpretation at the time and it may be totally unfounded and false. We reasoned that America had far more resources than the British. The Americans could afford to spend more on bombs and planes whereas the British had to be frugal with everything they had. The American Flying Fortresses (B-17) and Liberators (B-24) would be flying very high and would drop their bombs in a broad target area. The Americans by bombing a wide area must have figured that the actual target would be somewhere in the middle and thus be destroyed. The rest was mere collateral damage. That would be fine for German targets but not for us in Holland. On the other hand the British, flying at night and at a lower elevation would try to pinpoint the target more precisely. A problem that the American *Norden* bombsight did not necessarily take into account was the occasional strong wind current at ground level in *"flat as a pancake"* Holland.

A case in point was the bombing on March 31. 1943. In this particular case the bombers dropped their bomb load from a height of five miles. The picture you see here shows the area of Rotterdam - West from a height of five miles (8 kilometers)

307. A bomber's view of Rotterdam-West from a height of 5 miles.

308. Norden bombsight

It is easy to see that a bombing from this height with intermittent cloud cover over the target area could easily go awry. It's very well possible that a strong surface wind contributed to the disaster.

That is not to say that the British were always successful. They were not but the odds were definitely against the Americans.

Henry remembers:

"The raid on Wednesday March 31, 1943 was a lot worse than what we had experienced before. I had managed to get a roll of film, using paper negatives. When the air alert sounded I went in the backyard with the old Kodak box to take some pictures. I could see the bombers in the distance. When they got closer I saw them dropping their bombs. I hit the deck in a hurry, no pictures. There was a lot of smoke a few miles west of us; it looked like they tried to hit the Wilhelmina docks; however a lot of the bombs hit the houses nearby also near the high school where I used to go. Annie was going to that school and she was there when the raid started. So there I went again, running in that direction and looking for my sister. I had to get over a lot of rubble in the street, and detour to avoid the fires, but I did not find her. The school was still standing but had lost most of the windows. I went home again and there was Annie, shaken but safe and sound. More than 300 people were killed in that raid.

Then to Stokvis and up on the roof where I took pictures of all the smoke in the distance; several miles away.

309. Another bombing, another fire.

On the BBC that night they said the docks in Rotterdam had been bombed. Also that all aircraft were now equipped with new, very accurate, bombsights. You could practically drop a bomb in a bucket; that is: "If the bucket was large enough!"

There were other occasions in '43 and early '44 when the 8th Air Force made serious mistakes resulting in numerous civilian casualties. On October 10, 1943 the city of Enschede was bombed causing heavy damage to the city and killing 151 civilians. The following month, on November 7 Tungelroy near the city of Weert in Limburg was bombed causing much damage but fortunately no casualties. In both cases the bombers had assumed that they were over Germany. The Dutch government in London had pleaded with the American Air Force to attempt greater caution in the future. The Eighth Air Force was advised accordingly but on February 22, 1944 the warning proved to have had insufficient effect. Bomber squadrons had been instructed to bomb cities in West Germany, Osnabruck and Wesel. Several squadrons, however, dropped their bombs on Enschede (second time), Arnhem and Nijmegen. The bombing of Nijmegen, in particular, was devastating. The air-raid siren had given the alarm of approaching aircraft at 12:14 hours; American bombers flew over the city and there were also German fighters in the sky. After almost one hour, at 13:12 hours the *'all clear'* was given and many people were back on the street. The all clear was still in effect when from the east 16 bombers approached the city and dropped their load in the center of Nijmegen: about 150 heavy bombs. There was extensive damage; the railway station, five churches, numerous stores and many homes had been completely destroyed. Large fires added to the destruction; the fire department was unable to contain the fires because the water mains* had been hit as well. Approximately 800 people lost their lives and an additional 1,300 homes were completely destroyed.

The fault for not warning the people of Nijmegen was with the German authorities but regardless, the destruction had been such that a formal complaint was once again registered with the American Air Force. Even President Roosevelt got involved and the commander of the 8th Air Force received a serious rebuke. The Dutch Minister of Foreign Affairs in London, Mr. E. N. van Kleffens noted in his diary on February 24: *"The Americans are very sorry and there is much humility but the harm has been done"*.

*Natural gas and water lines were located next to each other, which resulted in completely filling the system's gas grid and causing the phenomenon of water spouting out of the gas lanterns in the lower part of the city where electric lights had not yet been installed.

CHAPTER SIXTY-SIX

THE DAMBUSTERS

310.

THE DAMBUSTERS

On May 17, 1943 under the leadership of Wing Commander Guy Gibson, of the Royal Air Force, a veteran of 170 missions, one of the most daring feats of the Second World War took place.

311. Guy Penrose Gibson VC, DSO and bar, DFC and bar (1918-1944)

Operation Chastise was the official name for the attacks on German dams using a specially developed *'bouncing bomb'*. The RAF No. 617

Squadron, subsequently known as the "Dambusters", carried out the attack.

The targets were the three key dams near the German Ruhr area, the Moehne, the Sorpe and the Eder Dam on the Eder River. The loss of hydroelectric power was important but the loss of water to industry, cities and canals was thought to have greater impact on German war production.

The aircraft were modified Avro Lancaster Mk IIIs. To reduce weight, much of the armor was removed, as was the mid-upper turret. The substantial bomb and its unusual shape meant that the bomb doors were removed and the bomb itself hung, in part, below the body of the aircraft. It was mounted in two crutches and before dropping it was spun up to speed by an auxiliary motor.

312. The Moehne Dam, inset Bouncing Bomb and Crew
upon departing for mission

In order for a dam to be breached, a bomb would have to explode against the dam itself and preferably at the foot of the dam where it would cause movement not unlike an earthquake. The big question was how to deliver a bomb that would have that effect.

The solution came from what all of us are familiar with and successfully performed many times when we were young and finding ourselves at a lake or other calm body of water. We'd take a flat rock and throw it parallel to the surface of the water. The flat rock would hit the water, bounce up, hit the water again farther down and repeat that several times until it would sink straight down to the bottom.

313. Rock skipping

Bombing from 60 feet (18 meters) at 240 mph (390 km/h), at a very precise distance from the target, required expert crews, intensive night and low-altitude flying training, and the solutions to two technical problems. The first was to know when the aircraft was the correct distance from the target. The two key dams at Moehne and Eder had a tower at each end. A special aiming device (a device with two prongs making the same angle as the two towers at the correct distance from the dam) showed when to release the bomb. The second problem was to measure the aircraft's altitude (the usual barometric altimeters lacked sufficient accuracy). Two spotlights were mounted; one under the nose and another under the fuselage, such that at the correct height their light beams would converge on the surface of the water. The crews practiced over the Eyebrook Reservoir in Leicestershire, the Derwent Reservoir, Derbyshire, and the Fleet Lagoon, Dorset.

The Lancasters were organized into three groups, two groups to attack the dams and one group in reserve. Nineteen Lancasters in total of which two returned to base before completing their mission. The outbound flights were flown at treetop level (between 75 and 120 feet) to avoid detection by the German air defense radar. The aircraft flew two routes, both over Holland. Formation 1 entered the continent between the islands of Walcheren and Schouwen (Province Zeeland), crossed the Netherlands, skirting the airbases at Eindhoven and Gilze-Rijen, curved round the Ruhr defenses and turned north to avoid Hamm before turning to head south to the Moehne. Formation 2 flew further northwards, cutting over the Dutch island of Vlieland and crossing the Wadden Zee before joining the first route near Wesel and then flying south beyond the Moehne to the Sorpe.

The first casualties were taken soon after the planes reached the Dutch coast. Formation 2 did not fare well: one plane lost his radio to flak and turned back over the Zuiderzee while a second Lancaster flew too low and lost his bomb in the water but recovered the aircraft to return to base. Two Lancasters crossed over the coast at the Island of Texel where one was hit by flak and crashed into the Wadden Zee. All seven of the crew perished. Two Lancasters heading for the Moehne and Sorpe Dams flew into high tension cables and crashed killing all on board. Two of the Lancasters were crippled by the explosions of their own bombs; subsequently hit by flak and crashed killing all on board. Three more planes were lost due to flak on their way back to base. In total, eight planes out of an effective total of seventeen Lancasters were lost totaling fifty-three crew killed and three taken prisoner. Squadron Commander Guy Gibson survived the raid and was awarded the Victoria Cross; the highest decoration on a par with the U. S. Medal of Honor. Gibson was subsequently killed on a mission over Holland in 1944. In spite of the terrible losses, the Operation was considered a success. Both the Moehne and Sorpe Dams were breached pouring around 330 million tons of water (equivalent to a cube 786 meters on each side) into the western Ruhr region.

314. Bouncing Bomb being dropped. Note the 2
spotlights under nose and fuselage.

315. Result of the bombing at the Moehne Dam

Mines were flooded and houses, factories, roads, railways and bridges destroyed as the flood waters spread for around 50 miles (80 km) from the source. In terms of deaths: 1,294 people were killed, 749 of them Ukrainian POW's from a camp just below the Eder Dam. After the Operation Barnes Wallis, the creator of the *'bouncing bomb'* wrote, *"I feel a blow has been struck at Germany from which she cannot recover for several years".*

CHAPTER SIXTY-SEVEN

CONFISCATION OF ALL RADIOS

On May 31, 1943 the population was notified that all radio receivers were to be turned in; *confiscated* is a better word. It is interesting how this came about. First of all, the confiscation of all radios was a clear admittance that the Germans and the local Nazi Party had failed in their attempt to propagandize their policies. Seyss-Inquart was not in favor of this action when it was first proposed to him because he recognized in doing so the clear failure of his policies.

The pressure came from an unexpected source; the German Wehrmacht (Army).

The German army foresaw the opening of a 'Second Front' in Western Europe, and they knew that such action would be heralded by detailed instructions from London to the population on the continent. A matter of fact, the BBC had said as much in their broadcasts. In the end, after much wrangling between the Army, the Sicherheitsdienst and Seyss-Inquart; the latter went to Hitler and proposed the confiscation of all radio sets with the exclusion of those owned by members of the Dutch Nazi Party, other Nazi organizations and individuals in official German functions. Hitler agreed.

At this point I need to tell you what our family's experience was when we received the order that before noon on Friday June 25, 1943 we were to place our radio in front of our house on the curbside. We would get a receipt from the Dutch State Police and German trucks would come in the afternoon to pick up the sets.

As I stated earlier in the book, our family had two radio receivers. In 1930 or about, my father had built his own radio set with the help of Uncle Anton my mothers cousin. Uncle Anton owned a lead cable manufacturing plant on the Westzeedijk, about a mile from our house.

Uncle Anton was an experienced engineer and was quite knowledgeable in electronics and machinery as well. (He had invented and constructed some of his own machinery).

316. A self-made radio receiver

Together they had built a radio set from a schematic. They had wound their own coil in the factory. This coil was very big and heavy and, in the end, so was the finished product. I remember it as a big wooden box with knobs and dials and a set of head phones. It worked but not as well as the new Philips radio that our family had purchased in 1938 a few years before the invasion on May 10, 1940. That was a beautiful set and with a sound to match. It had dials with station names that lit up and an interesting green eye that brightened when you tuned in to a station. If the eye lit up brightly you knew that you had the best reception. The set could receive both long and short wave broadcasts.

317. Our new Philips receiver

With a long, horizontal, antenna on the roof we were able to receive places all over the world. It depended a lot on the time of day and the weather. One station that stands out in my mind was Schenectady, all the way in the State of New York in the United States of America. To me that was the same as another planet.

There was never any doubt in my father's mind that what we would turn in was the *'old'* set and we would hide the new Philips in our basement.

On that Friday morning my brother Henry carried the old set and placed it neatly on the curb in front of our house. Every family in the Dunantstraat that owned a radio did the same. A few apartments down from us lived a family that only a few months before the German invasion had purchased a new set that combined both a radio and record player; a gorgeous piece of equipment.

The man of the house had proudly showed it to us and I remember looking inside and seeing all those mysterious tubes lit up.

318. Radio and gramophone combo

Our neighbor, who like us, hated the Germans with a passion had carried his beautiful set to the curb and then had returned to the house. When he returned he was carrying a hammer and I remember

393

him making a statement: *'If I can't have this radio, neither will those 'Goddamn krauts!'* With that he raised the hammer and beat the inside of the set and record player to smithereens. It must have been a terrible ordeal for him to commit such an act to an expensive and beautiful piece of equipment. There it was sitting at the curb, *'outwardly'* not showing the *'inside'* devastation. In advance of the pick-up by the Germans the Dutch State Police had gone around and issued receipts. (see picture of Empfangbeweis G854 issued by Staatspolitie Rotterdam on Friday June 25, 1943).

319. The receipt for our radio

With tears in his eyes but proud of what he had done and with the receipt in his hands, our good neighbor together with the rest of the street, waited for the pick-up by the Germans...

We waited and waited but not a German showed up. By 5 o'clock the State Police returned and told everybody that the Germans had forgotten our street and they suggested we take the sets back in the house.

"The Germans wouldn't be any wiser", they said.

Believe it or not.... our small street was accounted for but the Germans neglected to pick up the sets. Henry carried the set back in the house and so did our neighbor who by now was really sobbing and swearing like a dockworker. Once inside the house we couldn't help but roaring with laughter. That poor man!

Our Philips radio ended up in the basement where my brother Henry would listen covertly to the BBC. He would take the English news down in shorthand and type it up in Dutch, in six readable copies. From that point on it would be distributed to people we could trust who in turn would pass it on to others. A very dangerous practice, punishable by death.

CHAPTER SIXTY-EIGHT

TALES OF RESISTANCE

Henry remembers:

"The Russians defeated the Germans at Stalingrad; Rommel was defeated in Africa. Sicily had been invaded, followed by landings in Italy and the subsequent fall of Mussolini. The Italians turned on them and came to our side. But there would still be some hard fighting before it was finished. Things were looking up".

"I was glad to report some good news. We, the resistance, started seeing some weapons towards the end of the year. There were lots of coded messages transmitted, I picked them up and relayed them, but did not have the foggiest idea what they meant. I still remember; "Torino is a good wine". To this day I still don't know what it meant. Later I found out that a lot of fake messages were sent; only a critical few were meaningful. Just to confuse the Germans who were listening".

"Shortly after the Germans had occupied Holland they ordered the Dutch Army to go home and back to work. They were no longer prisoners of war. However when the situation in Holland deteriorated in 1943 they ordered them back to the prison camps. A large number went into hiding, but they needed ration cards and money. So the resistance started to rob the offices where the ration cards were distributed and a number of banks. This went generally smoothly; the people were cooperating and usually gave the 'robbers' at least a half-hour to get away. I never had to do that, but in a few cases I was a lookout. In May of 1943 I graduated and in July I passed my special English examination. Just in time because the Germans started arresting students, they were considered 'unreliable' and suspected of sabotage. Well, they were not far from the truth!"

"My salary at Stokvis had increased to the fantastic sum of 50 guilders a month; the maximum I could ever get from them. Pa and Ma thought

I could do better and make more money. I could get a job at the Optical Plant Oude Delft, but I was not about to make a daily trip on my bike from Rotterdam to Delft back and forth on a half-empty stomach. Then they did a stupid thing. Somebody had said that the Belasting Dienst (Dutch IRS) needed people. They had arranged with that 'somebody' I would get an interview. I went, but was really pissed. I just hated the idea to work for the tax people and I considered it far too dangerous. I was let into a room with a big desk and behind it a well-fed bureaucrat, who was wearing a golden swastika pin on his lapel. That really turned me off, especially when he asked me why I had not been in the Arbeids Dienst (Labor Service). I told him that I worked and also had to study. Then he questioned me why my first name was English. I told him I had no idea. At that point all I really wanted was to get the hell out of there. He blabbed on some more and told me he would let me know. He scribbled something on a piece of paper with my name on it, folded it, gave it to me, and said:" Give it to my secretary, you'll hear from us". "I left in a hurry and, of course, forgot to give that paper to the secretary. I never heard from them again. I did destroy that form with my name and other info on it. I told my Dad what had happened and that I would never work for those tax crooks and "dirty Nazi's". (vuile NSBers). He was a bit taken aback.

Also that year the Germans started to draft or confiscate dogs for the German army. Every dog with the owner had to show up at a field near the railroad tracks in Blijdorp. There was a long line of people with their dogs. I joined them with Tosca (a little mutt without a tail) He was not exactly a dog that the military would be interested in. I got a stamp on his dog license and walked away. Around the corner more people were waiting with dogs, such as German shepherds, which would be of far more interest to the Germans. A man with a shepherd asked me whether he could borrow my dog for a moment. We switched dogs, he got a stamp on his license, and came back, after which we switched dogs again. I did that only twice otherwise they might have recognized the dog. Later I found out that some of the Dutch dog pound people stamping the dog licenses were also involved in the resistance. I think that they would have given that stamp to anybody, even if you had shown them a cat.

It became pretty tricky to walk in the streets of Rotterdam. Of course I could no longer go to the library, but any large gatherings such as movie theaters, concerts, etc. attracted the Germans like flies to a you-know-what.

Annie often walked ahead of me to reconnoiter and see whether the road was clear of the Nazi vermin. She also did it when I had wrapped items on my bike's luggage rack.

One of our people had a 8mm-movie projector and on occasion I could get a movie, a good old American western, silent with titles. We all paid a quarter for the rental and spent a fun few hours at his home, in the basement.

In any war most of your time is spent in waiting, but then you can have short and violent action. My waiting was also listening to music and the spoken word from England. At one time I saw the start of a riot at the corner of the Binnenweg and the Claes de Vriese laan. Two WA characters were selling their party newspaper for a nickel. The people gave them dirty looks and for the rest ignored them. However one guy came over and bought one. He walked a few yards and stepped in a heap of dog do. He took the party newspaper, wiped his shoe with it and threw it back at the two Nazi's. The crowd cheered and chased them away. Nightsticks came out and the Dutch police tried very slowly to establish order.

The Dutch radio was terrible. Some traitor (Max Blokzijl) gave a weekly speech that would make you vomit. I decided to interfere at least locally. We had an electrical device with a coil, an interrupter and two handles. When you activated it with a 6Vbattery and held the handles, you could feel an electric current. The strength could be increased and the sport was to see who could take the highest current. I had hooked the handles to the 'gutter' antenna of the radio, which I had disconnected first. It sure worked; a guy who lived near the Havenstraat told me later that he could not hear Max 'the traitor' over the noise. That was a greater range than I expected, so I decided not to tempt fate and quit doing it. My very wide band transmitter could also interfere with the German transmissions, which might make them mad at me. They had a listening and lookout post on top of our only 30-story skyscraper in Rotterdam on the other side of the harbor from where we lived. At least I got it a little bit out of my system.

Towards the end of 1943 the Germans were in our opinion on the decline as well as the Japanese who were pushed back slowly to their main islands, all at enormous cost.

Doolittle's raid on Tokyo the year before was great, but experienced as we were with air raids, we knew that the damage would be minimal. It still would shock the living daylights out of them, as indeed it did. It also boosted our morale. Then I heard from the BBC that the American Air Force in the Pacific had intersected Admiral Yamamoto, the man who had planned the attack on Pearl Harbor. The Americans had shot down his plane and Yamamoto had been killed.

All in all, we were more interested in how to get rid of the Germans, how to foul them up and how to get food. The food situation was really getting bad and the worst was yet to come.

During the summer of 1943 I had to spend a week working on the 'Atlantic Wall'. All businesses had to provide workers for a week to work on the coast. I had the choice, not doing it and go into hiding, or just go and keep my eyes open. So I went with a bunch of other men. I was the youngest, so they thought, and the smallest. We went by train to Hook of Holland and walked to the dunes. There we had to carry poles and occasionally concrete bars. You carried them with three or four men; I was always in the middle, not much strain for me. I remember that the weather was fine and it felt more like vacation. There were no German police, just regular army, who were like most soldiers, had a lot of time when there were no officers around. On one occasion we had to go to Island de Beer, opposite Hook of Holland. When we were there they did not know what to do with us, so we sat around in the dunes and absorbed some sun. They also fed us and at the end of the week we were paid. The soldiers that were working there and watching us were very happy not to be at the Eastern Front; they were in constant fear of being transferred. A lot of them were older men, some of them at least around 50. I think they knew the outlook for them was not very good and that was before the invasion. All this was properly reported and I am sure I did not tell them anything new.

Towards the end of 1943 I had to start collecting license plate information of German cars. At first I did not know what it was all about, but figured it out pretty soon. The Allies wanted to know any troop movements in Holland and Rotterdam. Since I lived not far from the Park and the German Headquarters (Ortskommandantur and Kriegsmarine) were in some beautiful homes in a wide street just east of the Park. They had closed off some of the streets, but their staff cars had to come through the area near the Westzeedijk. I went to that area to take our dog, Tosca, for his walk. I had to memorize the information, numbers and letters. Carrying a notebook would have been a bit too obvious. After some time I could memorize about a dozen numbers and letter combinations. It depended on their length. I wrote them down once I was at home and dropped the list off at a house on the Heyman Dullaertplein at the corner of the Heyman Dullaert straat. My dead-drop!" "At one time I saw two German generals on horseback. I knew they were generals, because they had red stripes on their pants. No license number on the horses. They were looking at me, but I was just a skinny boy and Tosca was just doing what he did best, he lifted his hind leg so I had to stop. Then they totally ignored me, but I did report the sighting. All this was done before I went to work and again during Tosca's evening walk. So I guess I was a spy with my undercover dog.

They probably got a lot of that info from all over the place. I hoped it helped.

The Gestapo was getting more vicious, if that were possible. They got quite a few people of the Resistance, in most cases through traitors who infiltrated the resistance cells. After some well-published so-called trials, they were executed, often near The Hague in the dunes. We became very careful with people we did not know. If we found out that there was a traitor we were allowed to kill them. That was not my job. We had to get approval from our government in London, unless it was an emergency. Most of the time the traitors ended up in the harbor to float out to sea. (Without ID).

In the last part of the war our Government in London informed us by radio to add black marketers to the list. I believe I had to put that in one of my newsletters. We were not allowed to attack German troops, unless we were attacked. Our job was in general to collect information. If Germans were killed, they would arbitrarily kill dozens of innocent civilians or wipe out a whole village, such as they did in Putten on the Veluwe, when the Gestapo General Rauter was shot and severely wounded. He survived, but it took almost a year before he could walk again. By then the war was over, he was charged as a war criminal, convicted and executed. A waste of all that good medication!

We could sabotage the German military as long as it could not be traced to us. For example, a sealed glass test tube with acid (koningswater) slipped in front of the wheel of a German truck or car would eat through the rubber in one to two hours depending on the temperature and cause a blowout. The right front tire was best; maybe he would fly into a canal. At least he would be delayed.

CHAPTER SIXTY-NINE

WAITING FOR D-DAY

In Holland we had been thinking of our liberation ever since the war started. Not a day went by that we didn't talk of an expected Allied landing somewhere on the continent of Europe. The Germans had already been making preparations for such an event for a long time. When you are as eager as we were for *'things'* to happen then any *'wait'* is too long. Did we have to wait longer than necessary? Would it have been possible for the British and Americans to land in Western Europe and defeat the German army already back in '42 or '43? Had it really been the intention of the British and United States governments to prolong the fighting on the eastern front to not only break the power of the German army but also that of the Soviet Union as was suggested by their propaganda machine at that time? Was that the reason why London and Washington intentionally dragged their feet with the invasion?

From the point of view of the Soviet Union that is an understandable conclusion. In May '42 the British and Americans had publicly recognized that the creation of a *'Second Front'* in Western Europe was urgently required; instead it only came to Allied landings in French North Africa. Following North Africa, the Russians were counting on a 1943 allied landing in Western Europe but instead it only resulted in the Italian campaign. That campaign ground to a halt in October. To this day we don't know what was on Stalin's mind because nothing has come out of the Kremlin to say otherwise but it is almost a foregone conclusion that Stalin and his advisors interpreted the postponements of starting the *'Second Front'* in Western Europe as *'intentional'* foot dragging. The Russians had no idea of the complexities of a large cross-channel invasion but they may have reasoned that if they could cross the big Dnepr River why couldn't the Allies get across the Channel?

Naturally, there were people in Holland that felt the same way and I am sure that there were individuals in both England and America that were more afraid of the Soviet Union than Nazi Germany. They saw in the struggle between the Fascists and Communists an easy solution to rid them of both totalitarian regimes or at a minimum to weaken them sufficiently to guarantee an Allied victory.

Neither President Roosevelt nor the British War Cabinet and its ministers subscribed to that simple solution.

They did however consider that following the defeat of Nazi Germany, Italy and Japan, the interests of the two large democracies would be diametrically opposed to those of the Soviet Union. In this vein, the defeat of the Germans at Stalingrad became a stimulant to open up a *'Second Front'* on the continent of Europe as soon as possible. There were several other factors that contributed to this urgency. Firstly, the Allies were well aware of the enormous suffering of the people in the occupied countries living under German tyranny; worsening by the minute.

Secondly, in spite of the tremendous German losses on the eastern front, both England and America were sufficiently concerned with the *'V'* weapons that Hitler had been promising since 1942. The Allies knew from their intelligence sources that Nazi Germany was working on an atomic weapon and that they already had the capability of delivering such a bomb with their V-2 rocket. To these two factors the Allies added a third one; only after the defeat of Germany could they concentrate their resources to defeat the Empire of Japan.

The British had all along been in favor of an Allied landing in the Balkans. Churchill had been a great proponent of such action. The Americans, however, favored a more direct approach, a landing in force on the European continent. Americans at the Casablanca Conference (January 1943) had gone along with the British to try and eliminate Italy during 1943. The British argued that in doing so it would be possible to eliminate the Germans from the Mediterranean. It was clear that the British were aiming at a landing in force in the Balkans. Churchill had in mind that a successful landing in

Greece and a quick advance northward would prevent the Russians from advancing through all the eastern European countries and then establishing 'puppet' communist regimes. As it turned out, that is exactly what happened.

When it appeared that the Italian campaign was getting bogged down, the Americans had *'enough'* and they forced the issue with their British Allies to invade the European continent. The code name of the Operation would be *'Overlord'* and it would be executed on June 5, 1944; but because of the weather that date was changed to June 6, 1944 called D-Day*. Dwight D. Eisenhower was appointed by General Marshall to head all Allied Forces on the continent of Europe.

*D-Day stems from the two words: The Day meaning the specific day/date of a given operation, not just of Operation Overlord, the invasion of the European continent. Because of the enormity of Operation Overlord, the largest landing ever attempted, D-Day is directly and forever associated with that operation.

Henry remembers:

In 1944 the invasion came. As usual I was in the basement at the radio when the news came. In fact the BBC first reported from German sources that there were landings in France. Shortly after that allied headquarters announced the landings in Normandy. Then a Dutch news bulletin from London that we were now the Interior Forces of the Netherlands under command of Prince Bernhard, but General Eisenhower would give the orders. The orders for us were to wait and just go on with what we were doing.

Two days later the police (Dutch) came through the street and quite a few others and I were told to report at the police station. In our case the Harbor Police station. We were marched with about 30 other guys to the station on the Westzeedijk and from there accompanied by regular German soldiers marched through the Park and to the 'hill' (30 ft. high) facing the river. We were spread out and told to stand near pillboxes that were dug into the hill overseeing the Maas River.
The Germans were on alert, probably looking for some stray allied landing craft?
I figured we were hostages, who probably would get it first if the Allied Forces showed up. I did not think they would come that quick. Since I

405

had played in the Park as a kid I knew the way around there, I was already plotting an escape route. It was not needed. At around noon a German general showed up with his entourage, obviously on an inspection tour. They looked at us and the general asked one of the officers in the reception committee for an explanation. I think he told him we were their first line of defense. That general turned bright red and yelled at the officer loud enough that I could here it quite well at 50 feet. I also knew what he was saying. The mildest word I heard was 'Dumkopf' (a rough translation would be 'dumb shit'): "They did not need children to defend them". I normally would not agree with a German general, but in this case I thought he was right. He may have figured out that the war was lost anyway and that the Allies would take a dim view of civilian hostages. We were marched out of the Park and could go home. The police had never taken our ID cards. We had been in a normally closed area, but now I knew that there were some 88mm guns on the hill, as well as machine guns. That news got around quickly to the right places. Things were getting a bit more hectic now and I was getting military training. We first trained at a house on the Beukelsdijk. We were with about four people and had to learn the use of the 'stengun', a mass-produced British sub-machine gun. We learned how to handle it properly and safely, how to take it apart and put it together again blindfolded in not more than 15 seconds. I did not have any problems with that. You could easily carry the thing under your raincoat. After a few visits there we went to a parochial school somewhere at the end of the Gerrit Jan Mulder Straat, pretty close to the Marconiplein. There we trained in a large physical education hall. Running around with an unloaded stengun and learning how to operate a light machine-gun (brengun).

320. Bren gun

After we knew how to operate it, each of us had to sit at the top of the stairs with the machine gun aimed at the entrance doors. In case the Germans showed up we had to shoot them to give the others time to escape. This was the real thing, but the Germans never showed up. After the training we got a good lunch; mashed potatoes with vegetables, sometimes a bit of meat or bacon. (All taken from the Germans, who had stolen it from us to begin with) That was for all of us the best meal of the week. At one time I had to go to the ice factory in the Gouvernestraat. They were training with the bazooka and they needed an interpreter. It was an Englishman who demonstrated it. Everything went fine until someone connected the battery. He had left the safety pin in the warhead. When he squeezed the trigger, the rocket took off and crashed through a wall. It did not explode. It was quite exciting and we left quickly.

321. Soldier with a Bazooka

I remember one last major air raid and naturally I was on the roof of Stokvis; RAF heavy bombers with 12,000 lbs. bombs were attacking the concrete shelters for submarines and schnellboote (similar to our PT boats) in the Waalhaven.
When they dropped the bombs it looked as if half the plane broke off. The explosions were enormous and created mushroom clouds. A number of aircraft turned in our direction and that's when we got off the roof. BBC evening news reported that the U–Boat pens in Rotterdam and IJmuiden had been bombed."

322. Inside of U-Boat pen after the attack

Chapter Seventy

"They Have Landed!"

Numerous books have been written and continue to be written about the landing in Normandy on June 6, 1944. In my library I have at least fifteen publications that all cover this immense operation in great detail. Additionally, several films have been produced and it is probably true that just about every one has either read one of the books or seen one of the movies. The first picture I saw back in the 50s was "The Longest Day" from a book by Cornelius Ryan – a movie of epic proportions.

323.
Credits: Internet Movie Database

A more recent film is of course "Saving Private Ryan" starring Tom Hanks and directed by Steven Spielberg.

324.
Credits: Internet Movie Database

The first twenty minutes of that movie were the most gut wrenching of any war movie that I have ever seen and undoubtedly very close to what really expired on that early morning of June 6, 1944.

Recently I read: "The Bedford Boys", the poignant story of the boys from Bedford, Virginia – population 3,000. On June 6, 1944, landing craft dropped the boys in the shallow water off Normandy's Omaha Beach, part of the first wave of American soldiers to hit the beaches on D-Day. Within minutes nineteen were dead. No other town in America suffered a greater one-day loss. Later in the campaign, three more sons of Bedford died of gunshot wounds. It is a story that you cannot easily forget – and one that the families of Bedford will *never* forget. It was and still is, Bedford's longest day.

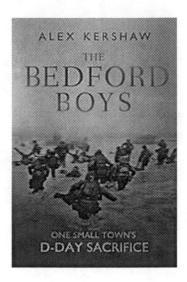

325.

The HBO series "Band of Brothers" from the book by the same name written by Stephen Ambrose depicts the invasion as seen from the famed 101st and 82d Air borne divisions that in the early hours of June 6 dropped behind enemy lines.

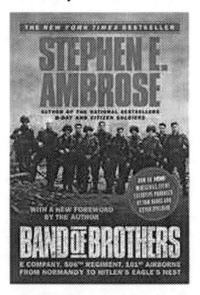

326.
Credits: Internet Movie Database

411

327. Eisenhower with the Screaming Eagles just before
they embarked on their mission. After the Battle of the
Bulge they will call themselves: "The Battling Bastards of
Bastogne"
Credit: US Photo Archives

Therefore, I have decided not to write about the bloody battles that took place on the Normandy beaches where thousands of American, Canadian and British soldiers were killed. Instead, I would like to share with you some historical anecdotes that changed the course of history.

OPERATION OVERLORD

For four consecutive years, thousands of soldiers of all nationalities underwent intensive training in England. Although millions of tons of material were prepared, and literally thousands of tanks, trucks and other vehicles were later dispatched on D-Day, its exact date remained a mystery until the very last moment. Nothing was left to chance. More than a year earlier, with the help of the Resistance, every detail of every possible plan had been scrutinized to test the feasibility of each mission. Three days before the launching of this immense operation, more than 200,000 soldiers embarked on about 5,000 ships. The best possible crossing conditions were necessary to make this landing a success, but waiting for departure was hard to bear for these men crammed into the vessels, many of them seasick and terribly anxious.

Several factors had to coincide perfectly in order for this massive operation to be launched and succeed:

A late moonrise: the paratroopers who would lead the assault had to arrive above their drop site during a perfectly dark night in order to preserve the effect of surprise.

A low tide: the first ships to arrive needed to be able to see the obstacles placed on the beaches by the enemy. The reinforcements that would arrive later in the day would also take advantage of the low tide. However, there were only 6 days in June when the tide would be low at the right time, and of these 6 days, only 3 would have moonless nights.

A calm sea: more than 5,000 ships would navigate side by side, which would only be possible with a perfectly calm sea that would avoid any risk of collision.

Good visibility: soldiers had to be able to identify the beaches where each military division was to carry out their precise mission.

A low altitude wind: this would help disperse the smoke from the explosions of the naval guns firing at targets on and beyond the beaches.

Finally, relative fair weather for 3 days prior to D-Day was also necessary to facilitate the rapid loading of men and material.

These were all the conditions General Dwight D. Eisenhower, Commander of the Allied Forces, needed to launch this modern-day crusade. With the constant input of meteorologists, June 5th appeared to be the most favorable day for departure. If the weather proved to be uncooperative, it would still be possible to leave the next day. As it turned out, this is exactly what happened. Had June 6th also needed to be cancelled, the soldiers would have to wait until July and everyone knew that such a late date would have considerably diminished any chance of success. June was clearly the most viable option.

328. General Dwight D. Eisenhower (1890-1969)

THE GERMAN REACTION

It was also good fortune that the German High Command utterly lacked any perception of what was coming. Although the Germans knew that a landing would occur very soon, they were convinced it would take place on the Pas-de-Calais beaches much farther north from Normandy.

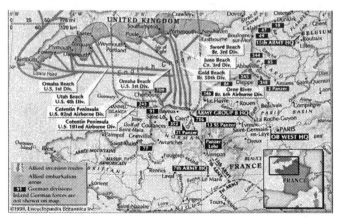

329. Operation Overlord map

The two reasons being that this was the closest point between England and France, and also the shortest path to invade the Reich. Besides they assumed that predicted bad weather conditions would certainly not allow any invasion in early June. After all, the Allied landings in North Africa, Sicily and Italy had all occurred in perfect weather. As a result leave was granted to all the German soldiers stationed in all the occupied coastal areas of France. The various commanding officers relaxed their attention, confident that no landing would take place this time of year. On June 4th, even Rommel returned to Germany to celebrate his wife's birthday on June 6th.

330. Generalfeldmarschall Erwin Rommel (1891-1944),
a great general and an honorable man. He was implicated
in the attempt on Hitler's life on July 20 '44 and was given
the option of standing trial or a poison capsule. To save
his family he chose the latter.

Ironically, several German generals were supposed to participate in army maneuvers, called *'Kriegsspiel'* (War Game), in Rennes on June 5th. The exercise was to enact the role of the Allies in a theoretical landing that would begin with an attack by paratroopers, followed by a landing from the sea. General Max Pemsel of the 7th Army Division worried about the commanding officers in Normandy all leaving at the same time. He tried to reach them and prevent them from leaving, but it was too late, most of them were already gone.

After D-Day, Hitler was so astonished by the coincidental timing of all these simultaneous departures with the landings, that he considered opening an investigation to assess if treason was behind it all. Indeed, this was also when the German High Command decided to transfer the last Luftwaffe flight squadrons remaining in France. The objective was to move them away from possible aerial bombings. When the startled German officers and soldiers with a front row view from their beach bunkers saw thousands of ships emerging on the horizon, they immediately knew that this was certainly not just a diversion maneuver. But none of their messages were taken seriously and the *'Fuehrer'* was not even awakened.

331. D-Day plus 6 hours

Actually, Hitler himself was no better informed than his generals, and it never occurred to any of them that an offensive would be launched that very day.

For weeks after the landing in Normandy Hitler continued to believe that the *'real'* landing would be at Pas-de-Calais. What strengthened Hitler's believe was the continued presence in southern England of General George C. Patton, Commander of the First U.S. Army Group; strategically placed right across from Calais. What Hitler did not know and would never have believed was that Patton had been relieved of his duties by General Eisenhower.

332. General George S. Patton (1885-1945)

While visiting several hospitals on Sicily Patton had slapped a soldier he deemed a coward because he claimed to be suffering from battle fatigue. Patton himself might have been suffering from battle fatigue at the time. When news of Patton's act was made public months later, there were calls for him to either resign or be fired. Instead, Eisenhower temporarily relieved him of his duties and returned him to England where he gave public talks as commander of the *'fictional'* First U. S. Army Group (FUSAG). This *'phantom'* army group was supposedly intending to invade France by way of Calais and was part of a sophisticated Allied campaign of military deception, called

Operation *Fortitude*. In order to facilitate this deception additional buildings were constructed; dummy vehicles, tanks and landing craft were placed around possible embarkation points. A huge amount of false radio traffic was transmitted, commensurate with a force of that size.

333. An inflatable tank

Thus, when the Germans learned that Patton*, who they considered the most outstanding general in the U.S. Army, was still in England Hitler was convinced that the Normandy landing was merely a ruse for the *'real'* landing to take place at Pas-de-Calais.

* The Germans had a great deal of respect for Patton. Patton was the **only** Allied general whose Army was referred to by his name and not its number; such was the Wehrmacht's respect for his skill as a combat commander.

THE DAILY TELEGRAPH

Mr. Dawe, a physics teacher living a simple life in a small English town, would also become emotionally involved in the plans for this memorable event. For more than 20 years, he had composed weekly crossword puzzles for the Daily Telegraph. However, he had no idea that the Allied commanding officers were deeply concerned about these crossword puzzles of his. Ever since May 2d, Mr. Dawe had been under close surveillance by Scotland Yard's counter- espionage unit. Some of his definitions that gave the Allies cold sweats were

'Feudal Lord', *'Red Skin of Missouri'*, *'Provokes revolutions in the nursery'* and *'He shares his kingdom with Britannia'*. The solutions were respectively: "Overlord", code name for the Allied invasion plan; "Omaha", name of one of the most famous beaches in Normandy; "Mulberry", code name for two artificial harbors that would be set up off the landing beaches; "Neptune", code name for all of the naval landing operations. Mr. Dawe astonished but absolutely sincere, could only guess that this was purely and simply the result of some extraordinary coincidences. He was then let off the hook.

RADIO LONDON

As early as 1940, the BBC transmitted a daily series of coded messages to allow the Allies based in England to communicate with the Resistance in France, to ask them to commit sabotage and, most importantly, to prepare for the upcoming landing in Normandy. A few days before D-Day, the commanding officers of the Resistance heard hundreds of messages, but only a few of them were really significant. When said twice, the first line of the poem by Verlaine, Chanson d'automne, *"Les sanglots long des violins de l'automne"* meant that *"the day"* was imminent, and when the second line *"blesse mon Coeur d'une langueur monotone"* was also repeated, the Resistance knew that the invasion would take place within the next 48 hours. Messages such as: *"Il fait chaud a Suez"* (It's hot in Suez), *"Les des sont sur le tapis"* (The dice are on the mat), *"Le chapeau de Napoleon est dans l'arene"* (Napoleon's hat is in the arena), *"John aime Marie"* (John loves Marie), *"La guerre de Troi n'aura pas lieu"* (The Trojan War will not take place) or *"La fleche ne passera pas"* (the arrow will not get through), all told the members of the Resistance it was time to go about their respective missions, which included: destroying water towers, blowing up trains or entire communication networks, or dynamiting selected roadways.

From FranceMonthly.com

As I have already written in previous paragraphs, not a day went by that we, in Holland, did not talk about the invasion and our liberation by the combined forces of the United States, Britain and its commonwealth (Canada, Australia and New Zealand), the Free French, the Poles, the Dutch, Norwegians, Danes and others. An amalgam of nationalities, all vehemently opposed to the Nazi regime and all working together to set us free. Already in 1942 people were predicting: *"they will come next week, I've been told by people that are in the know"*. When it did not happen we were disappointed but then someone would have the same prediction and we would look forward to next week and so on, and so on. It is a fact that by predicting this every week or month it will eventually come true. However, we had to wait a long time but we never gave up hope in spite of increasingly harsh conditions and the every day fear of death and destruction all around us. We were the lucky ones. Our immediate family remained intact throughout the war. Even I felt ashamed when thinking: *"Thank God I am not Jewish"*. We saw with our own eyes what happened to these poor people and there was little or nothing we could do about it. I remember the Jewish* children from my school and the ones that lived in our neighborhood when together with their parents and relatives they were rounded up by the Gestapo. They looked at us and we looked at them and I remember feeling so ashamed, so terribly ashamed and sorry. The one saving grace was that we did not know nor could they have imagined what their fate would be. We only learned of what had happened toward the very end of the war.

*At school I never knew who was Jewish. That was never an issue. We were not raised that way.

Since my *'big'* brother Henry was now in the Dutch Resistance and had access to more information than most we were somewhat better informed. For instance, we knew with a great deal of certainty that an invasion in Holland would be out of the question. The soil in Holland does not lend itself to the movement of heavy tanks and equipment. Too much water, too many rivers and very little cover from trees or hills. The Germans realized that as well and moved several infantry and armored divisions south to Belgium and France after inundating large areas in western Holland. We concluded that a landing would take place in either Belgium or France but we didn't know when.

Every day Henry would be in our 'cave' in the basement cavity listening to the BBC and I would often be with him in this cramped space with a large map of Europe on the wall. Every time the Russians made some further advances Henry would tell me where to insert the pins in the map. The pins had strings attached, extending from north to south providing a clear picture of the front lines. The Germans were falling back on their own country but in the German controlled Dutch press they would put a brave face on it all by stating: *"German armed forces have evacuated (this or that position) according to plan"*. Always: *"according to plan"*. Almost every day we would read this statement and it became a joke. When the Dutch Resistance robbed banks and ration card distribution centers they would very often leave a note for the Germans that read: *"Evacuated according to plan!"*

Henry had noticed that from the month of May on forward there was a marked increase in coded messages from the BBC. He still remembers one specifically: *"Torino is a good wine"*. We concluded that something was afoot and that we were getting closer to the invasion.

As long as I live I will never forget the morning of Tuesday June 6, 1944. I was with Henry in the basement. He had the headphones on his ears and I could only gaze over his shoulder to see what he was writing. Since most of it was his own brand of shorthand I could decipher very little. What I could do was look at his eyes and posture and deduct from that whether there was anything worthwhile being announced. The BBC news started as usual at a given time and I didn't notice anything unusual in my brother's behavior. Five or ten minutes into the news there was a sudden and unexpected move from Henry. He stopped writing for a moment, froze in his chair, reared his head, removed one of the headphones, looked at me with bulging eyes that were quickly becoming watery and said: *"My God, Wim, they have landed, the Allies have landed; they have finally landed. Soon we will be free!"* It was one of those emotional moments that happen in a lifetime; never to be forgotten and forever to be remembered and treasured. My reaction was immediate: *"Where, where, where did they land?" "In Normandy!"* he said and repeated it several times so that it would sink in. But I didn't know where Normandy was and I said: *"Where the hell is Normandy?" "In France, in France!"* and he repeated that a few more times. I turned to the map and quickly located the

421

French province of *'Normandie'* as we call it in Dutch. We were both so emotional that we cried from happiness and couldn't wait to tell our mom and dad. But first Henry had to get more details and when the news was done he turned to me and said: *"Wim, I was listening to this BBC announcer (whose voice was always low key and controlled) telling me the news from the Russian front, followed by a string of secret messages then the liberation of Rome in Italy and then in his usual quiet tone of voice said almost like an afterthought: "This morning at 06:00 hours Allied armies under the command of General Dwight D. Eisenhower have landed on the beaches of Normandy, France. The invasion has begun."* For a moment it was as if the world stood still and contemplated the impact of that event that would lead to the defeat of Nazi Germany and the liberation of all repressed people in Europe. Both of us literally ran upstairs and yelled: *"The invasion, the invasion, they have landed. The invasion has begun. Normandy, France. The American, General Eisenhower is the supreme commander"*. What was very interesting was that although few people had heard the news at that time, when we looked outside it was almost like people knew by osmosis that something fantastic was happening. There existed that unseen jubilation. It was like moving from a black & white movie to full color cinemascope.

The German controlled press made the announcement of the landing in a small article with the explanation that the landing had not succeeded and that the allies were being forced back into the sea. Naturally we didn't believe that but at Omaha Beach it came close to happening that way.

From this point on we would be counting down because the Allied armies had been able to establish a beachhead and were moving inland. Heavy fighting ensued with severe losses of men and materiel. Every day I would be in the basement cave with Henry and keep track on our map.

When the Allies finally broke through the 'bocage' (small fields surrounded by high hedge rows of almost impenetrable growth)

334. A typical road in Bocage country. General Omar

Bradley, commanding the US 12th Army Group, successfully completed Operation Cobra we knew that the Germans were practically finished. By that time Patton had returned as commander of the US Third Army. Field Marshall Montgomery had taken the city of Caen and combined Allied forces then just about destroyed the German 7th and 5th Panzer Armies in encirclement near the town of Falaise (Falaise Pocket). These two German armies had taken part in the Normandy campaign from the start.

335. Falaise pocket; death and destruction

336. More German wreckage.

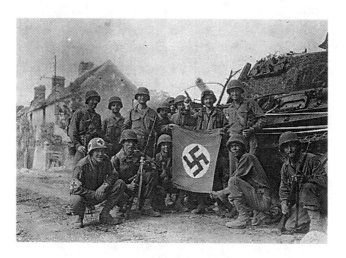

337. Captured German Swastika flag.

The next stop of the Allies would be the city of Paris where we meet a *'rotund old friend'* from Rotterdam: Dietrich von Choltitz, by now a full general. He had been put in charge of the German 84th Army Corps. However, his failure to stop the advance of the Americans led by Omar Bradley displeased Hitler and he was demoted and moved to the city of Paris where he became the city's military governor in August '44. Here von Choltitz disobeyed orders that came directly from Adolf Hitler. He was told to blow up all the bridges in the city which he refused to do. He was also ordered to destroy the city rather than surrender Paris intact to the Allies. This he also failed to do. Von Choltitz also negotiated with the French Resistance in the city to keep violence to a minimum – despite being ordered to fight to the last bullet. Why would an army man through and through disobey his commander-in-chief? While von Choltitz did have a very good military pedigree, he was a practical and logical man. It is possible that to him, the order to destroy Paris was anything but logical – hence it was not carried out.

Von Choltitz surrendered the city to the Allies along with the garrison that remained in the city. Those who were there said that Hitler was furious when he found out about the surrender. Von Choltitz became a prisoner of war and remained so until 1946.

338. Von Choltitz signing the surrender of Paris

Dietrich von Choltitz died in 1966 after a long illness. He was buried in Baden-Baden and his funeral was attended by a number of high ranking French army officers.

There is no doubt in my mind that the wanton destruction of Rotterdam that von Choltitz had been attempting to prevent on May 14, 1940 influenced his actions in the "City of Lights".

He is to be remembered as a true hero by all.

339. Barricades near the Notre Dame Cathedral

340. Barricades in Paris

341. Arc de Triumph

342. The triumphant entry of the Allies on the Champs-
Elysees.

343. A Day to Remember – August 25, 1944

344. Charles de Gaulle*

345. De Gaulle and General LeClerc, Commander of
the 2d French Armored Division that raced to Paris on
August 23d.

*What is interesting about this picture is that it shows Charles de Gaulle in 1938 with the
then President of France Albert LeBrun in office from 1932-1940.

The caption underneath the picture reads:

President Lebrun laat zich bij een bezoek aan het Franse
front inlichten door een officier van een tank-corps.

346. President LeBrun being informed by an officer of a
tank-corps while on a visit to the French front lines.

De Gaulle's name is not mentioned because he was unknown at the time, just an officer
in the French Army. He would later become President of France.

CHAPTER SEVENTY-ONE

"DOLLE DINSDAG" (MAD TUESDAY) SEPTEMBER 5, 1944

After the liberation of Paris the Allied Armies were moving rapidly toward the German border and through Belgium toward Holland. Rumors were rampant as were predictions that we would soon be liberated because the Germans were fleeing ahead of the advancing armies. Naturally, this was mostly wishful thinking caused in part by Seyss-Inquart and Rauter; the two Nazis in charge of Holland. On September 4th both Nazis had spoken on cable radio (300,000 subscribers) and announced a "State of Siege" for the Netherlands. The full text appeared in the newspapers of the following day, September 5th and it contained:

'The population must maintain order...it is strictly forbidden to flee areas that are threatened by the enemy. All orders from the military commanders must be strictly adhered to and without question...any resistance to the occupation forces will be suppressed with force of weaponry. Any attempt to fraternize with the enemy or to hinder the German Reich and its allies in any form will be dealt with harshly; perpetrators will be shot.'

This news was quite threatening but it contained hints of what the Nazis were expecting and that, in it self, provided hope.

Although the proclamation gave rise to the belief that the Nazis were prepared to stay and fight as long as they were able to, there were signs that they were actually preparing to do the opposite.

On the afternoon of Tuesday we noticed in our neighborhood a growing number of civilians pushing carts with their belongings and Germans in trucks loaded with furniture, carpets, food stuffs, even life animals; like pigs and chickens, fleeing the city. We concluded that they had to know something that we didn't; were our liberators on the way?

347. Collaborators waiting to leave by train.

348. Fleeing with their loot in a three-wheeler.

There were now reports circulating that the Americans and British troops had liberated Brussels in Belgium and had crossed the border into Holland at several points, Limburg and Brabant. They had been reported in the city of Breda in the province of North Brabant. That was only a mere 25 miles from Rotterdam and they could be in that city any minute. In Amsterdam people were reporting that the Allies were already in Rotterdam and moving toward The Hague. Everybody was going crazy with joy and preparing to greet the liberators. More and more Germans were fleeing in complete panic. In their haste to get to Germany they confiscated any kind of transportation they could lay their hands on. City busses, river barges, trucks, bicycles, handcarts and even baby carriages. All of this activity fed on itself and for the Germans and the Dutch collaborators it became a true Exodus. The Dutch collaborators knew that they were 'in' for it if they stuck around. Although it was only September and the weather mild there was smoke pouring out the chimneys of buildings on the Pieter de Hooghstraat occupied by the German Security police and Kriegsmarine (German Navy). It was obvious that they were burning *'sensitive'* incriminating papers and documents.

It is impossible to give a clear picture of all the rumors that circulated in the country from north to south and from west to east. All of these rumors had one thing in common: our liberation was at hand. The desire to be free was so great and intensely charged that in all the cities in the western part of the country every one was talking about the Allies being only a few miles away; in Dordrecht they said: they have crossed the Moerdijk Bridge, in Rotterdam: they have passed Dordrecht, in Delft: they are coming from Rotterdam, in The Hague: they have passed Delft, in Leiden: The Hague has been liberated, in Haarlem: they are on their way from Leiden, in Amsterdam: they are only a few miles away. It was almost impossible to verify any of the rumors because few people had operating telephones and, that day, nobody could get through to the three big cities in the west. But then again, who wanted to verify these rumors? Instead, people passed the news on in greatly embellished form.
Excitement was great; the national colors came out and thousands of people were at key points in the big cities waiting for the liberators.

What also contributed to the situation was an intelligence report that Eisenhower's HQ (SHAEF) had circulated on Sep 2: *"The German Army in Western Europe is no longer a cohesive unit but a disorganized and demoralized group of combat units that are on the run. These units lack weapons and equipment."* In response to this circular

Montgomery wrote to Eisenhower on September 4th (the day before Dolle Dinsdag): *"It is my opinion that we find ourselves at a stage when one big and energetic push in the direction of Berlin will quickly end this war."*

As it turned out none of the rumors of approaching allied armies were true with the exception that the British forces had indeed reached the Dutch border in Belgium. That was about as far as they got before running out of their supply lines.

When the population learned that little or nothing was factual it was like they had participated in the greatest party ever and were now waking up with the worst possible hangover.

The Nazis in Holland were also catching on to the rumors and quickly returned. Any gathering of people was brutally beaten down and any civilian found in the open after 8pm was shot without due process.

It is quite clear that Eisenhower's bulletin and Montgomery's opinion of the situation resulted in a campaign that would be called "Operation Market - Garden" but may be better remembered as "A Bridge Too Far".

Henry remembers:
After the great breakthrough in France and the fast advance of the Allies into Southern Netherlands, we thought it was almost over. We did see some Germans packing up and leaving, including some of the Dutch Nazi's, but there was no evidence yet of German army units pulling out. Notwithstanding that we had "Mad Tuesday"; wild rumors that the Allies were 30, 20, 10 miles away. People forgot there were 3 major rivers between them and Rotterdam. The Germans were not yet defeated and we had to fight on. Then came the airborne attack in September. We saw hundreds of aircraft flying over, we did not know where they were going, but we received very specific orders from Allied Headquarters. An immediate railroad strike, all Dutch personnel left their jobs or did not show up and went into hiding. We soon found out what was going on. The

airborne landings were to take the bridges over the rivers Rhine, Maas and Waal. The bridge at Arnhem was critical but could not be taken. Notwithstanding the information from the resistance that a German SS Panzer division was "at rest" in the Arnhem area, the British dropped their airborne soldiers right there and they lost the battle, Arnhem was destroyed in the process. However, Montgomery called it a victory.

CHAPTER SEVENTY-TWO

THE BATTLE OF ARNHEM
"A BRIDGE TOO FAR!"

SUNDAY, SEPTEMBER 17, 1944

On this beautiful Sunday morning in Rotterdam we were not yet aware of what was in store for us but we would soon find out.

In the south of England (less than 200 miles from Rotterdam), Sunday had dawned bright and sunny as well, a gorgeous day for flying. Paratroopers were in the process of boarding their Dakotas. The glider and tug combinations were all ready to go. They would be the first ones to take off; at 09:30 and the C-47 Dakotas would follow later.

British 1st AB British XXX Corps

US 82d AB US 101st AB

349. Insignias

The 101st Airborne Division, (Screaming Eagles), took the southern route into Holland, while the 82nd (All American) and British 1st Airborne Division (Pegasus) would fly the northern route. The two columns of aircraft stretched for 94 miles (150 kilometers) in length and 3 miles (5 kilometers) in width. There were a total of 1,051 troop carriers and 516 glider/tug combinations (2,083 aircraft in all). Escorts amounted to 371 Spitfires, Tempests and Mosquitoes on the northern route, and 548 P-47 Thunderbolts, P-38 Lightnings and P-51 Mustangs on the southern route.

The Stirling...   ...and the Horsa

One of the combinations by which the troops were flown to their destinations. The C-47 towing a Waco glider was an American variant.

350.

The cockpit of a Waco glider

351.

438

Shortly after 10am the air raid sirens sounded in Rotterdam and not long thereafter we heard the familiar sound of Rolls Royce Merlin engines; once you have heard the distinct rhythmic sound of these powerful engines, you will never forget it. First a few and then more and more engines joined the chorus. We sneaked a look outside and there high against a pure blue sky we saw heavy bombers of the RAF. We noticed something we had not seen before; these bombers were towing gliders; hundreds of them. They practically covered the sky overhead. I don't recall any anti-aircraft fire and the armada appeared to be flying very leisurely on an easterly course. All of us went out in the street and joined neighbors who, like us, were watching in amazement. The planes were flying east beyond our line of sight but they kept coming from the west. We had no idea where they were heading but they were definitely flying in the direction of the German border. It took a very long time for the gliders to pass and then we saw the C-47 Dakotas, undoubtedly carrying paratroopers. Interspersed were fighter planes and light bombers escorting these troop carriers and protecting them from the Luftwaffe. However, that morning we never saw a German plane in the sky. It reminded us of a time in May 1940 when we were invaded and the German Ju-52 transports had dropped paratroopers all over our immediate area. This was payback time. The disappointments of almost two weeks before, when we had experienced that "Crazy Tuesday", were quickly forgotten.

Unbeknownst to us "Operation Market-Garden" had begun. Its final outcome would turn out an unmitigated disaster for us in the west of Holland.

The US 82nd Airborne Division being
dropped at Groesbeek

352.

A paratrooper leaving the drop zone
is welcomed by the local people

353.

354. The commanders of Operation Market-Garden

The tactical objectives of Operation Market Garden were to secure a series of bridges over the main rivers of the German-occupied Netherlands by large-scale use of airborne forces together with a rapid advance by armored units along the connecting roads, for the strategic purpose of allowing an Allied crossing of the Rhine river, the last major natural barrier to an advance into Germany. The operation was initially successful with the capture of the Waal Bridge at Nijmegen on September 20, but was a failure overall as the final Rhine Bridge at Arnhem was never taken, and the British 1st Airborne Division was destroyed in the ensuing combat. The

Rhine would remain a barrier to the Allied advance until the Allied Offensives in March 1945.

The decision to launch Market Garden was influenced by several factors. After Normandy, the airborne forces had been withdrawn to re-form in England, forming the First Allied Airborne Army consisting of three US and two British airborne divisions, and an additional Polish Brigade. General Eisenhower had been under pressure from the US to use these forces as soon as possible; after Normandy eighteen airborne operations had been planned and then cancelled at short notice when ground forces overran the intended drop zones.

General Miles Dempsey's Second British Army would carry out the ground operation –(Garden) –. Dempsey selected Lieutenant-General Brian Horrocks's XXX Corps for the task of breaking through the German forward defenses and then pushing up a corridor containing just one road to relieve and join up the airborne landings. Highway 69 was a two-lane road and it would soon be dubbed *"Hell's Highway"*. Montgomery's order to Dempsey was that this move should be *"rapid and violent, without regard to what is happening on the flanks"*. No less than 2,300 vehicles loaded with bridging material and 9,000 sappers and pioneers to replace or repair any blown bridges were part of the operation. XXX Corps had fortunately captured a bridgehead over the Meuse-Escaut canal at Neerpelt, in Belgium, only three miles south of the Dutch border, which meant one less waterway to cross and also that almost all of the ensuing action would be in Holland. The distance by road from the start line at Neerpelt to the bridge at Arnhem was sixty-four miles, a far deeper airborne penetration than ever before contemplated. If the combined operations were successful, it was hoped that the British in Arnhem could be reached in three days or less and that a further advance could cut Holland in two by reaching the IJsselmeer on the fifth day. The two American divisions were to be withdrawn immediately to England, but the 1st British Airborne was told that it might be retained to remain in action as ground troops; Rotterdam was hinted at as the next objective for the division, and maps of that area were issued to the units.

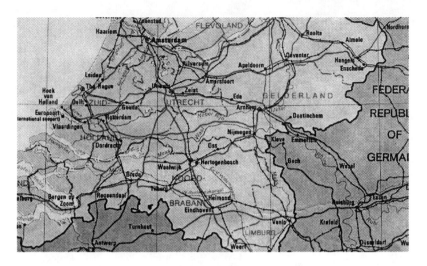

355. Map of Holland

The airborne part of the operation was called *'Market'*. The first gliders that we had seen crossing over Rotterdam were gliders of the British 1st Airborne Division. From Rotterdam to Arnhem is only 50 kilometers and once they had crossed over our heads the tugs and gliders would be making preparations for landing. They touched down just after midday followed by the divisional artillery and troops. Losses in gliders were light, the majority of which had landed in England and would arrive the following day. The only major loss was the failure of two gliders to arrive, each carrying a 17 pounder anti-tank gun. The 101st (Screaming Eagles), under Major General Maxwell D. Taylor, would drop in two locations just north of the XXX Corps to take the bridges northwest of Eindhoven at Son and Veghel. The 82nd Airborne (All American), under Brigadier General James M. Gavin, would drop quite a bit northeast of them to take the bridges at Grave and Nijmegen, and finally the British 1st Airborne Division, under Major General Roy Urquhart and the Polish 1st Independent Parachute Brigade would drop at the extreme north end of the route, to take the road bridge at Arnhem and rail bridge at Oosterbeek.

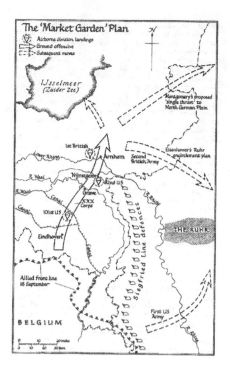

356. The Market Garden Plan

Market would be the largest airborne operation in history. It was the '*brainchild*' of Field Marshall Bernard Law Montgomery and for those interested in statistics, a total of 33,971 men would go into action by air – 20,190 by parachute, 13,781 by glider – together with 5,230 tons of equipment, 1,927 vehicles and 568 guns.

Garden

Garden consisted primarily of XXX Corps, and initially spearheaded by the Guards Armored Division, an elite British Armored Formation, with the 43rd Wessex and 50th Northumbrian Infantry Division in reserve. They were expected to arrive at the south end of the 101st area on the launch day, the 82nd by the second day, and the 1st by the third or fourth day at the latest. They would also deliver several additional infantry divisions to take over the defensive operations from the airborne, freeing them for other operations as soon as possible.

Four days was, and is, a long time for an airborne force to fight unsupported. In addition the Allied paratroopers lacked adequate anti-tanks weapons. Even so, it seemed to the Allied high command that the German resistance at this point had broken. Most of the German 15th Army in the area appeared to be fleeing the field from in front of the Canadians, and they were known to have no Panzer-Gruppen. XXX Corps would therefore be facing very limited resistance on their route up Highway 69, and little armor. Meanwhile the German defenders would be spread out over 100 km trying to contain the pockets of airborne forces, from the British 2nd Army in the south to Arnhem in the north.

The rout of the German forces in July and August led the Allies to believe that the German army was a spent force unable to reconstitute its shattered units, but all was not what it seemed. The failure of the 21st Army Group to clear or cut off the Scheldt from the mainland allowed the German 15th Army to move 86,000 men and 600 artillery pieces back into the mainland of the Netherlands, directly into the path of the planned attack. The arrival of Field Marshal Gerd von Rundstedt, who replaced Field Marshal Walter Model, was generally detested by Hitler, but well-respected by his troops, whom he had back in fighting condition within the week. Rundstedt immediately began to plan a defense against what Wehrmacht intelligence said were 60 Allied Divisions at full strength.

Finally, an unfortunate coincidence had resulted in German Panzer forces being sent to the Arnhem area on September 4th. Allied Command was informed of this from various sources including the Dutch resistance as well as their own intelligence. However, it seems that no one in authority was prepared to accept that the German forces were of sufficient strength to trouble Uruquart's 1st Airborne division. Rundstedt and his generals had agreed that Eisenhower would favor Patton in the anticipated offensive. Accordingly, in one of his final orders as Commander-in-Chief West, Model had ordered the II. SS-Panzerkorps, including the 9th SS and 10th SS Panzer divisions under the command of Lieutenant General Wilhelm Bittrich, to rest and refit in the rear. The place chosen happened to be the area around Arnhem with the 9th SS scattered in various towns and villages to the north of the city and the 10th SS stationed 15 km further to the east.

357. The German commanders

However, it should be noted that both SS divisions were very weak. Their combined strength amounted to no more that 7,000 men. In addition they retained few heavy weapons. Nevertheless, the fortuitous selection of Arnhem as a rest area meant that there was an additional 3,000 combat- ready troops immediately available for commitment against the British drop – troops that had received specific training in anti-airborne assault tactics.

PROBLEMS

Several reports from the Dutch resistance reported by September 10th on the German movements, with accurate identification of the German armor units. Although planning was in late stages, SHAEF (Supreme Headquarters Allied Expeditionary Forces) Chief of Staff General Walter Bedell Smith flew to 21st Army Group headquarters to suggest several possible changes in the plan, which Montgomery was unable or unwilling to institute. When an aerial reconnaissance flight returned with pictures clearly showing tanks* deployed only 15 km from the British drop zones, they were actively dismissed by Montgomery, with the (unfounded) assumption that they probably could not run and were broken down.

In the movie "A Bridge Too Far" this particular event is particularly close to my heart. The scene shows a young boy of about 14 years old, my age at the time. He is on his bicycle when he encounters the Spitfire that has just made pictures of the German tanks hidden in the woods. The Spitfire pilot noticed the young man on his bicycle. The pilot swoops down and comes flying directly at the boy who by now stops and watches the plane banking from left to right. The boy waves at the pilot and the pilot waves back. A very emotional scene. This also happened to me toward the end of 1944 when my brother Henry and I were on a small piece of land outside Rotterdam where we were attempting to grow some vegetables, potatoes and tobacco (for our dad). We were never able to harvest any of it. Others were there before us. What I remember vividly, however, is that on this particularly cold morning when both of us were miserable and hungry, a British Spitfire shot down a ME-109 near us and then circled around, saw us in the field and swooped down low while banking the plane from left to right. The pilot waved at us and we waved back. Tears in our eyes. Never to be forgotten!

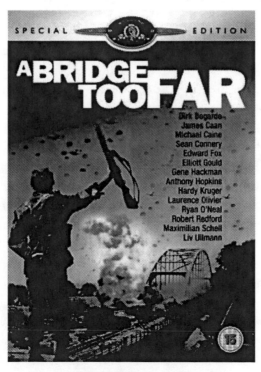

358. A Bridge Too Far
Credits: Internet Movie Database

Additionally, the inexperienced commander of the 1st Allied Airborne Army scheduled only a single drop on each of several days to allow for maintenance and aircrew rest. A precarious timetable at the mercy of the weather meant that the 101st Airborne Division would be without artillery for two days, the 82nd Airborne would lack artillery for one day (and its glider infantry regiment for three days) and the British 1st Airborne would be short a full brigade at the most vulnerable place until the third day.

Drop Zone selection was often poor, particularly at Arnhem where command inexperience placed drop zones 15 kilometers from the bridge; plans to take the bridge the first night ensured the force was split in two for over 24 hours. Unfortunately, air commanders refused to fly to the north of the target bridge because of flak guns at Deelen (Ede). Another suitable drop zone just to the south of the bridge was also rejected because it was thought to be too marshy for landing gliders containing the force's heavier equipment.

Realizing the seriousness of the problem, the plan was then hastily changed to task a small force of machine-gun equipped jeeps with seizing the bridge in a *coup de main* with three battalions following on foot.

In a period of one week, preparations were declared complete; by comparison the airborne plans for Sicily and Normandy had taken months to complete. Key planning tasks were done badly or not at all. The decision to make only one drop on September 17th was "disastrous" in the words of the United States Army's historical study of the operation. Communication planning was poor, and the 1st Airborne would be out of touch with most other headquarters for most of the battle.

Some loss of communication between the bridge and the drop zones was expected as 8 miles separated them, and the main radio used at all levels throughout the Division was Type 22 set with a 5 mile radius. However, the British radios did not function at any range, some had difficulty receiving signals from just a few hundred yards and others received nothing at all. Several theories have been advanced to explain the near-total failure of the 1ˢᵗ Airborne Division's communication net. Modern tests using 22 Sets have suggested that large deposits of iron in the soil could have been to blame. It is also possible that repeated operational stand-to's and cancellations (over a dozen drops were planned and then cancelled in the weeks prior to the operation) had led to sloppy battery charging procedures and lax supervision of this task.

As a consequence, communication between 1ˢᵗ Airborne units was poor at a time when German defenses were being coordinated and reinforced. This was partially due to the fact that the British 1ˢᵗ Airborne Division had been given a radio frequency that was similar to one belonging to a radio station in England. Additionally, Very High Frequency (VHF) sets operated by attached American units were tuned to an unused frequency and were rendered useless. Despite efforts to retune them, the sets were soon destroyed by mortar fire, cutting the 1ˢᵗ Airborne's only link with RAF fighter-bombers. The pilots were under orders not to attack on their own initiative, as there was no easy way to distinguish friend from foe on the airborne front.

In connection with this communication problem it is interesting to mention that when I served in the Netherlands army from 1950 through 1952 I had an opportunity to test the reach of the larger radio sets used during the operation Market Garden. In my capacity in charge of regimental communications of several batteries of 105mm howitzers stationed in Bergen op Zoom (in the province of North Brabant near the Belgian border) I equipped three jeeps with the aforementioned radio sets (Set 22) and routed them to three different locations approximately 35 km (20 miles) from Bergen op Zoom.

359. British Radio Set 22 used by the Dutch Army in
1951

360. Author in 1951 with the 22 Set

At a specific time when the three jeeps had reached their destinations
and had erected the highest antennas that were available, we called
in to HQ. I had been told that with the large antenna the sets would
be good for this specific distance. One of the jeeps was somewhere in
Zeeland on one of the small islands; another one was near Dordrecht
and the third was to the east of Bergen op Zoom. For the most part
this territory was flat countryside and we didn't think that we would
have any problem making connections. I think that you may already

have guessed the answer. We could not establish connection with Bergen op Zoom from any of these locations nor with each other. The distance was just too great. However, in our function of providing communication for the artillery observers these sets worked fine but it must be remembered that the distance during training exercises was never more than maybe 5 miles and only the sweeping antennas on the jeeps were used*. Even so, sets would break down frequently or battery power would be insufficient and the preference would be for the telephone lines that we strung from the howitzer batteries to the observers.

Never touch the antenna while transmitting; you burn your fingers.

Gavin, commanding the US 82nd Airborne Division was skeptical of the plan. In his diary he wrote, "It looks very rough. If I get through this one I will be very lucky." He was also highly critical of Browning, writing that he "…unquestionably lacks the standing, influence and judgment that comes from a proper troop experience…his staff was superficial…Why the British units fumble along…. becomes more and more apparent. Their tops lack the know-how, never do they get down into the dirt and learn the hard way."

Finally reinforcements arrive at Overasselt

361.

362. A crowded sky on Sunday, September 17, 1944

363. The Arnhem Bridge

The Battle
Day 1: Sunday, September 17, 1944

Early successes

Operation Market Garden opened with Allied successes all around. The first landing was in daylight for accuracy, and almost all of the troops arrived on top of their target drop zones without incident.

In the south the 101st met little resistance and captured four of the five bridges tasked to the Division. However, the bridge at Son was blown up as they approached it, after being delayed by a short engagement with two German anti-tank guns. To the north, the 82nd arrived and the small group dropped near Grave took the bridge intact in a rush. They also succeeded in taking one of the vitally important bridges over the Maas-Waal canal. The main effort of the 82nd was to seize the Groesbeek Heights and set up a blocking position there, to prevent a German armor attack out of the nearby Reichswald and to deny the height to German artillery observers. As it turned out they started too late and encountered many more German defenders. By the time the attack was mounted, they were stopped by just-arriving troops of the 9th SS Reconnaissance battalion. This left the Nijmegen Bridge in German hands. This bridge was of vital importance. Unlike some of the bridges to the south, which were over smaller rivers and canals and could be bridged by engineering units, the Nijmegen and Arnhem bridges crossed two arms of the Rhine, and there was no possibility of easily bridging either. If either of the Nijmegen or Arnhem bridges were not captured and held then the advance of XXX Corps would be blocked and Operation Market Garden would fail.

British Landings

The 1st Airborne, meanwhile, had landed without major incident, but problems with the poor plan began almost immediately. Only half of the Division arrived with the *'First Lift'*, and only half of these, in the form of the 1st Parachute Brigade, could advance on the bridge. The remaining troops had to defend the drop zones overnight awaiting the arrival of the *'Second Lift'* on the following day. Had these drops taken place on the same day when weather was still cooperating, the outcome of the ensuing battle would have been different to say the least. The Reconnaissance Squadron was tasked with racing for the bridge in their jeeps and holding it until the rest of the Brigade arrived. Many jeeps had been lost on the 38 1st Division gliders that did not make it to the landing zone; others were unloaded with difficulty. The unit set off to the bridge late, and having traveled only a short distance, the vanguard was halted by strong German defensive position and the Squadron could make no further progress.

Lieutenant Colonel John Frost's 2nd Battalion, however, were advancing far south of this position and so found their route largely undefended, and they arrived at the bridge in the evening and set up defensive positions at the north end. Of the other battalions, the 3rd had only covered half the distance to the bridge when they came to a halt for the night, the rear of their column being under attack and needing time to catch up. The 1st Battalion was similarly fragmented, yet they pushed on around the flank of the German line throughout the night, but frequent skirmishes resulted in their making little progress. Two attempts to take the entire bridge span including the south end were unsuccessful.

XXX Corps advance

General Horrocks refused to commit his troops until he received confirmation that the airborne forces had landed, having had experience of previous airborne operations that had been cancelled on short notice. XXX Corps therefore did not start its advance until 14:35, and soon ran into infantry and anti-tank units dug in on the road. Several division tanks were lost. As dusk fell at 17:00, they were still 15 km south of Eindhoven and behind schedule. The common doctrine for armor at that time was to halt at night, and although 21st Army Group in Normandy had made some night attacks with armor during Operation Totalise, no attempt was made here. *It is mere speculation what Patton would have done had he been in charge.* The Irish Guards commander, Col Joe Vandeleur was told by the Guards Armored Division Chief of Staff to *"take your time..."* because the bridge at Son has been blown. In fact, the loss of the bridge at Son made a fast advance more urgent, so that XXX Corps engineers could begin work on a replacement.

On the German side, it was soon clear what was going on. Walther Model, in direct command of the forces in the area, was initially confused by the British dropping in what appeared to be middle of nowhere, and concluded they were commandos attempting to kidnap him. Meanwhile, Bittrich, commanding the 2nd SS Panzer Corps, had a clearer head, and immediately sent a reconnaissance company of the 9th Panzer Division south to Nijmegen to reinforce the bridge defense there. By midnight, however, Model had gained a clear picture of the situation and issued orders that proved beneficial to the successful defense of Arnhem.

DAY 2: MONDAY, SEPTEMBER 18
BRITISH AIRBORNE FRONT

The 1st and 3rd Parachute Battalions pushed towards the Arnhem Bridge during the early hours and made good progress, but they were frequently halted in skirmishes as soon as it became daylight. With their long and unwieldy columns having to halt to beat off attacks whilst the troops in front carried on unaware, it was easy for the Germans to delay segments of the two battalions, fragment them, and mop up the remnants. Also, early in the day, the 9th SS reconnaissance battalion, sent south the day before, concluded it was not needed in Nijmegen and returned to Arnhem. Though aware of the British troops at the bridge, it attempted to cross by force and was beaten back with heavy losses, including its commanding officer, SS-Hauptsturmfuhrer Paul Grabner.

AMERICAN FRONT
82ND AIRBORNE

Grave proved to be well defended and German forces continued to press on the 82nd deployed on the Groesbeek heights to the east of Nijmegen. Early in the day, German counterattacks seized one of the Allied landing zones, where the second lift was scheduled to arrive at 13:00. The 508th Parachute Infantry Regiment attacked at 13:10 and cleared the LZ by 14:00, capturing 16 German flak pieces and taking 149 prisoners.

101st AIRBORNE

The 101st, faced with the loss of the bridge at Son, unsuccessfully attempted to take the similar bridge a few kilometers away at Best, finding the approach blocked. Other units continued moving to the south and eventually reached the northern end of Eindhoven. At about noon reconnaissance units from XXX Corps met them. At 16:00, they made radio contact with the main force to the south and told them about the Son Bridge, asking for a Bailey bridge to be brought forward.

XXX Corps soon arrived in Eindhoven, and by that night was bivouacked south of Son while they waited for the Royal Engineers to erect the Bailey bridge. At the end of two days the operation was 36 hours behind schedule, with both primary bridges still in German hands.

DAY 3: TUESDAY, SEPTEMBER 19
ARNHEM

During the early morning hours, the 1st Parachute Brigade began its attack towards Arnhem Bridge with the 1st Battalion leading, supported by remnants of the 3rd Battalion, with the 2nd South Staffordshire's on the 1st Battalion's left flank and the 11th Battalion following behind. As soon as it became light, the 1st Battalion was spotted and halted by fire from the main German defensive line. Trapped in open ground and under heavy fire from three sides, the 1st Battalion disintegrated and what remained of the 3rd Battalion fell back. The 2nd South Staffords were similarly cut off and, save for about 150 men, overcome by midday. The 11th Battalion, that had stayed out of much of the fighting, were now overwhelmed in exposed positions while attempting to capture high ground to the north. With no hope of breaking through, the 500 remaining men of these four battalions withdrew west in the direction of the main force three miles away from Oosterbeek.

The 2nd Battalion and attached units, by now amounting to approximately 600 men, were still in firm control of the northern approach ramp to the Arnhem Bridge. The Germans recognized that they would not be moved by such infantry attacks as had been bloodily repulsed on the previous day, so instead they heavily shelled the small British perimeter with mortars, artillery and tanks, systematically demolishing each house to enable their infantry to exploit gaps and dislodge the defenders. Although in constant heavy battle against enormous odds the British clung fiercely to their positions, and in the main, the perimeter remained unchanged.

Day 4: Wednesday, September 20
Arnhem Bridge

Lt. Colonel John Frost's force at the bridge continued to hold out and they established communication via the public telephone system with 1st Division at around noon. They learned that the Division had no hope of relieving them and that XXX Corps was stopped to the south in front of Nijmegen Bridge. By afternoon, British positions around Arnhem Bridge weakened considerably. Casualties, mostly wounded, were high from constant shelling. Also acute was a lack of ammunition, particularly anti-tank munitions, the absence of which enabled enemy armor to demolish British positions from point-blank range. Food, water and medical supplies were scarce and so many buildings were on fire and in such serious danger of collapse that a two-hour truce was arranged to evacuate the wounded (including Colonel John Frost) into German care and captivity. Frederick Gough took over as commander when Frost left.

The Germans overcame remaining pockets of resistance throughout the day, gaining control of the northern bridge approaches and permitting reinforcements to cross the span and reinforce units further south near Nijmegen. The remaining British troops continued to fight on fiercely; some with knives only, but by early Thursday morning almost all had been taken prisoner. Only German radio intercept operators heard the last radio message broadcast from the bridge –"out of ammo, God save the King"

While it was estimated that the entire 1st Airborne Division, 10,000 strong, would only need to hold the Arnhem Bridge for 4 days, in fact just 740 had held it almost as long against far heavier opposition than anticipated. While eighty-one British soldiers died defending Arnhem Bridge, German losses cannot be stated with any accuracy, though they were certainly extremely heavy; eleven units known to have participated in the fighting reported 50% casualties after the battle. In memory of the fighting there, the bridge has been renamed the "John Frost Bridge". General James M. Gavin, commander of the 82nd Airborne Division, called Frost's stand "the outstanding independent parachute battalion action of the war."

Operation Market Garden concluded officially on September 25, exactly a week after it started. It was decided to go over to the defensive with a new front line in Nijmegen. The Nijmegen Bridge had been captured on Wednesday, September 20.

364. The Nijmegen Bridge in allied hands.

365. Sherman tanks on Nijmegen Bridge

Boats ordered by the 82nd Airborne the day before failed to arrive until afternoon, and a hasty daylight assault crossing was ordered. At about 15:00, the 3rd Battalion, 504th PIR made the crossing in 26 canvas assault boats into well-defended positions. The unit had never seen the British-made boats before, and had no training on them. A shortage of paddles required some troopers to paddle the craft with their rifle butts. About half the boats survived the crossing under heavy fire; survivors then assaulted across 200 meters of open ground on the far bank and seized the north end of the bridge. German forces withdrew from both ends of the bridge, which was then rushed by Guards tanks and the 2nd Battalion, 505th PIR, securing the bridge after four days of struggle. The Germans had attempted to blow the bridge but the charges failed to ignite. The costly attack was nicknamed "Little Omaha" in reference to Omaha Beach in Normandy.

To the south the running battles between the US 101st and various German units continued, eventually with several Panthers cutting off the roads but pulling back when low on ammunition.

When General Dempsey of the 2nd Army met General Gavin, commander of the US 82nd Airborne Division, he is reported to have said (in reference to the Nijmegen Bridge attack), *"I am proud to meet the commander of the greatest Division in the World today."*

James M. Gavin (37),
the youngest Division
Commander in
"Market Garden"

366.

On Monday, September 25, employing every ruse to give the Germans the impression that their positions were unchanged, the 1st Airborne Division began its withdrawal at 22:00. British and Canadian engineer units ferried the troops across the Rhine, covered by the Polish 3rd Parachute Battalion on the north bank. By early the next morning they had withdrawn 2,398 survivors, leaving 300 men to surrender on the north bank at first light when German fire prevented their rescue. Of the approximately 10,000 men of the 1st Airborne Division and other units that fought north of the Rhine, 1,485 were killed and 6,414 were taken prisoner, of whom one third were wounded.

To the south, the newly arrived 50th (Northumbrian) Division attacked the Germans holding the highway and secured it by the next day. Allied positions in the *'Nijmegen Salient'*, as it became to be known, were manned throughout the rest of September and October by the 82nd and 101st Airborne units, then handed over to the First Canadian Army in November 1944 and remained unchanged until February 1945 when Operation Veritable was launched on the Rhineland, advancing east instead of north toward Arnhem.

Unseized Tactical Initiative

Arnhem Bridge was not the only available Rhine crossing. In fact, had the Market Garden planners realized that a ferry was available at Driel; Frost's paratroopers might well have secured that instead of the Arnhem Bridge, making a profound difference in the campaign. At a minimum, had XXX Corps pushed north, they would have arrived at the south end and secured it, leaving the way open for another crossing to the north at some other point. There was the smaller possibility of arriving with Frost's force intact. This perceived "lack of guts" caused some bitterness at the time.

Despite the heroism, bad choices were made throughout and opportunities ignored. The commander of the Glider Pilot Regiment had asked for a small force with gliders to land on the southern side of the bridge at Arnhem, to quickly capture it, but he was denied. This was surprising in light of the fact that in Normandy, the British 6th Airborne Division had used such coup-de-main tactics successfully to take smaller bridges. In Britain, the commander of the British 52nd (Lowland) Infantry Division, whose troops were slated to fly into a captured airfield, pleaded with his superiors to allow a Brigade to fly in with gliders to assist General Urquhart's trapped forces, this was also denied, though under the circumstances probably sensible as glider landings on undefended landing zones before the eyes of an alert enemy could result in disaster. However, there was another airfield near Grave, and if the 52nd Lowland had been landed there, they might have freed up British units that were supporting the 82nd Airborne, and might have allowed them to reach Arnhem sooner. Polish 1st Parachute Brigade commander, General Stanislaw Sosabowski was prepared to be dropped dangerously through the fog which held up his drop, but again he was refused.

The British forces at Arnhem ignored the Dutch resistance, although they did work with the US Airborne Divisions.

Reflections:

Eisenhower believed until his death that Market Garden was a campaign that was worth waging. Even so, Cornelius Ryan, the writer of "The Longest Day" and "A Bridge too Far", quotes Eisenhower as saying, "…I don't know what you heard in Britain, but the British have never understood the American system of command… I never heard from the British any golden paeans of praise. And you're not going to hear it now, particularly from people like Montgomery". But Eisenhower kept these views to himself, not revealing them until long after hostilities had ended.

For his part, Montgomery called Market Garden "90% successful" and said:

"In my prejudiced view, if the operation had been properly backed from its inception, and given the aircraft, ground forces, and administrative resources necessary for the job, it would have succeeded in spite of my mistakes, or the adverse weather, or the presence of the 2ⁿᵈ SS Panzer Corps in the Arnhem area. I remain Market Garden's unrepentant advocate."

Dutch Prince Bernhard responded directly to this to Cornelius Ryan:

"My country can never again afford the luxury of another Montgomery success."

LIBERATION

1 Canadian Corps finally liberated the city of Arnhem on 14 April 1945 after two days of fighting. The prized Arnhem Bridge did not survive the war. It was replaced with a bridge of similar appearance after the war, and was renamed John Frost Bridge for Colonel Frost in September 1978.

367. The John Frost Bridge today.

When in Oosterbeek, Holland, please go visit the British cemetery and find the grave markers of these three among all the other heroes. These three men received, posthumously, the highest British recognition for bravery in battle: the Victoria Cross (VC):

- Flight Lieutenant David S. A. Lord VC, DFC 271 Squadron Royal Air Force.
- Lieutenant John Hollington Grayburn VC Oxford and Bucks Light Infantry attached to 2d Battalion Parachute Regiment.
- Captain Lionel E. Queripel VC Royal Sussex Regiment attached to 10th Battalion Parachute Regiment.

368. Oosterbeek Cemetery

369. Oosterbeek Cemetery

370. With a personal message from his family.

371. The Airborne Museum in Oosterbeek

Holland will be forever grateful to the British 1st Airborne Division and will never forget and always remember their sacrifices in Holland so that we might be free.

CHAPTER SEVENTY-THREE

THE 'V' WEAPONS

First came the "Buzz bomb" or "Doodlebug". It was the first guided missile used in war and the forerunner of today's cruise missile. The *'V'* for *Vergeltungswaffe* came from the brain of the German Propaganda Minister *Goebbels*. It signified reprisal against the Allies for the bombing of the Fatherland. The V-1 was used between June 1944 and March 1945. It was fired at targets in southeastern England and Belgium, chiefly London and Antwerp. When the Allies overran launch sites along the French coast the sites were moved to the Dutch coast between Rotterdam and The Hague. They continued to be launched from there until the end of the war. Remember that with the failure of taking the Arnhem Bridge our area of Holland became isolated and was not liberated until the Germans surrendered on May 5th, 1945. I remember seeing these Buzz bombs quite frequently flying by. They were not very fast and the RAF fighters were able to fly along side of them and with their wings underneath the stubby wings and moving slightly up and down, without touching, the V-1 would topple prematurely to the ground. These V-1's made a buzzing and popping kind a sound. The sound was not continuous like the jet engines of today. It worked on the principal of taking in air with fuel much like a car engine, then closing the intake port and igniting the mixture. The resulting explosion of the mixture would open the intake ports and the process would repeat itself, fifty times per second. This produced a characteristic buzzing sound, which gave rise to the colloquial names "buzz bomb" or "doodlebug" (after an Australian insect).

The V-1's range was about 400 km (250 miles). It was about 8 meters long (25.5 feet) and 5.3 meters (17 feet 6 inches) in span. It weighed 2,180 kilograms (4,800 pounds). It flew at an altitude of 100 to 1,000 meters (300 to 3,000 feet) and carried an 850-kilogram warhead and held 150 gallons of fuel. The flying bomb was a relatively simple device, with a fuselage constructed mainly of welded sheet metal with wings built similarly or of plywood, and could be assembled in about 50 man-hours.

372. V-1's in production in an underground facility.

373. A V-1 in flight

374. The launch ramp being inspected by Allied soldiers.

On September 8, 1944 Henry and I were walking on the Pieter de Hooghweg, not far from our house, when we saw a quickly rising column of vapor shooting straight up in the sky. It was a clear sunny day and we could see it clearly. At the head of this quickly rising trail of white smoke we could see an object spitting fire. It was rising very fast and we were both fascinated because neither one of us had ever seen anything like it. It must have reached an altitude of at least 100 miles when the flame stopped and the object toppled over at an angle of maybe 80 degrees toward the west. Then we lost it. What we were seeing was the first successful launching to a target of Germany's second reprisal weapon, the V-2. V stood for *Vergeltungswaffe* (retaliation weapon).

All the time when we were watching it rise in the sky there was no sound and just at the point when the rocket toppled over toward England and the city of London, we heard a loud rumble that continued for quite some time. The launch site was somewhere along the coast between Rotterdam and The Hague, a mere 10 miles away.

Over the next few months the numbers of V-2's fired were at least 3,172, distributed over various targets in Belgium, France and England. Hundreds more were launched that blew up in mid-flight, and never made it into allied statistics.

Because the V-2 traveled at supersonic speed, it reached its target in total silence. To the civilians used to the idea that they might soon be blown up if they heard an enemy bomber or V-1 flying bomb, this new mode of attack was disconcerting.

It also meant that when the attacks on London began in September 1944, the British government could keep a lid on it. Explosions could be attributed to other causes or to no particular cause at all. In this way the Germans were unsure that their weapons were actually reaching England. The Germans themselves finally announced the V-2 on November 8, 1944 and only then did Winston Churchill inform Parliament, and the world, that England had been under rocket attack *"for the last few weeks"*.

375. A V-2 in flight

376. V-2 on its launch pad

At launch the V-2 propelled itself for a short time on its own power, and its navigation system directed it towards its target during this period. After engine shutdown it continued on what is basically a free-fall trajectory. It had an operational range of about 300 km (200 statute miles) carrying a 1,000 kg (2,200 lb) Amatol warhead, with accuracy 'Circular Error Probable' (CEP) of 11 miles (17 km). This meant that at a 200-mile (300 km) range, it would have only a 50% change of being within 11 miles (17 km) of the target. With that kind of accuracy, it could be aimed to hit a city, but not a factory. By comparison, the Minuteman missiles have a CEP of 100 meters at a range of 10,000 km (330 feet at 6,200 miles)

I can personally vouch for the fact that not all these V-2 were launched successfully.
Occasionally we could tell when something went wrong when they didn't reach sufficient height. They would topple over and come right back to within an area of maybe 10 to 15 miles from the launch site.

We had some chickens in the back yard that I took care of and tried to fatten up so that we could have them for supper sometime. I had to get some straw and with a buddy of mine we went to the area of Blijdorp where the Rotterdam Zoo is located and where I knew a place that sold straw for horses. (German horses). It must have been in November because it was already cold and I remember being hungry as well. While walking there, my peripheral vision picked up what I can best describe as a bolt of lightning. Immediately there were two distinct huge explosions, one right after the other. There had been no warning from air raid sirens, nor did I notice or hear any aircraft. Almost instantly I figured that it had to be a V-2 rocket that had failed. I had heard that when these rockets fail they still have a great deal of unburned fuel on board and this fuel would ignite following the explosion of the warhead. All of a sudden my buddy and I found our selves on the other end of the street we were on. We had been moved there by the concussion and a terrific gust of wind. I was not hurt, however, and whereas my friend turned tail immediately, I had to go see where it had impacted. I was always the '*nosy*' one. I ran toward where I saw huge dust clouds and at the first street on the left side I was just in time to see a three or four story apartment building folding in on itself. It seemed to go in slow motion, accompanied with a cloud of dust that spread all over. It was quite fascinating. Practically a whole city block had been obliterated. When the dust settled I saw what appeared to be body parts and debris in the surrounding trees, quite gruesome. At the far ends of the building that was now gone the walls were still standing with all the toilets still attached to their plumbing and sticking out from the wall. I don't know how many people were killed in this V-2 mishap.

Mother was happy to see me come home unscathed. I never got my straw for the chickens.

CHAPTER SEVENTY-FOUR

THE BIG ROUNDUP
DESTRUCTION OF THE HARBORS

On the afternoon of September 17, 1944 we had learned from the BBC that what we had seen flying over Rotterdam earlier that day was, in fact, the largest airborne assault ever attempted in the history of the world. We all agreed that what we had witnessed was gigantic in scope and truly unbelievable. Literally thousand of aircraft had filled the sky for hours on end and this was repeated the next day, the Second Lift to Arnhem. The BBC announcer provided little detail but the operation involved capturing a series of bridges from the Belgian border all the way to Arnhem where the British 1st Airborne Division would capture the bridge over the Rhine. We had little doubt that the Allies would succeed and it was clear to us that once on the other side of the Rhine river, the Allies would spread out in three directions, north to the Zuiderzee and Amsterdam, west to Rotterdam to capture this large port essential for supply and east, toward the heart of the German homeland.

We strongly believed that the war would be over before Christmas. Henry, my brother, kept us informed after listening to the daily reports from the BBC. After a few days it became clear to us that things weren't going as planned and that the British in Arnhem were slowly being decimated while waiting for the XXX Army Corps to come to their rescue over "Hells Highway".

On Sunday, September 24, we learned that the operation at Arnhem had failed with the loss of thousands of British paratroopers, either killed, wounded or captured. A heroic attempt to rescue a few thousand men holed up around Oosterbeek was for the most part successful. In the black of night small boats were launched from the south shore and were able to rescue what remained of the proud British 1st Airborne Division.

We were devastated by the news for several reasons. Firstly, the loss of so many lives, including many Dutch civilians. Secondly, who had thought that the Germans were still strong enough to win this battle? After Normandy, the slaughter of the Falaise Pocket where a whole German army had practically been annihilated and the subsequent rout of the Germans fleeing in front of the mighty Allied forces toward their own borders manifested our belief that the German Wehrmacht was done for. Obviously not true and in December we would be surprised again when the Germans launched their grandiose attack through the Ardennes in Belgium; a battle that would go into history as the Battle of the Bulge. Thirdly, we knew now that the war would go on and that we would be facing much harder times. The Germans were desperate and they would take it out on the Dutch population that had shown their unfailing support of their 'liberators'.

Already for months the Germans had organized razzias in the big cities in the west of Holland. Quotas for slave labor in Germany had to be filled and young men would be picked up at random, often times together with their bicycles. A favorite of the Germans was to wait outside a church on Sunday and pick out the able young men that were leaving the place of worship. These methods, however, were not satisfactory to the '*krauts*' and a better-organized way would have to be found that would assure at least 50,000 men from Rotterdam alone.

Dr. L. de Jong in his: The Kingdom of the Netherlands in the Second World War, volume 10b, The Last Year, writes about this as follows:

"*Indeed, it was determined that the first large-scale razzia would be executed in Rotterdam, the second in the Hague, the third in Amsterdam and the fourth in the city of Utrecht – Rotterdam had been chosen first because the Germans reasoned that in Rotterdam there were more able-bodied men that presented a danger too close to the German front-line on the north shore of the big rivers. The local German authorities meticulously organized the razzia in Rotterdam. The inner city of Rotterdam would be completely blocked off on November 10 and the razzia would take place on November 11. Men rounded up in the raid would be moved to several large buildings where the German SD (Sicherheitsdienst) would pick out the resistance fighters known to them. The men would then be transported to Germany by means of Rhine river barges, by train or by foot. The razzia would be 'protected' by about 8,000 soldiers of the Wehrmacht; they had machineguns, artillery and flak weapons at their disposal. Trucks with loudspeakers were directed to Rotterdam from all over occupied Holland; these trucks would play a very important role in rounding up the unsuspecting citizens. On Thursday evening, prior to the razzia, the commanders of the raid met and were given detailed maps of the various neighborhoods that were their responsibilities. They were also handed printed leaflets that were to be handed out door-to-door. On Friday morning at 4am (end of curfew) all the roads to Schiedam and Rotterdam were to be closed and the center of Rotterdam would be off-limits at 6:30am at the latest. All this was done in total secrecy. Several additional precautions had been taken: on Thursday afternoon the Rotterdam police force was stripped of their weapons and the city's Telephone Exchange had been ordered to shut down the exchange at midnight (with the exception of the lines used by the Germans). Some of this had leaked out to the Dutch resistance people. A German working on the staff of the Kamfcommandant maintained a connection with the local resistance group and it was he who alerted them that a large-scale razzia was in the offing. There was very little time to warn people but they were able to contact England and request that the RAF and US 8th Air force refrain from strafing large groups on men that were expected on the roads as a result of the razzia. No strafing took place.*

Already on Friday morning about 6:30am the city of Rotterdam had been cut off from the outside. People planning to enter the city were sent home. Early Saturday morning, November 11, the Germans had placed machine guns on practically all the large intersections, sometimes even pieces of artillery. Hundreds of Germans were moving from door to door handing out the leaflets (see below)

BEVEL.

Op bevel der **Duitsche Weermacht** moeten alle mannen in den leeftijd van 17 t/m 40 jaar zich voor den arbeidsinzet aanmelden.

Hiervoor moeten **ALLE** mannen van dezen leeftijd onmiddellijk na ontvangst van dit bevel met de voorgeschreven uitrusting op straat gaan staan.

Alle andere bewoners, ook vrouwen en kinderen, moeten in de huizen blijven totdat de actie ten einde is. De mannen van de genoemde jaargangen, die bij een huiszoeking nog in huis worden aangetroffen, worden gestraft, waarbij hun particulier eigendom zal worden aangesproken.

Bewijzen van vrijstelling van burgerlijke of militaire instanties moeten ter contrôle worden meegebracht. Ook zij, die in het bezit zijn van zulke bewijzen, zijn verplicht zich op straat te begeven.

Er moeten worden medegebracht: warme kleeding, stevige schoenen, dekens, beschermling tegen regen, eetgerei, mes, vork, lepel, drinkbeker en boterhammen voor één dag. Medegebrachte fietsen blijven in het bezit van den eigenaar.

De dagelijksche vergoeding bestaat uit goeden kost, rookartikelen en vijf gulden.
Voor de achterblijvende familieleden zal worden gezorgd.

Het is aan alle bewoners der gemeente verboden hun woonplaats te verlaten.

Op hen, die pogen te ontvluchten of weerstand te bieden, zal worden geschoten.

377. The original flyer.
(See English translation)

ORDER.

By Order of the **German Army**, all men of 17 to 40 years of age must report for labor in Germany.

Accordingly, **ALL** men of that age must immediately upon receipt of this order fall out in the street with the prescribed gear. All other citizens, also women and children, must stay in their homes until this action has ended. Men of the above age group, who are still found in the home upon house search, will be punished and their belongings confiscated.

Declarations of Free Passage from civilian or military government must be taken along. Also those who are in possession of such documents must report.

The following items must be taken along: warm clothing, strong shoes, blankets, rain gear, mess gear, fork, spoon, drinking cup and food for one day. Bicycles will remain the possession of the owner.

The daily reimbursement will consist of good food, cigarettes and five guilders.
Your family will be taken care of.

All citizens are forbidden to leave their premises.

Those who try to flee or offer resistance will be shot.

Rotterdam, 11 November 1944

378. Order to report for forced labor in Germany

Large speakers on German trucks loudly proclaimed the contents of the 'Order":

All men of 17 to 40 years of age must report for labor in Germany. They were to fall out in the street with the following items: warm clothing, strong shoes, blankets, rain-gear, mess-gear, fork, spoon, drinking cup and food for one day. Bicycles would remain the property of the owner. Those not answering the call and found in their home would be dealt with severely and their belongings confiscated. The daily reimbursement will consist of good food, cigarettes and five guilders. The family would be taken care of. Those who try to flee or offer resistance will be shot.

The population was completely taken by surprise. Very few succeeded in escaping the net. Everyone felt caged in. How to interpret the 'severity' of treatment of those still found in their homes? Did this mean that their homes would be burned down? This had been the case in previous razzias elsewhere. The result of such a fire was that adjacent homes would be affected as well and it was therefore understandable that people kept an eye on each other to ensure compliance with the razzia order.

Mother remembers:
It was the first week in November, on a Sunday, when Piet Bloemendaal, Annie's boyfriend and a friend of Henry and Wil van der Elsen, was over for a visit. Naturally we talked about the war. Piet Bloemendaal's father had been killed during the first days of the war. Piet said that he and his cousin had built a safe hiding place and that the 'krauts' would never get them. All of a sudden all hell broke loose outside. The Germans were blowing up all our beautiful harbor installations, cranes, harbor-quay walls, storage-facilities, everything. All this was happening less than a kilometer from our house and it would continue for a long time.

379. Germans are blowing up the Rotterdam harbor
installations (November 1944)

380. Destruction of harbor installations (a)

381. Destruction of harbor installations (b)

382. Destruction of harbor installations ©

383. Destruction of harbor installations (d)

384. Destruction of harbor installations (e)

385. Destruction of harbor installations (f)

386. Destruction of harbor installations (g)

387. Destruction of harbor installations (h)

388. Destruction of harbor installations (i)

389. More destruction of the harbor installations

390. Destroyed machinery at a shipyard.

We knew that the end was in sight. There was now daily bombing of Germany. Piet went home and we started to think of a hiding place for Henry. In the front room at the street side Henk sawed a lid from between the rafters of the floor. It was just wide enough for Henry to get in and the

483

rafters were just high enough. He would be lying on very thin lath and plaster. It was like a coffin. We rehearsed in order to find out how much time it would take to get him in this hole, put the lid on, then the tile and finally the carpeting and a chair. We were hoping that we would never have to use it. Toward the evening of November 10 we once again had electricity. The doorbell worked again and the bridge over the Coolhaven was raised.

I remember that my brother Henry, 20 years old, had left very early to search for food that was getting harder and harder to find. He must have been gone only about 15 minutes when a neighbor showed up at the door and told us that Henry should not leave because he had seen many Germans organizing a full-scale razzia in the Park along the Maas River. Mr. Sijp had also seen that on the Westzeedijk close to our home the Germans had picked up men that just happened to walk there on their way to work. Mother was beyond herself and prayed that Henry would return. Thank God, he did. He also had noticed all the activity; particularly the machine-guns at the intersections. He had returned by sneaking along the harbor and occasionally hiding in some bushes. But he had made it just in time. We now knew that the Germans were planning something big. Uncle Wim, who was past 40 years of age, had been sent back home but was not allowed to cross the bridge over the Coolhaven and he had to go back to his workplace. He only returned the following day. The pressure was on. We had rehearsed what to do and everyone had a specific task. Dad had Tuberculoses and stayed in bed. When the *'krauts'* would knock on the door, Anna de Jong, (the spinster who lived in our souterrain room) would go to answer the door but would not open it and tell the German that she would have to get the key first. That would give Henry more time to slide between the floors. My job was to hold our small dog, Tosca; we didn't want him sniffing where Henry was hiding. Henry was already sitting in the hole and was reading a book when there was a knock at the door. I remember the book was by Zane Grey and Henry was completely engrossed. No doubt reading about cowboys broiling steaks on a campfire somewhere on the prairie. It seems that when one is hungry you always read about food. Henry continued to read, and we were all nervous. It turned out OK. It was a German soldier who was distributing the leaflet containing the order that all men from the ages of 17 and 40 would have to stand in front of their houses. From there they would be transported to Germany to work. All homes would be searched. An hour later again a knock at the door and this time Henry was prepared and was safely between the floors. I remember that he had slight cold and we were afraid that he might cough. This time there were two Germans that came in the house, one was an older officer and the second a young soldier who could not have been more than 17 years old. Before the old guy went downstairs with Anna de Jong he told the young soldier to ask for our permits and also to look around. The young soldier just stood there and didn't move.

Mother remembers:

I looked at him and never will I forget that face. It was immensely sad. It was obvious that he had cried. His whole face was puffed up. It was strange but I did not feel any hatred toward him. I was sad for him but I thought of Henry lying there between the floors; one small cough would be enough to give him away. Maybe the boy had received a tongue-lashing from his superior or maybe he had lost his parents in the bombing of his country. Downstairs the old guy searched all over. He also looked in our cellar cavity. I believe that Henry had the radio with him in the hole. Not long ago I heard from Annie that Hen had been able to overhear what the old guy had said and that at several places he had punched his bayonet through the ceiling.

The young soldier asked mother for *'Ausweispapiere'*, our ID's. She was prepared with her small *Family Marriage Book* that recorded the birthdates of all the children born to the couple. The boy, who had been standing there with his rifle with bayonet on top, leaned the rifle against the wall in order to look at the book. I was holding the dog and was thinking: *"We can just hit this kid over the head and hide him somewhere. We will also have his rifle."* I was 14 years old and full of vinegar. The young soldier who had clearly been crying found the entry of Henry; born February 6, 1924. He pointed at the entry and looked at my mother. Without blinking an eye she said: *"He already works in Germany!"* The kid shrugged his shoulders and said: *"Danke schoen."* (Thank you, very well). Then he took his rifle that was still leaning against the wall and left through the hall where he met up with the old one coming up from the basement. On leaving I noticed that the young soldier was dwarfed by his rifle. A rather pathetic sight.

Henry stayed in his hole for a while longer. In the afternoon we saw hundreds of men walking south across our bridge. They were being marched to the new and not yet in use, Internal Revenue Building. They all looked so forlorn. All of a sudden Annie spotted Piet Bloemendaal (her boyfriend) and his cousin in the rows of men.

Mother remembers:

What a tragedy. Piet was dressed in a thin, short jacket and most likely had been picked up off the street. He and his cousin never had a chance to get into their hiding place. That night it was pitch dark, we heard loud singing. It was coming from thousands of voices. Exhausted men were being marched back across our bridge. What a day this had been. The next day Annie and I went to the IRS building to take some warm clothing for Piet but the men had all left that night and the building was completely empty. After this raid Henry could not leave the house at all. He stayed inside for a week and then went back to his job at Stokvis. He told people that he had managed to escape on the way to Camp Westerbork. Piet and his cousin never returned. At New Years Eve his aunt and sister came to tell us the sad news. They had been killed in an allied bombardment.

Annie was beside herself, completely heart-broken. I don't believe she ever got over it.

(Annie died from Alzheimer's disease December 2006; she was 15 days short of her 80ᵗʰ birthday)

During the night when thousands upon thousands of men came marching back from the IRS building across the Coolhaven Bridge, we went on our balcony to watch the 'exodus'. It was the saddest thing to see these men walking dejectedly. Although it was dark we could tell that some were wearing only a light shirt and it was clear to us that many had been picked up right off the street. They had had no time to prepare for their trip. Then, all of a sudden, we heard one strong voice starting to sing that hauntingly beautiful Dutch song: "Farewell, farewell, my dear fatherland, my dear fatherland farewell".

Immediately, this one man was joined by thousands of others and it seemed that now they were all walking more erect and purposeful. We all cried and sobbed. People on all the balconies overlooking the harbor joined in or applauded. How wonderful that feeling of defiance. Then just as quick there were shots being fired and the singing stopped. The Germans achieved their goal but they knew what was in the hearts of all these men.

391. The music of Farewell, farewell, my dear fatherland, farewell.

392. Columns of Dutch slave laborers on their way to Germany (Oudedijk, Kralingen)

393. Razzia victims on the Le Fevre de Montigny laan in
Hilligersberg.

Henry remembers:

*In November I would try to get over the river with my bike and try to
find some food. On the Westzeedijk, where I normally used to take the
dog, a German Army sentry stopped me. He told me very politely that the
police had closed off the city and should go home and stay there. The next
day the Germans went house to house and delivered a notice that all males
17 to 40 had to come outside and had to report for work in Germany. In
anticipation of such problem we had cut a hole in the floor between the
upper story and the basement. In there were the radios; my commando
knife and I would fit in there too. With the opening closed, the linoleum
and the carpet over it you could not see a thing. When they started to check
house-by-house I was between the floorboards; a good thing I was skinny.
It was like a small coffin and pitch dark. However, it was cold and drafty
so I could get enough oxygen. I was told later that two Germans came
in, one was a young guy and the other an older one. I heard them walk
above me and later below me. The older one was talking and banging on
the ceiling, right below me. Mother told me later that he had ripped the
sheet off the bathtub that was filled with water. Then they left, but I could
not come out yet, they were still roaming the street. The men from our
area were collected in a new building of the Revenue Service. They had
rounded up about 50,000 men in Rotterdam alone. They were marched
off to the east or put in barges. After a couple of days it had quieted down*

again and I could move around carefully and get the newsletter out. We also lost some members of the resistance, and it did hamper things for a while.

Dr. L. de Jong in his: The Kingdom of the Netherlands in the Second World War, volume 10b, The Last Year, in his summation of the Rotterdam razzia:

Approximately 50,000 men from Rotterdam and Schiedam were being shipped to Germany: probably 20,000 by foot, 20,000 by ship and 10,000 by train (a group of about 500 men went on bicycles to Amersfoort. The weather was cold – one day, Monday the 13th, was constant rain. Tired, loaded down with baggage that got heavier by the minute, they walked about 30 km (about 20 mile) a day. They were not allowed to rest and if so at all, for a very brief period. Their feet were wet, sore and blistery, they were hungry, their hands raw from carrying their heavy loads, and all this on mostly worn shoes that had known better times. Those who could go no further were loaded on wagons confiscated from the farmers along the way. Escape was nearly impossible. However, in Delft where the men spent the night in the Technische Hogeschool and where a Central Kitchen provided warm food, a few men from the resistance saw to it that about 250 razzia victims who had assisted with the food distribution found hiding places in the town. All along the route of these men citizens along the way provided similar assistance. It showed great solidarity that was very much appreciated. Even on the open highways hundreds of people from the small villages came with everything that they had been able to gather in a very short time. These scenes were most heartwarming. Men transported by barges experienced very much the same reaction from the citizens. Whenever the barges were moored along the side of the river (within Holland), word of the razzia victims quickly spread and people came in droves to bring them food and drink.

Chapter Seventy-Five

"Saved by a Collaborator?"

The next morning, after the curfew was lifted, my mother and I met in the street with some of the neighbors. Everyone was talking about the raid when, out loud, one woman said to my mother:

"Mrs. Ridder, I didn't see Henry go, where is he?" Mother and I were dumbfounded but before she could respond, another neighbor whom we knew to be a German collaborator and naturally didn't trust, said (just as loud): *"How can you say that, you must not have been looking very good, I saw him go myself. This morning they even went to see him in the IRS building."*

Both mother and I were stunned and she was at a total loss for words. Here was a Dutch woman spy who throughout the war had been visited by officers of the German Abwehr and she had answered the question of that ignorant woman. On the one hand we were glad for the support but on the other hand we speculated that she knew very well that Henry had not reported and that she would now inform the Gestapo. She had merely answered the woman to keep us quiet. We now knew what to expect. The whole family lived in fear and trepidation for several days expecting the worst. But there was no visit from the feared Gestapo, nothing happened and we relaxed somewhat but it continued to puzzle and concern us until we were finally liberated.

CHAPTER SEVENTY-SIX

THE HUNGER WINTER – PART I

The Hunger Winter for the population of western Holland officially started at the end of November 1944 and would last through the beginning of May 1945; almost six months of increasing starvation. Pressure from the German occupation forces continued unabated. From time to time the *Ordnungspolizei* would round up people to dig trenches to strengthen the German defenses around Rotterdam and along the North Sea coast. Plunder by the Wehrmacht was the order of the day. Anyone on a bicycle ran the chance of losing this valuable means of transportation. The population was exhausted: exhausted from the cold, exhausted from the hunger and tired of the war. If you were not able to augment your meager rations with some kind of additional nourishment you were doomed. Shipments from *Switzerland* and the *Swedish Red Cross* were only able to provide three-and-a-half million people a weekly loaf of bread of 400 gram with only 125 gram of margarine once a month. That meant that food intake was only 150 calories.

394. The actual wrapper of the Swedish margarine

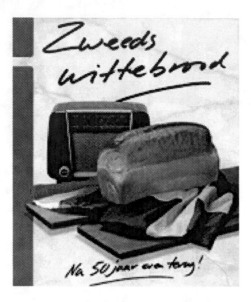

395. After 50 years still a wonderful memory!

Although food was rationed and supposed to provide weekly: 750 gram bread, 45 gram margarine, 125 gram meat, 1 kilo potatoes and 50 gram cheese, in reality, it was not available. Often enough, not even at exorbitant prices. As a result most people had that sallow grey complexion. Toward the end of March 1945 twenty thousand people had already died from starvation and the number of people suffering from malnutrition ran into the millions. That was the situation in March 1945 when the Canadians liberated the eastern provinces.

The west of Holland was not that fortunate and unless there would be a large-scale relief effort, it would lead to mass starvation and inevitable death. The large population centers in Holland were now completely isolated and nothing could be brought in to provide relief. There was no longer any coal, no gas and only two generators providing occasional electricity for the Germans. After April 9, 1945 even that stopped. Some small corporate-owned generators succeeded in keeping pressure on the water system and providing electricity to a few hospitals as well as the telephone system. Only the Germans and some selected few were still connected to that system. Several of the newspapers stenciled the news by hand. All of western Holland was descending in the abyss from which it could only be saved by a miracle.

In the Dunantstraat we suffered like everybody else. Severe hunger resulted in listlessness and apathy toward what was happening in the world around us. Our thoughts were primarily focused on food, food and again food. Anything that appeared edible*. A very close second was the need for heat. The winter of 1944/1945 was one of the coldest winters on record. The harbors were frozen solid, there was snow all around and people were dying in the streets.

* Charlie Chaplin ate the sole of his shoe in the movie: "Gold Rush".

Henry remembers:

After the Battle of Arnhem things became very difficult. The Germans in western Holland were very uptight. I saw one guy pulled off his bike. He had a package on his bicycle wrapped in some white cloth. They probably thought it was a parachute. The Germans did not allow any food transport, a little bit could get through by barge from Zeeland. This was when the "Starvation Winter" started. Shortly afterwards the Germans shut off all electric power for the civilian population, but we were in the harbor district with German facilities. At our house they removed the fuses, turned off the power and put a lead seal on the box. They also took the last meter reading. With a heated small screwdriver I wiggled the seal a little bit open to pull the wire out, open the box and put the fuses back in. I did the same thing on the meter and carefully loosened one of the gears so that the disc could not rotate and move the counter. You had to be careful not to turn on the lights because bulbs get hot and if they found that during an inspection, you were in deep trouble. An extension cord with a light bulb worked fine. Even for the Germans the power was on only a few hours a day so I had to find something for the radio. An acquaintance of ours had a radio store and made a simple battery radio but he did not have a battery. How to get one was tricky, but I managed to "liberate" a car battery. At Stokvis they had an automotive department and were forced to service German trucks. That's where I got the battery; fully charged. I had parked my bike inside the building and wrapped the battery in canvas and also changed the shape somewhat. I walked the bike home with Annie ahead of me to see that the road was clear. The radio worked fine and I was back in business, but always hungry. Tulip bulbs became a delicacy as long as you did not eat the green sprouts. Don't try daffodils, they are poisonous, even the deer here in Atascadero (California) won't eat them. The ration coupons were good for about 1,300 calories a week. That is if you could find the food. From December on till the end of the war you could see people dying on the street. We had a little garden, just outside the city and grew potatoes and some vegetables there, but most had been harvested before we could get them. Through Stokvis I managed to get a license to buy 70 kg seed potatoes for the garden. I managed to buy them but we never planted them. I carried them on the back of my bike home and put them in the basement. When I called mother you should have seen her face. There would not have been any food for us that day; maybe one sugar beet. Bill and I went to our 'farm' on January 1, 1945 and not long after we got there a lone German fighter roared over very low followed by a couple of Spitfires from the RAF. We hid the deck and the shrapnel was flying all around. Later I found out that the Me–109 had been shot down near Delft only a stone's throw from our 'garden'. One of the Spitfires came back to our area and must have noticed the two of us all alone in the dirt. He came roaring down at us, wiggling his wings and the pilot waved at us. It was a great moment. Our harvest was a few potatoes and some tobacco leaves.

Mother remembers

For all of us it was a terrible disappointment that the Allies had been beaten at the Battle of Arnhem. It got us into the hunger winter of 44/45. After that the situation in Holland got worse and worse, hardly any food and no coal, no gas or fuel for heat. Sporadic electricity. We were hungry and cold all the time. This particular winter seemed also much colder. The extra rations for your father didn't help because there was nothing you could buy. One evening, it was already quite late, loud banging on the door. We looked outside and there we saw a big German truck. We called: "Who is there?" "Open the door!" (In German) Your father opened the door and asked what they wanted. "Where is the Ras Company"? He told them and they left. That turned out OK but the fear stayed in our legs for a while. The next day we heard that they had confiscated all of Ras' supplies. We didn't know if these were Germans or the Dutch resistance dressed in German uniforms. Curfew required that everyone had to be inside at 6pm. Uncle Wim was on the bridge at precisely 6pm. The German guard on the bridge told him to go ahead and hurry but behind him walked a

German officer who was drunk and said something to him. Uncle Wim didn't answer and the Kraut took out his revolver and wanted to shoot him. But Uncle Wim ran away from him toward our street and remained in the shadow of Wijt Printing Company; he didn't want to go to our house because he did not want to bring the Kraut to our door. However, the German saw him and approached him in the dark. It was then that Uncle Wim ran for his life. He ran to the back of our apartment building to where the backyards are and to his surprise found our gate unlocked which it never was. He was able to get in and the Kraut who had followed him didn't know where he was and must have given up his pursuit. Of course, we didn't know any of this was going on and with some degree of humor we were talking that if he did not show up we would have more food. But a few minutes later we were frightened by a loud noise from someone running up the stairs from the yard below and then Uncle Wim stormed into our living room in a total state of shock. He then told us what happened. We felt so sorry for him and because of the excitement and in spite of his hunger he couldn't even eat. But he was saved by our negligence. The next day we heard that all the houses to our left had been searched. People were all frightened but nothing happened.

People who got the chance would cut down trees for fuel. We also cut down several trees at the Coolhaven and then drag these into our backyard. This was done at night after curfew. It sounds simple enough but it clearly was not. We were scared stiff. One time we had dragged a tree into our backyard when we felt danger. Quickly we went inside and then we saw a Kraut sticking his head over the fence. We will never know if he noticed the tree lying in the yard but he left. With a dull saw we went in the yard and sawed the tree in two. Then we dragged the two pieces in the cellar for further treatment. It was a tough job but it warmed our bodies. Getting food was next to impossible. For Henry it would be too dangerous. Annie, being a young girl, could not and we considered Wim at the age of 14 too young. In the Coolhaven there would be a barge now and then and we would see women leave with bags. That had to be a black marketer. Anna de Jong and 17-year old Annie went one time to find out and that bastard said to Annie: "Come back tonight, by yourself, and I will get you something." Yes, those things happened also and that way some women were able to obtain some food.

Willem (Bill) Ridder

CHAPTER SEVENTY-SEVEN

THE CEMETERY

Mother writes about cutting down trees along the harbor, in front of our house. When these trees had all disappeared, we had to venture out of our immediate area to find more trees. There was one place I remembered that had huge trees. Before the war we had played there. It was the Catholic Cemetery* on the Westzeedijk, behind The University of Economics. As I described it before, it was a rectangular cemetery surrounded by a moat of some 10 feet wide. There was only one way to get on the grounds and that was via a small bridge with a high wrought iron gate at the entrance. It was a very old cemetery and I never saw it used for burial. I suggested to Henry and Annie that we could go there in the dark during curfew and cut down some of the large branches off the trees. We didn't tell our parents because they would not have allowed us to go. We sneaked out of the house, being very careful not to make any noise that would attract attention. We moved stealthily along the Coolhaven for a few hundred feet, and then crossed the street to another parcel of land and after one more street we descended down a slight hill to the cemetery. It was very dark, overcast, windy and cold. Now and then the moon would show through. Annie was frightened to death because it was all very spooky. When we got to the big iron gate we noticed that it was open. Somebody had cut through the chain. That made it easier for us. When our eyes adjusted to the dark we saw more people that had the same thing in mind. The big grave markers served to hide the people from intruders (the German kind) and when they saw us three they came from behind the stones. It was like the living dead. I told Annie they had risen from the grave and I swear she wet her pants. With our few tools we went to work and were able to gather some good size branches. Then we heard hammering and I couldn't figure out who would be doing 'construction' work. I moved to where the noise was coming from and saw that a large piece of marble had been removed from a grave and a few men were standing in the grave hacking and hammering away at several oak coffins that were lying next to one another. Since it was dark, particularly in that hole, I was unable to see any *'remains'*. This did it for me and the three of us quickly left with the few branches that we had gathered. We made it home safe and then cut the branches in short little pieces that we could burn in the *'nood kachel'*. On this small contraption we did the cooking of what little we had to eat.

396. That's what our 'nood kachel' (emergency stove) looked like. You would blow in the small hole at the bottom to give it more oxygen and increased heat.

* When in Rotterdam in 2005 I went to see the cemetery but it was no longer there. It had made place for a big office building.

CHAPTER SEVENTY-EIGHT

SUGAR BEETS, TULIP BULBS AND WEEDS

First of all, beets and bulbs are edible but not all of them. When there were no longer any potatoes we could still get some sugar beets.

397. Sugar beets. Syrup, soup and cookies!!

We did everything with the sugar beets. First we cut them in small pieces, mashed them into pulp and then boiled the results in a pot with water. After boiling for a while we would strain the pulp and remove it from the pan. A slimy kind of goop was left. This concoction still contained much water and needed to be boiled out. If done right you would end up with pure brown syrup. It was very sweet and nourishing. The problem was that if you waited just a little too long before taking the pan off the stove, the syrup would start to burn and dense smoke would be the result. The stink of that was awful and would hang around for a long time. We would use the remaining pulp to make soup or to make small cookies. A word of caution to anyone trying to eat sugar beets in the raw. When you do you will end up with a sore throat and be hoarse for a long time.

398. Tulip bulbs. Just like chestnuts

Tulip bulbs were a delicacy. Peel off the immediate layer of skin around the bulb and cut off the sprouts on the bottom. Roast them on a fire and it is like eating chestnuts. Not bad at all.

Weeds were another vegetable that we would cook before eating. It was green stuff, bitter but people in the know insisted it was nutritious.

399. Dandelions

Some people even ate nettles but I didn't want any part of it. I had too much experience coming in contact with these plants when we were playing behind our apartment building.

400. Nettles. Edible when cooked and they won't sting anymore.

They sting like the dickens and your skin would get red and be irritated for a long time. However, when cooked, they are said to be *"superb, non-stinging, cooked vegetables"*.

CHAPTER SEVENTY-NINE

A MASS KILLING

In spite of the miserable conditions in Rotterdam and the rest of western Holland, I would still try to go to my High School. It had very little to do with my academic desires but everything with the possibility that one of my classmates would have managed to get some food and would be willing to share it. Additionally, in front of the school there were always some black marketers that sold some miserable looking apples. My mother had given me some guilders and occasionally I would buy one and had myself a feast: a small sour apple cost 15 guilders. In time the price went to 25 or 30 guilders. I don't quite remember, as I didn't have that kind of money anyway. Another reason for going to school was the hope that the potbelly stove would be fired up and there would be some heat in the classroom. The teacher was suffering like the rest of us and if he taught us anything it was the English language. This was against the rules, of course, but at that point we didn't care anymore.

If the resistance killed one German, the Gruene Polizei of the Gestapo would immediately respond and kill innocent people left and right.
I was unfortunate enough to witness one of those killings.

On Monday, March 12, 1945, (54 days before we were liberated) with several of my schoolmates we were making our way to school located in a side street of the Kruiskade near the Hofplein. We didn't stick to the road but rather took shortcuts over the ruins. When we got to the intersection of the Coolsingel and the Kruiskade, we observed some activity and it stopped us dead in our tracks. It must have been around 10:30am when we observed several German trucks coming from the direction of the Coolsingel at great speed. They stopped near the Doelwater, across from the Kruiskade. My guess is that about

40 members of the Gestapo police (Gruene Polizei: their uniforms were green) left the trucks and quickly secured the area around the Hofplein. Then we saw another group of Germans enter the Police Headquarters on the Coolsingel. On the corner of the Kruiskade and Coolsingel as well as the streetcar tracks machine guns were set up. Passersby were ordered to go back. That order included us as well and we moved toward a building where we hid in the high weeds that had sprouted on the ruins adjacent to the bare wall of the building. From our vantage point we observed a group of civilians, all men of different ages that were driven in the direction of the Schiekade where they halted in front of an air raid shelter. At the same time we saw a group of Gruene Polizei coming from the Coolsingel carrying their rifles. They were heading for the Hofplein. Then some short but loud orders were heard coming from the Germans.

From our hiding place we watched with bated breath. Suddenly we heard staccato machine gun fire: *"rat-tat, rat-tat"*. It is quiet for a moment and then again: *"rat-tat, rat-tat"*. Again there is a moment of stillness when once again the gunfire erupts. A little later the Germans spread out and another group heads for the trucks. Together with other people we slowly rise to our feet. There is an eerie silence. There is no traffic whatsoever. We walked in the direction of the Hofplein and the Germans ordered us to hurry along. There was no other way than to pass the air raid shelter. There we observed what we had all been afraid of. In the grass in front of the shelter are the lifeless bodies of 20 men. All this had taken a mere 15 minutes from beginning to end. I remember one young man in blue overalls. He had been on his way to work when he was apprehended for this 'reprisal'. He could not have been older than sixteen.

There was talk that day that a similar incident had taken place on the Pleinweg with 20 men having been murdered. These were reprisals for the shooting of a member of the Ordnungspolizei (Order Police) on Friday, March 9 at 1 pm. It had happened at the Hofplein and the perpetrator had managed to escape.

401. The scene of the killing on Het Hofplein. The bodies are lined up against the slope of the air raid shelter on the right.

Chapter Eighty

Fishing

402. The 'Parksluizen' in Rotterdam

In my quest for food I remembered that when watching ships entering and exiting the locks near our house I had observed a lot of fish at one end of the locks when the Maas water was being lowered to the level of the Coolhaven. These fish would be jumping up and down in the water. I figured that we could catch those fishes with a big enough net. My friend and I constructed a net by attaching some thin cloth between a rectangular frame of metal tubing.

Together with one of my friends we put this contraption together and at the right time we threw it in the water where it sunk. When we pulled it back up it was full of little silver fishes.

We had a bucket full and we went to my friend's home to cook them, including their insides. It tasted like sardines, not bad at all. It helped to satisfy our hunger. We went back the next day but other people had the same idea. These were some rough characters and we were pushed to the side never to get another chance. These roughnecks had constructed large nets covering the width of the locks. After a while there were no more fishes left. The fishes either got smart or the supply was exhausted.

CHAPTER EIGHTY-ONE

DOGS & THE DINING ROOM

During the winter our dog *'Tosca'* disappeared.
We never saw him again. We surmised that perhaps somebody ate him. Sad but under the circumstances quite understandable. It's just that we couldn't do it ourselves.

In 2005 when I was in Rotterdam I talked with Frans van de Berg who like myself had experienced the Hunger Winter of 44/45. At 15 he was a year older than I. He had experienced the *'Hunger Winter'* and had kept a small diary. He was kind enough to share several parts of it with me. It was in Dutch and I translated it:

DOGS DURING THE HUNGER WINTER

(Frans van de Berg's diary)

"Father is home again and he finds temporary work in Terbregge as a greengrocer. With his carrier tri-cycle he visited customers. We would sometimes go find him to see if there was something left to eat. One day an old lady customer asked my dad: "Greengrocer, don't you know a good home for my dog because I have no more food for him"." That's a stroke of good luck!" my father thinks. There were very few dogs and cats left in the city. He knows of an immediate solution and the next day tells the old lady that he knows of a good home and that a young girl will come to pick up the dog. Daughter picks up the dog (a fat one at that) in Terbregge. At home, Uncle Leen is waiting anxiously. With a struggle he gets the dog on the attic and in neat pieces and in a bucket it comes back down from the attic. The bucket is overflowing and the animal is cooked in its own grease. For a couple of days we have something good to eat".

"The second dog (not very big) is lured away from an aunt in Overschie by my sister and my cousin Corrie. The next day we split the beast".

THE DINING ROOM

(Frans van de Berg's diary)

"Next to our Elementary School building in the Pootstraat was the dining room belonging to a children's nursery. Before going home in the early afternoon we could get some food there. Not all the kids made use of the facility thinking it was below their dignity to be seen there. It was really for the poor people. (Just like the wooden shoes and the clothing ration card). But this was the hunger winter of 44–45 and everyone went there to eat whatever he or she could get. When the school whistle blew at 11:45 we would run outside, through the gate of the nursery and into the dining room. In our school were two separate schools. It was therefore important to get inside quickly because otherwise you would have to wait outside in the cold weather. A woman behind a desk that was covered with lists of names stood at the entrance to the dining room. You would say your name and the name of the principal of your school (because of the two schools). The woman would check off your name and you were allowed to enter. From a large container you were given a ladle of some kind of stew in a metal bowl. And now my misery! You would be sitting on wooden benches at long wooden tables. One day there was pea soup: very tasty but full of pieces of bacon. Square pieces as large as dice covered with pig's hair. My cousin was sitting next to me and he also didn't like this bacon. To the extent we could we removed the bacon while eating and put them on the table between our bowls. But... there was also supervision. When the woman was finished ladling the soup she would walk between the tables to make sure everyone had eaten all the food. Here is what happened next. My cousin had finished sooner and had already left the room. The woman notices the heap of bacon pieces and had an immediate solution. Either I eat the bacon or weren't allowed to leave to go home. She would also register a complaint with the principal of my school. I had to do a lot of swallowing and very little chewing. I was able to get rid of a few pieces under the table. My eyes were rolling around in my head and I was

gagging all the time. Suffice to say, I was the last one to leave the dining room, retching all the way home".

CHAPTER EIGHTY-TWO

THE HUNGER WINTER – PART II

403. Hungry kids looking for something edible.

404. Breaking up the wood blocks between the rails.

Henry remembers:

515

After a short interruption as a result of the November razzia our weapon training resumed. I also got my stengun with two fully loaded magazines. I tested the gun in our basement when there was enough outside noise. It worked and after the war I heard something about it. Mother had a small suitcase ready in case we would have to leave in a hurry. She had filled it with sheets and put in the basement with some other stuff. I had fired through the wall and put a few holes in the suitcase. Sometime after the war she took the sheets out and found nicely matching holes in every sheet. She was not pleased.

Early in 1945 the Swedish Red Cross managed to get everyone a half loaf of bread, a stick of margarine and half a pound of artificial honey. The Germans allowed it to go through after Eisenhower told them that if they did not, he would hang them as war criminals. Eisenhower was our hero. After the war he was greeted with wild enthusiasm wherever he visited. The Gestapo, however, did not let up. A most gruesome murder of our dentist, his wife and young children occurred. They lived in a nice house on the Mathenesserlaan. The dentist was accused of having connections with the resistance. This may have been true. I don't know. The Gestapo raided the house and took the family outside. They burned down the house with gasoline and a hand grenade. Then they shot the children in front of the parents, then the mother and finally the father. These murderers were later caught and executed by the resistance. Sometime in February I managed to buy a crate of lettuce. It tasted good, raw without any dressing. At least it filled the stomach. The Army of the Interior started planning an all-out uprising if the war was not over by May. The situation was desperate. The Canadian Army had crossed the Rhine River and Eastern, Central and Western Holland, part of the province of Utrecht and several small islands of Zeeland and South Holland were completely isolated.

Mother remembers:
Now there were daily bombing raids on Germany and all those planes would fly over Holland where some of them were shot down. The resistance saved some of the crew that survived. And so it went. We exchanged things for food but the farmers wanted gold. I wanted to use our wedding rings but your father didn't want to do that. Annie had made a beautiful dress in her Sewing class at school. She exchanged that dress for food voluntarily.

* Magazijn Nederland was the new name of N.V. Kattenburg & Son, a Jewish owned business. The owner was in hiding and my father was the only one who would keep contact with him. He was one of the few that survived the war.

I felt so bad for her because she was missing already so much of her youth. Some of her friends had pretty dresses and shoes. One of these girls' fathers worked for the Krauts at the Coolhaven. That man stole what ever he could from them and would sell it on the black market at exorbitant prices. That way he was able to buy nice clothing and shoes for his family. Honesty would put you in the ground. We tried to buy on the black market but our money was quickly exhausted. A pint of milk was $25. A 70-kilo bag of potatoes cost $1,000. Only those who were rich could still buy on the black market. And yet we had to move forward. We couldn't allow the Krauts to destroy our spirit. Things got increasingly worse with the food supply. Henry wanted to go and find food somewhere but that would be too dangerous. But our distress was increasing by the day. Fortunately Uncle Wim had found a job at Magazijn Nederland and occasionally he would be sent on a secret mission for potatoes. That way he was able to bring some potatoes home with him and one time both your father and Anna would each get 5 kilos. Occasionally Henry would leave, where to we didn't know, and he would come back with some cooking oil and a few onions. We felt so immensely rich then. Henry was very close-mouthed and we never asked him where he got it. We had no gas and no electricity. We were all so terribly cold and because of malnutrition we felt the cold even more. The extra coupons for your father couldn't buy anything. When would we be liberated? The Krauts were also having a harder time feeding their soldiers. Uncle Wim came home one time and told me that he had to pick up a load of coal for the business from a place near the Oostkousdijk. That was about a half hour walk from our house. I went with Uncle Wim and on our return would pass by our house to offload some of the coal. I realized that would be dishonest. Henry had wanted to go but it was too dangerous from him to be out in the open. Besides, the area where we had to go was teeming with Krauts. Uncle Wim had a few black sheets that he would cover the coals with. We filled up the handcart and I found a few briquettes that I put in my pockets. We then went on our way but that was easier said than done. The cart was too heavy and we couldn't get it going. Our main goal was to get away from those Krauts. At last we got the cart going albeit very slowly. When we got to a slight incline we couldn't move any farther. We were becoming desperate and didn't know what to do. But *there came a tough-looking young woman who said she would help us to get over the incline. That succeeded. She must have noticed how exhausted we were and asked: "Where do you guys need to go"? I told her and this tough-looking young woman brought us to the front door of our house. I was so thankful and offered to give her some of our potatoes. She looked at me and said: "I don't want anything." And then looking at Uncle Wim said: "Just give it to that skeleton." Thank God for those kinds of people that you would never forget. Now we had again some fuel for our small stove.*

Mother continues:

Everything had to be done in the dark after curfew. We were scared all the time.

The year had come to an end and the lack of food had reached unimaginable proportions. The winter was worse than ever and we had no more fuel for heating. Beyond this food we kept ourselves alive with tulip bulbs and during the month of March with some greens that we bought at exorbitant prices. We would eat that raw. Toward the end of March many people started to die from 'hongeroedeem' (hunger oedema). In front of our house a 12-year-old boy had collapsed from hunger and we saw him die. He had been able to tell us where he lived and your father with a few other men from the street put him in a wheelbarrow and carted him to his house at the Schietbaanstraat. While I am writing this I can see it all again clearly in front of me and again feel the anger and frustration. At our neighbors, the Smit's, their old father had died from malnutrition and they came to our house asking if your father could get him ready for burial. There were no other means like doctors or mortuary people anymore. Your father was sick and so Uncle Wim and I went instead. There was Mrs. Smit with her two daughters. Smit had died that night. His body was already showing rigor mortis. This was the first time in my life but I got the strength to do it. Uncle Wim shaved him and I washed him. All of a sudden, when I got to wash his knees, his legs went straight up. It scared me to death. He finally got buried more than 2 weeks later because there were not enough coffins. There were so many dead bodies all over the city. Some of the dead went in coffins but when the relatives had left the cemetery the gravediggers would dump the body in the grave and use the coffin again. In early April we were able to buy some white bread with our otherwise worthless coupons. Sweden had sent us flour and margarine. Can you imagine what that meant for us? It was like manna from heaven like it says in the bible. But for too many people it was too late including your uncle Jan.

Several pictures of starving children saved just in time from malnutrition and starvation.

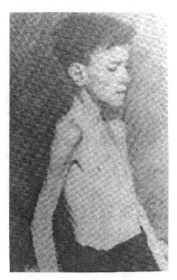

405.

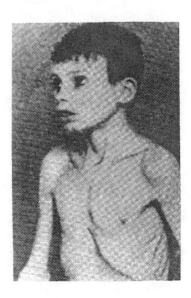

406.

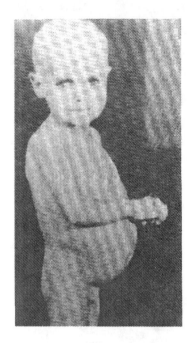

407.

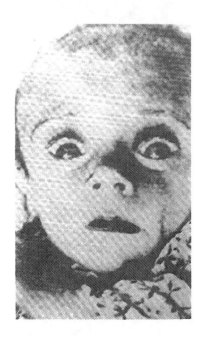

408.

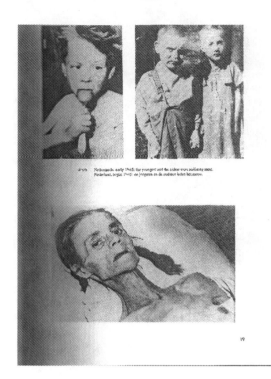

19

409.

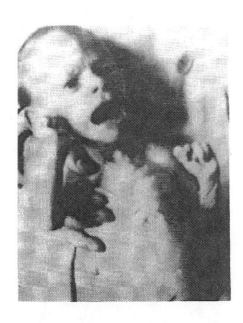

410.

CHAPTER EIGHTY-THREE

A QUEST FOR FOOD

Mother remembers:

*Before 1940 we would go on vacation to Rockanje near Oostvoorne on
the coast. For 14 days we would rent a few rooms of a farm owned by
Mr. Jaap Looy. The last time we went there was August 1939. We were
there when the Dutch Army was mobilized. The pleasure of a vacation
was gone. You felt the threat of war. In 1944 you couldn't get there any
longer. We would write occasionally but during the hunger-winter they
were unable to help us with food. Their farm had been confiscated because
it was in the dunes near the North Sea beaches. With the three of them
they now lived in a chicken coop.*

*We knew that occasionally young children were smuggled across the bridges
by people who would declare the children theirs. Those people lived on the
islands and had a permit. Our situation was so bad that we decided to
try and get Wim across the bridge. He would then be able to get some food
and not starve to death. Don't ask a mother how I could have done that.
Wim was only 14 years old, he was so very thin but he was feisty and
determined. The day before we would try to get Wim across the bridge he
came home all excited. He had a small plate of warm food, a few potatoes,
some vegetables and a small meatball. He said: "I will stay here until you
eat it all and then I will get some food also." That's the way it happened
but that night Wim got sick and threw it all up. The next morning, Henk,
Wim and I, on bicycles got on the way. First with a small boat across
the Maas to the Heiplaat. The small boat was filled to overflowing with
people like us who were hoping to find some food on the almost barren
fields. I had sewn some money in Wim's inside coat pocket. He would have
to cross the Spijkenisse Bridge and only people that lived on the other side
were allowed to cross with the right papers. Your father and you went up
to the Krauts at the bridge but were immediately sent back. The only way
would be to go as the child of somebody who lived on the other side. We*

asked several but they didn't want to take a chance. When you were caught you could be shot on the spot. All of a sudden some women came up to me and said: "Thank God your son wasn't killed". What had happened was that a large German truck had hit Wim on his bicycle. His bicycle had been demolished but Wim was safe. The small and only sandwich that I had given him was lost in the mud. In spite of that Wim wanted to get across. Your father and I finally found a man who agreed to take him as his son. Your father gave Wim his bicycle and together with that nice man Wim paddled to the bridge and the other side. Henk and I then made the trip back home where we arrived just in time for curfew.

At 14 years of age I felt quite capable to go on this quest for food. A matter of fact, I was looking forward to it. As mother described, the three of us, Dad, Mom and I, went on our bicycles; the bikes had no tires and we rode on the rims. After crossing the Maas River we ended up at the *Spijkenisse Brug*. This was a *Hefbrug* (a vertical lift-bridge).

411. A picture of the new bridge after the war. A big
German trailer truck on the road on the left demolished
my bike. I was able to jump off the bike up the grass slope.
In '45 it was all mud.

There were a lot of Germans at the head of the bridge. They were not friendly and as we had no permits they shouted at us to get back: "Machen Sie schnell!" We did as ordered but lingered a few hundred

525

feet back on the side of the road. There were a lot of people like us. Some had baby prams, wheelbarrows or two bicycle wheels with a wooden box resting on the axle. It was a motley crew of starving men, women and children. They had made attempts to cross but like us had been rudely rejected. We did, however, notice that occasionally people on bicycles were seen crossing the bridge and we figured that they must live on the other side. You could tell because they appeared sure of themselves and they also looked better fed. When we noticed one of those people paddling his way to the bridge my dad approached him. The man stopped and my dad must have asked him if he would pretend that I was his son and get me across. He agreed and told me to stick close to him. Dad gave me his bicycle; a big German truck had demolished mine. From that point on I was on my own. Nervous but determined. The German sentry raised his arm for us to stop and apparently the sentry knew the man and waved us through. I remember paddling across the bridge. I didn't dare to look back in fear that they would call me back. The closer I came to the other side the more elated I became. Once on the other side and out of sight of the Germans my surrogate father went to the left and I continued toward the town of De Brielle, a very old and historic town. My first visit would be to the sister of Oom (Uncle) Anton, my mother's cousin. The one who owned a factory making lead pipes and wiring? His sister Hennie ran a yarn store downtown De Brielle. I located the store on Main Street quickly. Hennie recognized me and welcomed me with open arms. One of her nephews, whom I knew, was there also. She fed us and this time I kept it all in my stomach. Both of us slept at her roomy apartment and the following day I went on my way. *Hennie* had given me some woolen socks and other things to trade for food. She had also given me some real tea to take home. The next town on my way to *Rockanje* would be *Oostvoorne.* These towns are very close to the coast and the beautiful sandy dunes where we would go on vacation in better times. While paddling my way on the steel rims to the area of the dunes I was almost blown off my bicycle. It felt that way when at least six or more British *Mosquitos* were on a bomb run and came roaring down behind me, zipping over me at a terrific speed and whipping up a strong air current.

121. British Mosquito Airplane

412. Mosquito medium fighter/bomber. Almost the entire
plane was built of wood. At almost 400mph it was the
fastest aircraft in Bomber Command until May 1951. The
plane could carry the same bomb load as a B-17 and only
with a two men crew.

It looked like these "balsa wood" fighter-bombers knew where they
were going. I saw them swoop down even lower and drop bombs over
some installations in the dunes followed by huge explosions. They
must have hit what they were after because then there were secondary
explosions, worse than the bombs. It could have been the Biber
Bunker, the German Luftwaffe night-fighter control post. That whole
area was the heaviest defended terrain in the whole Atlantikwall with
a labyrinth of bunkers. I was far enough away not to be in any danger
and I must readily admit that I enjoyed it. It was January 1945, the
Krauts were on the run; Berlin was being bombed daily; I had a full
stomach, a warm coat; our liberation could not be far off and here
I was in an area where there was still food and on top of that I was
enjoying the fireworks of those *"stinging"* Mosquitos. At that moment
I remember feeling that life could not be better. From *Oostvoorne* I
rode to *Rockanje* and found the chicken coop where the Looy family
lived. It was a big chicken coop but no chickens. Mr. and Mrs. Looy
and their son also welcomed me and wanted me to stay with them. I
told them that I would be more than pleased but that I had a duty to
perform. I had to find food and take it back home. They promised to
help me and for their generosity I gave them a couple pairs of socks.
I was there maybe five days and every day I did my negotiating for
potatoes, carrots, cabbage, lettuce, onions, flour, apples, bacon, beans

and other foodstuff that I can't remember now. When I had gathered all this food and spend the money mom had given me, my concern turned to how to get it back to Rotterdam on my bike. On top of that I would have to cross two big rivers. Between Rotterdam and where I was on the island of Voorne & Putten there was another small island called Rozenburg. First I would have to cross the Oude Maas River, cross over the island and then get across the New Waterway. Once on that side I would practically be home. The problem was that nobody was allowed to cross these rivers. German boats patrolled the rivers and anyone caught would end up dead. The Germans were much on edge at that time and were under instruction to be ruthless. It was clear that I couldn't haul all my loot on the bike. Mr. Looy knew a barge captain who occasionally made a trip to Rotterdam transporting supplies for the Germans. I met with this man and he agreed to take the large sack of potatoes and several other big sacks on his next trip to the city. Usually he would be in the Coolhaven near our house. That was good fortune. Once I had that organized my concern turned to getting across those rivers. The only way would be after curfew when it was dark. Again I was in luck. Some other person, a friend of Mr. Looy, knew of a man who had a large rowboat and occasionally rowed people across the Oude Maas to the island of Rozenburg. He only asked 10 guilders. My friend in Rockanje would arrange it for me and told me to be at the side of the river at 7pm and only on a night when there would be no moon. The day was decided upon and during '*D-day*' I walked my bike through sleet and snow, loaded with bags on the handlebars, the main frame and across the rear fender, for about 10 kilometers (6 miles) to the designated side of the river. There I hid in some bushes and waited until it was sufficiently dark. I didn't have a watch and had to guess the time. It must have been well past 7pm when I heard the swooshing of oars. Pushing the bike ahead of me I moved to where I saw the rowboat. It was a large one and there were already quite a few people seated in the boat holding their bikes. One of several oarsmen helped me with my bike and I joined the other people. Both men and women but no young people like myself. In a whispered voice the skipper told us to be very quiet. *"Don't make a sound!"* We readily obeyed. He came on board and was just about ready to push off when the silence was broken by a voice from the shore. A shout in German ordering the skipper to return to shore: *"Zuruck, Zuruck, kommen Sie sofort zuruck!"* All of us kept deadly quiet but we knew that this would be the end for us in this world. I recognized this tall German officer in his long leather coat and in full regalia complete with a dagger on his side to be from the German Kriegsmarine (German Navy). Immediately I thought: *"Thank God, he is not from the Gestapo"*. Our skipper jumped ashore and was obviously debating some issues but we could clearly hear this kraut ask the skipper where he thought he was going. The skipper tried to act innocent telling him that he was going nowhere. It was obvious that the officer was not accepting that. At long last the skipper admitted that he was taking us *'poor and hungry people'* to the other side, to the island of Rozenburg. And then this kraut who had clearly been drinking because he was rather unsteady on his feet said something that was music to ours ears: *"Dort muss Ich ja auch sein, Ich muss noch etwas zum trinken haben"*. *"That's where I need to go, I need another drink!"* With that he got on board the rowboat and there he stood in the front of the boat. The skipper pushed the boat off and the two oarsmen got to work. As stated before, this winter was just about the coldest winter on record and there were many ice floes. All the time this kraut is standing straight up and in spite of his condition seems to be taking the waves in stride, as a good Kriegsmarine officer should. With this guy standing in front of the boat, us people hunkering down from the cold, ice floes all around, it was a reenactment of Washington crossing the Delaware on Christmas night in 1776 for a surprise attack on the Hessian forces in Trenton. To top it all off, we had our token Hessian* on board.

413. Washington crossing the Delaware on Christmas
night in 1776.

When we finally got to the Island of Rozenburg the officer was the
first one to get off and low and behold he even said: "Vielen dank, auf
Wiederzehen!" Then he disappeared into the dark night trying to find
another bar that would only be open to the occupiers because it was
well after curfew. Now there was an example of a *'good'* German.
*The term Hessian refers to the inhabitants of the German state of Hesse.

That night, in spite of the curfew that would be in effect until the
morning at 6am, I worked my way across the island to the shore
of the Nieuwe Waterweg (New Waterway). There I found a place
between two buildings that provided some shelter from the awful
weather but I don't believe I slept at all. When it got light I walked
my bike to where I saw a string of barges. One of these barges was
getting ready to leave up the river. I shouted my request for passage
to the skipper but I was not the only one. There were other people
with the same idea. The skipper agreed to take all of us but the only
place where he would be able to hide us was underneath the planks
over the keel on the bottom of the ship. That area is usually filled
with water and there is certainly not much headroom. Actually none
at all. I readily accepted the offer because I was short enough and
only had to bow my head somewhat. By sitting on the upward slope
of the keel I almost stayed out of the water as well. By the way, that
water was freezing cold. The skipper gave the people some cement
blocks, used for ballast, and by resting their bodies on those blocks

they could keep themselves and their feet out of the water. Not the best and most comfortable arrangement but it was free travel to the city of Vlaardingen, less than 7 miles from Rotterdam.

The trip to Vlaardingen was relatively uneventful; the German River Patrol stayed away. To say I was relieved to get out of that dungeon is an understatement. For a while I felt like a pretzel and took me some time to warm up. The weather had improved somewhat and it was relatively dry. Everyone got his or her bicycle back and I started on the final lap of my quest.

Mother remembers:

I will never forget when on January 12, 1945 in the afternoon of that terribly cold winter Wim stuck his head over the back fence and yelled: "Mother, mother, I have food for all of us". I ran downstairs and unlocked the gate. There he was. We had you back. I remember that you brought us some beans and some precious tea that Hennie had given you. We had not tasted tea for 4 years. You, yourself, know of course how you made it back. I know that it had not been without danger. Later that week the skipper arrived with his ship in the Coolhaven and we got our potatoes. He also had some packages destined for other people whose relatives on the islands had addressed the packages to us because of Wim's connection with the skipper. These people gave us part of what they received. Wim's doings saved us from starvation.

Chapter Eighty-Four

"Nuts!"

During the period of December 1944 and the end of April 1945 the population in western Holland was preoccupied with trying to stay alive. It was the infamous *'Hunger Winter'*. The weather did not help either. It was by far the coldest and most miserable winter on record. This preoccupation led to a lessened interest of what was happening on the battlefronts. When on December 16 the Germans opened their offensive through the Ardennes forest of Belgium we paid little attention.

414. American soldiers of the 75th Division photographed
in the Ardennes during the Battle of the Bulge.

Only later when the news we were receiving from the BBC was less than stellar, we became increasingly more alarmed. On top of our misery in Holland we worried about the Americans fighting one of the biggest battles of WWII with the German Army that for some reason didn't want to give up. It was outright scary. Much has been written about what became called: *"The Battle of the Bulge"* and I will not attempt to describe the horrors of that battle that at the start on December 16 involved the following:

The German side:
At the start of the battle: about 200,000 men, 5 armored divisions, 12 infantry divisions, and about 500 medium tanks, supported by 1,900 guns and Nebelwerfers.
Casualties:
15,652 dead
27,582 captured or missing
41,600 wounded

The American side:
At the start of battle: about 83,000 men, 242 Sherman tanks, 182 tank destroyers, and 394 pieces of corps and divisional artillery
Casualties:
19,276 dead
23,554 captured or missing
47,493 wounded
British:
200 dead
1,400 wounded and missing
Numbers provided by Wikipedia.org

One story needs repeating however. It is the result of an interview by Patrick O'Donnell of Lt. General Harry W. O. Kinnard. At the time of the siege of Bastogne in the Belgian Ardennes, a Lt. Col. and Division G-3 of the 101st Airborne Division.

415. Lt. Col. Harry O. Kinnard G-3, 101st Airborne
Division. Photo through Kenneth McAuliffe

*"We got into Bastogne late on the night of 18 December 1944. We were
not well equipped, having just gotten out of combat in Holland. We
were particularly short of winter clothing and footwear. On the 21st of
December we became completely surrounded by Germans and our field
hospital was overrun by a German attack. We had put the hospital in
what would normally have been a safe place, but no place is safe when
you are completely surrounded. At this time we were not able to receive
air resupply because the weather was absolutely frightful. It was very,
very cold and snowy. Visibility was often measured in yards. Our lack of
winter gear was partially offset by the citizens of Bastogne who gave us
blankets and white linens that we used for camouflage.*

*While we were still surrounded, on the morning of December 22, a
German surrender party, consisting of two officers and two NCOs, and
carrying a white flag, approached our perimeter in the area of our Glider
Regiment, the 327th. The party was taken to a nearby platoon command
post. While the enlisted men were detained the officers were blind folded
and taken to the command post of the 327th where they presented their*

surrender ultimatum. The ultimatum in essence said the 101st's position was hopeless and that if we elected not to surrender a lot of bad things would happen.

Major Alvin Jones, the S–3, and Colonel Harper, the Regimental Commander brought in the message to the Division Headquarters. They brought the message to me, the G–3 and Paul Danahy, the G–2. My first reaction was that this was a German ruse, designed to get our men out of their foxholes. But be that as it might, we agreed that we needed to take the message up the line. We took it first to the acting Chief of Staff of the Division, Lt. Col. Ned Moore. With him, we took the message to the acting Division Commander General Tony McAuliffe. Moore told General McAuliffe that we had a German surrender ultimatum. The General's first reaction was that the Germans wanted to surrender to us. Col. Moore quickly disabused him of that notion and explained that the Germans demanded our surrender. When McAuliffe heard that he laughed and said: "Us surrender? Aw, nuts!" the date was December 22d, 1944".

416. General McAuliffe at Bastogne

To the U.S.A Commander of the encircled town of Bastogne.

The fortune of war is changing. This time the U.S.A. forces in and near Bastogne have been encircled by strong German armored units. More

German armored units have crossed the river Our near Ortheuville, have taken Marche and reached St. Hubert by passing through Hombre-Sibret–Tillet. Libramont is in German hands.

There is only one possibility to save the encircled U.S.A. troops from total annihilation: that is the honorable surrender of the encircled town. In order to think it over a term of two hours will be granted beginning with the presentation of this note.

If this proposal should be rejected one German Artillery Corps and six heavy AA.Battalions are ready to annihilate the U.S.A. troops in and near Bastogne. The order for firing will be given immediately after this two hours' term.

All the serious civilian losses caused by this artillery fire would not correspond with the well-known American humanity.

The German Commander.

"But then McAuliffe realized that some sort of reply was in order. He pondered for a few minutes and then told the staff, "Well I don't know what to tell them." He then asked the staff what they thought, and I spoke up, saying, "that first remark of yours would be hard to beat." McAuliffe said, "What do you mean?" I answered, "Sir, you said 'Nuts". All members of the staff enthusiastically agreed, and McAuliffe decided to send that one word, "Nuts!" back to the Germans. McAuliffe then wrote down:

To the German Commander,
Nuts!
The American Commander.

"McAuliffe then asked Col. Harper to deliver the message to the Germans. Harper took the typed message back to the company command post where the two German officers were detained. Harper then told the Germans that he had the American commanders reply. The German captain then asked, "Is it written or verbal?" Harper responded that it was written

and added, "I will place it in your hand."
The German major then asked, "Is the reply negative or affirmative? If it is the latter I will negotiate further."

At this time the Germans were acting in an arrogant manner and Harper, who was starting to lose his temper, responded, "The reply is decidedly not affirmative." He then added that, "If you continue your foolish attack your losses will be tremendous."

Harper then put the German officers in a jeep and took them back to where the German enlisted men were detained. He then said to the German captain, "If you don't know what 'Nuts' means, in plain English it is the same as 'Go to Hell'. And I'll tell you something else, if you continue to attack we will kill every goddam German that tries to break into this city."

The German major and captain saluted very stiffly. The captain said, "We will kill many Americans. This is war." Harper then responded, "On you way Bud," he then said, "and good luck to you." Harper later told me he always regretted wishing them good luck.

The battle officially ended on January 25, 1945 with the total defeat of the German forces. Their lack of fuel for tanks and trucks did them in and those not taken prisoner walked back to Germany.

417. Battle of the Bulge Memorial in Bastogne, Belgium

In May/June 2003 I went on a two week Stephen Ambrose tour to England, France, Belgium, Holland and Germany. The tour guide was Ron Drez, the author of several books. The trip followed the route of the Allies from England to Normandy, Paris, Brussels, Arnhem, and Bastogne. Luxemburg and finally Germany. It was a most interesting tour. While in Bastogne, Belgium sometime in early June Ron Drez told us a story that I thought was hilarious. Ron was in Bastogne on the 50th Anniversary of D-Day, June 6, 1944. It was a hot and sunny day. At that time there were still many WWII veterans participating in these anniversaries and Bastogne was no exception. One of the roads in Bastogne slopes down and from that direction a large group of veterans of the Battle of the Bulge are coming up the hill. They are obviously having a tough time making the climb; they must all be in their seventies by now. Ron and his entourage are waiting on the top of the road near the center of town waiting for these veterans. Ron is holding a large stein of beer in his hands. When after a lot of huffing and puffing the veterans reached the top of the hill, one who is sweating profusely steps out of the line, comes up to Ron and takes his beer. Ron is more than glad to give it to him and then asks the question: "How come you guys are celebrating the anniversary of the battle in June instead of December?" whereupon the old vet says: "Sonny, have you ever been here in December?"

CHAPTER EIGHTY-FIVE

WIERDEN REVISITED

Wierden, the small town where I had lived on a farm for some time during the early part of the war was one of the places liberated in April 1945. However, there had been some heavy fighting and the Germans, before retreating, had plundered the area of everything that wasn't nailed down. When visiting there in 2005 I met with Hennie and Bertha, the twin daughters of Jan en Miene Waalderink, who I wrote about in the beginning of the book. I attended Jan en Miene's wedding on May 7, 1942. It was a grandiose party and I have vivid memories of that event. Miene was like a mother to me. Jan Waalderink drove a horse-drawn milk wagon with rubber tires that were a lot better on the kidneys than wagon wheels. He was a great guy and sometimes I would accompany him on his runs. However, theirs is a sad story. On Friday, February 24, 1978, Jan and Miene together with Miene's brother Jan were in their car traveling from the hospital where their brother-in-law had just passed away when they were involved in a terrible accident with a large German truck. All three were killed instantly. The twins were 22 years old then.

418. Picture of the extended family Beverdam and Waalderink in 1967. Jan Beverdam is in the top row, fourth from the left. Jan's sisters Bertha and Tine are

to his left, sixth and eighth from the left. Miene and Jan Waalderink are the couple celebrating their 25th Anniversary. They are seated in the middle with their parents on either side. The twins, Hennie and Bertha, are sitting on their knees in front of their parents.

419. Picture of Hennie and Bertha with their respective families in recent times. Hennie is the second and Bertha seventh on the top row. Two delightful families.

In 2005 Hennie handed me a few pages of notes handwritten by her dad on Easter Monday, April 2, 1945 when the Germans were retreating in front of the Canadian Army. These handwritten notes are particularly interesting in that they paint a firsthand picture of the widespread plunder by the German Army:

Wednesday, March 28 – I saw the bodies of 10 dead civilians at the factory of Ten Bosch on the Almelosestraat. Thursday, March 29 – Germans captured three members of the resistance at widow Albert's house and took bicycles and parts from Stiena Wild and John Bolk. J. Buitenweg was ordered to transport the plunder.

March 30 – observed 30 heads of cattle and several pigs taken from the Beverdam farm March 29/30 at 11:30pm observed 3 trucks with V-2's, machine parts and stolen goods. At 12 midnight 8 trucks with plunder including my brother's car and the horse of Morsink.

March 30 5:30pm 10 German gendarmes are searching homes and stealing furniture.

Saturday – volleys of gunfire, bullets whizzing past – a pig is killed at J. Loohuis. Plunder is getting worse with bicycles, horses and food supplies fair game.

April 1 in the morning 3 farmers coming from Markelo. They had left their homes leaving all their belongings behind.

At night rumors that the Canadians were at the canal but not true. In the afternoon English fighters strafe a German car and train. At 8:15 knock at the door. Four men ask to stay overnight.

April 2 – today did not drive the milk wagon because of all the stealing and mayhem.

I hear that the Canadians have reached Hengelo. Tanks and infantry between Hengelo–Borne. We are in full anticipation of our liberation.

J. Waalderink 2d Day of Easter 1945

THE TRAIN

In a small publication celebrating the 60th Anniversary of Wierden's liberation there is the detailed story of the strafing of a train on Christmas Day 1944 similar to the one Jan Waalderink wrote about. It is an example of what can go wrong during a war:

"Christmas 1944. It is bitter cold; the thermometer shows 12 degrees below zero. Around nine o'clock in the morning of Christmas Day the people in Wierden are startled by the staccato sound of heavy machine gunfire. Spitfires of the Royal Air Force are seen flying low over the railway station; the target is a long train that had left Kampen in the early morning. The train is full of Dutch slave laborers on their way to a Forced Labor Camp in Germany".

When on September 17, 1944 Operation Market-Garden started, the Dutch Government in London had on September 16 requested a national railway strike in anticipation of the airborne operation. It would hamper the Germans in transporting their troops to the battlefield. The Dutch Railway system went on strike in the whole country. This would have been fine if the Allies had won the Battle of Arnhem and taken the bridge but they had lost that battle. However, the railway strike remained in effect. The Allies wrongly concluded that any train still running would now hold Germans and be fair game. Allied intelligence, however, knew of the *'razzias'* in November and December and was aware that Dutch men were rounded up and transported to Germany to perform slave labor. The Dutch resistance had at that time alerted the Allies not to shoot at big columns of men. They had heeded that warning but what about the trains?

"The long train came to a halt just outside Wierden Station and the Spitfires had a field day. They shot up the train from all sides. Four men were killed instantly; there were screams of wounded people everywhere; more than one hundred and sixty men see a chance to escape into Wierden where a great number enter a church and afterwards are hidden by the churchgoers.1) At the same time the population in Wierden is gathering and preparing food for those that were unable to escape; they have been rounded up and are kept under heavy guard at the plant of Scholten on the Violenhoeksweg. In the evening they are forced to enter another train to continue their trip to Germany. While being marched over the Stationsweg to the train, people from the EHBO (Eerste Hulp Bij Ongelukken) i.e. First Aid, is successful in hiding some thirty men in the boiler room of the factory; several more will hide in the bushes along the route but for the rest there is only one thing they can do and that is to continue their journey. Forty of these men will never return".

1) In an act of reprisal for helping these slave laborers to escape the Germans rounded up Wierden citizens and executed them on Christmas Day. A monument commemorating this reprisal killing is located at the Wierden railway station.

CHAPTER EIGHTY-SIX

OPERATIONS MANNA & CHOWHOUND

Credits: Memories of a Miracle by Hans Onderwater

As I stated in an earlier chapter: *"All of western Holland was descending in the abyss from which it could only be saved by a miracle."* We didn't know it but that *"Miracle"* was getting a lot of attention from Air Commodore Andrew James Wray Geddes attached to the Operations and Plans Section at the Headquarters of Second Tactical Air Force in Brussels.

Of all the events during WWII Operation Manna/Chowhound has been for me the most emotional experience of my life and to this day when I talk about it I still get teary eyed. It is extremely difficult to express how I felt that Sunday, April 29, 1945.

It has to be seen in the framework of almost five years occupation by the German Nazi Regime; the ever-increasing brutality of the occupying forces, particularly following the Battle of Arnhem that the Allies clearly lost; the hunger winter when I saw so much misery and starvation all around me; women rampaging over the Binnenweg and attacking anything that may have contained some kind of edible things. They had practically given up hope but their children and babies at home turned them into angry lions and they no longer cared for their own lives; the extreme cold and lack of fuel to keep warm; but above all the hunger. Not unless you have ever endured a total lack of sufficient nutrition for weeks on end it is impossible to imagine a shrinking stomach that screams for something, anything, just anything at all. People going crazy, walking on the street totally dazed and just falling over and sitting in the gutter mumbling to them selves. Not a cat or dog was to be seen on the street. Birds weren't even around as if they knew that it would be wrong to sing in such a totally hellish environment. No more trees along the streets and avenues, all had been cut down. Most of the younger male population had been taken away to Germany to work as slave laborers leaving many families with only the women to cope. That was the situation at the end of April 1945 and only a miracle could save us.

"DO IT, BUT DO IT QUICKLY".
THE STORY OF OUR "MIRACLE WORKER"

420. The 'Miracle Worker' Air Commodore Andrew
James Wray Geddes

"In 1945 I was Air Commodore Operations and Plans at the Headquarters of Second Tactical Air Force in Brussels. Since my appointment on 1ˢᵗ April 1943 I experienced many mixed feeling when dealing with the variety of widely conceived plans which had to turned into successful operations. In detail, every operation had its lethal aspect with the horrible underlying question, which had to be considered in each case: – Can we ensure that this operation will kill more of the enemy than of our own people? The one question where this question did not apply, as far as I remember, was Operation Manna; the allied drops of food from the air with the positive expectation that about 3,500,000 of our friends in the Netherlands could be saved from almost certain death by starvation. I vividly remember how on 17ᵗʰ April 1945 I was summoned to Reims, to General Eisenhower's Headquarters for an urgent assignment. I had no idea what they expected from me until I was ushered into the room of General Walter Bedell-

Smith, Ike's Chief of Staff. He was a great man. He looked as stern and serious as ever but he always showed great compassion with people. What he said caught me by complete surprise. 'Geddes, the Dutch are starving, their food is running out, the Germans can not feed them any more. We are pushed by the whole Dutch government, by the President and by Churchill. Something has to be done to put an end to this tragedy. I want to see you again with a plan to feed 3,500,000 Dutch by air, drop zones, corridors, the lot. You have my full support. Bert Harris has been told to give you two Bomb Groups and sufficient Pathfinders; the 8th Air Force has three Wings at your disposal. We need a prepared agreement for Jerry, no negotiations, just instructions. Do it, Geddes, do it quickly. If you need any help, come to me. I will make sure that Ike backs you all the way. We have cleared an office for you at HQ SHAEF here. Tell me what you need and who and I will get it for you'. 'Thank you'.

That was all; I had no idea as to where to start. We worked all through the week, the room covered with maps of Holland and the latest Intelligence reports about that part of the front. I knew that the outline had to be simple: it had to done like a bombing raid, targets had to be selected, firm rules had to be laid down and, above all, aircrews had to be told what I expected from them. I knew they would not be happy at first; who was going to trust the Germans? But I gathered that once the first day went according to plans the crews would be excited. We decided to call it 'Manna'. By late morning one day everything was ready. Clerks had prepared the documents, which had to be signed by all concerned. The next day I saw Bedell-Smith again and briefed him on the plan. He said he was happy with it. Maori Cunningham, Commander in Chief of the 2nd Allied Tactical Air Force, my boss, had been told to do without me for a while. I was to be flown to Gilze-Rijen in Holland and then by Auster to Nijmegen. A staff car would be waiting for me and take me to a village called Achterveld, where a conference would take place on 28th of April. Frankly, I was exhausted, yet I was determined to do this job. What a way to end the war!!! That afternoon I received my written credentials, which would take me through any Military Police barrier and which would virtually give me authority to get whatever I wanted. An hour later I was on my way to Holland. In the Dakota to Gilze-Rijen, I wondered what it would be like to stand opposite the Germans again. Would they be same arrogant bastards that I escaped from in May 1940, when I evacuated my

Squadron just before the German tanks reached Abbeville? At the airfield near Gilze-Rijen I changed into an Auster AOP aircraft. We landed at a strip near Nijmegen. A Canadian staff car waited for me and escorted by two MP's on motorcycles we drove through the town, across the bridge to Arnhem. I crossed the Rhine Bridge and saw the place where poor John Frost had been battered by the SS Panzer troops. We headed northwest until we reached the village of Achterveld. The Canadians had set up a field kitchen and a sealed-off perimeter around the village school where the conference was to take place. I had a meal, talked to some of the officers and went to see Freddie de Guingand, an old friend, now the Chief of Staff of Montgomery. We discussed next day's procedures and had a few drinks before I went to my room in a local house. I got up early the following day. Freddie told me that the Germans had arrived at the railway east of Amersfoort and that they were on their way in Canadian staff cars. When they arrived I stood under the trees where the cars stopped. They all carried white flags. The Germans were escorted into the building and told to wait to be presented to Freddie. I had a chance to have a good look at them. They were four chaps. One looked like a Party boss, the others were officers. They showed their credentials to Freddie, who handed them to me. Not a word was spoken. Their names were Dr. Schwebel, who seemed to be the number 2 man after Seyss-Inquart. The others were Dr. Plutzar, Major Stoeckle and Leutnant von Massow. Stoeckle was the only one who gave the Nazi salute. Plutzar spoke English fluently and protested vigorously for having been called 'Fritz' by the Canadian soldiers. Freddie said nothing but just looked at me. Schwebel was a Junker-type of officer with a big nose and dueling scars from his student days on his face. Plutzar looked like a gentleman. Von Massow did not say much; he was a paratrooper and clearly present to see if he could gather some intelligence about our strength. That was exactly what we wanted him to do. When the meeting began Freddie de Guingand explained that he had full authority to speak on behalf of the Supreme Commander and that he was not going to spend too much time on details. 'The Dutch are starving, you cannot help them, so we will. The Air Commodore here has a plan. If you carry it out to the detail we can alleviate the plight of the Dutch. Speed is essential, so I suggest we all get to work in a hurry'. Then Schwebel replied, through Plutzar, that he was not present to make any deals. The Reichskommissar had sent him to hear what we had to say. All he was to do was to report back to his superiors. Freddie was very annoyed. But he could do little else but to go through my proposals, and ask the Germans to return with proper people, chaps he could deal with. Then Plutzar translated that, if there was to be talk about a truce, the Reichskommissar wished to speak with General Eisenhower himself. If he was to make a major decision, he wanted to confer with the highest allied general. There was little left for Freddie than to ask Schwebel to meet again as soon as possible and tell him that Eisenhower had decided that food drops were to begin the next day. The Germans left as they came; in Canadian staff cars, curtains closed and white flags streaming. I have no idea if they were called Fritz again when they returned to their own lines. On Monday 30th April another cavalcade entered Achterveld. A Canadian convoy arrived like two days earlier. This time the German delegation also included Dutch civil servants and members of the resistance, who had come in separate vehicles following the Reichskommissar's party.

421. The German delegation arriving at the Manna meeting

422. The German delegation leaving the meeting

They were to give us first hand information about the situation in Holland and to report about the drops on the day before. Seyss-Inquart himself had come as well. He brought a large group of Army, Air Force and Naval Officers. But first the Austrian was in for a nasty surprise. The man who caused that surprise was HRH Prince Bernard.

423. Lieutenant-General HRH Prince Bernard of the Netherlands

Early that morning, a large black Mercedes staff car entered the village, escorted by a jeep with soldiers carrying machine guns. It was quite unusual to see a typically German official vehicle arrive with an allied officer behind the wheel. Besides it had a very odd license plate: RK-1. The driver was Prince Bernard, Commander in Chief of the Dutch Forces under allied command and those of the Resistance inside Occupied Territory. The Mercedes had been Seyss-Inquart's pride and joy. It had been 'liberated' by the Dutch Underground and presented to the prince as a gift. It was clear that HRH planned a prank on the chief of the people who had occupied his country for five years. He had the Mercedes parked exactly at the spot where Seyss-Inquart was expected to get out. I did not see the incident, but later I spoke to Colonel van Houten, Prince Bernard's chief of staff, who told me that Seyss-Inquart was very upset indeed. It was quite a humiliation to get out of a Canadian Packard to see your own standing there, with big white stars on the hood and the bonnet, a shield saying CNF-1 and a young allied General leaning on it, clearly showing off that he is the new proprietor.

424. HRH Prince Bernard arrives in Seyss-Inquart's
Mercedes.

A lot of allied staff officers had come to the Saint Joseph School at Achterveld. Bedell-Smith had arrived; he was in a bad mood as he thought it was very bad manners for the Germans to insist on Ike coming to see them. Freddie de Guingand was there too, as was General Galloway, the Canadian who was to take charge of the B-2 area after the German surrender (B-2 was the famine area of Holland). The Russians had sent General Suslapurov to watch over their own interests and to make sure that we were not accepting separate surrenders without notifying them. There were sailors to take care of food supplies by sea and army chaps who were to carry out the road operation, transporting the food which had been piled up in Brabant, by road to occupied territory. Bedell-Smith made working groups. Each group had to carry out its own task. In these groups were allies, Dutch and Germans. They had to do the practical job. At the same time Bedell negotiated with the Reichskommissar who still did not seem to understand that Germany was collapsing on all fronts. At about 1200 hrs we took a break. The Germans were put under guard in a classroom were we served them a straightforward meal of combat rations. The Dutch were invited to join us for lunch. We entertained them, gave the best food we had and almost embarrassed them with cigarettes, sweets and other goodies. Prince Bernard had a long talk with one of the Resistance Commanders, a bright young civilian, with whom the Prince

549

looked to be very cordial. The Dutch civilians were a bit shy at first. One of them explained that he was afraid to be called a collaborator, once the war was over. 'But, you must understand, General', he said to me. 'If I had left my post, a Nazi would have taken over'. I was not sure what to say. I do remember he was intensely pleased when I gave him my pouch filled with pipe tobacco. After lunch we got together again. General Reichelt, who was the Chief of Staff to Blaskowitz, the German CiC, signed the Manna documents without much comment. I trust the same thing happened with the army and the navy. As far as I was concerned I had done my job.

On the next day I was to have one more meeting with the Germans, between the lines, west of Wageningen, I left rather early for my quarters. Therefore I was not present when a rather funny incident took place at the main meeting, the one between Bedell-Smit and Seyss-Inquart. Later that afternoon Freddie de Guingand told me what had happened. Bedell-Smith wanted to make it absolutely certain to Seyss-Inquart that the war was lost. He explained where the allies were, what was left of the German army and more of these things. However, Seyss-Inquart did not seem to believe that he was fighting a lost battle. Then Bedell-Smith played his last card. He looked the Austrian straight in the eyes and said: 'now listen, Herr Reich minister. You have lost the war and there is no way you will get out of it but by surrender. Besides your name is on our list of war criminals and it is very likely that you will be shot. So, be a realist and surrender'. The prospect of being shot did not seem to surprise Seyss-Inquart for he looked at Bedell, said something in German and Plutzar translated: 'That leaves me cold'. Bedell from his side snapped: 'That is exactly what it will do'.

In the afternoon all arrangements had been agreed. I was to cross the Canadian lines the following day to exchange documents and maps with the enemy. My trip to No Men's Land was on 1ˢᵗ May. It also was my last involvement in the drops. Escorted by Captain McAlpine of the 1ˢᵗ Canadian Corps and a RASC driver, Group Captain Hill and I passed the first Canadian positions and drove slowly along the long straight road called the Wageningseweg. In the distance I could see the hills where the German positions were. At a small cottage, I remember the number was 118, Von Massow, who had brought an interpreter and several officers of the 6th Para Division, met us. We exchanged our maps and documents and then I decided to play my trick against the cocky behavior of Von

Massow. We had excellent intelligence on the Germans and this I would use to shock Von Massow. While we smoked a cigarette I asked him to come with me for a moment. Some distance away from the others, who were smoking and chatting with Hill and McAlpine, I showed him the latest 'Stars and Stripes'. It had a map showing our advance into Germany. 'Propaganda', he said. 'That may be true', I replied, 'but I want you to know that your brother General Kurt von Massow is OK and well. We bagged him near Kassel a few days ago'. Von Massow's mouth fell wide open. He turned round, said something to the others, jumped into his jeep and roared off. On our way back Hill asked what the matter was with that German lieutenant. 'Nothing', I said, 'I gave him his brother's best wishes...'

That evening I returned to Nijmegen and then flew to Reims to report. Two days later I was back at Headquarters 2ⁿᵈ Tactical Air Force in Brussels, business as usual".

Supreme Headquarters Allied Expeditionary Force

ANNOUNCEMENT
to the Population
of occupied Netherlands

1. The enemy, who is responsible for your food supply, has lost the opportunity to obtain sufficient stocks while the communications with Germany were still open. Now that he has been isolated and besieged by our campaign and has made the criminal decision to resist to the end, he will not be able to save you from starvation.

2. As your food supplies have been exhausted, the Supreme Commander has ordered that food will be dropped by aircraft over occupied Netherlands immediately.

3. We warn the enemy that this is about to happen and that he shall not hamper or hinder our attempts to help you. Even if he should do so we will continue to do all we can to save your lives.

4. The food stuffs will be dropped by aircraft of all types, mainly heavy bombers. These aircraft will fly low and drop their cargo where it is easiest for you to collect it. We can not tell you exactly when and where food supplies will be dropped and you therefore have to take into account the following instructions:

a. Expect food parcels by day as well as by night. From now on take notice of our aircraft.
b. Form, under the direction of responsible persons, groups to watch out for the aircraft and to collect the parcels. We will give instructions to the enemy to help you as much as possible.
    Do not deny this help; it could ease your burden.
c. When you hear our aircraft approaching you are to take cover at places where the aircraft could drop the parcels. The parcels will not come down by parachutes and will be heavy enough to cause serious injuries or even kill you if they hit you.
d. Post sentries at fixed points when our aircraft approach to establish where the parcels come down.
e. Distribute the food fairly among yourselves.
f. If the enemy tries to steal your food, or if he tries to shoot at our aircraft, make careful notes of all possible details and above all of the names of those who do this. Report these particulars. Members of the enemy forces who are guilty of this will be considered war criminals and we will treat them as such.

5. Mind you - we can not promise to drop the right share of parcels in each area. In some parts the share will be too big, in some too small. Therefore ensure a fair distribution among yourselves.

6. Do not forget - we are your friends and we will continue to do all we can to help you.

425. Bulletin to the Population

The following bulletin appeared in *'Het Volk'* on May 1ˢᵗ, 1945. In this publication the Germans tried to prove that the food drops were a futile propaganda stunt of the allies

Food from Aircraft

The Höhere SS und Polizieführer Nordwest und Generalkommissar für das Sicherheitswesen ') announces:

It is brought to the attention of the population that in a few areas, designated by the Reichskommissar, food stuffs will be dropped by the allied air force. These food stuffs will be received and distributed by the Netherlands Food Distribution Service. The general public is strictly forbidden to enter the areas where the food stuffs will be dropped. Violations of the prohibition will be punished with the utmost severity.

As has been remarked in an earlier edition, it is virtually impossible to ensure a really effective supply of food by air to the Western Netherlands. As, however, it seems to be impossible to realise food supply transports by ships, air transport has been agreed upon. Thanks to the cooperation of the German Supreme Command in the Netherlands, it has become possible that allied aircraft drop food at designated areas, via previously determined routes without being shot at. This way the danger of scrimmages, unfair distribution and losses by food stuffs ending up in the water, has been prevented.

True enough the quantities will of course be limited, but the fact that on the first day in South-Holland at the designated areas already 600 tons of valuable food stuffs (flour, meat, cheese, margarine and sugar) could be dropped, shows that this emergency measure, thanks to all cooperation, will be of great importance for the three provinces that are in such serious need.

Undoubtedly the distribution authorities will circulate the available food stuffs as quickly as possible.

We trust that these authorities will be aware of their duty to ensure that these food stuffs stay absolutely off the black market and that they create the possibility for a realistic control.

(From 'Het Volk', 1st May 1945. In this publication the Germans tried to prove that the food drops were a futile propaganda stunt of the allies)

) The highest German law inforcement agency in occupied Hollal death of Jews and resistance workers.

426. In this publication the Germans tried to prove that the food drops were a futile propaganda stunt of the allies.

SUNDAY, APRIL 29, 1945

On a sunny Sunday morning I found myself, as usual, with my brother Henry in our cave in the basement. Henry, headphones on his ears, was listening to the BBC. As always I kept my eyes on his face for any type of expression that might indicate something important being said on the radio. Henry would usually be busy writing the news in his own shorthand; he was busy doing so that morning when all of a sudden I noticed a change in his expression. He removed the headphones and turned to me: *"My God, Wim, will you believe it, Lancaster bombers are on their way to Rotterdam and other places in Holland to bring food. They will drop it on designated fields. Eisenhower's Headquarters has arranged it all. Hundreds of planes have taken off from all over southern England and they are on their way. Right now, Wim, they are on their way!"* With that unbelievable news we both went upstairs to where the rest of the family in their coats was sitting around the smallest stove you have ever seen.

Henry told them the news and my mother's reaction was one of total disbelief: *"How can that be. Dropping food from airplanes? It will all fall apart. They wont do that!"* Henry insisted that it was true and that the planes were actually right now on their way and might arrive anytime. The distance from the south of England to Rotterdam is not that great. Henry then added that the planes were ordered to fly at rooftop level. We all looked at each other and knew that if all of this was true a miracle had happened; the miracle that we had hoped for.

All of us went on our balcony that overlooked the Coolhaven. We had a good view to the left and right as well. There we waited in anticipation of some sound from those beautiful Merlin engines. Four of those engines on one Lancaster and there would be hundreds of them. We knew that sound very well from the many Lancasters flying over on their way to Germany. It has that deep throaty roar that resonates through body and soul. We were all still and listened, but nothing, not yet, not yet, no not yet and then I imagined hearing something from far, far away!

A Lancaster Base near Haverhill, East Anglia

The full crew of the Mk III Lancaster with the markings XY and the "S" for Sugar is watching the loading of its bomb bay. The pilot Alex Howell, an Australian, Chris Poole, the Bomb Aimer, Denis Down, the Navigator, Peter Weston, the Radar and Radio man, Flight Engineer Charles Damey, Mid Upper Gunner William Hughes and

Rear Gunner Bernard Shaw. They are all standing together watching this unusual scene.

427. A Lancaster being loaded with sacks of food.

428. This shows a sling before being put together and loaded. There were four more slings in front of this one, as per Peter Weston, Radar and Radio Operator.

In a short time they will leave on another mission together with hundreds of aircraft like their own. But this mission is not like the one they flew four days earlier when they blasted Hitler's "Eagle Nest" at Berchtesgaden. No, this will be a mission they will never forget as long as they live. This time hundreds of Lancasters are not loaded with bombs to 'destroy' but with food to 'nourish'; for the starving people in occupied Holland: to Rotterdam, the Hague and Amsterdam areas.

The Mk III Lancaster XY-S flown by Alex Howell has been assigned to the Rotterdam drop on Waalhaven Airport on the south side of the River Maas. Peter Weston, 20 years old and already a veteran with two years in the RAF, is adjusting his radio and radar controls. There is some apprehension about the low level of flight and the uncertainty of the Germans not sticking to the agreed upon truce. The North Sea below them looks a bit choppy but quite peaceful on this sunny Sunday on April 29, 1945. To the left and right, above and below, other Lancasters string out and are getting into position for their drop zones. In the far distance they can see the by now familiar Dutch coastline. Lanc XY-S is heading for the Maas river delta and is now about 5 minutes away from Rotterdam.

Back on the balcony in the Dunantstraat we can't be sure what we hear. We just can't be sure. It could be anything at all. But then all of us thought we heard something more distinct and it had to be the sound of engines. It now became obvious that we were hearing approaching bombers. The sound level increased and increased further but we didn't see any planes. Where were they? Well, Henry had said that they would be flying at rooftop level and we had always seen them high in the sky. Rooftop level, by golly, that is low. The sound was now such that one of the planes must be on the roof and sure enough; all of a sudden that first Lancaster bomber flies past our apartment. I will never in my life forget it. I cried and so did all of us. We waved at that plane with anything we could grab. Towels, handkerchiefs, paper, anything. It was and always will remain the most emotional event in my entire life. The plane seemed to be banking from left to right and back again*. The plane had the distinct markings of XY-S on the side. We saw the crew; they were waving at us from the small windows and doors. It was as if we could reach out and touch them. They were smiling and maybe crying as well. For them it also was the most beautiful mission they had ever been on. We now saw planes everywhere. They didn't seem too far apart. They were all flying on much the same altitude. It seemed like maybe 50 feet above the buildings. Above our house they were making a turn that took them over the Pieter de Hooghstraat; the street with the buildings occupied by the Germans. All of us wanted to follow the planes and we ran outside through the Dunanstraat to the left then right on the Pieter de Hooghstraat and sure enough the planes were heading for the Maas River and Waalhaven Airport at the south side of the Maas River. On the Westzeedijk we saw the bomb bays open and a mass of what looks like confetti whirling down. What a sight!

429. We saw the plane open the bomb bays and drop the food.

When in my run over the street I saw the reaction of the Germans in the buildings. Some were hanging out of the windows and were waving at the planes; at the University of Economics building the sentries were donning their gas masks and running into their shelter. It was clear that not all Germans had been advised of what would be happening but some knew that low-flying planes could mean gas attacks. More planes were flying over and repeating the performance of the first one we had seen. It was unbelievable. Lots of people were on the street and we all rejoiced; the war would soon be over. It had to be, the Germans were licked; why would they otherwise allow these planes to drop food. They had to realize that the war was lost for them. When we returned to the Dunantsraat I realized that I had no shoes on. I had run all the way on my socks.

* When I talked with Peter Weston and told him that we had appreciated his Lancaster greeting us by rocking back and forth, he said he was sorry but that had not been their

intent. The truth was that all the planes flying so close together were whipping up air currents and the pilot had a tough time keeping the plane flying straight.

In 1996 Peter Weston mailed me his memories of the droppings in Holland:

"The first two drops we did were both in Rotterdam onto what looked like a football field, very close to a hospital marked with a large red cross on the roof, the people must have known we were coming. Large crowds surrounded the field, we were only about 100 feet or so and we see the sacks falling from the planes ahead of us and people running in to get them while others were still falling. It looked absolutely crazy from the air, but I guess we would all do the same if we were in the same state as they were. As we zoomed over the hospital, nurses were on the roof waving towels, sheets or anything they could lay their hands on. We felt very gratified afterwards; it was a change from dropping bombs. These 2 drops were done on 29th and 30th of April 1945. Flight time for each was 2hrs 40mins".

"The very last operation that I took part in was to The Hague, on the 2nd of May 1945. It was a food drop just like the others, but two things happened to make it different. The first was, we were approaching the dropping zone when we had to avoid a Lancaster that swerved in front of us from starboard, it appeared that he was trying to avoid a shower of sacks being dropped from another Lancaster slightly above and in front, this caused us to overshoot and we tried to have another go at it. It may seem that it would be a simple thing to do, but to try and get into position amongst a constant stream of aircraft, all at low level, is not easy. We eventually found a gap and got rid of our load, or so we thought, one sling had not released, we had no alternative but to turn on our exit course towards home.
We were engaged in very low level flying, over the villages and dikes, in fact we were so low that we had to pull up to go over the dike walls. In one village we were whizzing by, nearly everyone in the place was waving at us, so between the crew we decided to try and give them a present. We came back over and tried twice to dislodge the hung-up sling by a slight dive and then a sharp pull up, on the third try it worked and the sacks went hurtling down, right through the roofs of houses located on

the only road between the dikes, it was a very narrow zone with nothing but water around it. We came round again to give them a wing waggle and we laughed so much, the sacks had made large holes in the roofs and people were poking up through the holes waving like mad, they were not bothered, food had dropped from the heavens".

"Finally, we set off, following a narrow straight road leading to the coast and home. We were still at low level, I was standing on the step, a boxed in metal affair, with my head in the astrodome, looking ahead there was a girder type bridge and just beyond that was a group of German soldiers marching in line along the side of the road, they began to scatter (who wouldn't?) but one went to the middle of the road and put his rifle to his shoulder. At that point he was out of my sight and I felt a tremendous whack on the sole of my left foot, at the same time the rear gunner yelled out "did you see those soldiers run, we must have scared the (obscenity) out of them". After landing we went round to the front of the Lancaster, and sure enough, underneath between the nose and the bomb doors was a large dent with a hole in the middle. A bullet had come through and hit the underneath of the step I was on, causing a bump of about three quarters of an inch on top. My crew and the ground staff started to make remarks, such as: "My gosh! I wonder what would have happened (to certain parts of my anatomy) if the angle had been slightly different". So that was the end of our last operation for us, at least it ended happily".
(See also the Excerpt from Chapter Eleven 'Manna' No.186 Squadron for confirmation of the rifle bullet)

Mother remembers:
"Then on a Sunday, April 29, 1945, planes were flying over Rotterdam and the Germans were not shooting at them. They had agreed to these planes dropping food packages to us. We ran to the Westzeedijk and saw the packages coming down but they did not fall in our area. But now there was hope and our liberation could not be very far away".

Henry remembers:
"The Germans still had two 'Coastal' Divisions in the area. Towards the middle of April the Army of the Interior was ordered to stand down by SHAEF (Supreme Headquarters Allied Expeditionary Forces). A few

days later the BBC and the US Armed Forces Radio announced that heavy RAF and US bombers were going to be dropping food for us on designated areas near the big cities. If the Germans would interfere they would be treated as war criminals. When I told Ma and Pa, they didn't want to believe it. A few hours later in another broadcast we were told that the aircraft had taken off half an hour ago. Dad, Bill and I went on our neighbor's roof and a short time later there they came, flying not higher than a few hundred feet. They had already dropped their loads on open areas around the city. They were waving at us and we were waving back with anything we could find. It must have been quite a sight for them to see a crowd of dancing skeletons! The crews also dropped candies and chocolate (probably from their own rations) over the city. When the bombers roared over, the Germans dove in their shelters and stayed there. That was one of the best sights. It took a while before the food was distributed, lots of crackers and military ration packages. The soldiers may not always have liked those, but for us it was manna from heaven".

Crackers out of tin cans, for sure, *"Manna from Heaven"*

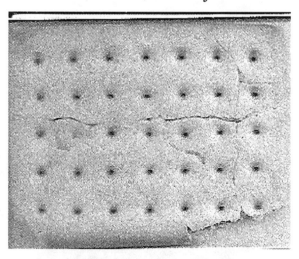

430. One of the crackers I saved but it broke in several
pieces and I glued it together for posterity.

431. Lancasters flying over Terbregge in the vicinity of Rotterdam. Probably the most famous picture of all Operation Manna.

432. B-17's after dropping the food returning to base.

433. Two Lancasters flying over a village on their way to
the drop zone

434. A Flying Fortress making a drop.

'Below I saw people running to collect the food . . .'

435.

436. Collection of food

437. A concrete barrier, part of the Atlantic Wall, at the
crossing of Hoofdweg and Terbregseweg.

438. View of the dropping from the Bergse Linker
Rottekade

439. Rejoicing at a mountain of food!

440. Food being loaded on a barge for shipment to
Rotterdam for sorting.

441. Gathering the food from the fields

442. Dried eggs, milk powder, dried yeast, cheese, chocolate, dried meat, meat and vegetables, spam, mustard, margarine, luncheon meat, tea, coffee, beans. Treasures!!

443. Then I dove down to 300 feet and released 2,000 loafs of bread – by Roland Davies

Excerpt from Chapter Eleven 'Manna', 'Exodus', Baedecker', 'Post –Mortem' C-flight and the end of No.186 Squadron

The excitement of the aircrews was only matched by the emotions of the Dutch people who, at first watched in stunned disbelief as the beautiful great aircraft, bomb doors open, approached in perfect formation, roaring in low over the flat, flooded land, but who then broke into wild excitement as thousands of packages cascaded down onto the white crosses or smoke markers of the drop zones. Wave after wave of aircraft came in, unloaded, pulled up and headed away for a return trip. The Dutch police and the authorities who organized the collection and distribution of supplies, had asked for all forms of transport to be made available including small boats which were used to recover any packs which had fallen onto dykes and in the canals. Nothing was wasted.

The greatest rewards for the aircrews was the sight of crowds of civilians lining the roads and packing the towns, all waving madly with anything which came to hand, especially Dutch and Union flags, which for years had been hidden away. Messages soon began to appear in fields or on rooftops, the most common being 'Thanks Tommy' or 'Tabac'. One section of the population received special attention from the crews were the children, the real victims of a terrible war. Chocolate and sweet rations were pooled and packaged for delivery, often by way of a small parachute thrown from a gun turret or cockpit window.

The German troops generally behaved themselves, no doubt hoping to sample the goods as well, but there were instances of aircraft being hit by small-arms fire. Alf Crowley, an Australian pilot from Chedburgh, had some control wires of his Lancaster severed and had to divert to Woodbridge, but not before his crew had parachuted chocolate and sweets with the message: "From Alf Crowley and crew, good luck". Many years later when in Holland, Alf met the Dutchman who, as a boy had retrieved the package and who still possessed that magic piece of paper. Flying so low in daylight over lines of German troops and vehicles, proved a strange experience for the crews especially the air-gunners, and many fingers strayed instinctively towards the triggers of silent guns. In the midst of such thoughts, one rear gunner heard as if by telepathy, his air-bomber saying: *"don't you dare you bugger"!* The final International agreement had been for the ground guns to lay their barrels horizontally and those in the aircraft to be vertical, an agreement that in general worked well.

At HQ.31Base, RAF Stradishall was in the thick of the operations with its own three Stations and squadrons' participants in the drops. 186 Sqn was ready to fly its first 'Manna' sortie on April 25, but a frustrating spell of poor weather prevented the 15 Lancasters from leaving. After two further cancellations, the first flight was made on the 29th. The diarist summed it up well.

"The Dutch had been warned to keep a good look out, both for food parcels and to avoid being hit by them. Each aircraft carries five containers, enough food to supply over 100 people for one month, so from our squadron alone sufficient supplies for over 1,500 starving Dutch men, women and children were dropped".

"Thousands of the excited population were watching and waiting". "Although there were a few hang-ups, most of the parcels fell satisfactorily and safely. Crowds rushed to the aiming area to collect them". "Despite the agreement with the enemy, the Hun lived up to his tarnished reputation and three aircraft were hit by small-arms fire". *'There were no casualties and in spite of these irregularities, it was an encouraging start'.* Newspapers announced the following day that 600 tons of food had been dropped – a good beginning. *"A 600-ton Dutch Food Shower"* was the headline in one daily paper of 30 April 1945.

NF995/B one of the damaged aircraft, was that flown by P/O Rose, who took off at 12:46 hours to drop five packs of POW rations near Rotterdam. He off-loaded four packs on his second run over the area by red TI's but had to return with suspected small-arms fire damage to the bomb-doors. For safety, the offending package was released near to Base and the pilot elected to land at Woodbridge where damage to the bomb-doors and the undercarriage was confirmed. The jettisoned pack was never found and it is assumed that some larders in the Hundon area were boosted by its unofficial, unexpected but welcome arrival!

P/O Onus suffered a hang-up on his first run in LM697/A and went round again. After further problems he managed to drop the 5th pack on the second run, but the crew's problems were not over, for the Lancaster was hit by small-arms fire as it flew over a pillbox at Battenoord. With incorrect oil and temperature showing for the starboard-inner engine, Fred Winch, the engineer, shut it down. For encouragement, the pilot of a Mosquito, which joined up with them, promptly feathered one of his engines and proceeded happily on one before parting. They landed safely at Stradishall at 15:26 hours with a nice collection of bullet holes in the fuselage and the starboard engine nacelle, plus a punctured oil-sump. Sgt Weston*, the wireless operator in W/O Lex Howell's aircraft, had a narrow escape when a rifle bullet passed through the fuselage, very close to where he was sitting.

F/O Forand's RF126/V was loaded with 6270lb food. The Lancaster crossed out over Orfordness, delivered its mercy load over Rotterdam airfield and was back at Base three hours after leaving.

Another trip was called on the 30th but after the initial detail for 12 aircraft was cancelled, 14 actually left when conditions improved. The weather was classed as poor but the official view was that: *"owing to the urgency of these relief flights being so great, only IMPOSSIBLE weather conditions were considered as a suggestion for cancellation"*.

The crews began to notice improvements in the efforts of the Dutch authorities in collecting the supplies and in controlling the excited crowds. The few German miscreants soon ceased their pointless activities but there were still risks from unexpected quarters.

F/Lt Idle's XY-P was hit fair and square by a bag of sugar: *"Dropped by some OTHER squadron"*, which embedded itself in the wing, broke some Perspex and injured two of the crew. LM543 returned safely to Stradishall for the ground crew to ponder over its unusual battle damage.

186 Sqn dropped 61 tons of supplies during the latter part of April. John Hart delivered his supplies on 30 April, a just reward for the crew who had started their low-level training on the 15th.

On 1 May, and in better weather, 14 Lancasters headed for The Hague, where the delighted crews saw the crowds waving Dutch,

British and American flags plus many messages of thanks or simply: *"Good luck Tommy"*.

Fourteen crews supplied The Hague again on 2 May, and on this trip a new innovation was officially sanctioned, whereby the mid-upper gunners relinquished their grandstand seats to members of the ground crews, a move welcomed by all as a token of appreciation for men who had toiled long and hard to keep the bombers serviceable. *"Both crews and passengers were thrilled with the new novelty"* (official). Even some of the German troops seemed as enthusiastic as the Dutch, for on one occasion as the Lancasters thundered over the coast on the way home, five soldiers emerged waving from their dugout.

On May 3rd, a dozen Lancasters, 10 with their ground crew passengers, made a morning run to the Ypenburg drop-zone near The Hague dropping 1,154 packages, some of which were seen to break open on impact. One large white message: *'Tabac SVP'* was almost certainly attended to on a later trip. The same drop zone was visited again next day, five aircraft dropping twenty-four packs between them. F/Lt Cusson's crew improvised a private delivery, parachuting 200 of their own cigarettes to try and satisfy the never-ending demand for 'tabac'.

A new mechanical release system fitted to six of the aircraft on The Hague drop on 6 May, proved successful when 27 of 30 packs landed close to the white-cross marker. Several crews who had dropped their own chocolate rations near Delft must have been elated to read a huge but heartfelt: *"Thank you Boys"*, on a factory roof. After a cancellation on May 6, 15 aircraft flew to The Hague on the 7th when some of the 67 packs dropped ended up in the trees due to faulty marking. Phil Gray, who dropped his 6,820lbs from NG148/T; *"near to The Hague"* logged the trip as a third of an op. Harold Peake, in F/Sgt Les Baker's crew, recalled their *'Manna'* trip as a fond memory and also remembered that during their low-level training, his pilot had the opportunity and subsequent pleasure to completely out-fly a B-17 pilot who tried to take them on; the tighter turns of the Lancaster finally forcing the American to break off.

8 May 1945. The day for which everyone had waited and prayed for finally dawned. The European war had ended. The aircrews were

briefed at 11:00 hours, but before leaving, all Base personnel listened to impressive addresses given by the Base and Station Commanders and then observed a one-minute silence, standing bareheaded and in deep thought. Aircrews then left the briefing rooms and once more were taken out to their laden aircraft. Significantly, this trip, the last in the *'Manna'* program was made in excellent weather, and as might be expected, the Dutch who were now aware of their true freedom, were even more enthusiastic.

The food drops made over Holland in those closing days of the European War forged a unique and permanent bond between the Dutch people and Allied aircrews. Operation *'Manna'* was recorded for posterity in many ways, including a series of beautiful Delft tiles depicting scenes of the times, but it was from the hearts of the Dutch people themselves that the strongest and most binding memorial would emerge, this being exhibited time and again by the warm receptions given to any returning airman who might make himself known. The countless reunions held over the years are legendary, and throughout Holland, often in quite unexpected places, are memorials recording the gratitude of the Dutch people who suffered so much during the conflict.

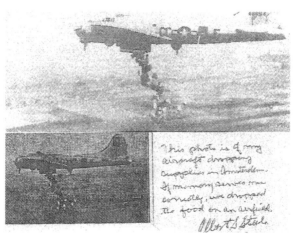

444. Pilot Albert S. Steele recognized his aircraft from
the above photo. It was in the Stars and Stripes, London
Edition of Monday, May 7, 1945

445. THANK YOU BOYS!

446. Lancaster Crew 'H' for Harry, No.7 Pathfinder
Squadron Oakington Cambs.

Left to Right:
Nav/Radar ....Flt/Lt. Vincent* **
Nav/Plotter....................Fl/Off. Andrews
Mid-Upper Gunner..........Fl/Sgt Edwards
Pilot (Skipper)...............Fl/Lt Wilson
Flight Engineer..............Fl/Sgt Roberts
Radio Operator..............Pilot/Off. Bateman
*I had an opportunity to meet Bill Vincent, the Navigator of the Lanc. 'H' for Harry
(see photo 466). He told me about his first Manna flight to The Hague and related to me
what they did after they had dropped the food and were leaving on their return flight.
He pre-empted it by saying that whenever they went on bombing missions they would
bring bottles of beer on board which naturally was not allowed and they had to be very

circumspect in dealing with the empty bottles; they stored these bottles at the tail gunners position. When they were just outside The Hague they noticed a German encampment and buildings teeming with soldiers of the Wehrmacht. The pilot called the tail gunner on the intercom and told him to quickly turn the gun cupola all the way to the left and shove the empty bottles out of the gap that would appear. They watched with glee when they saw the bottles hitting tents and the roofs of the buildings.

**He told me another story that I thought was hilarious. After completing his Navigator training and not yet having flown as well as being a rather naïve young lad, he was assigned to his first Lancaster. The veterans told him that before each flight it would be best to eat a hearty meal of eggs and bacon. He did as told and when they were well on their way Bill Vincent got stomach cramps and needed to go potty. This uncomfortable potty is located toward the back of the plane. Bill went there and when it was the proper moment the pilot took the plane in a steep angle drop. Without a seat belt Bill Vincent hit the ceiling of the plane together with the digested ham, bacon and eggs. Boys will be Boys!

On November 18, 2000 I received a very nice email from Mrs. Judy M. d'Arcy Thompson in Harrogate, North Yorkshire, England. She wrote me in connection with the research for this book.

Dear Willem Ridder:

I have just come across an Internet site, which says that you are writing a book about your experiences as a child in Holland during WWII and are researching Operation Manna,

By a strange coincident my parents were visiting with me and knowing that my father flew on the mission I asked him to give me some more details. My father was married to my mother Peggy in December 1944 and she was pregnant with me when he flew with Pathfinder Force and when he flew on Operation Manna. I was born the following January 1946.

He has told the story of Operation Manna to me and his grandchildren, my children, many times. He was so moved by the plight of the people of Holland and, especially, the children.

source: Mrs Peggy Priestley
Peggy Meek, 207 Squadron, was photographed at RAF Langar

447. Peggy Meek, Judy d'Arcy-Thompson's mother,
loading bombs onto a Lancaster bomber.

I am sending you the details as he gave them to me only yesterday, 13th November 2000, and hope that they will be of some use to you.

Operation Manna
As remembered by Flight Lieutenant Harry Priestley from Selby in North Yorkshire

My father, who had flown Lancasters on number 207 Squadron, had already done over four years of 'ops' flying Lancaster bombers before he transferred to number 582 Pathfinder Squadron. It was with this squadron that he flew from Little Staughton in Bedfordshire on the 1st of May 1945 to participate in the Operation Manna food drop at Rotterdam. His aircraft was A/C Lancaster H966, piloted by Flying Officer Coombes. My father was the engineering officer, Flying Officer Harry Priestley, then five days short of his 22d birthday. His birthday is May 6th. One of his most abiding memories is of the Briefing, before the Operation. The crews were told by their commanding officer that they were, under NO CIRCUMSTANCES to fly above 300 feet. For crews who faced the German anti-aircraft barrages every night this was quite

573

something! They were all praying that the Germans would remain true to the temporary truce agreement, which was allowing the food drop to take place. My father has told us many times that when they dropped the food they could read the words "Thank You" written in whitewash on farm buildings and that when they also saw the children, lined up to form the words "Thank You", all of the air crew were in tears. So moved were they by what they saw that they threw their own rations and emergency rations, anything they had on them, or in the aircraft, out of the open bomb bays when they had dropped the supplies they had been sent with.

Many years later, while still in the RAF, in the early 1960's he visited Arnhem with my mother. Talking in a bar he was asked about his wartime experiences and he told the tale of Operation Manna to the Dutch people they were talking with. When he had finished telling of his feelings when he saw all the starving little children lined up in the words "Thank You" a man got up, took his hand and said, "I was one of those children, now I thank you personally"

I hope that this has been of some use to you and your research and I wish you well with your book. It will make fascinating reading I am sure.

On November 18, 2000 she wrote me some more and I wish to write just a small excerpt from her letter because it is so poignant:

"Although I am an only child I have had six children myself and they all adore their grandfather. When one of the my boys had his 21ˢᵗ birthday he turned to his grandfather and asked him, "What were you doing on your 21ˢᵗ birthday, Granddad?"
My father thought for a moment, then said: "Bombing Berlin actually!"

Frans van den Berg who wrote about the *'Dog'* and the *'Dining Room'* covered in a previous chapter had an interesting 'Manna' experience as well. "Het Rotterdamsch Parool" of September 25, 1948 devoted the following article entitled: "Flying Grocer" in Rotterdam.
Here follows the translation:

"Flying Grocer" in Rotterdam

We had the good fortune to meet a former RAF pilot at the house of family van den Berg in the Van Rheynstraat 47. He was one of the flying grocers who in April/May 1945 saved the population of Rotterdam and other cities in West Holland from certain starvation. The pilot's name is Walter McNeil from Heaton near Newcastle. He didn't just show up at the family in Rotterdam. His presence here has a much more romantic beginning.

In April/May 1945 Pilot McNeil made 5 flights as "flying grocer" above West-Nederland, two of those above Rotterdam. Pilots and crewmembers would make small parcels from their own rations and drop those as well. During his last flight McNeil asked the tail gunner to drop his parcel from the plane. In this parcel he had enclosed his name and address as well as: "Greetings from the RAF". The parcel containing chocolates and sweets fluttered down and two young boys in their small sailboat on the Kralingse Plas retrieved the parcel from the water. One of the boys, 15-year old Frans van den Berg living in Crooswijk held on to the message from Pilot McNeil. It was but 1.1/2 years later, after Frans had learned enough English at the MULO School, when he was able to write to McNeil in English. Promptly he received a response from Newcastle. The pilot wrote that even the papers in Newcastle had made mention of the contact between a pilot of the RAF and a boy from Rotterdam.

In time there was a regular exchange of correspondence between the two. Frans van den Berg is now 18 years old and this past summer was a guest of the family in Newcastle. And presently Mr. McNeil is the guest of the family van den Berg. Surrounded by the family, McNeil told us that he had made several bombing missions above Germany. In spite of heavy anti aircraft fire from the ground McNeil had never been wounded. His Lancaster, however, received numerous hits from shrapnel. "Once a large piece of shrapnel penetrated the wing right next to the gas tank. If it had hit the tank I would now not be sitting here", McNeil tells us with a wide grin on his face. His luck held out throughout the food droppings although it was not without danger because of their low altitude. Another Lancaster was not that lucky, when a friend of McNeil received whole load of food in his cockpit from a plane flying above him. His best memories come from the missions as "Flying Grocer" above Rotterdam and other

Dutch cities. He will never forget the sight of hundreds of people on the ground waving to the planes with anything they could find. We are convinced that Rotterdam will never forget the "Flying Grocers". Again thanks to you, Pilot McNeil and all your comrades who flew these missions with you.

Chapter Eighty-Seven

Free at Last!

448. Field Marshall Montgomery accepting the German surrender of all German troops in Holland, Denmark and West Germany, including Heligoland and the Frisian Islands.

449. The surrender document signed on May 4th, 1945
effective 8am May 5th, 1945
Credits: U.S. National Archives

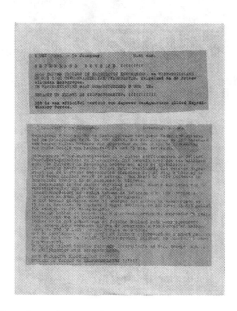

450. Henry's Bulletin of Friday May 4, 1945, 8:40pm and
Saturday, May 5, 2pm giving the news of the German
surrender going into effect on Saturday, May 5th at 8am.

The following is a translation of both documents:

4 May 1945 – 5th Year of Publication   8:40 hours

THE NETHERLANDS LIBERATED!!!!!!!!!

ALL GERMAN TROOPS IN HOLLAND, DENMARK and WEST GERMANY, INCLUDING HELGOLAND and THE FRISIAN ISLANDS HAVE SURRENDERED UNCONDITIONALLY.
THE ARMISTICE WILL GO INTO EFFECT TOMORROW MORNING AT 8AM

STAY CALM AND KEEP YOUR COOL!!!!!

This is an official announcement from Supreme Headquarters Allied Expeditionary Forces

5 May 1945 – 5th Year of Publication   Saturday, 2pm

This evening at 8pm HM the Queen will address the Nation by radio. The BBC has announced that Princess Juliana and Prince Bernard will visit Amsterdam and The Hague. The broadcast of Radio Orange for tonight has been extended by 15 minutes.
This morning at 8am all German troops in Holland, North-West-Germany and Denmark have capitulated. More than a million men are involved. The Germans in Norway have not yet surrendered. Admiral Doenitz declared in a radio address that further resistance to the western powers is senseless. However, he urged to continue the fight against Russia. He ordered all Germans in Denmark to stay in their barracks. A new government was formed in Denmark including members of the resistance. The Germans between Magdeburg and Berlin have also capitulated. Yesterday the Russians took 45,000 prisoners. The RAF torpedoed and sunk another 14 ships and damaged 15 in the Oostzee. During the last 5 days the Germans lost a total of 150 ships and 215 planes. In Berlin the Russians captured 6 generals, including the President of Police for Berlin.
Any radio transmitters in the west of Holland are urged to only air the programs of Radio Orange and the BBC. The 7th American Army

have forced entrance to the Brenner Pass and made contact with the 5th Army in Italy. Berchtesgaden, Salzburg and Innsbruck have been captured. Australian and Dutch troops fighting on Tarakan have penetrated the city by the same name.

NO PREMATURE FLAG WAVING!!!!!!!

STAY CALM AND KEEP YOUR COOL!!!!!

Henry remembers:

For the Germans everything was starting to fall apart fast. Hitler committed suicide. Berlin fell to the Russians and the Allies broke through in all directions, except the western part of Holland. But then on May 3rd we were alerted to start checking German troop movements. I had to go with several others to the railroad overpass at the end of the Albrechtskade close to the Beukelsdijk. There was a trade school (Ambachtschool) close by, which was occupied by the Dutch SS. Another resistance group was keeping their eyes or rather machine guns on that school. A German car tried to go through their checkpoint to the crossing where we were. The Germans did not stop so they came under fire. They were about 500 feet from our position. All we had were sten guns and they would not be effective at that range. However, the other group had a light machine gun (bren) that did the trick. They came out with their hands up and a few were somewhat damaged in the process. Our group went back to the Park area and in the evening I picked up the news that the Germans were negotiating to surrender in Holland and Northwest Germany, Denmark and Norway. On the 4th of May we had the news that the surrender would be at 8am the next morning, May5th. Communications for the Germans were almost non-existent so they needed some time to alert their troops. On the 4th of May the machine gun posts on our bridge were gone. The day before we used the ferry across the Schie near the Hooidrift. Towards the evening we went to our assigned positions and our task was now to keep order until the Canadians would arrive. The Dutch police was too 'contaminated' to do the job. About four days later the Canadian Army arrived to a tumultuous welcome. They set up their base camp on the Heemraadsingel just past the Binnenweg. The Germans had installed themselves in some very nice homes there, which now became the Canadian Headquarters. They needed an interpreter and I was sent for. The officer to whom I reported looked at me and asked how old I was. 21 and I weighed a little over 100 lbs. He called one of his men and told him to feed me first. I got real food and ate things I had not seen in a long time. I gained weight in a hurry. They also gave me a bunch of K or C rations to take home. What was also very much appreciated was a liter of uncut cognac (60%) and the cigarettes. I did this for a few weeks and the Canadians moved on. The city was pretty orderly. We had to step in when a bunch of characters had shaved the heads of some ladies of doubtful virtue and wanted to remove the plucks of hair by holding them over a bonfire. Shaving them was one thing but burning them was going too far. It was resolved by a burst of Sten gun fire in the air. We had to guard some areas where food supplies were stored. By that time police was back minus the German appointees.

Mother remembers:
It was now the beginning of May and I remember Henry coming up from the cellar and in an exciting voice telling me that we were free. The Germans had surrendered. But watch out! Henry left and shortly thereafter he was putting out the flag with the beautiful orange banner and he put orange bulletins on the walls. In front of the window was a big "Welcome Liberators" sign that Wim had painted showing the flags of the Allies including the Russians. All of a sudden several German soldiers stormed in our house. They tore down the flag as well as all the orange posters and the Welcome sign. We were so in shock and didn't say a word. That was a good thing and they left. However, on the corner of the street where the Printer Wijt has their offices the two krauts started to fire their weapons and wounded a young girl. We took her home to the Havenstraat where she lived.

The Germans had surrendered Western Holland on May 5th but the Canadians and British forces did not show up until May 8. Until they arrived there reigned total anarchy. The Resistance Forces were now in control but they couldn't be everywhere. On the morning of the surrender, May 5th, mother, Annie and I had an appointment at the hospital on the Westzeedijk in connection with my father's TBC, we had to be checked occasionally as well. It was after 8am and we started our trip to the hospital. We passed the buildings on the Pieter de Hooghweg still occupied by the Germans. The sentries were still there but what we noticed was that they carried their rifles upside down, a sign of surrender. That made us feel good but we still weren't sure about some of them, particularly the characters from the Gestapo and Sicherheitsdienst, including even the Kriegsmarine (German Navy). When we reached the end of the Westzeedijk close to the hospital we heard a lot of shooting. Quickly we went behind one of the many air raid shelters and I peeked around the corner to see what was happening. I saw two drunken Germans who had just left a bar on the Westzeedijk and they were doing the random shooting. I don't believe they were aiming at anyone in particular but it was dangerous enough. I remember my mother saying: *"Where are the resistance people when you need them?"* The two Germans continued their shooting and appeared to have lot of fun falling all over themselves, reloading their pistols and continuing their fire. Somebody must have gone for the resistance people because we saw some them come running up the incline from the Westersingel. They had Sten guns that were not very accurate at a distance. Therefore they had to get closer and about seven resistance fighters opened fire at pretty close range. One of the Germans was literally shot in half. His body was actually in two parts, shot straight through his midriff. The other German had been shot as well but he was lucky, he lived. He had raised his arms in surrender and one of the resistance men tore the buttons of his pants, which caused this kraut to hold up his pants from going down over his knees. It was an unreal sight. One a bloody mess and the other one crying for his 'muttie'.

On May 4th when we had been notified that the surrender would go into effect the next day, I had painted a large sign on a piece of cardboard or plywood. It said: Welcome to our Liberators and it showed the flags of the USA, Britain, France, Canada, Australia, New Zealand and the Russians. It was a beauty and I was proud of it. We put it in front of the window facing the Dunantstraat and there it sat until a detachment of Germans came through the street. They were carrying their rifles and acted quite ugly. We were all at the window and saw this bunch coming to the door. They banged on the door and my father went to answer it. I could overhear what was being said: "Wir muessen das Schild haben". (We have to have that sign). My father, quite cocky now because they had surrendered, although it would only go into effect the next morning at 8am, said: "Nein, Sie koennen das Schield nicht haben, Sie haben kapituliert!"

(No, you can't have the sign you have capitulated!) Whereupon this German officer said: *"Ja, das ist ja so aber night an die Russen!"* (Yes, that is true but not to the Russians!) It was true they were still fighting the Russians. We no longer argued and gave them the sign. We never saw it back. We were really lucky. They could just as easily have killed us.

On May 6th people were on the street and groups were forming, eager to take revenge on Dutch collaborators and particularly the members of the hated Dutch Nazi party, the NSB. There was this penned up frustration and hatred accumulated over a five-year period of suppression, killing, hunger and persecution that needed an outlet. Some people had kept lists of those they considered traitors but what to do with them after you nabbed them? They had no weapons and the Resistance Forces were trying to maintain some kind of order. These mobs of people reminded me of pictures from the French Revolution when the guillotine was used so effectively. What the crowd did have, however, was hair clippers and they went after the women that had cavorted and fraternized with the Germans. Everyone knew their names and where they lived. I joined one of those mobs in the Willem Buijtenwegstraat. In short order our mob had collected more than five of these women. Doors had been bashed in and people had entered apartments and dragged them out on the street. They were frightened as can be and were sure that they were going to be killed but something else was in store for them. It is hard to imagine now but at the time I was, like the rest, full of hatred toward anything German and I wanted revenge like everyone else. At the south end of the Willem Buijtenwegstraat was an air raid shelter covered with grass. The women were dragged on top of the shelter, a chair and table were set up and the first woman was held down on the chair while the "barber" shaved her completely bald. Her struggling to get free had no effect. Another person then painted a red swastika on her head from a bucket of paint they had brought along for the purpose. I remember seeing the red paint run down the faces of these women after they had been roughly clipped. After the paint job they were given a good kick in the rear and were sent on their way. One of these women was defiant to the end and with the red paint running over her face raised the Nazi salute and yelled out loud that we were all stupid and ignorant people, that pretty soon we would have to fight the Russians and then we would need the Germans again. I must admit it made we wonder some. She was not completely wrong. However, all this got lost in the headiness of the moment.

450a. Shaven heads

From the time of our liberation until the arrival of the Canadians and British forces we were in a state of suspended animation. People dancing in the street, mobs of people seeking revenge, others breaking into buildings and stealing what ever they could. Complete anarchy. People were still hungry however and so far the only nourishment that I had received from the food drops was a lick of yellow mustard that somebody had brought to our street. We all thought that was funny. It must have come from the Americans, someone said. *"They must have thought we had hot dogs and lacked the mustard"*. Lancasters and Flying Fortresses were still flying over continuously and were dropping food on fields near the big population centers. No longer was Waalhaven being used; too many of the parcels had fallen in the water of the Maas River and adjacent harbors. For weeks the Coolhaven had a yellowish color. The cause had been a big load of egg powder that had split open upon impact with the water. The new drop zone was in Terbregge near where Henk Dijkxhoorn lived, a 12-year-old boy in 1945 who would in his later years become my good friend. Like myself he never could forget the miracle from the sky and for many years worked on and pursued the idea of a monument honoring the crews of the RAF and US 8th Air Force that had brought us manna from heaven. His tenaciousness paid off after eleven years and with the support of the city and public donations a unique monument was inaugurated in 2006.

451. Henk Dijkxhoorn and Secretary of State Van de Knaap cutting the ribbon of the Monument during its inauguration on April 28, 2006.

452. The steel monument resembles the many food parcels in the belly of the bomber. It is located along the Freeway A-20 in New Terbregge on land that in 1945 was polder land and perfect for the droppings.

During this period I roamed the area with a friend and we visited places that everybody else shied away from. We had been warned not to touch any suspicious looking parcels or objects. Those things could be booby-traps. Of course, that only stimulated us to look for them.

Near the Catholic Cemetery where we had harvested firewood a month or so earlier we got lucky and noticed in the bushes something rather bulky wrapped in sailcloth. We poked at it with a stick but it didn't explode. Then we got the courage of pulling it out of the bushes. The parcel was tied up in twine. We were quite curious; who wouldn't be? We slowly unwrapped it and what we discovered was a cache of small arms and ammunition. This package was discovered right behind the University of Economics building and the Gestapo must have hid it there. If I had known at that time that fifty years later there would have been an auction house by the name of EBay I would have held on to the ample supply of 'lugers' in holsters, with enough grease to last for a lifetime. But we were good kids; we reported the find to the Resistance people and they eagerly took possession. I often wondered what they did with it.

453. The Parabellum-Pistole, popularly known as the
Luger pistol taking a 9mm Parabellum cartridge.

Frans van de Berg, who experienced the liberation very much the same as I did had a similar experience but with heavier equipment. In 2005 he related: *"The Germans had abandoned their quarters and equipment in our area. Our playground was the Kralingse Plas area where, in the woods, the Germans had left behind several small armored cars with grenades and bandoliers of machine gun bullets. We managed to twist the bullets out of the shells, removed the black gunpowder and lit it with a match. Great fun to watch it burn. We found several stick hand grenades and we did some fishing in the lake. Then we went back to the tanks and removed the machineguns. We hid those in the woods but with the guns first scared off a man who was collecting 'Manna' food from the lake. One morning however the police came to our house after we had an accident with one of the grenades. They took us to the woods where we had hidden the machineguns and with the guns took us to the police station on the Boezemsingel. We had a lot of people staring at us. We received one day detention".*

"Our Canadian liberators were in tents on land near the Boezemsingel. I did some washing of their socks for cigarettes".

(From Frans van de Berg's Diary)
Now the waiting was for the arrival of the Canadian liberation forces. On the 8th of May I was on the Rochussenstraat and noticed an unusual green motorcycle approaching fast from an easterly direction. It was definitely not a Zundapp or BMW. It turned out to be an English made Norton with a Canadian on it. "My first liberator". There were more people waiting for the arrival of the Canadians and when the people saw this man they practically stopped him in his tracks. Once he was forced to stop, a crowd you wouldn't believe overwhelmed the poor guy. They wanted to lift him off his bike and the jubilant crowd wanted to carry him around. The man begged the people to let him go and although I didn't understand much English it was clear to me that he was in a hurry to go somewhere and it was German HQ. The crowd understood and allowed him to continue on his way. I hope he made it. We should have known that he was only a single Canadian and not the vanguard of the liberation army because on his motorcycle there was a sign that said: Provost. He was an MP to take control of the German HQ. By the next day all the main roads in Rotterdam were lined with people waiting for the grand entrance of "our liberators".

454. The advance party.

455. An amphibious tractor LVT4

456. A scout car M3

457. A Sherman Tank

458. A medium tank entering the city.

Finally, on May 9th we saw them coming and what a sight it was! They came in bren-carriers, DUKW's, tanks, trucks, jeeps, motorcycles, but no horses, nobody walked, it was all motorized. Some small boats entered the Coolhaven; these boats were flying the Canadian flag, the Maple Leaf. What emotion. It was unbelievable to see these healthy looking and smiling young men that had come from so far away. The ones I saw were from Saskatoon, Saskatchewan, all 'stocky' wheat farmers. How we loved them. Within short order vehicles were crowded with people climbing all over them.

459. Underneath it all is a Bren Gun Carrier

The drivers couldn't see where they were going and the columns just stopped. For these Canadians it must have been the most wonderful experience of their lives; the war was over in Europe and the Dutch population, who adored them, welcomed them with open arms.

460. Nurses and police dancing on the Coolsingel

They encamped on the grass along the Heemraadsingel near the Nieuwe Binnenweg.

591

461. Canadian encampment on the Heemraadsingel

Big and small pup tents and field kitchens with massive burners for cooking. They had roped off this area for some privacy but they didn't get much of that. Scores of kids like myself were lined up and watching. The soldiers were waiting in line at the kitchen and were receiving white bread, ham and eggs & bacon and tins of steaming hot coffee. I still remember the aroma of it all. One of the soldiers, a huge guy, looked at me. He was sitting in his jeep and eating his fare. He motioned for me to come to him, lifted me into the jeep next to him and handed me his mess kit with some of his food. I had died and gone to heaven. The taste of those eggs, even if it was from egg powder, and the ham and bacon was like nothing I had ever tasted in my life. I remember him looking at me with that big grin on his sunburned face. At that point I knew we were free again and everything would be all right from now on.

Before I left the area to go home and tell my parents about my experience, this big guy gave me some cigarettes: *"for your dad"*. Several brands: Players and Sweet Caporal. Dad was delighted!
In front of our house in the Coolhaven a small boat displaying the Canadian flag had berthed.
I immediately went there and was invited on the ship. It turned out to be a supply ship of the Quarter Master. Lots of uniforms, boots, clothing, etc. This time a very short Canadian with the distinctive "Saskatoon" tag on his uniform sleeve sized me up and gave me a new battle jacket. It was really too big for me but I wore it with pride and

kept it for a long time. He also gave me some K rations that I brought home. It contained cans with corned beef hash. Delicious!

462. Children are taking joy rides in a DUKW, an amphibious truck.

463. Everywhere in the city the population is overjoyed

464. How can you forget a welcome like that?

465. Our liberators are welcomed by girls in their Dutch costumes.

466. Nurses dancing in front of Rotterdam City Hall

467. The Resistance people in action.

468. Another picture of the men of the Resistance.

469. I remember 'shorty'. I believe he was a reporter. Every one loved the children.

470. Distribution of crackers out of tin cans.

471. A Canadian column of trucks laden with food supplies working its way toward Rotterdam. A typical Dutch scene.

"Joe, those are the ones we want!"

Several days later, the British arrived on the Pieter de Hooghweg and occupied the buildings vacated by the Germans. These troops, I remember, were from the "Royal Engineers".
A friend and I went to see what was going on and tried to communicate with several of the soldiers at the barbed wire barricade in front of the University of Economics. Our English was not quite sufficient for a decent conversation but we did get the meaning of things. One of the soldiers suddenly looked away from us and pointed at some young women with turbans all around their head. We knew what they were; they were several of the women that we had watched being shaved a few days earlier. In my best English I explained to these soldiers that these were: *"Not good, bad German women!"* The soldiers understood and then one looked at the other and said: *"Hey Joe, those are the ones we want!"* I was disappointed; they obviously didn't share the same 'feelings' toward these women. "Boys will be Boys".

Secret Service MI6

597

The resistance people knew of the woman who lived in our street and who was considered a spy for the German Abwehr. Therefore we fully expected her to be arrested by the British Secret Service. On May 10th we spotted a half-ton truck stopped in front of our apartment building. Several high-ranking British officers in their dress uniforms left the vehicle and entered the apartment occupied by Miss M. After a little less than an hour the officers came down the stairs with our neighbor in tow and before leaving in their small truck our neighbor was embraced by the three officers. What was going on here? Then we learned that throughout the war our neighbor had been a certified MI6 spy for the British planted there prior to hostilities in 1940.

On November 12, the day after the razzia, she had saved Henry and the rest of our family. We asked her about the November 12 incident and she told us that she realized that by answering the question of whether or not Henry had reported for duty in Germany, she would throw us for a loop and might cause us to panic but considered it a risk well worth taking. We were of the same opinion. She had also been the one in May 1940 who had fired shots from her apartment in the hope that she would be considered a collaborator and should be shunned at all cost. A total set-up. Her shots were always aimed at the sky proving the fact that nobody of the soldiers or for that matter Henry, who had brought food to our Dutch soldiers, were ever hit. Of course, there were certainly other *'real'* collaborators. They were quite numerous in the Willem Buijtenwegstraat, the street behind the Dunantstraat. That street was known for its German infiltrators, the "Fifth Column" *, prior to the outbreak of war.

* The term originated in 1936 and came from a nationalist general during the 1936-1939 Spanish Civil War. As four of his army columns moved on Madrid, the general referred to his militant supporters within the capital as his "fifth column", intent on undermining the Republican government from within.

One last act that comes to mind during these few days following our liberation was when the Canadians together with people from the resistance had nabbed the Mayor of Rotterdam, Frederik Mueller together with his complete city council. They were locked up but during the day they were put to work dismantling barbed wire obstructions left by the Germans. One of those barricades was near the Museum Booymans on the Rochussenstraat. My friends and I were roaming the streets at that time because there was so much of interest going on and we hit upon this motley group in their best Sunday suits picking away with their bare hands at these barricades. We knew many of these people; they were all members of the Dutch Nazi Party (NSB) and been the ones that had executed the orders of the Gestapo. It is understandable then that these men were hated even more than the Germans. These were Dutchmen, our own kind.

Some very nonchalant Canadian soldiers were keeping an eye on them. They didn't know about these people or what they had done to us; had no axe to grind, but we did. We started to pelt them with stones and bricks. I hit the mayor with a good one. The soldiers quickly put a stop to our attack and told us that they were ordered by their superiors to return these Nazis in one piece because they would have to stand trial: *"Please kids, don't kill them now!"* Several of these 'dignitaries' were found guilty and later executed.

Toward the middle of May we were getting more food from both Operation Manna and food supplies brought in by truck from the already liberated area. All of us started to feel better. With a full stomach of crackers and spam we started to think of the freedom we had regained. It was once again possible to say what you wanted, to move around where you wanted, to express your religion, to meet in groups, to complain, to read the truth instead of lies. With that came 'disunity" as well. Where before everyone had had but one goal and was of one mind, i.e. getting rid of the hated *"Hun"*, now the nation became once again a people with their own personal beliefs, likes and dislikes, be it: nationalists, royalists, liberal democrats, social democrats, communists, rich and poor, blue blood and blue collar. The mixture from before the war, that amalgam of people calling itself: "The Kingdom of the Netherlands".

472. Je Maintiendrai
"I will maintain", is the motto of the House of Orange
and Nassau, the Royal Family of the Netherlands

Chapter Eighty-Eight

The Final Surrender

473. General Alfred Jodl, Chief of the Operations Staff in the German High Command signs the document of unconditional German surrender at General Eisenhower's Headquarters in Reims, France, May 7, 1945.
Credits: U.S. National Archives

474. The Document of Surrender signed by Jodl in Reims on May 7th, 1945
Credits: U.S. National Archives

475. German Field Marshall Wilhelm Keitel signs the surrender document at Soviet Headquarters in Berlin, May 9, 1945. The Soviets had insisted that a second ceremonial signing take place in Soviet-occupied Berlin.
Credits: U.S. National Archives

476. During the Battle of Berlin, the Red Flag was raised over the Reichstag, May 1945.

477. Deposition of captured 1ˢᵗ SS Division Leibstandarte
SS Adolf Hitler standards by Soviet soldiers near the
Kremlin Wall during the Victory Parade, June 24, 1945.

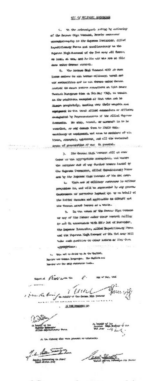

478. Document of Surrender signed by Keitel in Berlin on
May 8ᵗʰ, 1945
Credits: U.S. National Archives

CHAPTER EIGHTY-NINE

"I REMEMBER THE GERMAN SURRENDER"

BY KATHRYN WESTCOTT
BBC NEWS

Susan Hibbert was one of the first people to know that World War II in Europe was over.

479. Susan Hibbert in 1945.

Long before the countries that had been locked in the struggle against Nazi Germany rang with cheers of victory, Susan, a young sergeant based in the French town of Reims, quietly celebrated with *Veuve Cliquot* champagne served in a tin cup.

In May 1945, Susan was a British sergeant in the Auxiliary Territorial Service (ATS) based at General Dwight D. Eisenhower's temporary HQ – a small redbrick schoolhouse in northeastern France. Early in the morning on May 7, in a windowless room in the corner of the building, Susan witnessed history being made, the full capitulation of all Nazi forces. As a secretary for the Supreme Headquarters Allied Expeditionary Force (SHAEF), she played an essential role – typing and retyping the final surrender document for 20 hours.

NEGOTIATIONS

"In the days leading up to the surrender, we knew something was happening – there was a real feeling of excitement in the air", Susan told BBC News.
"For five days we were typing documents. We started early in the morning and finished late at night. I typed the English documents, three other secretaries typed the French, Russian and German versions." Drafts were sent to Washington, London and Moscow.

With Hitler's death at the end of April, leadership of Germany had devolved to Grand Admiral Karl Doenitz. On May 6, General Alfred Jodl, Commander in Chief of the Wehrmacht, arrived to represent him in Reims.

Susan began typing the Act of Military Surrender on 6 May and finished some 20 hours later in the early hours of 7 May.

"Staff officers and interpreters were coming and going. We were not allowed to leave the room. There were constant changes and amendments. I often had to start again from the beginning. The British version of the surrender was quite basic, although a lot of people had worked on it."

The documents were finally taken to the "war room", which was covered floor to ceiling in maps.

THE TABLE

In the centre of the room stood a large, black wooden table. One reporter present described it as the *"Most important table on earth"*. Pencils, papers and ashtrays had been placed on the table with military precision, their positions having been measured with a ruler by an American captain. At about 0230 on 7 May, 10 Allied officers came in and took their places at the table. The Germans were called in. General Eisenhower remained in another room for reasons of protocol.

Susan and a group of her colleagues had been waiting for a long time outside the room, before being invited in to watch history being made.

"We were very, very tired. We had been waiting for ages. We came into the room; there were a lot of journalists and photographers. The actual signing was carried out quietly and solemnly. There was no celebrating," said Susan.

An interpreter read out the surrender terms – probably more for the benefit of the journalists.

General Jodl then rose stiffly and turned to General Eisenhower's Chief of Staff Lt. General Walter Bedell Smith. He said in English: *"I want to say a word"*. Then proceeding in German, he declared: *"With this signature the German people and the German armed forces are for better or worse delivered into the victor's hands. In this war, which has lasted more than five years, they both have achieved and suffered more than perhaps any other people in the world. In this hour I can only express the hope that the victor will treat them with generosity."*

There was no answer. No salutes. The Germans got up and left the room.

CHAMPAGNE

Those left inside the war room celebrated quietly. *"We had some champagne but we didn't have any glasses so we had to drink it out army mess tins. We passed the tins around and had a few sips. We were so pleased it was happening – it was wonderful to be part of it. But, we were so exhausted, all I and the other secretaries wanted to do was go to bed. But I was asked to do one more job. I had to type the signal informing the War Office in London that the war in Europe was over."*

The most momentous wartime message simply read: *"The mission of this Allied Force was fulfilled at 0241, local time, May 7ᵗʰ, 1945"*.

According to General Bedell Smith, in his book Eisenhower's Six Great Decisions, there were attempts to make the historic communication less prosaic. The general and his colleagues *"groped for resounding phrases as fitting accolades to the Great Crusade and indicative of our dedication to the great task just completed."* But General Eisenhower apparently rejected a stack of draft messages proposed by his staff and opted for the simpler message.

While millions celebrated, Susan Hibbert slept. *"When the surrender was over, we just disappeared. I went to bed and didn't get up for two days. I was so exhausted,"* she recalls.

Sixty years later, in 2005, she was honored at a reception hosted by French Prime Minister Jean- Pierre Raffarin in Reims. She is believed to be one of only two people still alive who witnessed the final surrender. The war ended at 2301 Central European Time on 8 May. For Europe, it marked a new beginning. For Susan, it remains a vivid memory. *"I feel very privileged to be part of history,"* she said.

480. Germany Quits.
Credits: U.S. National Archives

122. German prisoners on the Autobahn (USA)

481.
Credits: U.S. National Archives

482. The Wehrmacht leaving Rotterdam
Credits: U.S. National Archives

483. Walking back to 'der Heimat'
Credits: U.S. National Archives

484. Some even have transportation

124. Pen for holding German prisoners of war. (USA)

485. Credits: U.S. National Archives

486. Canadian soldiers breaking up a bunker of the
'Atlantikwal'

487. Henry, dad and I in the summer of 1945. I am
wearing the battle jacket given to me by the Canadian
supply sergeant from Saskatoon.

CHAPTER NINETY

THE DAY AFTER

The war was over. The occupation had lasted almost five years and we had not known freedom for 1,451 days. All of a sudden the cloak had lifted and everything we experienced was once again in Technicolor. It was truly a strange sensation to wake up in the morning and realize that the bombings and fly-overs had stopped; the air raid sirens had been silent. We were still somewhat hungry but we were not starving any longer. Slowly but surely the realization of freedom manifested itself. The Newspapers once again related the facts. The radio could be turned on 'loud'. Dance music could be heard, all the latest songs from the U.S. and Britain. *"Don't Fence Me In!"* comes to mind. Movies that had already been out for years were now shown in the theatres; I went to see *The Thief of Baghdad* with Henry. *Bambi* from Walt Disney Studios was another movie I remember. We could walk the streets after dark and once again we could talk freely and say anything we pleased. We were allowed to travel again. That is if there was transportation. The trains were running again albeit on a very limited schedule. My mother took the train to Amsterdam to visit her older sister Kaatje and her cousins. She came back with a story that even after our liberation was very unsettling. Without realizing it we had had a brush with death. Mother's niece Stien had a girlfriend by the name of Jo Landzaad. Her job during the later years of the occupation had been collecting money from the cable radio subscribers. She had gotten to know her customers quite well. On one occasion during the past winter she had talked with a customer about the difficulty of mailing her winter coat to Rotterdam to be altered at my father's place of business. The man said that he might be able to help; occasionally he had the means of transportation to Rotterdam. She had been delighted with the offer. But there was a condition, he had told her: "What I am doing is very dangerous and I need to know if those people in Rotterdam can be trusted." *"Oh, yes*", she had assured him. *"They hate the Germans and their oldest son is even in the Resistance!"* The man was now keenly interested and asked for our address in Rotterdam. Jo Landzaad who had known us for many years and had visited us many times could for the life of it not remember our address. The man insisted that she come back to him with the address and the coat and he would take care of the rest. This was in either February or March 1945. For some reason Jo didn't get to it and other events had overtaken the urgency of the coat. A week following the liberation she was once again collecting the bills and called on her 'friend'. However, he was no longer there and a neighbor told her that he would never come back because the resistance people had nabbed him. He had been a member of the Dutch Gestapo and been responsible for the death of many a patriot in Amsterdam. Had it been fortuitous fate that she had a moment's lapse of memory? We will never know but the tale gave us all a cold chill of what might have happened to us. We would have been killed for sure and never have known from what corner it had come. We had been lucky once again.

Henry remembers:
We could go home and back to our jobs but I took a test for the air force. I passed and went to Island de Beer, where we received primary training from Dutch marines. The marines were guarding German prisoners who had to clear the beaches of anti-personnel mines. We also cleared the anti-tank mines; they were not as sensitive. However, if we found a booby-trapped one, we left that area to the Germans. In August the war with Japan was over with a bang. We were told; no pilot training in the USA, you can sign on as sailor 3rd class or something. The honor was declined and since several others and I were former Resistance we could join the Stoottroepen Regiment. That was in Weert (Limburg) and we there hopping from one military base to another. The Regimental Commander. A Colonel in US uniform with the SHAEF badge interviewed each of us. And now we come to an amazing coincidence. He asked me where I lived during the war and I told him the Dunantstraat. "Oh", he said: "then you must know the Heyman Dullart Plein". I told him: "sure, I also worked at Stokvis". He used to live in a house at the corner of the Heyman Dullaert straat. That's the place where I dropped information off! He laughed and said: "So, you were one of them". He asked me some more questions, such

as: "How did you get a car battery?" I told him that I had liberated a German one. After that I was accepted into the Regiment. Towards the end of November I received a notice to give to my commanding officer and get travel papers to go to Harderwijk for a test. This was for officer training and since the school in Breda was destroyed it would now be held in the Jan Willem Friso Kazerne in Harderwijk. It was built in 1944 by the Germans and barely used. There would be three days of testing and physical activities for about 120 men. We all got a big number to put on our backs. At the end of the third day, assembled in the auditorium, they called two numbers; one of the two was mine. We were told to stay and the rest could go back to their units. We were told that we were accepted and should report on the 2nd of January 1946. By that time it was 6pm. We had to leave for our units right away, because a new group was coming in. I made it back in time for the 7 o'clock report. Then the battalion commander had to see me and congratulated me. Later I heard from the sergeant in the office that he had sent half a dozen of his men, but they were all rejected. It obviously pleased him that one of his men had been accepted; he had saved face. A year later I was 2nd Lieutenant and that was the start of my military career. In 1950 I was demobilized as a 1st Lieutenant and transferred to the reserves where I made Captain. I got my honorable discharge a year after I was in the US.

Mother remembers:

Yes, we were liberated but I never felt the happiness and exhilaration that I thought I would feel upon being liberated. Maybe that feeling would come later. Too many people had lost their lives so that we might live. Not because we were better but because we were lucky. We had been saved but just look at our city, one big pile of rubble. So much had been destroyed. People had torn up their homes for anything that was combustible and would keep them warm, only small stumps where beautiful trees had been before. What I have written here is only what was experienced by one family and then only a small part. I think again of the fear and sorrow when our Wim lived for one and one half year on a farm in Wierden so that he would have enough to eat. We missed this happy child so much and Henry went and brought him back. It is now 48 years since all this happened. Every family has a story to tell, one more terrible than the other. None are exaggerated. It is incomprehensible that just because they were Jewish, little babies and children direct from a deep sleep were thrown in trucks, hauled away and gassed. I had hoped that people would have learned their lessons, but alas, there is still war.

It was not long after the liberation that thousands of people were anxiously waiting for the return of their loved ones and friends from Germany. Soon barges were coming in our harbor loaded with men that had been slave laborers. There were many happy scenes of family being re-united but in many ways it was a sorry sight. All these emaciated people coming ashore dressed in rags and carrying bundles of more rags. Many were crippled and unable to walk. The Red Cross and several other Relief organizations were at hand to welcome these people, feed them and get them on their way home. Relatives had come in droves in the hope that they might find their husbands and fathers. Many of the scenes that played out were heart rending. I remember one occasion when a mother recognized her son among the throng of people, ran to him, embraced him and then collapsed when told that her husband who had been picked up together with her son would not come back. His son had been on his side when he died in Germany. Hundreds of notices were posted on the surrounding buildings and fences containing names and messages of the people that had arrived and moved on. Relatives and friends of people that were still missing posted hundreds of messages as well.

During the war we had witnessed thousands of Jews being rounded up and shipped to Germany. We expected them to return but none did. We had heard rumors of the death camps but our minds could not accept the reality of the Holocaust. When not one Jew returned on these barges realization set in that all these men, women and children had been slaughtered. None of our Jewish friends returned. Only much later were we notified of the fate of Jacob Hamel, his wife, son and daughter-in-law. They were just one family out of millions. We can comprehend twenty people or maybe one hundred but millions? No, numbers like that are impossible to comprehend. It becomes more realistic when you think of a city like Chicago or New York being totally wiped out. All of us had lost friends and it would take a lifetime for wounds to heal. But we would never forget and it would be next to impossible to forgive.

CHAPTER NINETY-ONE

TEN CHAPTERS

In 1942 when Field Marshall Bernard Law Montgomery was appointed to command the British forces in North Africa he started a little book and at the end of the war entitled it:
Ten Chapters

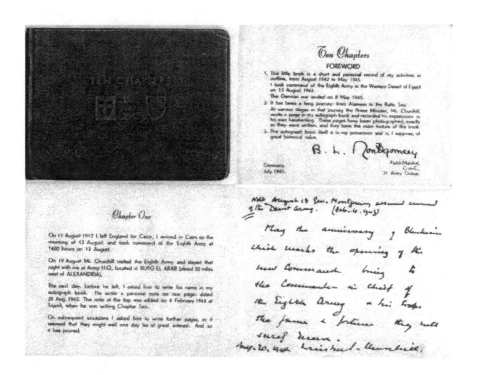

chapter II

On this night at Tripoli the Desert army reported the completion of all tasks hitherto set them; the enemy being driven out of Egypt, Cyrenaica, & Tripolitania and all his establishments capabilities & destroyed.

These memorable events prefix the brisk with I expounded on an earlier page & see that prelude to a still more glorious. Chple

Feb 4. 1943   Winston Churchill

chapter III   Algiers June 3. 1943

The total destruction & capture of all enemy forces in Tunisia, culminating in the surrender of 248,000 men, marks the Triumphant end of the great enterprises set on foot at Alamein & by the invasion of N.W Africa. May the future reap in the utmost fullness the rewards of hard achievements & arms endurance.

Winston Churchill.

Chapter Two

The battle of ALAMEIN began on 23 October 1942.

It was won by 4 November.

The Eighth Army swept forward across the Western Desert of Egypt, across Cyrenaica, into Tripolitania and captured Tripoli on 23 January 1943.

The Prime Minister visited me at Tripoli early in February, and wrote Chapter Two on 4 February, 1943.

Chapter Three

By May 1943 the war in Africa was over. Early in April the Eighth Army had linked up with the Allied Forces in N.W. Africa under General Eisenhower, and one month later the German forces surrendered in the TUNIS area.

I visited Algiers on 2 June to meet the Prime Minister and the C.I.G.S.

The Prime Minister wrote Chapter Three at Algiers on 3 June 1943.

488. This little book was published in 1945.

Chapter Four

Chapter IV   Marrakesh. January 1. 1944

The immortal march of the Eighth Army from the gates of Cairo along the African shore through Tunisia, through Sicily has now carried its ever victorious soldiers & those words & honoured Commanders far into Italy towards the gates of Rome. The scene changes & vastly expands. A great task accomplished gives place to a greater in which the same unfading spirit will live for all true men in full & glorious renown. Winston Churchill

On 10 July 1943 the Eighth Army and the Seventh U.S. Army invaded SICILY; the capture of that island was achieved in 38 days.

On 3 September 1943 the Eighth Army, alone, invaded ITALY across the Straits of MESSINA.

One week later, on 10 September, the Fifth U.S. Army landed at SALERNO, on the west coast of ITALY.

The two armies linked up eventually.

On 31 December 1943, I left the Eighth Army for England to take command of 21 Army Group: the British Group of Armies for the liberation of Europe.

I stayed that night at MARRAKESH in Morocco with the Prime Minister. He wrote Chapter Four on 1 January 1944.

Chapter V

On the verge of the greatest Adventure with which these pages have dealt I record my confidence that all will be well & that the organization & equipment of the Army will be worthy of the valour of the soldiers & the genius of their chief. Winston Churchill,

19.5.44

Chapter Five

From the beginning of January until the end of May 1944, 21 Army Group was planning and making final preparations for the invasion of western Europe.

Just prior to our assault across the Channel, on 19 May 1944 the Prime Minister visited me and wrote Chapter Five in my book.

The Dominion Prime Ministers were in England in May. Three of them wrote in my autograph book:

Field-Marshal Smuts   (South Africa)
Mr. Mackenzie King   (Canada)
Mr. Peter Fraser   (New Zealand)

Goodluck in your new task

J C Smuts F.M.

15.5.44

[illegible]

15-5-44 [illegible signature]

The New Zealand Division valued the leadership of General Montgomery. They admired and loved him personally, with their own Commander, the intrepid General Freyberg, they trusted Montgomery and went forward in North Africa to victory with confidence, determination and cheerfulness.

Under his leadership they did great deeds and added to their fame.

On what may be the eve of the Great Invasion I pray that the Commander-in-Chief will be given strength to use his genius as before in directing and leading his armies to sure and swift victory for God and man. Peter Fraser, P.M.

Conference of Army Comds before "Overlord"

1st American Army	Omar N. Bradley
3rd American Army	G S Patton Jr.
2nd British Army	M C Dempsey
1st Canadian Army	H D G Crerar
C-in-C	B. L. Montgomery General

1st June 44

489.

Chapter Six

On 6 June 1944, 21 Army Group invaded western Europe, landing in NORMANDY. The landing was successful.

Mr. Churchill and Field-Marshal Smuts visited me at my H.Q. at CREULLY in Normandy on 12 June 1944.

The Prime Minister wrote Chapter Six on that day, and Field-Marshal Smuts added a note.

General de Gaulle visited me on 15 June, and he also wrote in the book.

At the end of Chapter Six are the names and signatures of the Supreme Allied Commander and his three Cs-in-C. Of the three Cs-in-C I am now the only one left alive; Ramsey and Leigh-Mallory were killed in air accidents during the campaign in western Europe.

Chapter VI

Creully June 12 1944

As it was in the beginning so may it continue to the end.

Winston S. Churchill

And so it will!

J C Smuts

12.6.1944

Au Général Montgomery, l'excellent ouvrier de la Victoire

15 Juin 1944

C. de Gaulle

The armed forces of the Allies landed in France on 6 June 1944. The H.Q. of the Supreme Comd and his Cs-in-C was at Portsmouth.

Supreme Comd	Dwight D. Eisenhower
Naval C-in-C	B. H. Ramsay
Army C-in-C	B. L. Montgomery General
Air C-in-C	T Leigh-Mallory
Tactical Air Forces	A Coningham

The initial operations were very successful and a good lodgement area was soon got.

Chapter Seven

By November 1944 the Allies had liberated France and Belgium, and had opened up the Scheldt as the main supply channel leading to ANTWERP.

I visited England early in that month and the Prime Minister wrote Chapter Seven on 6 November 1944.

Chapter Eight

By March 1945 the Allies had won the battle of the Rhineland, and had reached the Rhine itself on a broad front.

Preparations for crossing the Rhine were in full swing.

The Prime Minister visited me at my H.Q. in Holland, just west of the MEUSE, early in March.

He wrote Chapter Eight on 4 March 1945.

490.

Chapter Nine

On 23 March 1945 the 21st Army Group attacked across the Rhine.

The Prime Minister was present at my H.Q. in Germany for the first stages of the Battle of the Rhine.

He wrote Chapter Nine on 26 March 1945.

The word "Germany" was added in red ink, after he had written the chapter.

The Surrender in N.W. Germany and Holland

Having crossed the Rhine the British Group of Armies swept eastwards; it crossed the EMS, the WESER, and the ELBE; it captured the great cities of BREMEN and HAMBURG, it reached the Baltic Sea at LÜBECK and WISMAR on 2 May 1945.

On 3 May a German delegation came to my H.Q. on LÜNEBURG HEATH to discuss terms of surrender; they were informed that there were no terms and that surrender must be unconditional.

The delegation consisted of:

    General-Admiral von Friedeburg.
    General Kinzel.
    Rear Admiral Wagner.
    Major Friedel.

The surrender was finally signed at 1830 hrs on 4 May 1945.

491.
Credits: 'Ten Chapters' by Hutchinson & Co. Ltd

The words that you read are the exact words written in their own handwriting by Montgomery and Prime Minister Churchill and many of the Allied Commanders as well as the enemy who were asked to sign the book as well. It is very interesting for <u>what it says and even more interesting for what is does not say.</u>

Under Chapter X, at the very end, Winston Churchill makes the statement that:

"The fame of this Army Group like that of the Eighth Army will long shine in history & other generations besides our own will honour these deeds and above all the character, profound strategy & unrelenting zeal of their commander who marched from Egypt through Tripoli, Tunis, Sicily & Southern Italy, & through France, Belgium, Holland & Germany to the Baltic & the Elbe <u>without losing a battle or even a serious action</u>."

I repeat: *"<u>without losing a battle or even a serious action.</u>"*

With my comments I do not want to minimize all that had been achieved but if, by now, you are questioning how much of a success or disaster Operation Market Garden really was, then you are right on target. As concerns Operation Market Garden (September 17 - September 25, 1944), the free encyclopedia, Wikipedia states:

"The operation was initially successful with the capture of the Waal Bridge at Nijmegen on 20 September, but was a failure overall as the final Rhine Bridge at Arnhem was never taken, and the British 1ˢᵗ Airborne Division was destroyed in the ensuing battle. The Rhine would remain a barrier to the Allied advance until the Allied Offensive in March 1945. The defeat of Allied forces at Arnhem is considered the last major German victory of the Western Campaign."

"When an aerial reconnaissance flight returned with pictures clearly showing tanks deployed only 15km from the British drop zones, they were actively dismissed by Montgomery, with the (unfounded) assumption that they probably could not run and were broken down."

"In a period of a week, preparations were declared complete; by comparison the airborne plans for Sicily and Normandy had taken months to complete. Key planning tasks were done badly or not at all. In the words of the United States Army's historical study of the operation the decision to make only one drop on September 17 was "disastrous". Communications planning was poor, and the 1ˢᵗ Airborne Division would be out of touch with most other headquarters for most of the battle. No arrangements were made for close air support. The drops were scheduled with a south-to-north priority to ease XXX Corps' advance, but this put the units at Arnhem at a disadvantage in terms of surprise and time to complete their missions".

Losses:	KIA	WIA	MIA	POW	Total
Germany:	**8,000**	**5,000**			**13,000**
British:	6,484	851		6,450	13,785
American:	3,542	458			4,000
Polish:	102	309			411
Allies T.	**10,128**	**1,618**		**6,450**	**18,196**

Much has been written about Montgomery's difficult personality. It says that he was insensitive, conceited and boastful. In the movie "Patton" I remember Patton talking with Omar Bradley who by that time was his superior. With reference to Montgomery, who Patton despised, he said:

"Brad, I know I am a Prima Donna. I am willing to admit it. What I can't stand is that Montgomery is a Prima Donna and he wont admit it."

I took a lot of this talk with a grain of salt and contributed a lot of it to rivalry between senior officers. But then I came in possession of Montgomery's little booklet: *"Ten Chapters"*. There, in black on white are his own words and those of Winston Churchill, and what is missing is probably the only significant battle he clearly lost as it had been the intention to cross the river at Arnhem and push on to the Ruhr area. It had failed. Why then did Churchill have to support Montgomery's arrogance by saying: ... <u>without losing a battle or even a serious action</u>. Operation Market Garden, Montgomery's idea, is not mentioned at all. On the other hand, if Montgomery considered the operation 90% successful, why then did he not mention it as such in the booklet and make it Eleven Chapters?

Not recognizing Market Garden at all is a slap in the face of all who participated in this heroic battle. Particularly, the British 1st Airborne Division, that so valiantly fought at the Arnhem Bridge. Not recognizing these brave men who died by the thousands is a travesty. It speaks of Montgomery's great insensitivity, selfishness, and self-aggrandizement and in the end, a lack of character.

CHAPTER NINETY TWO

THE ATOMIC BOMB

The Tokyo control operator of the Japanese Broadcasting Corporation noticed that the Hiroshima station had gone off the air. He tried to re-establish his program by using another telephone line, but it too had failed. About twenty minutes later the Tokyo railroad telegraph center realized that the main line telegraph had stopped working just north of Hiroshima. From some small railway stops within 16 kilometers (10 miles) of the city came unofficial and confused reports of a terrible explosion in Hiroshima. All these reports were transmitted to the headquarters of the Japanese General Staff.

Military bases repeatedly tried to call the Army Control Station in Hiroshima. The complete silence from that city puzzled the men at headquarters; they knew that no large enemy raid had occurred and that no sizable store of explosives was in Hiroshima at that time. A young officer of the Japanese General Staff was instructed to fly immediately to Hiroshima, to land, survey the damage, and return to Tokyo with reliable information for the staff. It was generally felt at headquarters that nothing serious had taken place and that it was all a rumor.

The staff officer went to the airport and took off for the southwest. After flying for about three hours, while still nearly 100 miles (160 km) from Hiroshima, he and his pilot saw a great column of smoke. In the bright afternoon, the remains of Hiroshima were burning. Their plane soon reached the city, around which they circled in disbelief. A great scar on the land still burning and covered by a heavy cloud of smoke was all that was left. They landed south of the city, and the staff officer, after reporting to Tokyo, immediately began to organize relief measures.

492. The Fat Man mushroom cloud rises 18 km (60,000 ft) over Nagasaki.

PRELUDE TO THE BOMBINGS

The United States, with assistance from England and Canada, designed and built the first atomic bomb under what was called the Manhattan Project. The project was initially started at the instigation of European refugee scientists, (including Albert Einstein) and American scientists who feared that Nazi Germany would also be conducting a full-scale bomb development program (that program was later discovered to be much smaller and further behind). The project itself eventually employed 130,000 people at its peak at over thirty institutions spread over the United States, and cost a total of nearly US$2 billion, making it one of the largest and most costly research and development programs of all time.

493. General Leslie Groves and the physicist Robert
Oppenheimer led the project.

The first nuclear device, called "Gadget", was detonated near
Alamogordo, New Mexico on July 16, 1945. The test was called:
"Trinity".

It was successful and two additional bombs were then prepared for
actual usage against Japan. On August 6, 1945, the nuclear weapon
"Little Boy" was dropped on the city of Hiroshima followed on
August 9, 1945 by the detonation of the "Fat Man" nuclear bomb
over Nagasaki. The bombs were of different construction

494. Little Boy, the 'Gun type' fission weapon

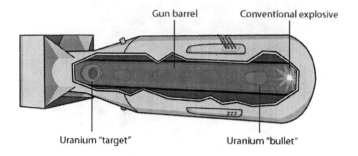

495. Little Boy, the "gun" assembly method.

496. "Fat Man"

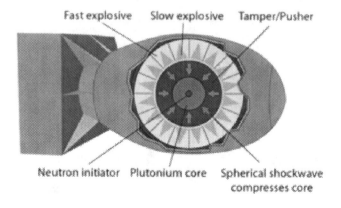

497. "Fat Man" schematic

498. Map of Japan

499. A view of Hiroshima following the bombing. The
bomb killed an estimated 90,000 people instantly. The
radius of total destruction was 1 mile with fires raging
over an area of 4.4 square miles.

500. A view of Nagasaki following the bombing. The bomb killed an estimated 70,000 people instantly. Another 60,000 were severely injured. The radius of total destruction was 1 mile with fires raging over an area of 2 square miles.

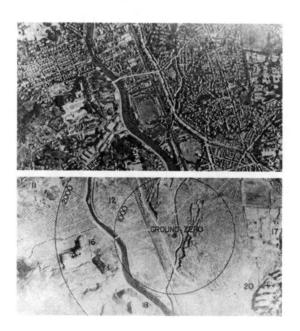

501. Nagasaki before and after.

On August 15, 1945 Japan announced its surrender to the Allied Powers signing the Instrument of Surrender on September 2, which officially ended World War II.

My cousin Henry Kriete served in the air force on the Island of Tinian. He took a picture of the B-29 "Enola Gay", the plane piloted by Paul Tibbets. The Enola Gay dropped the atom bomb on Hiroshima. There is also a picture of Henry in front of the B-29 "Bocks Car". This plane dropped the bomb on Nagasaki.

502. The Enola Gay, picture taken by Henry Kriete

503. "Bocks Car" and my cousin Henry Kriete

CHAPTER NINETY-TWO

THE NUREMBERG TRIALS –
OCTOBER 1945

"We must establish incredible events by credible evidence."
U.S. Chief Prosecutor Robert H. Jackson, June 7, 1945

504. The Nazi Criminals on trial
Credits: U.S. National Archives

The Nuremberg Trials were a series of trials most notable for the prosecution of Nazi members in the political, military and economic leadership of Nazi Germany. The trials were held in the city of Nuremberg, Germany, from 1945 to 1946. The best-known trial was the Trial of the Major War Criminals before the International Military Tribunal (IMT), which tried 24 of the most important captured leaders of Nazi Germany.

Nazi Germany planned and implemented the Holocaust within the devastating maelstrom of World War II. It was in this context that the IMT was created, a trial of judgment for war crimes. The IMT was not a court convened to mete out punishment for the Holocaust alone. The tribunal was designed to document and redress crimes committed in the course of the most massive conflict the world has ever known. In October 1945, the IMT formally indicted the Nuremberg defendants on four counts: Crimes against peace, war crimes, crimes against humanity, and conspiracy to commit these crimes.

The Holocaust was considered "a crime against humanity". The verdicts were delivered on October 1, 1946:

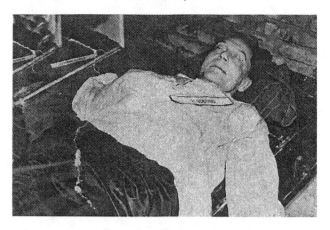

505. Hermann Goering
Credits: U.S. National Archives

Hermann Goering, Reichsmarschall, Commander of the Luftwaffe, and several departments of the SS. He committed suicide the night before his execution. He had been found guilty on four counts out of four.

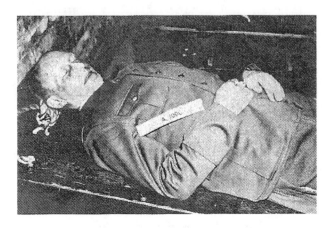

506. Alfred Jodl

<u>Alfred Jodl</u>, Wehrmacht Generaloberst, Keitel's subordinate. On February 28, 1953, Jodl was posthumously exonerated by a German de-Nazification court, which found him not guilty of crimes under international law. He had been found guilty on four counts out of four and hanged.

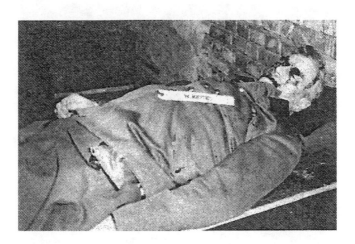

507. Wilhelm Keitel

<u>Wilhem Keitel</u>, Head of Oberkommando der Wehrmacht (OKW). He was found guilty on four counts out of four and hanged.

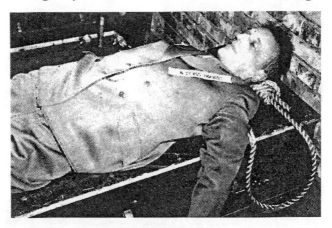

508. Arthur Seyss-Inquart

<u>Arthur Seyss-Inquart</u>, instrumental in the Anschluss of Austria with Germany. Later Gauleiter of occupied Holland. He expressed repentance. He was found guilty on three out of four counts and hanged. He got his wish when he told Bedell Smith at the 'Manna" meeting that death would leave him cold.

509. Albert Rosenberg

<u>Alfred Rosenberg</u>, Racial Theory Ideologist. Later, Protector of the Eastern Occupied Territories. He was found guilty on four out of four counts and hanged.

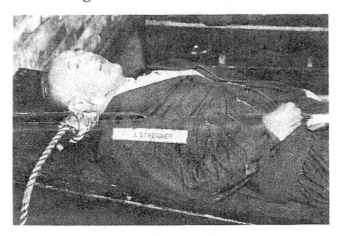

510. Julius Streicher

Credits: U.S. National Archives

<u>Julius Streicher</u>, Incited hatred and murder against the Jews through his weekly newspaper, Der Stuermer. He was charged on two counts and found guilty on one. He was hanged.

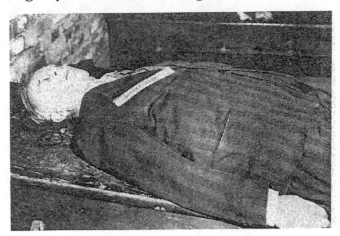

511. Joachim von Ribbentrop
Credits: U.S. National Archives

<u>Joachim von Ribbentrop</u>, Nazi Minister of Foreign Affairs. He was found guilty on four out of four counts and hanged.

512. Hans Frank
Credits: U.S. National Archives

<u>Hans Frank</u>, Ruler of the General Government in occupied Poland. He expressed repentance. He was charged on three counts and found guilty on two. He was hanged.

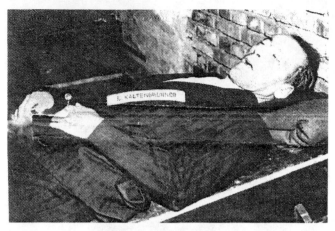

513. Ernst Kaltenbrunner
Credits: U.S. National Archives

<u>Ernst Kaltenbrunner</u>, highest surviving SS-leader. Chief of RSHA, the central Nazi intelligence organ. Also commanded many of the Einsatzgruppen and several concentration camps. He was charged on three counts and found guilty on two. He was hanged.

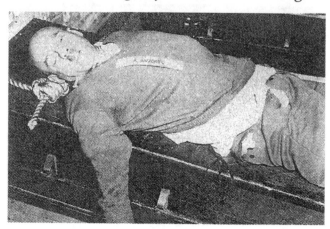

514. Fritz Sauckel
Credits: U.S. National Archives

<u>Fritz Sauckel</u>, Plenipotentiary of the Nazi slave labor program. He was charged on four counts and found guilty on two. He was hanged.

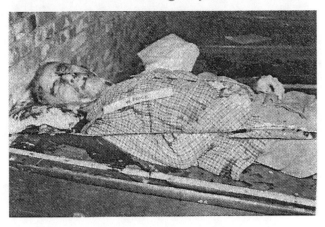

515. Wilhelm Frick
Credits: U.S. National Archives

<u>Wilhelm Frick</u>, Hitler's Minister of the Interior. Authored the Nuremberg Race Laws. Charged on four counts and found guilty on three. He was hanged.

<u>Martin Bormann</u>, Successor to Hess as Nazi Party Secretary was sentenced to death in absentia. His remains were found in 1972.

<u>Karl Doenitz</u>, Leader of the Kriegsmarine. He succeeded Raeder. Initiator of the U-Boat campaign. Became President of Germany following Hitler's death. He was found guilty on two out of three counts and received a 10-year sentence.

<u>Hans Fritzsche</u>, Popular radio commentator, and head of the news division of the Nazi Propaganda Ministry. He was tried in place of Goebbels who had committed suicide. He was acquitted.

<u>Walter Funk</u>, Hitler's Minister of Economics. Succeeded Schacht as head of the Reichsbank. He was found guilty on three out of four counts and received a life sentence. He was released due to ill health on May 16, 1957.

Rudolf Hess, Hitler's deputy, flew to Scotland in 1941 in attempt to broker peace with Great Britain. He was found guilty on two out of four counts and received a life sentence. He died in Spandau Prison in 1987.

Gustav Krupp von Bohlen und Halbach, Major Nazi industrialist. Medically unfit for trial. The prosecutors attempted to substitute his son Alfried in the indictment, but the judges rejected this. Alfried was tried in a separate Nuremberg trial, thus escaping the worst notoriety and possible death.

Robert Ley, Head of DAF, the German Labor Front. He committed suicide on October 25, 1945, before the trial began.

Konstantin von Neurath, Minister of Foreign Affairs until 1938, succeeded by Ribbentrop. Later, Protector of Bohemia and Moravia. He resigned in 1943 due to a dispute with Hitler. He was found guilty on four out of four counts and received a 15-year sentence. He was released as a result of ill health on November 6, 1954.

Franz von Papen, Chancellor of Germany in 1932 and Vice Chancellor under Hitler from 1933. Later he became ambassador to Turkey. Although acquitted at Nuremberg, von Papen was reclassified as a war criminal in 1947 by a German de-Nazification court, and

Erich Raeder, Leader of the Kriegsmarine until his retirement in 1943. He was succeeded by Doenitz. He was found guilty on three out of three counts and received a life sentence. He was released on account of ill health on September 26, 1955

Hjalmar Schacht, pre-war president of the Reichsbank. He admitted to violating the Treaty of Versailles. He was acquitted.

Baldur von Schirach, Head of the Hitlerjugend from 1933 to 1940, Gauleiter of Vienna, Austria from 1940. He expressed repentance. He was found guilty on one out of two counts and received a 20-year sentence.

<u>Albert Speer</u>, Hitler's favorite architect and personal friend, and Minister of Armament from 1942. In this capacity, he was ultimately responsible for the use of slave laborers from the occupied territories in armaments production. He was found guilty on two out of four counts and received a 20-year sentence.

CHAPTER NINETY-FOUR

THE MARSHALL PLAN – JULY 1947

On June 5, 1947, Secretary of State George C. Marshall spoke at Harvard University and outlined what would become known as the Marshall Plan. Europe, still devastated by the war, had just survived one of the worst winters on record. Something had to be done, both for humanitarian reasons and also to stop the potential spread of communism westward.

516. George C. Marshall, (1880-1959)
He served as Chief of Staff from 1939-1945

The United States offered up to $20 billion for relief, but only if the European nations could get together and draw up a rational plan on how they would use the aid. For the first time, they would have to act as a single economic unit; they would have to cooperate with each other. Marshall also offered aid to the Soviet Union and its allies in Eastern Europe, but Stalin denounced the program as a trick and refused to participate. The Russian rejection probably made passage of the measure through Congress possible.

The Marshall plan benefited the American economy as well. The money would be used to buy goods from the United States, and these goods would have to be shipped across the Atlantic on American merchant vessels. But it worked. By 1953 the United States had pumped in $13 billion, and Europe was standing on its feet again. The Plan included West Germany as well, which was thus reintegrated into the European community. The Marshall Plan led to what we now know as the European Union.

In 1947, Jo Spier (1900-1976) a well-known Dutch Jewish artist and writer who had survived the Holocaust put together a small booklet of illustrations depicting the Marshall Plan and what it meant for the people in Holland.

"The Marshall Plan and You"

517

517

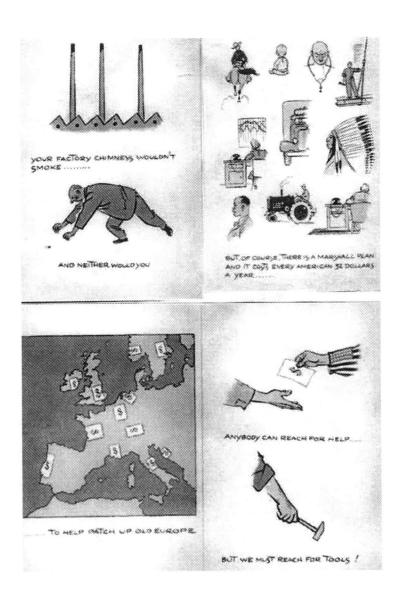

518

... IF YOU THINK THIS JOB IS A
LIGHT ONE, THEN THE OUT-
COME IS SURE TO BE A
DARK ONE .... !

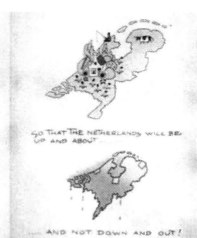

SO THAT THE NETHERLANDS WILL BE
UP AND ABOUT ....

... AND NOT DOWN AND OUT!

BECAUSE BY 1952 WE
MUST STAND ON OUR
OWN TWO FEET ....

BECAUSE THAT'S WHEN
THE MARSHALL PLAN
STOPS!

518

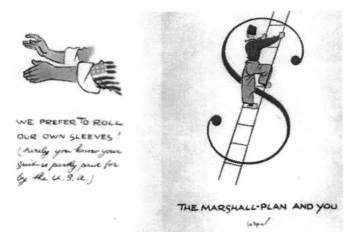

518.

519. Marshall Plan Poster

Epilogue

Family and Friends

As for our immediate family in the Dunantstraat, all seven of us survived the war but we mourned other friends and family members. Tom van de Meer had died as a result of the bombing of Rotterdam on May 14, 1940. My father's oldest brother Jan, who lived in Rotterdam, died from starvation during the horrible winter of 44/45. My sister Annie's boyfriend, Piet Bloemendaal and his cousin, died in an allied air raid while slave laborers in Germany. My parents' friend from the Hooidrift, Mrs. Van Wingerden and her daughter Annie found a tragic death in an air raid shelter that took a direct hit in the first U.S. 8th Air Force bombing of Rotterdam on March 31, 1943. The Gestapo for harboring Jewish possessions killed our dentist and his whole family. Jacob Hamel, the prominent children's choir director, his wife, son and daughter-in-law had all died in the Sobibor death camp. Our neighbor in the Dunantstraat, Mr. Smit, had died from starvation during the hunger winter.

Both Henry and Oom Wim were enlisted in the new Dutch Armed Forces immediately after the liberation and would serve time in the Dutch East Indies until this country's independence from the Netherlands. They returned safely to Holland. Oom Wim returned to his old job at Magazijn Nederland and retired at age 65. He died in 1990. Dad recovered from Tuberculoses and he also returned to Magazijn Nederland. Max Kattenburg, the owner of Magazijn Nederland returned from hiding and once again managed his company. Dad retired at age 65 and died from emphysema at the age of 83 in 1982. My mother's cousin Anton Zee went back to managing his Lead Cable Factory on the Westzeedijk and prospered. First thing he did after the liberation was to dig up his 1938 Chevy. I learned to drive in that car. Anton died in 1978. Miss de Jong, our spinster, moved out of the Dunantstraat and I lost track of her. Annie and I finished our schooling and found jobs. In 1950 I was drafted into the Dutch Army (part of NATO) and attended the Military Academy in Breda. I graduated as 'Wachtmeester' and was assigned to a Battalion of 105mm howitzers. In 1953 I migrated to the United States where I was promptly drafted in the U.S. Army but I was lucky, the Korean War had ended by that time and I stayed stateside in Fort Lewis, Washington where I served in the U.S. 2nd Infantry Division (Indian Head), 40th Tank Battalion. On May 15, 1956 I married Diny C. Sorber to whom I was engaged back in Holland before migrating to the US. I was discharged from the army in 1956 and continued my 30-year career with Bank of America. Diny and I had two children, Lynette and Steve, both born while on assignment for the bank in Europe from 1964 to 1974. I left BofA in 1985 and founded First Collateral Services, Inc. (FCS). Presently a wholly owned subsidiary of Citigroup. I retired from FCS in 2002 at the age of 71. In 1958 Henry, his wife Sofia and their two young daughters, Ineke and Judy, migrated to the USA. Henry had an outstanding career as an electronical engineer in non-destructive testing techniques. He worked with both NASA and the U. S. military. Henry retired and with Sofia, his elementary school sweetheart, lives in Atascadero, California. Both daughters are married. My mother Coba, who cared for all of us during those dreadful years, continued her role as a homemaker. In spite of several health problems she lived to a ripe old age. She died in Rotterdam at the age of 97 in 1997. Annie married Johan Viergever and they had two children, Annelies and Jan Willem. Annie died of Altzheimer disease in 2006, just a few weeks shy of her 80th birthday. Our children, Lynette and Steve, are married to respectively: Jeff Nolen and Bernadette Maes. Lynette and Jeff live not far from Clayton in Concord, California. Steve and Bernadette have three sons: Henry, Willem and Miles. They live in the wine country: beautiful Healdsburg, California.

THE COST OF WAR

(1)Casualties

Country	Military	Civilian	Total
Soviet Union	12,000,000	17,000,000	29,000,000
China	1,324,000	10,000,000	11,324,000
Germany	3,250,000	2,440,000	5,690,000
Poland	597,000	5,860,000	6,457,000
Japan	1,506,000	300,000	1,806,000
Yugoslavia	305,000	1,350,000	1,655,000
Rumania	450,000	465,000	915,000
France	245,000	350,000	595,000
Hungary	200,000	600,000	800,000
Austria	380,000	145,000	525,000
Greece	19,000	140,000	159,000
Italy	380,000	153,000	533,000
Czechoslovakia	7,000	315,000	322,000
Great Britain	403,000	92,700	495,700
USA	407,000	6,000	413,000
Holland	13,700	236,000	249,700
Belgium	76,000	23,000	99,000
Finland	79,000		79,000
Canada	42,000		42,000
India	36,000		36,000
Australia	29,000		29,000
Spain	12,000	10,000	22,000
Bulgaria	19,000	2,000	21,000
New Zealand	12,000		12,000
South Africa	9,000		9,000
Norway	5,000		5,000
Denmark	4,000		4,000
Totals	21,809,700	39,487,700	61,297,400

(2)Death Distribution of Both World Wars

War	Military Dead	Civilian Dead
WWI	95%	5%
WWII	33%	67%

(3)Civilian Air Raid Deaths

Country	Deaths
Germany	543,000
Britain	60,400

(4)D-Day Statistics

Unit	Allies	Germans	Ratio
Ground Troops	1 million	.7 million	1.43:1
Replacements	.12 million	.02 million	6:01
Other	1.75 million	.78 million	2.25:1
Total	2.87 million	1.5 million	1.92:1

Unit	Allies	Germans	Ratio
Tanks	5,500	1,400	3.93:1
Artillery	4,800	3,200	1.5:1
Other	2,000	800	2.5:1

Air Force	Bombers	Fighters	Total
RAF	624	2,172	2,796
USAAF	1,922	1,311	3,233
Luftwaffe	400	420	820
Ratio	6.4:1	8.3:1	7.4:1

(5)Civilian Casualties in the United Kingdom during WWII

Means	Killed	Seriously Injured	Total
Aircraft Bombs	51,509	61,423	112,932
V-1	6,184	17,981	24,165
V-2	2,754	6,523	9,277
Artillery Fire	148	255	403
	60,595	86,182	146,777

(6)German Plane Losses in the Netherlands from May 10 through May 17, 1940

Type	So.Holland	Gelderland	No.Brabant	No.Holland	Limburg	Zeeland	Utrecht	Groningen Friesland Drente	Overijsel		Crashed in Germany Dutch Action	Total	Type
Do-17	3			1	3	1	1		1			10	Do-17
Do-215				2					1			3	Do-215
FW-58				2								2	FW-58
He-111	10		12	6	1	8	4	1	1		3	46	He-111
He-115	1			1		1					5	8	He-115
He-59	5			1								6	He-59
Hs-123					1						1	1	Hs-123
Hs-126	3		2		5						1	11	Hs-126
Ju-52	243	22	7		3		2				11	288	Ju-52
Ju-87	2		2		6						1	11	Ju-87
Ju-88	6	3	2	5		3		5			4	28	Ju-88
Me-109	12	10	8	7	2	1		4			1	45	Me-109
Me-110	5	1	1			2					1	10	Me-110
Unknown	10	9	7	8	1		5	2				42	Unknown
Planes	300	45	41	33	22	16	12	12	3	0	27	511	Planes
	So.Holland	Gelderland	No.Brabant	No.Holland	Limburg	Zeeland	Utrecht	Groningen Friesland Drente	Overijsel		Crashed in Germany Dutch Action	Total	

(7)Dutch Plane Losses from May 10, 1940 through May 14, 1940

Type	Destroyed on Ground	Dogfights	Other	Torched	Total
Fokker T-V	2	5	2		9
Fokker G-1	12	9	2		23
Fokker D-21	5	11	9		25
Douglas 8A-3N	2	8	1		11
Fokker C-V	9	8	0		17
Koolhoven FK-51	4	0	2		6
Fokker C-X		2	1		3
	34	43	17	45	139
Type	Destroyed on Ground	Dogfights	Other	Torched	Total

Flying Personnel Killed in Action: 39
Ground Personnel Killed in Action: 36

(8)Number of Sorties Flown by Dutch Air Force in May 1940.

10-May	51
11-May	31
12-May	48
13-May	23
14-May	18
Total	171

(9)Royal Air Force Bomber Command Losses in Planes in Holland 1940 - 1945							
Type	1940	1941	1942	1943	1944	1945	Total
Lancaster			26	166	148	19	359
Wellington	6	68	135	75			284
Halifax		3	42	141	66	2	254
Blenheim	27	94	14	0	0	0	135
Stirling		7	39	66	4		116
Hampden	15	40	23	0	0	0	78
Whitley	11	51	9				71
Mosquito			6	7	18	7	38
Ventura			11	10			21
Boston			10	2			12
Manchester		3	9				12
B-17					2		2
Hudson					2		2
Mitchell				1			1
Total	59	266	324	468	240	28	1385

(10)Number of divisions available for these countries over the course of the war:								
Country	1939	1940	1941	1942	1943	1944	1945	End
USSR	194	200	220	250	350	400	488	491
USA**	8	24	39	76	95	94	94	94
Romania	11	28	33	31	33	32	24	24
Poland	43	2	2	2	2	5	5	5
Italy	6	73	64	89	86	2	9	10
Great Britain	9	34	35	38	39	37	31	31
Germany*	78	189	235	261	327	347	319	375
France	86	105	0	0	5	7	14	14

*towards the end of the war, many of these divisions were either incomplete or poorly equipped

**including both Army and Marine divisions and accounting for the Pacific theater

(11)Aircraft Available in Europe

Date	British	US	Soviet	Total	German	All. Ratio
Jun-42	9,500	0	2,100	11,600	3,700	3.14
Dec-42	11,300	1,300	3,800	16,400	3,400	4.82
Jun-43	12,700	5,000	5,600	23,300	4,600	5.07
Dec-43	11,800	7,500	8,800	28,100	4,700	5.98
Jun-44	13,200	11,800	14,700	39,700	4,600	8.63
Dec-44	14,500	12,200	15,800	42,500	8,500	5.00

(12)Aircraft Sorties in WWII

Campaign	Allied	Axis	Allied Kills Per 1000	Axis Kills Per 1000	Allied Lost Per 1000	Axis Lost Per 1000
France 1940	4,480	21,000	28.6	12.5	58.5	6.1
Britain 1940	31,000	42,000	21.8	29.5	29.5	9.6
Pre D-Day 1944	98,400	34,500	12.7	29.3	10.3	36.1
Post D-Day 1944	203,357	31,833	17.3	16.2	2.5	110.6

(13)Major Warships Sunk in WWII

Country	Aircraft Carriers	Battleships	Cruisers	Destroyers	Sub marines	Total
Germany	0	4	9	53	994	1060
Britain	9	5	29	142	75	260
Italy	0	2	15	99	116	232
USA*	11	2	10	82	52	157
France	0	5	10	58	65	138
USSR	0	0	2	34	95	131
Holland	0	0	3	11	15	29
Poland	0	0	1	4	2	7

*includes figures from the Pacific War

(14)German Flak

Unit	1939	1940	1941	1942	1943	1944
Heavy Guns	2,66	3,164	3,888	4,772	8,520	10,600
Light Guns	6,700	8,290	9,020	10,700	17,500	19,360
Searchlights	2,988	3,450	3,905	4,650	5,200	7,500
% Luftwaffe	50%	61%	54%	64%	74%	70%

(15)German Occupational Forces, 1939 - 1940

Country	Population	Area in Sq. Mi.	German Forces	Ratio to Pop.
Balkans	21 million	403,000	200,000	1:105
Belgium	8 million	30,400	100,000	1:80
Denmark	3.6 million	22,700	40,000	1:90
France	40 million	550,700	500,000	1:80
Holland	8.5 million	34,200	100,000	1:85
Norway	2.8 million	324,000	150,000	1:19

(16)Location of German Divisions in June of Each Year

Country	1941	1942	1943	1944
USSR	34	171	179	157
France, Belgium, Holland	38	27	42	56
Norway & Finland	13	16	16	16
Balkans	7	8	17	20
Italy	0	0	0	22
Denmark	1	1	2	3
North Africa	2	3	0	0
Total	95	226	256	274

(17)**German U-Boat Losses**

Sunk By	1939	1940	1941	1942	1943	1944	1945	Total
Aircr. Car.	0	2	3	37	136	83	40	301
Ships	5	11	24	34	57	83	17	231
Bombs	0	0	0	2	2	24	36	64
Mines	3	2	0	4	2	11	7	29
Submarines	1	2	1	2	4	5	3	18
Miss./Other	0	7	7	7	41	44	17	123
Total	9	24	35	86	242	250	120	766

* 40,000 men served on German U-Boats during WWII, 30,000 never returned.

(18)**Percentage of All Allied Bombs Dropped**

Year	%
1940	0.80%
1941	2.00%
1942	3.00%
1943	12.80%
1944	57.90%
1945	23.50%
Total	100.00%

(19)**Oil Production in Million Tons**

Year	Germany	USA
1939	8	n/a
1940	6.7	n/a
1941	7.3	n/a
1942	7.7	184
1943	8.9	200
1944	6.4	223
Total	45	607

(20)**Convoy Battles**

Date	Convoy Code	Ships	Sunk	Tonnage	U-Boats	Sunk
Oct-40	SC-71, HX-79	79	32	154,600	12	0
Sep-41	SC-42	70	18	73,200	19	2
Jul-42	PQ-17	42	16	102,300	11	0
Nov-42	SC-107	42	15	82,800	18	3
Dec-42	ONS-154	45	19	74,500	19	1
Mar-43	SC-121, HX-228	119	16	79,900	37	2

* 800 U-Boats sank 2,640 ships in the Atlantic

(21)**Allied Merchant Shipping Losses during WWII**

Year	No. of Vessels	Tonnage
1939	221	755,237
1940	1,059	3,991,641
1941	1,299	4,328,558
1942	1,664	7,790,697
1943	597	3,220,137
1944	205	1,045,629
1945	105	438,821
	5,150	**21,570,720**

(22)**U.S.Armed Forces Total Strength and Casualties in WWII**

Service	Total Strength	Battle Death	Deaths Other Causes	Wounds[1]	Captured or Missing
Army[2]	11,260,000	234,874	83,400	565,861	135,524
Navy	4,183,466	36,950	25,664	37,778	2,429
Marine Corps	669,100	19,733	4,778	67,207	1,756
Coast Guard	241,093	574	1,345	955	
	16,353,659	292,131	115,187	671,801	139,709

[1] Not Mortal [2] Includes Army Air Force

(23)**Peak Strengths and Battle Deaths
of the Principal Allied Powers**

Nation	Peak Strengths	Battle Deaths
Australia	680,000	23,365
Belgium	650,000	7,760
Canada	780,000	37,476
China(1)	5,000,000	2,200,000
Denmark(2)	25,000	3,006
France	5,000,000	210,671
Greece(2)	414,000	73,700
India	2,150,000	34,338
Netherlands	410,000	6,238
New Zealand	157,000	10,033
Norway	45,000	1,000
Poland	1,000,000	320,000
USSR	1,250,000	7,500,000
South Africa	140,000	6,840
United Kingdom	5,120,000	244,723
United States	12,300,000	292,131
Yugoslavia(2)	500,000	410,000
	35,621,000	11,381,281

(1) Casualties beginning with the Japanese invasion of 1937.
(2) Most of these casualties were suffered in guerilla warfare.
In the case of Denmark they include more than 1200 merchant
sailors in the service of the allies.

(24) Peak Strengths and Battle Deaths of the Axis Powers

Nation	Peak Strengths	Battle Deaths
Bulgaria(1)	450,000	10,000
Finland	250,000	82,000
Germany	10,200,000	3,500,000
Hungary	350,000	140,000
Italy(2)	3,750,000	77,494
Japan	6,095,000	1,219,000
Romania(1)	600,000	300,000
	21,695,000	5,328,494

(1) A limited number of these casualties occurred after the country joined the Allies

(2) Of these, 17,494 were killed after Italy became a co-belligerent with the Allies

(25)Total Ships Sunk and sunk by U-Boat

Year	Ships Sunk	By U-Boat
1939	222	114
1940	1,059	471
1941	1,299	432
1942	1,664	1,160
1943	597	377
1944	205	132
1945	105	56

(26)US Daily Ammunition Expenditure in Tons

Action	Armor Divisions	Infantry Divisions	155mm battalions
Attack	436 - 832	353 - 658	66 - 121
Defense	596 - 969	472 - 768	86 - 142
Pursuit	107	83	15
Delay	321	256	51

(27)Mid-Year Manpower on the Eastern Front in Millions

Year	Soviet	German
1941	5	3.3
1942	5	3
1943	6.2	2.9
1944	6.8	3.1

(28)Operation Manna/Chowhound April 29,1945 - May 8, 1945						
	Royal Air Force		**USAAF**		**Total**	**Total**
Date	**Aircraft**	**Tonnage**	**Aircraft**	**Tonnage**	**Aircraft**	**Tonnage**
29-Apr	239	526.5	0	0	239	526.5
30-Apr	482	1005.3	0	0	482	1005.3
1-May	488	1095.9	392	776.1	880	1872.0
2-May	483	1081.6	393	767.1	876	1848.7
3-May	383	869.7	395	739.1	778	1608.8
4-May	204	449.9			204	449.9
5-May	193	433.6	402	744.4	595	1178.0
6-May			378	703.1	378	703.1
7-May	543	1222.9	229	426	772	1648.9
8-May	143	344.5	0	0	143	344.5
	3158	7029.9	2189	4155.8	5347	11185.7
	Aircraft	**Tonnage**	**Aircraft**	**Tonnage**	**Aircraft**	**Tonnage**

RAF	Avg. T. per plane	2.2
USAAF	Avg. T. per plane	1.9

(29)Royal Air Force Bomber Command Losses in Crew in Holland 1940 - 1945						
Year	**Fatal**	**POW**	**Evaded**	**Injured**	**Unknown**	**Rescued**
1940	158	70	1	1	2	0
1941	879	308	0	5	0	0
1942	1,490	316	9	3	0	5
1943	2,464	616	33	10	0	0
1944	1,255	274	76	4	0	0
1945	105	23	3	7	0	0
Total	**6,351**	**1,607**	**122**	**30**	**2**	**5**

540. "A City Destroyed". This almost 19 feet high sculpture by Ossip Zadkine was unveiled on May 15, 1953. It is located in Rotterdam. It shows the person "Rotterdam" in a stance with his arms and hands extended to the sky in a vain attempt to ward off falling bombs. Where the heart should be is a gaping hole.

Printed in the United States
92320LV00003B/43-249/A